Jim L

CW00919210

'The Australians who served here in Papua New Guinea fought and died, not for defence of the old world, but the new world. Their world.

They died in defence of Australia and the civilisation and values which had grown up there. That is why it might be said that, for Australians, the battles in Papua New Guinea were the most important ever fought.'

Former Prime Minister Paul Keating, Bomana War Cemetery, Port Moresby, Anzac Day, 1992

Also by Peter FitzSimons

Basking in Beirut
Little Theories of Life
Hitchhiking for Ugly People
Rugby Stories
Everyone But Phar Lap
Everyone And Phar Lap
Nick Farr-Jones: The Authorised Biography
FitzSimons on Rugby
Beazley: A Biography
Nene
Nancy Wake: A Biography of Our Greatest War Heroine
The Rugby War
John Eales: The Biography
The Story of Skilled Engineering and Frank Hargrave
Tobruk
The Ballad of Les Darcy
Charles Kingsford Smith and Those Magnificent Men

KOKODA

PETER FITZSIMONS

hachette
AUSTRALIA

Every effort has been made to acknowledge and contact the
owners of copyright for permission to reproduce material
which falls under the 1968 Copyright Act. Any copyright
owners who have inadvertently been omitted from
acknowledgments and credits should contact the publisher
and omissions will be rectified in subsequent editions.

hachette
AUSTRALIA

First published in Australia and New Zealand in 2004
by Hodder Australia
(An imprint of Hachette Australia Pty Limited)
Level 17, 207 Kent Street, Sydney NSW 2000
www.hachette.com.au

Hardback edition published 2004
Original trade paperback edition published 2005

This updated edition published 2010

20 19

Copyright © Peter FitzSimons 2004, 2010

This book is copyright. Apart from any fair dealing for the purposes of private study,
research, criticism or review permitted under the *Copyright Act 1968*, no part may
be stored or reproduced by any process without prior written permission. Enquiries
should be made to the publisher.

National Library of Australia
Cataloguing-in-Publication data

FitzSimons, Peter
Kokoda / Peter FitzSimons

978 0 7336 1962 5

World War, 1939-1945 – Campaigns – Papua New Guinea.
World War, 1939-1945 – Participation, Australian.
Kokoda Trail (Papua New Guinea).

950.5426

Maps by Kinart
Front cover image courtesy of AWM 061859
Front and back cover image courtesty of The Australian Picture Library
Cover design by Nada Backovic
Text design and typesetting by Bookhouse, Sydney
Printed and bound in Australia by Griffin Press, Adelaide, an Accredited ISO AS/NZS
14001:2004 Environmental Management System printer

The paper this book is printed on is certified by the Programme
for the Endorsement of Forest Certification scheme. Griffin Press
holds PEFC chain of custody SGS - PEFC/COC-0594. PEFC promotes
environmentally responsible, socially beneficial and economically viable
management of the world's forests.

To my late parents, Lieutenant Peter McCloy FitzSimons and Lieutenant Beatrice Helen Booth, both of whom proudly served with the AIF in New Guinea: my mother at Lae, helping to put back together some of the men who were wounded in the Kokoda campaign, and my father at Finschafen and Dumpu in the actions which followed it, after he had previously served in the Middle East and North Africa.

And to all the warriors of the Kokoda Track and Milne Bay— including my father's late twin brother, James Marsden FitzSimons, who fought in the final stages of the Kokoda campaign in the clean-up at Buna with the 2/6th Field Regiment.

Finally, I dedicate this book to the brave war correspondents and cinematographers of both sides who first documented this extraordinary saga, thus ensuring that the story can be told to the generations to come. I cite particularly the greats: Osmar White, Chester Wilmot and Damien Parer from Australia, and Japan's Seizo Okada, who was with his forces throughout their campaign.

CONTENTS

PROLOGUE

It was on a bitterly hot and humid morning on the outskirts of Port Moresby in the early days of September 1942. As sweat trickled down his exhausted, shaking arms—and occasionally to the very fingertips he was pecking at his typewriter with, the great ABC Correspondent Chester Wilmot tried to give some sense to just what it was that he had so recently seen . . .

He wrote:

One day late in August we stood on a spur of the Owen Stanleys and looked down the deep valley which leads to Kokoda, five thousand feet below. All we could see was a blanket of dark green treetops broken only here and there by the white waters of the turbulent creek at the bottom. The valley was almost as deep as it was wide and its sides swept up from the creekbed steeply and in some places precipitously. Somewhere under those treetops wound the track which leads from Kokoda up the valley and over the range to Port Moresby. And two miles away somewhere under those treetops in the dark damp forest Australian and Japanese troops were fighting desperately for the possession of this track. It didn't look much to fight for. It was just a series of muddy footholds in the mountain side . . . so slippery that you had to sling your rifle and leave your hands free to grab the nearest vine or branch as your feet slid from under you . . . so steep that in some places you could scale the mountain face only by using both hands and both feet . . . so muddy that at times you sloshed through a quagmire more than ankle deep and felt the cloying mud suck your feet back at every step. That was the track they were fighting for down there . . .

Looking at what he had written, it was all Wilmot could do not to weep. Given his recent experience, he couldn't even be sure that this report would make it onto the airwaves before it was quietly killed in the night by the authorities, but it changed nothing of the question that kept gnawing at him . . . All that valour, all that courage, all those *lives* . . . lost. How, how had it come to this? How was it that such a small number of Australian men without much of a military background had been thrown up against a vastly superior, superbly trained Japanese force . . . when the fate of Australia might very well be hanging in the balance?

PREFACE

In the spring of 2001, I was taken to lunch by Matthew Kelly of Hodder Headline. He came to the point fairly quickly. On the strength of the success of the book I'd written on the war heroine Nancy Wake, aka 'the White Mouse', he would like me to write a book on the Kokoda Track.

My answer was succinct: 'No.'

Even though my Uncle Jim had fought on the Kokoda Track and both my mother and father had served in New Guinea in WWII, like most Australians I only had a foggy idea what the fighting along the Kokoda Track had been all about. Sure, I knew our blokes had gone up against the Japanese—and I gathered that they had done pretty well—but that was close to all I knew. Only a short time later, though, I was having lunch with my friend Daniel Petre and mentioned the Kokoda offer to him.

Daniel fired up in a manner I have rarely seen. Usually a very calm, considered kind of bloke, he was insistent. I *had* to do this book. Did I have *any* idea how extraordinary the story was, what had been achieved there? No? Well let me tell you . . .

In another conversation shortly afterwards with my former biographical subject Kim Beazley—a military aficionado to beat them all who, among other things, had been this country's long-time defence minister—he said that in his view the fighting on the Kokoda Track was some of the toughest in the course of all human conflict. Kim began to add some fascinating details, reeled off the names of five books I should read to get a grasp of it, and promptly sent me two of them.

And things moved from there. Once bitten by the same Kokoda bug that had got to Matthew, Daniel and Kim, I soon embarked and have been on the case ever since. In November of 2002, I was with Daniel and sixteen mates on the Kokoda Track itself, pushing hard from Ower's Corner to Kokoda in a little under six days and surviving, just, the hardest physical ordeal of my life. My respect for what had been achieved there by the soldiers of the 39th Battalion, the 2/14th, 2/16th and others, now knew no bounds, and though with every tortuous step up the towering Maguli Ranges I swore I would never set foot there again, I know I'll go back, perhaps at the point when my now young children are strong enough to accompany me, and I am not too weak to accompany them.

One final thing. On the subject of the Kokoda campaign, there is a continuing discussion about whether it is the Kokoda *Track* or the Kokoda *Trail*, with many passionate adherents on both sides. It has been explored so often I won't go into it again here, if only to say I have plumped for 'Track' on the simple grounds that every Digger I spoke to referred to it as that, and if it was good enough for them . . .

ACKNOWLEDGMENTS

In many ways much of the ground I cover in this book has already been well covered, not only by the Diggers themselves, but by a variety of eminent historians and writers, and this book owes their exacting work a great debt. I am not an historian, and this is not a history book, but it has been their work which has either delivered the pearls I was looking for, or pointed me in the direction where I might find them.

For this book I was heavily dependent on the splendid researching skills of Glenda Lynch who was able to work the wonderful resources of the Australian War Memorial and National Library for me. (And if you haven't seen the superb Kokoda section of the War Memorial, you should.) To her, my enormous gratitude, most particularly for finding the songs sung by the Japanese troops on the Kokoda Track and the diary entries of the 144th Regiment's 2nd Lieutenant Noda Hidetaka. I read it and wept.

In essence, what I have tried to do in this book is to take these established points of historical fact and then join the dots, before taking out my colouring pencils, fleshing this into a story that hopefully reads at least a little like a novel. An example is my prologue about what the correspondent was feeling when he wrote his report on the fighting he had seen. Of course I cannot know for sure whether it is an accurate account of his emotions, but after two years of research, that is my best reckoning.

In his introduction to Raymond Paull's 1958 book, *Retreat From Kokoda*, Lieutenant General Sir Sydney Rowell, K.B.E., C.B., C.B.E., wrote: 'There is surely sufficient drama in this without clouding the issue by a discussion of the personalities of commanders, however intriguing this might be to lovers of sensation.'

For what it's worth, I have taken the directly contrary view, trying as much as possible to fill out the personalities of some of the key and minor players to help make the story—and them—live again. Certainly, in an effort to achieve this to my own satisfaction, I have had to occasionally take out my poetic licence and, for example, postulate what the final thoughts of a man who has just been shot might have been. But as much as possible I have stayed with what is on the historical record, right down to what the Diggers nicknamed their detested cans of herring—'goldfish'.

In the endnotes and bibliography, I hope I have fully acknowledged all the writers and historians whose work I have drawn upon, but it is appropriate that I also 'dips my lid' here.

In the course of researching this book I became so enamoured with the work of Osmar White, Chester Wilmot and Damien Parer—who recorded the actions of the Kokoda campaign for newspapers, radio and film respectively—that I decided to make them characters in the book. With these three outstanding journalists there was very little need for me to use any poetic licence, for they recorded their feelings for posterity at the time, and how. I might say in passing that spending many a late night going through transcripts of Chester Wilmot's reports for ABC radio, particularly, was a delight. Osmar White's book *Green Armour* is equally a gem, and though getting into Damien Parer's head was not as easy, the work of his principal biographer Neil McDonald, who wrote *War Cameraman*, went a long way towards bridging the gap. I also appreciated Neil's warm support of this project and his valuable advice. It was also he who first played me recordings of Wilmot's ABC reports, which was a great thrill.

To my eyes, all of us who have written about Kokoda since the time of White, Wilmot and Parer—and there will be many more to come after me—are building on foundation stones laid by three historians in particular.

Official historian Dudley McCarthy's book *Australia in the War of 1939–45: South West Pacific Area First Year, Kokoda to Wau*, which came out in 1959, sets out in clear language all the key movements of the major battles and is a first-class bit of work. W. B. Russell's official *History of the Second Fourteenth Battalion* was also invaluable. The other man was Raymond Paull, who accomplished a similar feat with his book *Retreat from Kokoda*, published in 1958, with even more detail, albeit within narrower parameters.

Among contemporary writers about Kokoda, there is none finer than Peter Brune, who has written *A Bastard of a Place, Those Ragged Bloody Heroes* and the biography of Ralph Honner, *We Band of Brothers*. Time and again, in the course of writing this book, I turned to Brune when trying to understand what happened in specific actions. Let me also place on the record how much I appreciated the fact that when I had completed the manuscript, both Peter Brune and Neil McDonald were kind enough to carefully go through it, spotting errors and giving valuable advice on how to improve it. (That said, whatever brute mistakes remain in the text are my responsibility alone.) The book is far better for their generous input, and I am deep in their debt.

Another contemporary writer whose work I found valuable was Lex McAulay, who wrote *Blood and Iron: The Battle For Kokoda 1942*. My knowledge of Arnold Potts and his actions in the war were filled out by Bill Edgar's *Warrior of Kokoda: A Biography of Brigadier Arnold Potts*.

Much of the information concerning General Douglas MacArthur in this book came from two key biographies. First, and most important, is William Manchester's classic, *American Caesar: Douglas MacArthur*, and I also drew upon *Old Soldiers Never Die: the Life and Legend of Douglas MacArthur*, by Geoffrey Perret. On the subject of both General MacArthur and Major General Sir Thomas Blamey, I found Jack Gallaway's book *The Odd Couple: Blamey and MacArthur at War*—which focuses on both commanding officers—useful for information and influential in the way I approached looking at their relationship. On the subject of Sir Thomas Blamey specifically, I constantly referred to Professor David Horner's book, *Blamey: The Commander-in-Chief*, and I also warmly thank Professor Horner here for his time and advice in helping me to pin down the specific details of Blamey in which I was interested.

David Day's work on Australia's primary wartime prime minister, *John Curtin: A Life*, was revelatory from first to last, as was his book *The Politics of War*, which helped me to put the Kokoda campaign in its political context.

The great Stan Bisset, the oldest living Wallaby, has been a wonderful help to me throughout the course of writing this book, and I have treasured the time I have been able to spend with him and his wife Gloria, for which I warmly thank them now.

After Damien Parer's Oscar-winning film *Kokoda Front Line*, which documented the Kokoda campaign at the time, there have been two outstanding documentaries, both of which I devoured. The first came in 1992 and was called *The Bloody Track*, produced by George Friend and presented by Patrick Lindsay, both of whom have been helpful. The second was a Four Corners' documentary which came out in 1995, called *The Men Who Saved Australia*, produced by Jacquelyn Hole and presented by Chris Masters. Chris, who I am proud to call a friend, was a great source and sounding board on this project, and I also thank him. As a matter of fact something that greatly struck me in the course of writing this book was just how helpful other 'Kokoda people' have been, sending me information, ideas and advice and doing everything they could. In this field I particularly cite Bill James who sent me some wonderful material on Tom Grahamslaw that I had not previously spied.

Beyond information, I cite a particular influence in the way this book was shaped. Well into the writing of the book, my friend Bill

James sent me a paper published by Professor Emeritus Hank Nelson, of the Australian National University, where the professor cogently argued that the story of the Kokoda campaign was strong enough in truth, that it didn't need some of the trappings of mythology that have been attached to it over the years. I contacted the professor and he graciously advised me thereafter, sending me some of the academic papers you will see referred to in the bibliography. If anyone was helpful in my getting the Japanese side of the story, and in pinning down the true conditions that the native porters worked under, it was Professor Nelson, and I cannot thank him enough for it.

Many other people helped me in specific areas of the book. I thank Trevor Robertson for his expert advice on submarine warfare during World War II and Richard Seeto for his help with the fascinating language of Pidgin. My former editor at the *Sydney Morning Herald*, Max Prisk, proved to be a collector of many WWII Battalion magazines, books and the like, and he very kindly lent many of them to me, pointing out exactly where the best information could be found. Equally, Charlie Lynn, of the New South Wales Upper House—a Kokoda devotee to beat them all—was a wonderful source of information and of material for me to go through. My friend Michael Cooper, with whom I walked the track, proved to be an aficionado of matters medical on the track, and sent me everything he had.

Both the 2/14th Battalion Association and the 39th Battalion Association were wonderfully welcoming when I attended their reunions, and I warmly thank all the Diggers I talked to, both at those reunions and in subsequent interviews. From the 39th, Joe Dawson of Forster was a wonderful find. He was with the battalion from its first days at Darley; he travelled on the *Aquitania* to Fairfax Harbour in January of '42 and was unloading the *Macdhui* when Japanese bombers got it in their sights in June '42. He was with the 39th when they took their first steps up the track three weeks later; was there when Sam Templeton met his fate at Oivi, and was just ten yards away when Captain Owen stood too tall at Kokoda.

Throughout all of the Battle of Isurava Joe was in the thick of it; he was standing in the front rank when Ralph Honner made his speech at Menari, and he was still with the 39th when they stormed Gona in December of 1942.

I thank Joe for the time he accorded me to interview him and affirm how much I enjoyed it all. I particularly thank Joe's wider family who were so wonderfully accommodating to me, none more so than his wife, Elaine. Joe's two daughters, Leigh Vaughan and Toni Hoekstra, together with Joe's granddaughter Caitlin Vaughan had already done a lot of painstaking and professional work getting Joe's experiences recorded and written down, and I was very lucky that the family was happy to share that with me and allow me to draw from it.

It was also very kind of Ralph Honner's family to allow me to see some of his remaining papers and I record my appreciation to them here.

This is my fifteenth book, and by this time I have been blessed to have a very good team of people helping me put it together. My thanks as always to my principal researcher, Kevin Brumpton; my transcriber of interviews, Margaret Coleman; and my help in all things to do with the form and texture of the book, my indefatigable and treasured colleague at the *Sydney Morning Herald*, Harriet Veitch, who put many weekend and evening hours into the project. I record my appreciation and professional respect to the people at Hodder Headline—most particularly Matthew Kelly and Deonie Fiford, who was a Trojan when I most needed her—and my editor for this book, Belinda Lee. She and I have now worked together on four books, and she consistently manages to strengthen my stuff.

In all my books I have called on the professional editing skills of my wife, Lisa, and this book is no exception. Her input was as invaluable as ever, and the book is all the better for her many suggestions.

Peter FitzSimons
May 2004

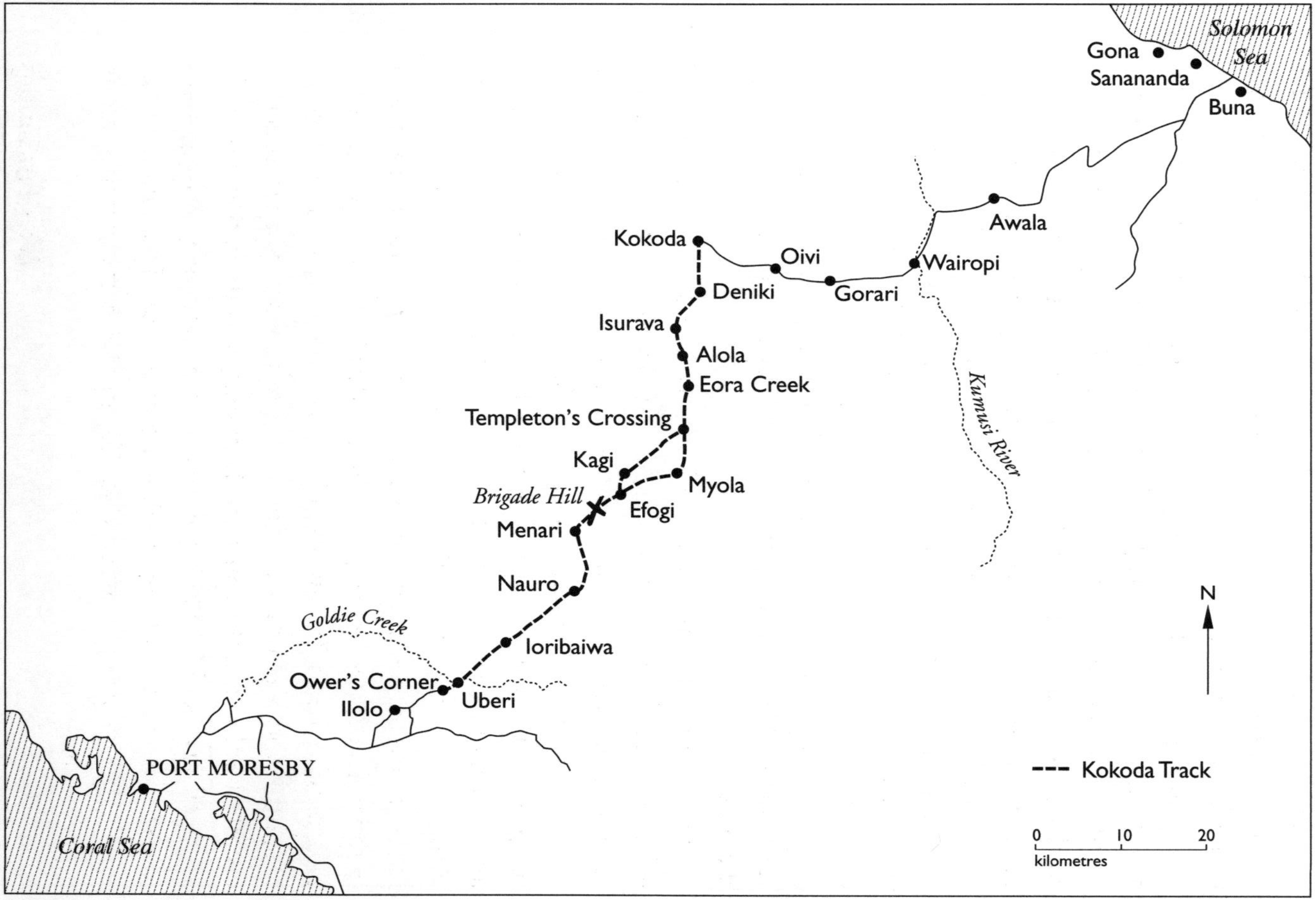

THE KOKODA TRACK

Solomon
Sea

Buna
Sananda
Gona

Awala
Wairopi

Kumusi River

Gorari
Oivi
Deniki
Kokoda
Isurava
Alola
Eora Creek
Templeton's Crossing
Myola
Kagi
Efogi
Brigade Hill
Menari
Nauro
Ioribaiwa
Uberi
Goldie Creek
Ower's Corner
Ilolo

PORT MORESBY

Coral Sea

N

Kokoda Track

0   10   20
kilometres

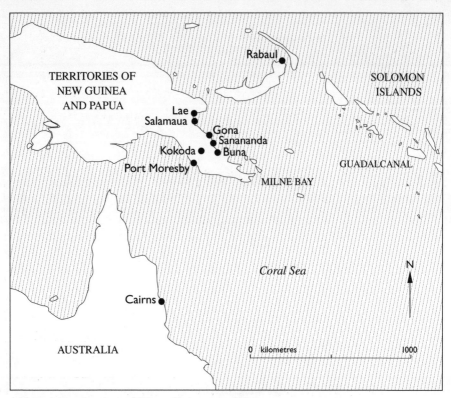

(*Above*) Territories of New Guinea and Papua

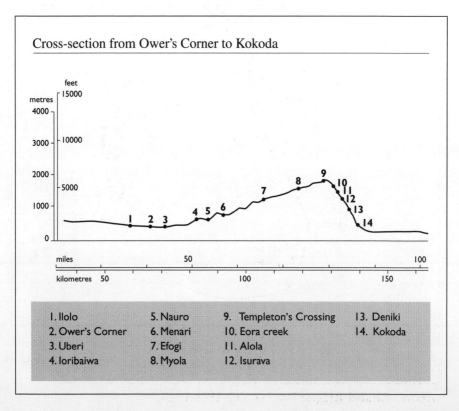

Cross-section from Ower's Corner to Kokoda

feet
metres 15000
4000
3000   10000
2000   5000
1000

miles   50   100
kilometres 50   100   150

1. Ilolo	5. Nauro	9. Templeton's Crossing	13. Deniki
2. Ower's Corner	6. Menari	10. Eora creek	14. Kokoda
3. Uberi	7. Efogi	11. Alola	
4. Ioribaiwa	8. Myola	12. Isurava	

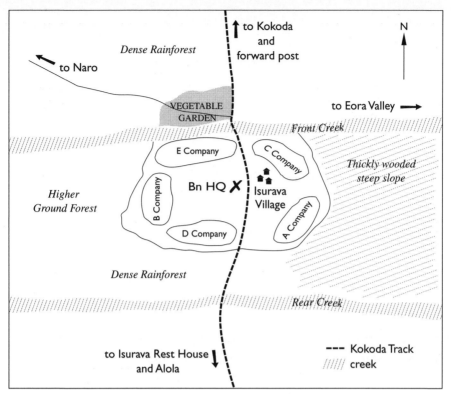

(*Above*) The 39th's Positions at Isurava 18–27 August

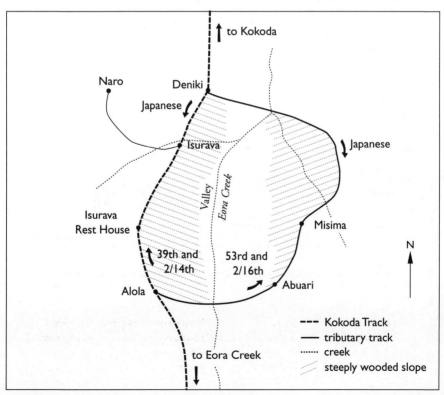

(*Above*) Parallel Ridges: Isurava and Abuari

It was an infantryman's Calvary, where the pain of effort, the biting sweat, the hunger, the cheerless, shivering nights were made dim by exhaustion's merciful drug . . . Surely no war was ever fought under worse conditions than these. Surely no war has ever demanded more of a man in fortitude. Even Gallipoli or Crete or the desert.

Osmar White, *Green Armour*

CHAPTER ONE

IN THE
BEGINNING

The ancient Japanese culture, once built of wood, bamboo, paper, straw and silk, is today a civilisation built of iron and steel, of factories and machines. Yet even today Japan's strength rests more on its ancient culture than on the civilisation of the 20th Century

From *The Secret of Japanese Strength*[1]

Not only to develop the resources of the Territory, but also to preserve the Papuans and to raise them eventually to the highest civilization of which they are capable. Not to make the brown man white—but to make him a better brown man than he was before.

The stated goal of Sir Hubert Murray, Australia's Administrator of Papua New Guinea from 1908 to 1940[2]

The mid-1920s . . . There is a special kind of drone teachers assume when they are giving a lesson about something they don't particularly care about, and know that their students care for even less. So it was on this hot afternoon at Warrandyte High School in the old mining town some twenty miles northeast of Melbourne, as ol' Mr Hallett was pointing out to his students just one more bit of the map of the world that was coloured in red because it was another part of the British Empire, on which the sun never set.

'And here, boys and girls,' he was saying, 'are the territories of New Guinea and Papua, which as you can see, are squarely in the tropics. The "Papua" part in the territories of New Guinea and Papua came from Jorge de Meneses, a Portuguese seafarer who arrived in 1526 and is thought to have been the first European to discover it. He gave the land the name "Papua" after the Malay word which means "fuzzy-haired man". It wasn't until 1884 that the Germans and British established colonies on the northeast and southeast sections respectively of the island. In 1906, Australia took over control of the British colony and in 1914, when the Great War started, it also occupied the German areas. In 1920 the League of Nations formally decreed that it should be a territory of Australia. There are no fewer than eight hundred tribes in the territories of New Guinea and Papua, and one-third of the world's languages are spoken there. All in an area of no more than 500 000 square miles. Its average rainfall, in some places, incredibly, rises to as high as 150 inches!'

Stan Bisset, all of twelve years old, listened and paid attention as best he could, because he was generally a conscientious kind of student, but it tested even him. New Guinea was a place that sort of brooded at the top of the map of Australia, but it wasn't somewhere that quickened his interest the way, say, London, or New York or Paris did. New Guinea was just a bit of a blob that might be geographically close to Australia, but that was about it.

Anyway, already Stan's thoughts were turning to that afternoon after school when he would get back to the family farm by the Yarra River and, with his beloved older brother Butch, go fishing, or play cricket or football. Or maybe they'd go after rabbits, using their uncle's shotgun, or have a competition to see which of them could shoot out the flame of a candle at a distance of 25 yards. One of their favourite games was to take it in turns to pretend being Ned Kelly, setting up ambushes in the nearby forest. But they'd be hard put to match the most fun they ever had, which was when, with a couple of boys from the Howden family, they'd wagged school and used some old gelignite and fuse wire they'd found in one of the abandoned mines to blow it up . . . but anyway. Whatever they did, that night after dinner Stan and Butch would likely sing everything from chorus-line songs to favourite hymns in front of the fire with their two older brothers, younger sister and parents.

On Sundays the whole family would walk together to the local church—where his mother was the pianist and his father the leading tenor in the choir—to worship before returning for the boys' favourite Sunday roast with all the trimmings that their mother and sister cooked up for them.

Life was simple and good for the young Stan, rather in the image of Australia itself. He and Butch were young blokes just about to get into their stride, growing up in a young nation just about to get into *its* stride . . .

Every now and then when Stan and Butch were taken into Melbourne by their parents, they passed by the Melbourne suburb of Malvern's small hospital—and it was in this establishment that, a decade-and-a-half earlier, one Damien Parer had been born.[3] He was the tenth child of the fiercely Roman Catholic couple John and Teresa Parer, of King Island in Bass Strait. After her confinement, Teresa returned with her tiny and precious bundle to the island where her husband ran the only hotel, and life for Damien began. It was not an easy existence. While the family life was warm, and the immersion into heavy Catholicism lifted and nourished Damien's spirit rather than weighed him down, the fact was that his father was a compulsive gambler. This was another way of saying he was frequently absent from home and lost a lot of money that the family could ill-afford. Damien was by nature a notably happy, confident and up-beat sort of fellow, but as money dwindled and his mother wept, as his father tried one 'fail-safe' gambling scheme after another to restore the family fortunes, which did in fact fail anyway, there were many things which tried his natural spirit. Always, Damien's devotion to Catholicism and the strength he drew from praying saw him through and, somehow, the combination of it all bred enormous courage in him, together with an ability to withstand great hardship.

There was just something about Footscray football team that thrilled young Joe Dawson to the core. Most weekends when 'the Bulldogs' played 'at home', young Joe would scrape together the sixpence necessary to get into the Western Oval to watch them take on the likes of Carlton, Collingwood, St Kilda or South Melbourne. He knew in his tribal bones that none of those other teams were as good as Footscray, had the *soul* of Footscray, the *spirit* of Footscray. The mere sight of their famous red, white and blue colours made young Joe shiver with pleasure every time he saw them run onto the field. There could be no finer thing than one day, maybe, to wear their jersey. Who better to represent?

Sometimes the crowd would roar 'Up There Cazaly!' if anyone leaped particularly high to take a mark—a catch-cry that had taken off several years before, when St Kilda's Roy Cazaly would leap fair to the heavens, a cry which had such a nice feel about it that it had not dissipated since his retirement.

Joe called out his support, maybe a little shyly at first, but then with greater gusto as the game went on. He was a quiet kid, but spirited in his own way. With his father's menswear store on Nicholson Street going pretty well, the family of seven lacked for not too much. Joe was a fairly bright student at school, and the future seemed pretty fair, even if he wasn't quite sure what he was going to do.

Over in the Japanese city of Kochi on the spectacularly beautiful island of Shikoku, the young lads growing up didn't wonder what they'd do, they pretty much knew. They knew that at least for a certain part of their lives they would be going into the military. And they were already getting a headstart in preparing for it. In their schools the basic military skills of marching, firing rifles and hand-to-hand combat were taught as a matter of course, just as they were taught what they were learning to fight for. Every school day began with a collective prayer to the Emperor, the national anthem and a ceremonial raising of the Japanese flag. Directly and innately, these lads were made to understand that Japan had a destiny to be militarily strong and to use that strength for the greater glory of the nation. Their *duty* was to be worthy of helping fulfil that goal.

Japan, which only seventy-odd years before had emerged from near total isolation from the West, was indeed at a notable point in its history, poised between two worlds, each struggling for supremacy. While Europe had been torn apart by the Great War, Japan had remained essentially uninvolved, apart from the odd task for the Allies—like escorting Australian troopships on their way to Gallipoli across the Indian Ocean in early 1915. One result was that Japan's economy had received an enormous surge as its manufacturing industries provided the things that Europe no longer could.

The tension in the times though was twofold. For despite its growth, Japan remained dependent on importing natural resources such as rubber, iron ore and, most notably, oil. And the more the economy grew and the population expanded, the more this need grew, including the most urgent requirement for food. This caused a great struggle between those in Japan who advocated—in the grandest of samurai traditions—ruthlessly using their superior military force to invade and subjugate resource-rich neighbouring countries like China, and the more moderate, modern forces, who maintained that normal forms of simple trade would give Japan the resources it needed. The cause of the moderates was weakened when many countries of the West imposed heavy tariffs on manufactured Japanese goods, limiting Japan's capacity to pay for the raw materials. And the moderate cause was further weakened with the gruelling effects of the Great Depression when the Japanese people ceased to trust normal market operations to secure the country's future prosperity.

This battle in the highest realms of Japanese Government between the moderates and the militarists—all of it under the sometime nervous gaze of the Emperor himself—would dominate Japanese political life for two decades.

There is no doubt that the militarists had the structural advantage in the struggle. First, the need for resources grew more urgent with every year, underlining the need for drastic measures. And secondly, it was always going to be easy to assert military control over a people with strong militaristic traditions, a people who had been ruled for centuries by shoguns (the Emperor's top military commanders) and samurai warriors. There was practically a cultural imperative for the Japanese population at this time to automatically obey high military authority, no matter in which direction it steered them.

It was in such circumstances that, effectively, the military remained almost a force unto itself, answerable neither to the *Diet* (parliament) or the government.[4] A particularity of the Japanese Constitution since 1900, strengthened by subsequent amendments, was that the government minister controlling the navy and the army had to be a serving officer, thus effectively eliminating traditional civilian control of the military. In fact, given that the resignation of the Minister for the Navy or Army could bring down a government— and frequently did so—they clearly had exceptional power. But what the military could not do was bring down the Emperor because, as affirmed by this same constitution, he was a divine power—a direct descendant of *Amaterasu,* known to Westerners as the Sun Goddess, the almighty being who created Japan.

On all but one of the above, the passage of time changed both the subjects and the circumstances in which they could be found.

By the early 1930s, Stan Bisset had blossomed into a scholarship winner at the Melbourne Conservatorium of Music on the strength of his extraordinary bass-baritone singing voice, and was also turning into a very fine cricket and rugby player on the strength of his great athletic gifts. Butch Bisset, meanwhile, after heading off to Western Australia with one of his older brothers to work on their uncle's sheep station—before also having a stint cutting sleepers for the railway line they were building over that way—had returned as a very tough man with the capacity to ride horses, shoot and swim all day long, and carry on into the night when he was in town. Butch soon joined Stan in Melbourne's famous Powerhouse Club, where he played rugby in the front row—right at the 'coalface' of the action—with Stan pushing directly behind him in the second row.

At this time, too, another young Australian was finding his feet. His early ambition to become a Catholic priest had given way at his Bathurst boarding school to a passion for photography. Now, as an apprentice to a noted Collins Street photographer in Melbourne, Damien Parer began experimenting with moving pictures. As a matter of fact, by this time he had already shot his first tiny 'film', a ten-minute roughly put together sequence of shots of his and brother Adrian's Catholic hiking club going on a long trek through the forest. Sure, it was rough, but somehow it had something. Somehow Damien just *had it*, could splice together the right footage taken from the right angles, with just the right perspective, and was able to not only evoke time and place, but give a real impression of just what it was like. He was even then working his way towards what would become practically his first commandment of documentary making: 'We shall find most of our gold in the hidden detail of expression of our men by watching carefully, noting expression and gestures and shooting circumspectly at the dead right moment.'

At another 'coalface' of action—St John's Catholic Church debutante ball—young Joe Dawson was making an impression on young Elaine Colbran. And she on him . . .

Although he'd known Elaine since they were at primary school together Joe had never thought about her in a particularly romantic way, but there was no denying that the red-haired Elaine had turned into a singularly pretty young woman. And she was kind. And she was fun.

As to the young men of Shikoku, they too had changed. For in the image of the country around them, they had grown, developed new muscles and were increasingly eager to test them out. The fact that Japan had grown both in industrial and military might year by year now meant that all able-bodied young boys went into the universal service of the Imperial Japanese Army and underwent intense training. As soldiers in Japan, they were thus heirs to the tradition of the samurais, the uniquely Japanese warrior class which for so many centuries had been regarded as embodying the nation's highest virtues.

While the samurais of old, however, had lived a life with a rigid code of ritualised behaviour and highly refined sense of honour and ethics known as *Bushido*, what was left to these young men in the 1930s was not quite that . . .

They were proceeding through far and away the most brutal army training system in the world, where beatings from non-commissioned officers were part of the daily fare, and not simply for individual transgressions. It was enough that a member of your platoon had committed even a minor infraction that the whole corps was beaten by superiors, some to the point of unconsciousness. The focus was always discipline, absolute discipline, the need to obey orders instantly without question, whatsoever those orders might be. Individual initiative was not only left unrewarded, it was severely punished both physically and by public humiliation in front of your peers.

One aspect of the samurai tradition that survived intact was that the recruits were taught that they must be willing to give their lives in the service of the Emperor. Each morning, at the first lustre of the pre-dawn, each recruit rose, bowed respectfully in the direction of Tokyo's Imperial Palace, and repeated the famous declaration of the Emperor Meiji: 'Duty is weightier than a mountain, while death is lighter than a feather.' This did *not* mean that those soldiers were to throw their lives away, merely that the principal weapon they possessed as a body of fighting men was that death must hold no fear for them.

While they had been taught this idea from infancy, it was now beaten in: death on the battlefield was a beginning, not an end. Death on the battlefield transformed one into a type of god, a

'Kami', who remained among the living with the ability to nurture and protect loved ones from that spirit world. And for that transformation, one would be honoured by all, revered forever by ensuing generations for their sacrifice for the good of the nation and the Emperor.

It was nothing if not intense, and it created an extremely tightly bound military machine of formidable capacity. The bonds between these Japanese soldiers were all the greater because many had known each other from early childhood onwards. This, too, was a part of the carefully constructed Japanese military system, the reckoning being that because soldiers' families were known to each other, no soldier would visit disgrace and dishonour on his loved ones by deserting during a battle.

All, *all* had changed, except Papua New Guinea.

The island still just sat there—immovable, a dark green, impenetrable silhouette, perched above the Australian continent exactly as it always had been. If, at any time in its past, an open calendar had been tacked to a tree in the New Guinea highlands, it would *not* have fluttered over page after page as the years rushed by, the way it often did in the new genre of 'movies' which by the 1930s were taking a faraway place called 'Hollywood' by storm. For although time *did* pass in New Guinea it didn't actually change anything substantial from one wet season to the next . . .

Various powers and forces, from Germany, to Great Britain, to Christian missionaries to the twentieth century had done their level best to gain a foothold on the island—and just managed to do so— but never succeeded in doing anything more than that. Always, it was a place where so much energy was expended just holding on to the one foothold, that trying to find a spot to put down the next foot was all but out of the question.

Even for such a timeless place as New Guinea, though, a force was building that would cause an event so cataclysmic that nothing, absolutely nothing, would be left unchanged by it . . .

•

On 26 February 1936, extreme militarists in Japan, in the form of a group of ambitious army officers, shot two of Emperor Hirohito's key advisers, before other militarists of the same bent, seized key Tokyo installations, including the Japanese Foreign Office. They then handed out leaflets which were a veritable call to arms for Japan's citizens to rise up with them and recognise that the essence of Japan was rooted 'in the fact that the nation is destined to expand', and that those who did not embrace that concept were guilty of 'treason'. Though that attempted coup failed, the notion that expansion by military means was Japan's destiny did not.

In July of the following year the Imperial Japanese Army, which four years earlier had occupied the resource-rich Manchuria in neighbouring China, went after the rest of the country, including Peking. Still, Chinese resistance continued to be strong, nowhere more so than in the city of Nanking, the capital of the Nationalist Chinese. When finally the Chinese soldiers defending Nanking surrendered, the Japanese soldiers showed no mercy. Many thousands of the Chinese were put up against the wall and cut down by machine-gun fire, while hundreds were used for bloody bayonet practice and unceremoniously thrown into the Yangtze River. Still, the Japanese were not done. For weeks afterwards the victorious soldiers looted the city, destroying more than a third of its buildings, while murdering many of the city residents and raping, almost as a military policy, some twenty thousand women. Dreadful stories emerged of Japanese soldiers forcing fathers at gunpoint to rape their own daughters, and sons to rape their mothers. Many civilians weren't simply shot, but were disembowelled and decapitated by soldiers who seemed insane with bloodlust.

This riot of death and destruction reached its apocalyptic apogee when at the city quay, before assembled foreign correspondents, Japanese soldiers began butchering Chinese prisoners of war almost as part of a show, happily posing for photographs with the slain at their feet. The whole episode became known as the 'Nanking Massacre' or the 'Rape of Nanking' and, given the delight the Japanese had in demonstrating their brutality to foreign correspondents, its news spread far and wide. Later calculations established that somewhere between 100 000 and 300 000 Chinese had been killed.

In response to events such as the Nanking Massacre, the United States of America was quick to impose economic sanctions on Japan until such times as it withdrew from China. Henceforth, the United States government, led by an enraged President Roosevelt, began to limit exports of oil and scrap iron to Japan.

The same approach was not taken by the ruling political class in Australia, though there was no doubt which way the sympathies of the workers lay, setting the scene for a major political brawl which occurred in November of 1938.

Down at Port Kembla, just south of Sydney, the waterside workers refused to load a cargo of pig-iron into a ship bound for Japan on the grounds that they thought that it would likely end up in bullets and bombs that the now supremely militaristic nation of Japan were then firing and hurling at China in a notably vicious war. The workers further argued that once Japan had finished with China, it was quite possible that Australia might find itself on the receiving end of this same pig-iron.

In reply, the Australian government, most particularly Attorney-General Robert Menzies, took a heavy hand. For Menzies the issue was simple: it was *not* for the wretched trade unions to determine Australian foreign policy, and the government would sooner close down the steelworks on which the workers depended for their employment than cede to them any say whatsoever.

So the steelworks were indeed shut down, and after a bitter campaign which included new legislation being passed which forced the workers to cooperate or lose their jobs in the whole industry, Menzies won the day. Just before Menzies became Prime Minister of Australia on 26 April 1939, the pig-iron went to Japan, and Menzies had found a nickname that would stay with him for life: 'Pig-Iron Bob'.

Growing alarm in Australia about Japanese intent in the region, coupled with an equal alarm about Hitler's new designs on the map of Europe ensured that all over Australia men began to join up with their local militias or, as they were formally known, Citizens Military Forces, a kind of antechamber for the army proper.

Down in Melbourne, for example, no fewer than 250 members of the Powerhouse Club—including Stan and Butch Bisset—joined up to form C Company of the 14th Militia Battalion, based at Prahran, and proudly became 'Weekend Warriors'. A couple of times a week, often just before rugby training, or perhaps on the morning before the game, they would form up at a spot close to their clubhouse at Albert Park Lake and practise basic military skills like marching, saluting and shooting at the miniature rifle range they had built. Butch Bisset was always the stand-out performer in the last endeavour, taking on all-comers and always winning. The blokes reckoned that if he wanted to, Butch could wing a flying sparrow at a distance of a hundred yards. For every twenty shots, Butch would get at least nineteen bullseyes.

The men also learnt how to use a gas mask, what the basic military regulations were and what happened if you disobeyed them. Some of the more interesting stuff was when they were given battle formations with miniature soldiers on model terrains, and were asked to work out how to manoeuvre the soldiers to maximise damage to the enemy. Very occasionally they'd go out and practise actual war games against other militia battalions to see who could adapt the quickest and move most effectively.

There is something stirring in the vision of men on horseback charging forward that stiffens the sinews, stirs the blood and awakens an atavistic spirit long dormant. Out on the sandhills of Cronulla in southern Sydney on this summer's day of 1938, the great Australian film-maker Charles Chauvel and his production crew were thrilled as they captured scenes for Chauvel's film *Forty Thousand Horsemen*, based on the famous charge of the Australian Light Horse Regiment in the Great War, where they had covered themselves in glory at the Battle of Beersheba. Amid the thundering hooves the only real worry for the delighted Chauvel and his staff was for one of the cameramen, a Damien Parer, who seemed to be taking extraordinary risks jumping around amidst the galloping nags, taking footage from ground level.[5] This fellow Parer did, admittedly, provide extraordinary vision, but the *risks* he took! Just one veering horse at full tilt and that would have been the end of him.

For Damien Parer this episode was simply one step on the way of a busy life pursuing his passion of capturing reality in a box, both through still and moving photography. Such was his overall talent, that in short order, by the end of 1938, he had gone to work for the leading still photographer of his day, Max Dupain, working out of his Kings Cross studio, learning ever more about how to frame a shot for maximum effect, the kind of light that was most effective, the level of exposure and so on . . .

A lot of what Parer learnt there he found useful for his cinematography craft as well, though what interested him more and more at the time was not the Chauvel re-creation of something that had occurred a long time before, but something even more powerful. What he loved was the idea of capturing important events, live as they actually happened, and then cutting them together exactly as you would for a fictional film, in such a way that the event *lived*.

Meanwhile, far from Australia, the 1939 Wallabies Test team had just disembarked from the P&O liner *Mooltan* on the first leg of their ten-month, five-test rugby union tour. The eight-week trip had been a long haul for Stan Bisset and the team and they were excited and bursting with the energy of the newly landed. The team had just settled into the Grand Hotel on the esplanade of the picturesque British seaside resort of Torquay on this Sunday morning, 3 September 1939, when the word went around that the British Prime Minister, Neville Chamberlain, was about to make some kind of national address and they should turn their radios on in their rooms.

'I am speaking to you from the Cabinet Room at 10 Downing Street,' he began in his clipped, but still rather unsteady tones. 'This morning the British Ambassador in Berlin handed the German Government a final note stating that unless we heard from them by 11.00 a.m. that they were prepared at once to withdraw their troops from Poland, a state of war would exist between us. I have to tell you that no such undertaking has been received, and that consequently this country is at war with Germany . . .

'At such a moment as this the assurances of support that we have received from the Empire are a source of profound encouragement to us . . .

'Now may God bless you all. May He defend the right. It is the evil things that we shall be fighting against—brute force, bad faith, injustice, oppression and persecution—and against them I am certain that the right will prevail.'

Bloody hell! What was all but immediately apparent was that the Wallaby tour was off, and the war was on. At a team meeting called immediately after the announcement, some members expressed a desire to join up with the British forces and get stuck into the Germans right away, but after discussion they reconsidered. They had left Australia as a team and would return in the same manner, only then would blokes go their own ways.

While they waited for their return passage to Australia they set themselves to work. To keep themselves busy, Stan Bisset and ten of his strongest teammates began building for the delighted hotel proprietor a wall of solid sandbags around the windows facing the waters of the English Channel, from which any German fire would come. As he worked, Stan's mind raced as he considered his future.

Within hours of Neville Chamberlain's announcement to Britain, the stentorian tones of Robert Menzies went out across Australia, and his words were reported in the gratified English press.

'Fellow Australians,' the new Australian prime minister said, 'it is my melancholy duty to inform you officially that in consequence of a persistence by Germany, and her invasion of Poland, Great Britain has declared war upon her and that as a result Australia is also at war.'

Of course Australia was also at war. Britain was at war, therefore Australia, her loyal dominion, was at war. Australia was in fact so loyal to Britain that under Prime Minister Menzies's guidance,

Australia's navy was effectively placed under the control of the British Navy and sent to northern climes, while much of the Royal Australian Air Force was also sent to Europe to fight the good fight for the King and the Empire. It would not be long before two entire divisions of the Australian Army, which were then and there being quickly raised for overseas duties, were also put essentially at the service of British interests.

Against it all, only very few voices were raised, though one of particular significance was the Leader of the Opposition, John Curtin. Before the war, he had made many speeches in Federal Parliament to the effect that Australia should not be sending forces to Europe for an Imperial war, and that remained his view now (even if in the exigencies of the moment the expression of these views had to be somewhat milder, compared with earlier declarations of Labor policy). In Curtin's view, Australian forces should be devoted to defending *Australian* soil.

As to Stan Bisset, he was now in two minds. He felt certain that he wanted to serve in some fashion, but was simply not sure in what form. On the way back to Australia the *Strathmore* zig-zagged through the ocean for much of the journey to avoid possible submarine attacks. All the while the Wallabies discussed what they were going to do, and they were never so emotional as in the first flush of dawn when the ship pushed through Port Phillip Heads. The Wallabies had been up chatting and carousing all night and now, as the lights of Melbourne appeared ahead in the distance, the realisation struck that with the winds of war likely to push them in thirty different directions, this was undoubtedly the last time they would all be together.

And then Stan Bisset started singing 'Danny Boy' in that deep bass baritone that could just send a bolt right through you:

Oh Danny boy, the pipes, the pipes are calling
From glen to glen, and down the mountain side
The summer's gone, and all the flowers are dying
'Tis you, 'tis you must go and I must bide.

But come ye back when summer's in the meadow
Or when the valley's hushed and white with snow
'Tis I'll be here in sunshine or in shadow
Oh Danny boy, oh Danny boy, I love you so.

And if you come, when all the flowers are dying
And I am dead, as dead I well may be
You'll come and find the place where I am lying
And kneel and say an 'Ave' there for me . . .

It was the kind of melancholy, beautiful song that captured so perfectly the way they all felt, and when Stan sang it, he sang it for them . . . and by the time he'd finished, it wasn't just Stan who was crying but most of the Wallabies with him. Fare thee well, good chum. Keep your head down, and yourself in touch with me. Strong handshakes, rough embraces and then they really were all scattered.

While the Wallabies had been on the water, Prime Minister Robert Menzies had made the key appointment for the age. The General Officer Commanding of the Australian Army, soon to be known as the Second Australian Imperial Force, was to be a man by the name of Major General Sir Thomas Blamey. As Menzies would later write, in explaining his reasons for the appointment, none of Blamey's rivals for the post 'nearly matched him in the power of command—a faculty hard to define but impossible to mistake when you meet it.'[6] Blamey had a distinguished war record, but he also had recent experience in commanding and administering a large body of men with the Victoria Police Force, albeit in controversial circumstances.

Blamey had taken over as police commissioner on 1 September 1925, after a military career that included such impressive credentials as having made that legend of landing on the shores of Gallipoli with the First Australian Imperial Force at dawn on 25 April 1915, and rising to be Chief of Staff of the First Australian Division in France a year later. But only shortly after assuming his new civil post in Victoria, police raided a a notable 'house of ill-repute' in Fitzroy and a particular gentleman was caught 'on the job', as it were. The police were about to take the rather short, stocky, moustachioed gentleman into custody when he produced a police badge, told them he was a detective, and bally-hooed his way free.

The badge was embossed with the number eighty, and when the policemen got back to the station they discovered that Badge 80 had been issued to none other than . . . the new police commissioner, Thomas Blamey. He survived this debacle by resolutely insisting that someone had stolen the badge and done the dirty on both the girl and his good self, in a different way, before he could raise the alarm. In this post, Blamey had nevertheless proved to be an extremely capable administrator. It was said of the oft-abrasive officer that his main failing was a lack of empathy and common feeling with the men beneath him.

After yet another scandal in which he committed perjury at a Royal Commission, *Sir* Thomas Blamey, shortly after being knighted, had finally stood down from his position as Commissioner of Victorian Police in 1936, and gradually worked his way back to his base career as an officer with the Australian Army.

Despite Blamey's controversial reputation, perhaps another factor in Menzies's appointment of Blamey was that he had a great deal of experience with the English, with whom he had done substantial military training, and Menzies knew that it was they, after all, who would be once again running the show. Menzies pushed the appointment through, the whole thing being formalised while Blamey was out one weekend wandering through the Dandenong Ranges looking for a particular type of wild orchid that he had long coveted for his collection.

It would be some time before the military man would again have the time to pursue this passion, as the task ahead of him was a mammoth one. In the time since the Great War Australia's state of military preparedness had sunk to such an abysmal level that not only was its army a mere rump of a few thousand men, but it possessed not a single tank, no machine guns to speak of and very little in the way of modern artillery or even radio equipment. In fact, the country had precious few resources other than an emerging band of citizens who had already expressed their willingness to fight for King and country. But to process, accommodate, train and send them into battle, the government would have to open recruiting offices, build barracks, order and manufacture weaponry, make uniforms, produce rations, the lot.

Blamey set to with a will, beginning by making the strategic appointment of Colonel Sydney Rowell, a fellow Gallipoli veteran, who was known as a superb manager of men and who had a strong feel for military tactics. Regarding his professionalism highly, Blamey made him his chief of staff and the two began to build an Australian army around them, almost literally from the ground up.

All across the nation then, the courses of lives began to alter slightly and then change direction entirely as the call to arms, the call to fight for Australia, took hold . . .

CHAPTER TWO

STORM CLOUDS GATHER

The Japanese would act quickly, they would all be regulars, fully trained and equipped for the operations, and fanatics who like dying in battle, whilst our troops would consist mainly of civilians, hastily thrown together on mobilisation, with very little training, short of artillery and possibly of gun ammunition.

General Vernon Sturdee, predicting in 1933 that Japan would pose the major threat to Australian security[7]

Our country is firmly determined to set up a Greater East Asian order by eliminating those who continue their resistance against us and by collaborating with those who make common cause with us . . .

Prince Fumimaro Konoye, Prime Minister of Japan, 1941[8]

And that'd be about bloody right. There was the world going to hell in a handcart, and here he was selling bloody sheets, furnishings, and women's undies! Somehow, Joe Dawson just knew it didn't fit. A keen reader of Melbourne's *Sun News-Pictorial* newspaper, which he bought every day up at the corner store, Joe'd been following very closely the shenanigans in Europe, and was aware just what kind of carnage Hitler and his stormtroopers were causing. Some blokes acted as if nothing at all was going on, and tried to ignore it, but Joe never could. One day, while running an errand into the city for the Footscray store he was working in, he passed by the recruitment centre at Melbourne Town Hall. It was an instant decision: selling more women's undies or going off to war. War won.

The only problem was that because he looked, and was, so young—he was still only seventeen years old—the recruiting officer said he would have to get one of his parents to sign a form giving him permission. So he tried his mum first.

'Mum, I'm going to join the army and I just need you to sign this form.'

'See your father . . .'

That was his mum's way—end of story—but as it happened, Joe never got time to ask his father, for as soon as he found out, he came and saw Joe.

'*No!* Not on your bloody Nelly. When you're a legal adult you can do what you damn well please, but until then, no!'

His dad wasn't the kind of bloke you could argue with—especially since his menswear shop had gone bust during the Depression and he'd had to work in the building trade since—so Joe festered for a while, until just a few nights later he was passing by the Footscray drill hall where the 32nd Militia Battalion Footscray Regiment was going through its stuff. There was a bloke outside who gave him the drum.

'Look,' he said to Joe, 'what you do is join the militia, get to know a bit about the army, and then transfer to the AIF. They won't worry about your age then. You can join the militia at eighteen years without any parents' signature.'

On the spot, Joe went in and told a warrant officer he wanted to join up.

'When were you born?' the officer asked.

The question hung there for a moment, while Joe looked at his options and realised there was only one. He told a white lie . . .

'The third of January, 1921,' he said, instantly making himself a year older. Done. After a medical established that he was healthy, he was told to report the following Saturday to the drill hall, where he would be issued with all his kit. It left him with only one minor problem . . .

That Saturday, after taking proud possession of his service jacket, breeches, long puttees, tan boots, felt hat, .303 rifle, bayonet, water bottle, ammunition pouches and pack—and having done his first training session—Joe decided he would just have to front his mum and dad, dressed in full regalia, and take it from there. So he did.

Predictably, his dad hit the roof.

'We'll see about this!' he roared and then launched into a long tirade about how no son of his was going to defy him, and the only way he could have joined was to lie about his age and once he told the authorities Joe's true age they'd kick him out again and . . .

And just then, the redoubtable Auntie Nell, who lived next door and had heard all the noise—like half the neighbourhood—popped her head in the door. Informed of the situation, she shot Joe's dad down as surely as if he were a Zeppelin air balloon and she a hard-rising bullet.

'Good on you,' she said to Joe, 'it's good to see someone with a bit of *guts* around here!'

It might have been the way she said '*guts*', or maybe just that Auntie Nell was the kind of woman you didn't cross, but one way or another all the wind indeed went out of Joe's dad and that was the end of it. Joe stayed in the militia, and that was fair dinkum *that*.

One breezy summer's night, in early 1940, Max Dupain turned the corner off Bondi's Campbell Parade when he saw coming towards him someone he thought he knew, but dressed like he had never seen him before. It was his recently departed employee and still great friend, Damien Parer, dressed from top to toe in the uniform of a war correspondent.

'What do you know, Maxie!' Damien greeted him, 'I'm off to the bloody war!'[9]

And he was that. In 1939, Damien had gone for an interview with the Cinema Branch of the Department of Commerce, which at the outbreak of war had been subsumed by the newly created Department of Information. At the interview they had asked Damien what his goal would be if he were to become a war correspondent and he had replied with characteristic honesty, quoting from his catechism: 'To know God, love and serve Him here on earth and to enjoy Him forever in Heaven.'[10]

It wasn't quite what they were expecting, but in any case he'd got the job, and now, a new uniform and kitbag later, he was suddenly on his way to cover the first actions of the Australian forces in the Middle East.

True, it would be a great wrench to leave the side of the young woman he had been getting so close to—her name was Marie Cotter, she worked at the David Jones beauty salon on the corner of Market and Castlereagh in Sydney, and maybe it was true that he hadn't fallen in love with her until he'd taken her photo and saw her beauty peering back at him from the bottom of the developing tray—but it had to be done. The war, and enthralling documentary possibilities beckoned. Within a week of running into Max, Damien was on a troopship called the *Empress of Japan*—an unlikely name for a ship taking the first Australian troops to action in what would shortly become known as World War II—heading to Palestine.

On the ship he wrote a letter to Max and Olive Dupain, setting out his views on his new role.

I think I have told you before what I reckon I should aim at in this job—that aim has not been achieved yet.

To build a true picture of the Australian soldier in movie and stills.

To make good movie single reelers showing cause and effect. Something after March of Time idea of why we are here and what we are doing in the long range perspective as it affects us in Australia.

To keep newspapers and newsreels supplied with really hot spectacular news.[11]

Butch Bisset was gone. Not long after brother Stan had returned to Australia with the Wallabies, Butch had joined up, farewelling his partly tearful, partly proud parents and officially becoming a soldier of the 2/14th Battalion, 7th Division of the 2nd AIF. (The First Australian Imperial Force which had been formed up for World War I had consisted of five divisions—with each division numbering fifteen thousand men—and the Second Australian Imperial Force had continued the numerical series, with the first division formed for World War II becoming the 6th Division and so on.)

Against the magnetic pull of his own beloved brother already having joined up, Stan held out for as long as he could. If there was one thing that finally prompted him, it was news of Dunkirk . . .

In late May 1940 more than 300 000 Allied troops were pinned on the northwestern beaches around the French town of Dunkirk, as seemingly the entire German army and Luftwaffe bore down upon them. On the edge of complete catastrophe, a flotilla of tiny English boats, ferries, large ships and just about anything that could float, made its way across the English Channel and, due to the extraordinary courage of the captains and crew, successfully plucked the troops to safety. In some ways the exercise was a massive defeat for the British, in that their forces had been so clearly routed in the face of the German Blitzkrieg through the Low Countries and France. But, on the other hand, the fact that the evacuation had been successful, and that such a massive number of troops had escaped to fight another day, was inspirational to the Allied cause. What *was* clear was that Britain was going to need help, and it was for the sons and daughters of the English-speaking world to answer the call.

An editorial in the *New York Times* immediately afterwards reflected the overwhelming joy with which the success of the amazing operation was greeted and the hope it generated.

So long as the English tongue survives, the word Dunkirk will be spoken with reverence. For in that harbor, in such a hell as never blazed on earth before, the rags and blemishes that have hidden the soul of democracy fell away. There, beaten but unconquered in shining splendour, she faced the enemy. They sent away the wounded first; men died that others might escape. It was not so simple a thing as courage, which the Nazis had in plenty. It was not so simple a thing as discipline, which can be hammered into men by a drill sergeant. It was not the result of careful planning, for there could have been little. It was the common man of the free countries rising in all his glory from mill, office, mine, factory and shop and applying to war the lessons learned when he went down the mine to release trapped comrades; when he hurled the lifeboat through the surf; when he endured hard work and poverty for his children's sake. This shining thing in the souls of men Hitler cannot attain nor command nor conquer. He has crushed it where he could from German hearts.

This is the great tradition of democracy. This is the future. This is victory.[12]

And this was Stan, making the decision of his life just a few months after arriving home. It was obvious Britain urgently needed assistance against the rampaging Germans and—put together with the fact that Butch had already joined up—Stan knew there was only one thing to do. In rugby if ever there had been a 'blue' on, his place had always been standing shoulder to shoulder with Butch and, given that this was a blue that all of Australia was in, there was no doubt his place was in Australia's armed forces . . . right beside Butch. Stan reached this conclusion on a Friday night while having a few beers with friends; on the spot he headed off to the nearest recruitment office at the Melbourne Town Hall. By the Monday morning Private Stanley Young Bisset was reporting for duty at the Puckapunyal training camp.

Consisting of many wooden barracks, each housing twenty-two men, and acres of sweat-drenched red clay on which to parade and perform military manoeuvres, Puckapunyal was to be their home for the next few months as they prepared for war. Both Stan and Butch were soon part of the 2/14th Battalion, which was the sole battalion raised from Victoria as part of the 21st Brigade, which was in turn one of the three brigades which made up Australia's 7th Division. Those who had joined up immediately war was declared had gone into the 6th Division—and were promptly committed by Prime Minister Menzies to fight beside Britain in the Middle East— and this promptitude had earned the men of the 6th the right to refer mock-derisorily to those in the 7th as 'the deep thinkers'. But for many it just wasn't possible to walk away from all their commitments in civilian life and join the armed forces. But for all the problems of extrication, many like Butch and Stan had simply not been able to resist the call to duty and, within six months of war being declared, Australia had raised no fewer than a hundred thousand volunteers, meaning that one in six able-bodied Australian men was under arms. Which, in a way, was as well, because things were definitely stirring, and not just in Europe, where Hitler had already laid waste to Poland, Denmark, Norway, Belgium, Luxembourg Czechoslovakia, Holland and France.

Even more pertinently from Australia's point of view, in July 1940 the Japanese government had effectively been taken over by its military and, just one month later, Japanese Foreign Minister Matsuoka Yôsuke announced his grand idea in very plain language. From this point on, he said, Japan would devote itself in its area of the world to establishing a New Order called the 'Greater East Asia Co-Prosperity Sphere'—essentially an autonomous bloc of Asian nations which would trade with each other, entirely exclusive of Western powers. As he put it in a speech to the Diet: 'We have thus maintained an attitude to surmount all obstacles for the purpose of establishing a sphere of co-prosperity throughout greater East Asia with Japan, Manchukuo and China as its pivotal point.' What Matsuoka and his Prime Minister, Prince Fumimaro Konoye, were essentially proposing was a 'United States of Asia', with Japan as its pivotal point.

Both the Japanese prime minister and the foreign minister made it clear that Japan would not endure the American and European powers dividing up the Asian nations between them. It was time for Asia to be 'liberated from Western Imperialist powers', albeit under strong Japanese leadership. Still heavily engaged in their war with China, Japan's industry desperately needed the raw materials that Europe and America had been trying to deny it for the previous two decades. Specifically, in the last few years, the United States had imposed an embargo against selling Japan oil or steel. Concerned at being denied full access to such crucial products as oil from the Dutch East Indies and rubber from Indochina, Japan's government felt that that the Co-Prosperity Sphere was the answer, and the tone of Foreign Minister Yôsuke's speech made it clear that Japan would consider using military force to simply take what it needed.

After all, back in 1905 Japan had been the first Asian nation to engage in a war with a western power and win, when it had trounced Russia in the Russo–Japanese War of 1904–05. If it came to it, Japan had little doubt it could do it again. A similar disdain for any quibbles that other nations might have about the whole notion of the 'Co-Prosperity Sphere' was apparent when Japan began to flex its military muscles in Asia and install puppet regimes who— wouldn't you know it?—thought sending Japan raw materials was the highest priority of all. Those Asian countrymen who protested, risked torture and execution, and many others were herded into forced labour at the point of a bayonet.

The Japanese move into French Indochina at the invitation of the pro-Nazi Vichy Government in September 1940, was Japan's first foothold in Southeast Asia, but there were many more worrying things to come. Just a few days after this invasion, the news broke that Japan had formed a 'mutual defense' alliance with Germany and Italy, known as the Tripartite Pact, meaning that Japan was now sitting squarely on the side of Hitler, whom the Allies were struggling to contain. (The American Secretary of State, Cordell Hull, gave the definitive Allied response to the Pact when he described it as the 'joining of the bandit nations'.)

Apart from freezing all Japanese assets in the United States, the Roosevelt administration now widened its previous sanctions against Japan, making it illegal to export *any* oil or rubber to that country, and the American lead was followed by Britain and the Commonwealth of Nations, as well as the Dutch Government in exile—the last, particularly significant, because it denied Japan the resources of the oil-rich Dutch East Indies. All up, the land of the Rising Sun now felt isolated and alone, up against what became known as the 'ABCD Powers', as in America, Britain, China and the Dutch.

The bottom line was that within a month of Japan's incursion into Indochina, the country was effectively being starved of all but twenty per cent of its previous supply of oil, and most of the raw resources (including rubber) that it needed to fuel its aggression. And while against this possibility Japan had previously amassed a certain stockpile of necessities, clearly it would not be enough. Japan would either have to back down, withdraw and renounce its aggression, or it would have to increase its hostilities to the point where it could simply take what was being denied it by market trade.

Despite those clear aggressions, the alarm bell was not ringing shrilly everywhere. As a matter of fact, on 3 March 1941, a full nine months after Japan had declared its establishment of the Co-Prosperity Sphere, the Australian Prime Minister, Robert Menzies—who was in England on a sixteen-week visit—addressed an international audience of movers and shakers from the worlds of business, media and diplomacy, and made Australia's position on Japan clear. Not only did Australia have no emerging problem in the Pacific, he said, but in fact it wanted to 'draw closer to Japan and appreciate its problems'.

As it turned out, of course, it wouldn't be long before Japan—which had by that time built up the strength of its army to fifty-one infantry divisions—was the one who was drawing closer to Australia, and other countries besides . . .

The news came through. The 2/14th had been called up. Together with the 2/27th Battalion from South Australia and the 2/16th Battalion from Western Australia, the 2/14th would make up the 21st Brigade, and would be going to the Middle East to sort out the Germans and Italians, who had been rampaging through much of North Africa. They needed to be sent back whence they came, and the men of the 2/14th—including the newly installed Sergeant Major of B Company, Butch Bisset, and his brother Stan, the Corporal of Section 9 of 12 Platoon—felt they were the men for the job. As did most of their comrades. They were young, strong, well trained and off to war to do their bit for King and country. A great mood of euphoria swept through the troops at the news that they were off to battle.

So it was that on 19 October 1940, just over a year after signing up, Stan and Butch Bisset stood close together in their new uniforms on the bow of the good ship *Aquitania*. The ship, side by side with the *Queen Mary*, sailed out of Sydney Harbour amid a tumultuous farewell of tooting ferries, tugboats and pleasure craft.

Just over 170 years before, Captain James Cook had sailed to this continent to ultimately claim Australia for Britain. This then, was the sons of the soil that Cook and his followers had tilled, heading from that continent to help Britain out . . .

A one-time cruise ship of the Cunard line, the *Aquitania* was once the second largest ship in the world, all the more impressive for the fact that the largest, the *Titanic*, now lay on the ocean floor. Converted to a troop carrier, the *Aquitania* could transport just under eight thousand men, sweating among its oak panelling and beams and Louis XIV-style restaurant, now known rather more simply as 'The Mess'. Below decks, first-class cabins, which used to sleep an imperial one, now slept as many as ten soldiers, with two five-tier bunks crammed into it, with just three feet between, but no one was complaining. This, many of the soldiers felt on the day, was the adventure of their lives . . .

One who definitely felt like that was a bloke called Alan Haddy, whom Stan and Butch met about ten days into the voyage, after they'd stopped to pick up the 2/16th Battalion in Fremantle. To keep the mass of soldiers on the ship both busy and fit, boxing competitions had been staged, and Stan had just been marginally bested by an enormous Kalgoorlie miner in the heavyweight division, when this bloke came up to congratulate Stan on having done so well against a bloke who was so much bigger than him.

'I thought he was going to knock your block off!' Haddy told him with an enormous grin, while proffering his hand, 'but you nearly knocked *his* off.'

Haddy had been born and bred in Western Australia and possessed a warm and generous disposition, despite having known many hard times growing up in a succession of orphanages. A superb physical specimen, with a chin like a clenched fist, he projected strength, confidence and capability, a veritable physical force of nature. Yet, he was also the kind who, once it seemed likely that German aggression would inevitably lead to war, had taken himself off to night school to learn the German language as he thought it might come in useful.

One expression that had sort of taken off from the days of the Great War was to say of someone 'he's the sort of bloke you wouldn't mind being in the trenches with', and from the first, both Bisset boys felt instinctively that Haddy was like that.

The *Aquitania* continued to plough to the west . . .

Damien Parer had never been busier, nor more professionally fulfilled. Since arriving on the other side of the world with the AIF, he had been always in the thick of the action, from the 6th Division's first intensive training activities in Palestine (whose 16th Brigade was under the command of Brigadier Arthur 'Tubby' Allen), to their R and R activities in Cairo, to the brief debacle in Greece where

Australian forces had been routed by the oncoming Germans, to the actions in Syria, to the mighty siege of Tobruk. Along the way he had not only achieved extraordinarily graphic footage of Australian troops in action, but also photographed—and to a lesser extent got to know—some of the key figures in the war, such as General Blamey, Tubby Allen, General Morris and a man by the name of Captain Ralph Honner of the Western Australian 2/11th Battalion . . .

Far and away the most important relationship Damien formed though, was with the ABC Radio war correspondent Chester Wilmot, who was also covering the Australians in the Middle East and Greece. Thirty years old, and himself the son of a famous journalist, Chester was close to the cream of the ABC crop. Educated at Melbourne's Church of England Grammar School and Melbourne University, he was worldly, articulate and forthright, as might be expected of one who had captained the university debating team— on one occasion condemning Fascism against the arguments of his opponent, one Bob Santamaria—and then taken the team on to great success on a tour encompassing universities in Britain, Europe, East Asia and North America. While in Europe he had been to an Adolf Hitler rally at Nuremberg, billeted with a family of devoted members of the Nazi Party, and been to Italy to see the land of Mussolini. On returning to Australia, convinced there was going to be a world war, he had decided to become a journalist.

What most commended Reginald William Winchester Wilmot to Damien though, was his shared passion for reporting from the frontlines, for getting the story absolutely right, for perpetually trying innovative ways to tell a story so it achieved maximum impact on his audience at home. Both men were highly motivated to make the Australian public aware of exactly what the Australian troops abroad were facing, and how magnificently the nation's sons had performed under often difficult circumstances.

Wilmot had an equal regard for Damien, so much so that on occasion he would interview him for his ABC radio reports to get his expert eyewitness accounts. On one notable occasion, Damien returned the honour by putting his camera over Chester Wilmot's shoulder for a close-up, as, using his patented two-finger 'hunt-and-peck' method, the ABC's finest typed the following words:

> *The spirit which has made Australia is the spirit which has held Tobruk. The inspiring and binding force in Australian life isn't tradition or nationalism or social revolution. It's quite a simple thing. Henry Lawson called it MATESHIP . . . the spirit which makes men stick together. In Australia by sticking together, men have defied drought, bushfire and flood. In Tobruk they've scorned hardship, danger and death, because no digger would ever let his cobbers down. In Tobruk for the first time in this war the Germans were thrust back by a spirit that even tanks and dive-bombers could not conquer.*[13]

And indeed it was, Tobruk marking the first time also, in the whole war, that the might of German arms was significantly checked. The mateship of Damien Parer and Chester Wilmot, though, would get them through steeper and more dangerous obstacles yet.

And then, the last moderate in Japan crumbled. Having fought a losing battle for too long against a military that he now viewed as out of control, in October 1941, Prime Minister Fumimaro Konoye resigned. He was immediately replaced in the post by the famously brutal Army Minister, General Hideki Tojo, the same man who had been Chief Of Staff of Japan's Kwantung Army during both the occupation of Manchuria and the Nanking Massacre, as well as the former chief of the Manchurian Secret Police.

Known to his colleagues as 'Razor', Tojo had long been an advocate of Japan simply taking by military force anything, and even any *country,* that it coveted in its region, and had been personally instrumental in forming up the detailed plans for the conquest of Southeast Asia.

For the militarists generally, Japan's historical calling was '*Hakko Ichiu*', to gather the people of Asia under one banner—it translated as 'all the eight corners of the world under one roof'. Much of the

Japanese military leadership taking over had quite openly studied the best of the Western military ways—and in fact copied the way the Germans organised their army and the British their navy—and many had taken a shine to the West's ideas of establishing colonies. Not for them to be like India, Burma, Malaya and the East Indies and find themselves subjugated by a foreign system—they were much too proud for that. For well over a decade it had been Tojo's view that it was for Japan to *liberate* such countries from the yoke of the West and essentially establish Asia for the Asians, under Japanese leadership, of course. And if this put them on a collision course with the West, as well as those Asian countries who didn't see things their way, then so be it.

Now that he was not only prime minister, but also the minister for war, and a full general of the army, there was nothing and no one left to stop Tojo. The militarists in Japan had won a comprehensive victory over the moderates. Tojo was now the most powerful figure in modern Japan besides the Emperor.

Too few in New Guinea had the barest inkling that the war might reach its isolated shores and the most likely suspect to do it was the increasingly warlike Japan. The ascension of Tojo to the top political post was a clear sign of increasing militarism. So too was the fact that two months earlier the Japanese had followed up their invasion of northern Indochina with the invasion of the southern half of the country. Given Japan's shortage of natural resources, they were obviously looking covetously at the oil-rich Dutch East Indies. The question had to be raised: did Japan's interests in Southeast Asia extend all the way to New Guinea?

From Australia's point of view, New Guinea was something of a colonial outpost, and one of only medium value—a value determined mostly by its natural resources. Since Europeans had first settled there, a kind of white 'squattocracy' had developed in those scattered parts of the island where the wild environment could be tamed enough to produce some economic benefit. The Europeans had established rubber plantations, the odd mine and a few scattered copra farms, while in other parts many missions had been set up to harvest native souls for Jesus. Typically, each white household had a retinue of black domestic servants attached to it and it was they who provided hard labour.

The Australian administrative authorities essayed to continue to 'civilise' as many of the natives as it could and as part of that aim they published a newspaper called the *Papuan Villager*, which gave the latest news. In that October of 1941 the *Villager* broadcast what was happening in the European theatre of war between the Allies and the Germans, and also informed them of what to expect should the Japanese arrive on New Guinea shores. One article was as clear a manifestation as any of the view which had suddenly crystallised among Australians in that part of the world, that the true value of controlling New Guinea was not just supply of rubber and gold and copra, but the fact that New Guinea would be the ideal launching pad to invade Australia.

'The Japanese are not white men,' this article went. 'Their skins have a rather yellow colour, sometimes pale brown. They are often small men, but well-made and strong . . . The Japanese are a very warlike people. They are brave men, but they make a lot of trouble . . . So far the Japanese have not entered our war. They have done a lot of talking, but they have not begun to fight. We do not want them to fight; but if they do we shall be ready for them.'[14]

An example of the Japanese 'them' at this very moment were the men of the 144th Regiment. In much the same manner as some Australian battalions had been formed by taking bits and pieces from other units, so too was the 144th brought together in November 1941 from units of the 55th Division from No. 11 Army Depot at Zentsuji, Japan. Most of the men were drawn from the city of Kochi on the island of Shikoku. At their head was Major General Tomitaro Horii, who received his promotion from the 11th Brigade after brilliantly brutal service in China. The men of the 144th were for the most part hardened veterans who had already seen a lot of action and victory. In this moment, they were being formed up for duty somewhere in the South Seas. Just where and when they would see action, they neither asked, nor were told.

Just where and when the young Aussie Diggers would likely see action, they most definitely *did* ask, but still were not told. All that the young men of the newly formed 39th Battalion knew—as they gathered at Camp Darley about forty miles west of Melbourne, near the tiny town of Bacchus Marsh—was that their battalion had just been created by order of the Military Board in early October 1941, with a possible view to serving overseas.

There was nothing specifically stirring there at the moment, but the noises coming from the increasingly aggressive Japanese meant that the Australian military authorities had decided that it was a good idea to gather up some of the militia—they were all that was left at home after Australia's fighting finest had been sent to the Middle East and Singapore—and train 'em up the best they could, and quickly haul them up north, just in case.

And this was 'them'! Victoria's 3rd and 4th Infantry Division, as well as the 2nd Cavalry Division, had kicked in the few men they felt they could spare, and they were thrown in with several hundred raw recruits who didn't necessarily know the butt end of a rifle from the pointy bit. Finally, to complete the mix, the authorities also added a few old stagers regarded as not good enough for the AIF, but who Australia was now getting desperate enough to allow back under arms. This was the new 39th Battalion.

And one old stager, now standing at the front of the battalion in the Camp Darley parade ground on this dusty morning in mid-October 1942, was the Battalion's Commanding Officer, the vastly experienced Colonel Hugh Marcell Conran who had been a lieutenant with the 1st AIF in the 23rd Battalion. He was not a bad sort of fella to be leading a newly formed outfit like this. For while he was very much old school and had all the fortitude and command of one who had successfully hauled himself up in life by his own bootstraps—and believed that others could do the same—he was also a family man with a strong streak of compassion and a high sense of duty to Australia. And not without reason . . .

After the last war he had settled on land in the Red Cliffs district which the government had opened up for soldiers like him who had served their country well. He had raised his family and prospered but now that Australia was in trouble, and needed him once more, like many of his ilk he made it his business to jump straight back into the fray and give service. Many of his erstwhile military mates from the last war had felt the same, for flanking him as he spoke were many of the older officers who had served with Colonel Conran, friends and former associates who would be useful teaching both the new soldiers and some of their younger officers everything they knew about establishing a good battalion. And in his book, by the book, that started with them learning that they were there to serve Australia in whatever capacity was demanded of them.

'And what I hope,' the Colonel continued as he surveyed with military bearing the assembled mass, 'is that over the next few months we will be able to raise your levels of physical fitness, give you an understanding of how the army works, an appreciation of military tactics, and turn you all into good soldiers worthy of bearing arms for this country. Australia deserves no less, and you will deliver no less.'

Still, to look at them, Colonel Conran could see that they really did have a *lot* to learn. Physically, he could see that they came from disparate militia units, as well as straight off civvy street, because they were dressed in a range of outfits—the 39th's new uniforms had not yet arrived. But more significantly, having looked at the personnel files over the previous fortnight, he knew . . . well, he knew that the raw material he had been given to work with was not straight from the top drawer.

All put together, they were a rum lot these blokes of the 39th, essentially a snapshot of the very young Australian male population at that time who had been left behind by the AIF—some so young they didn't need razors, and the rest chosen from older generations, including a few *really* old codgers who in turn had been just about taken from the retirement home. One young bloke there was blind in one eye, the bugler had just one arm, another was an epileptic, yet another was a severe asthmatic, while others were reasonably physically fit but had résumés that wouldn't get them a job anywhere else. Lined up for their first parade it was not straining fancy to say that within their ranks could be found all of the 'butcher, baker, candlestick-maker, rich man, poor man, beggar man and thief' of popular folklore.

As one, however, they were bound by their common oath, which was taken with their right hand raised (if they had one), their left hand stiff by their side and their eyes staring straight at the Australian flag.

'I swear,' the new blokes had intoned as one, 'that I will well and truly serve our Sovereign Lord, the King, in the Military Forces of the Commonwealth of Australia until the cessation of the present time of war or until sooner lawfully discharged, dismissed, or removed, and that I will resist His Majesty's enemies and cause His Majesty's peace to be kept and maintained, and that I will in all matters appertaining to my service faithfully discharge my duty according to law. So help me God.'

So help them, God. And so they began. For the next two months they trained the best they could.

One among them was Joe Dawson—now *Sergeant* Dawson, if you please—who had lied about his age to join the militia a couple of years earlier, and had been one of fifty or so who had transferred from the 32nd Battalion, Footscray Regiment, to join the 39th Battalion. Joe figured it was his best chance to see some action overseas, just as he had always wanted to do with the AIF, and he was delighted to be there.

Another was a rough 'n' ready kinda bloke by the name of Smoky Howson, one of nineteen children who had at last found a way out of working all day in the bloody market garden his alcoholic father had run. The kids at school had called him 'Smoky' because he always smelt of smoke, 'cos at home the only way he could get warm was to practically get right *in* the open fireplace the family also used as its stove, and it wasn't as if his clothes got a wash too often anyway. Smoky had come to the 39th by way of the 52nd Battalion and, all up, he just couldn't believe how luxurious the army life was! Three meals a day! A real bed! Weekly pay! Frankly, he had never had it so good, and he couldn't quite believe it when the other guys sometimes complained about having to get up so early, train so hard, and eat such ordinary grub in the Mess Hall. Plenty of them, to be sure though, simply weren't fit, whereas Smoky was as strong as a mallee bull. For most of his twenty years he had worked like a human bullock, carrying bags of spuds, and bags of fertiliser weighing 180 pounds, and now that strength was going to be useful.

While by this time the likes of Joe Dawson were familiar with much of military life, most of the wet-behind-the-ears newcomers had a lot of learning to do. And so it began . . .

Each morning at 5.30 a.m. the newly formed battalion band, led by their one-armed bugler, marched up and down between the huts thumping out the one martial tune they'd been able to master, 'Sussex by the Sea'. After that the soldiers' days would be filled with instruction in basic military skills and endless training to improve their physical fitness. Over the coming weeks they learnt such things as how you set up a defensive perimeter; how you could penetrate such a perimeter when you were attacking; how you set up an ambush; how you reacted when ambushed; how you cleaned a .303 rifle; and how to operate and maintain Lewis and Vickers machine guns left over from the Great War. (The men would have liked to work with more modern guns, but there simply weren't any available.) At a cost of great fatigue and terrible blisters, they came to understand what a 'route march' was, and how you could move overland in a straight line by the dead reckoning of a compass. They learnt to fire three-inch mortars, and how to dig trenches quickly to take shelter when the enemy were firing mortars and bullets at you. They also received rough instruction on how to stem the flow of a bloody wound, should the last lesson not have worked for everyone.

Most of their military manoeuvres were done out in open fields with a few sparse trees scattered here and there. At other times— and the men liked these best—it involved the troops being moved into different positions with trucks, with an official 'umpire' to decide who had won.

They spent time in what was called 'the bull ring', essentially an open-air spot where some straw dummies swung from a rope beneath a tree, and you had to practise slashing the bayonet into its gizzard, pulling the bayonet out and swinging the rifle butt into its face in two very quick movements. Speed was everything in this, it was explained to them. If ever it came to it, you had to kill the enemy soldier not only quicker than he could kill you, but *so* quickly that you would have time to kill the next one coming at you. It was a matter of life and death, both your own, and that of the enemy. Again and again and again, they went at the grisly business of it, most of the soldiers of the 39th at least quietly wondering how they'd go if ever they were ever obliged to stick those cruel bayonets into an actual person. How would they go, *then*?

In the course of the early days of the formation of the 39th Battalion, many soldiers who were in the military for the first time were also learning something of the building blocks of the army structure, and the way this structure ideally worked. Each of them was a private, and it usually took ten privates to make up a section. The section was composed of four riflemen, two scouts (whose job it was to get themselves in forward positions and act as the eyes and ears), a machine gunner and his 'number 2', a second-in-command (2IC) called a lance corporal and the section commander, who was a corporal. Three sections made up a platoon, which was commanded by a lieutenant, with a sergeant as his second-in-command. Three platoons formed a company, under the command of a major, with a captain 2IC and company sergeant major—a warrant officer class 2. As well, each company would have its retinue of cooks, medics and the like.

Four companies, usually designated A, B, C and D, formed a battalion—although the militia, like the 39th Battalion, also had a machine-gun company called E company. And each battalion, incidentally, had its own colours which it was their job to—both metaphorically and physically—hoist high in the course of their actions. In the case of the 39th, the colours were a mélange of brown and red, which the men knew colloquially as 'Mud Over Blood'. These were always visible as a patch on their lapels, as well as on the battalion flag, which was used for ceremonial occasions. And speaking of blood, if they were injured in the course of a battle they were to fall back to the RAP or Regimental Aid Post, for a preliminary assessment. But moving along . . .

Battalions were usually commanded by a lieutenant colonel, known as the CO or commanding officer, and his wider staff included a major as 2IC, and other officers with such responsibilities as intelligence, logistics, operations, mortars, medical services, signals and administration, while transport formed essentially the fifth 'support' company. Battalion HQ was an entity in its own right and the nerve centre of the battalion. Each soldier learnt that in any battle it was essential to protect battalion HQ as it was the brain of the whole body—now composed of over five hundred men—which gathered in all intelligence from the battlefront and issued hopefully intelligent instructions. Three battalions formed a brigade, commanded by a brigadier, and higher still than a brigadier— way up high in charge of a division of three brigades—was a major general, then further up a lieutenant general and general. All put together, it could get very complicated from a lowly private's perspective and, for many of the new recruits, the only safe way forward was to snap off salutes to anyone with insignia on their shoulder indicating that he wasn't a private, and try to work out their rank and significance later on.

Mind you, it could be a lark sometimes to have a go at officers the men didn't like—and there were a few of them—by lining up one after the other and walking up and down the street past the targeted officer to make him salute till his bleedin' arm near fell off. Ah, how Smoky and the boys laughed, most particularly if the officer had a sheila on his arm and he had to let go of her every time to do it properly.

Naturally enough, as they trained and learnt the mechanics of military killing, each and every man thought about death. The possibility of a sudden and violent end changed men, made them keen to put as much into their remaining life as possible. Oh, a bloke didn't really think *he himself* was going to die—it was mostly other blokes you worried about—but the fact that you might die kind of gave justification for doing things you otherwise wouldn't. There were at least two or three of the 39th who went on an '11.59' pass—meaning they had to be back before midnight—to Melbourne, and came back with a glazed expression on the Sunday night . . . and not a few thereafter would be visiting the battalion doctor shortly afterwards, complaining that it burned every time they pissed. (A popular expression at the time was to say someone was 'all dressed up like a pox doctor's clerk', and now many of them were finding out just what that meant, for real.)

One who didn't make such trips to St Kilda for such a purpose was Joe Dawson. He'd been extremely happy going steady with Elaine Colbran for a couple of years now, they were both devoted to the teachings of Catholicism, and apart from all that, he just wasn't that kind of bloke.

In mid-November 1941, General Thomas Blamey returned briefly to Australia from the Middle East to have, among other things, consultations with John Curtin—the new prime minister who had just taken over the helm from Robert Menzies. General Blamey also took the opportunity to make a nationwide radio address to inform the Australian people of how the AIF was faring against the Germans, the Italians and the traitorous Vichy French, and also to achieve something else besides.

Since his return from Europe Blamey had been staggered by how little worried Australians seemed by the still far-away war; how they continued to go to the pub, the races, their dances and the football as if nothing was happening, as if his men weren't then and there putting their lives on the line every day in the desert. It angered him, the more so because the only way the Australian troops could prosper at the front was if there was a committed war effort at home and the nation as a whole was behind them, aware of the sacrifices they were making and prepared to make their own sacrifices in at least some small way. Blamey was conscious also, even if the people weren't, that Australia risked having more enemies in the near future than the aforementioned and he felt obliged to make at least oblique reference to it, though diplomatic niceties prevented him from making direct statements.

Still, after preliminaries, he got to the nub of his message:

'And to come from that atmosphere and its scenes back to Australia gives one the most extraordinary feeling of helplessness,' he grated in his rather clipped military tones. 'You are like—here in this country—a lot of gazelles grazing in a dell on the edge of the jungle, while the beasts of prey are working up towards you, apparently unseen, unnoticed. And it is the law of the jungle that they spring upon you, merciless . . .'[15]

CHAPTER THREE
BATTLE STATIONS

The Japanese warriors—the samurai—had always lived to die. Their maxim was to expect death every day and to comport themselves in a fashion to be ready for it. That was also the way in which the Japanese soldiers lived in this new army, and it explains why the Japanese had the attitude they did towards dying in battle and taking or being taken prisoner. There was no place in the Japanese military code for prisoners. If you won, you were victorious. If you lost, you were dead. It was as simple, and as cruel as that . . .

Edwin P. Hoyt, *Warlord—Tojo Against The World*[16]

It is now generally agreed that the Australian defence policy between the wars and until the fall of Singapore was at the best, naively optimistic, and at the worst . . . close to treason.

Professor David Horner, *Crisis of Command*[17]

As Sunday mornings went, it was a typically quiet one at Pearl Harbor in Hawaii on 7 December 1941. Many of the regular residents were just getting ready to head off to church, and many military personnel were trying to shake off hangovers from the previous night's carousing when, almost as one, they turned to the northwest to the noise of a sudden massed droning. What was that?

It was the Japanese . . .

Bombers. Torpedo planes. Escorting fighters. Two hundred in all, coming their way from a secretly assembled pod of six aircraft carriers, some 250 miles to the north of Hawaii. Japanese intelligence had predicted that most of America's Pacific Fleet would have returned to Pearl Harbor for weekend leave and, sure enough, there they were! Just before 8.00 a.m. the Japanese arrived above the American airfields and harbour and—on the direct orders of Prime Minister Hideki Tojo—unleashed hundreds of tons of bombs. (And this, despite the fact that at that very moment Japanese diplomats were in Washington, ostensibly to discuss peace.)

While the Japanese bombers and torpedo planes were busily sending the many occupants of the US Navy dock's 'Battleship Row' to the harbour bottom, the escort fighters were not busy at all. Simply put, so complete had been the surprise of the attack that barely one American plane was able to scramble in response before it was quickly shot out of the skies. When the first wave of Japanese planes had completed their work, they were quickly replaced by a new wave which unleashed its own thunder, and so on. Less than two hours after the first bombs hit, the sky cleared of Japanese planes, though the smoke from the destruction they had wrought would still be there four days later. The pride of the American Pacific Fleet—including seven battleships, three cruisers, two destroyers and four support vessels—lay on the bottom of Pearl Harbor. No fewer than 188 planes were wiped out, two thousand American military personnel were killed, over one thousand were wounded, and many military buildings were reduced to rubble.

One small blessing for the Americans, at least, was that the US Navy's three aircraft carriers of the Pacific Fleet had been out of the Harbor at the time of the attack and had therefore been spared, which would shortly prove to be of great significance.

Not for nothing would President Roosevelt quickly declare 7 December 'as a day that will live in infamy', in the process of declaring war on Japan. Prior to the bombing, the Americans simply had not wanted to become involved in this World War—now, there was no question. For his part, Prime Minister Hideki Tojo addressed his own people in a national radio broadcast to make them aware that the war would be long and arduous, but that it would be worth it to 'construct a glorious tomorrow'.[18]

A mighty giant, now enraged, stirred itself after two years of neutrality.

While Pearl Harbor was shaken to its core in the wake of the Japanese attack, one part of the Pacific where blind panic did *not* take hold was the Philippines where General Douglas MacArthur was in charge. In fact not only was there no panic, nothing much at all happened. Just after midday local time—some ten hours after the Pearl Harbor raid—most of the personnel on duty at Clark Field, the principal American base fifty miles north of Manila, had just finished their lunch and were lazing around on the lawn before resuming their duties, when a very funny thing happened. At least it seemed funny at the time . . .

A soldier burst forth from the barracks and with high hilarity yelled: 'Hey, you guys. It's just come over the radio, Japanese planes are bombing Clark Field! Can ya believe it?'[19]

Everyone laughed and looked around at the perfectly placid scene, and marvelled at the ludicrous report. No sooner was the laughter just starting to ebb though, than air-raid sirens sounded. Moments afterwards—*run for your lives!*—an angry swarm of fifty-four Japanese bombers with their thirty-six Zero fighter escorts broke through the clouds and bore down upon the American base. There, directly below the Japanese bomb-bay doors was the collected might of a good chunk of the US Air Force—B17 Flying Fortresses, B25 Mitchell Bombers and Kittyhawk Fighters—neatly lined up on the ground and waiting to be blown out of existence, in much the same manner as the US Navy had awaited its fate at Pearl Harbor. Again, not a single plane scrambled to meet the Japanese aggressors. No anti-aircraft fire raked at their bellies. Consequently, almost all the American planes were wiped out. Somehow, even though the attack on Pearl Harbor had occurred ten hours earlier, and General MacArthur was fully aware of it, his forces remained totally unprepared to counter a likely follow-up Japanese attack.

The raid perfectly softened up the American defences so that tens of thousands of Japanese troops could storm ashore shortly thereafter to take over the Philippines. The attack on Pearl Harbor had destroyed much of America's naval power in the Pacific, while the bombing of the Philippines destroyed much of its air power in the same theatre.

Under normal circumstances such a debacle might have seen the immediate dismissal of the unprepared commanding officer who allowed such defeat, but these were not normal times, and MacArthur was no ordinary man.

To most American military men, MacArthur was already in fact the most famous man in the army. Born in 1880, the son of a famous general who was himself a Congressional Medal of Honor winner for his exploits in the Civil War, Douglas MacArthur had graduated first in his class at West Point. His grade point average had been beaten only twice before and one of those had been the famous contemporary of his father, Robert E. Lee.

Of the many things MacArthur had pursued in his military career one of the most significant was that he had virtually pioneered army public relations when, during the Great War, he had worked as a major for the Secretary of War, Newton D. Baker, and was responsible for drumming up public support. He had risen from there to be the Chief of Staff of the entire United States Army. It was his skills in public relations that now came to the fore. For, despite the debacle, few details of it were yet known, and to the American public MacArthur emerged almost overnight as the key defender of all that was good and American in the south seas against everything that was evil and Japanese. And even if President Roosevelt had wanted to, how could he sack an American hero while he was under siege; for less than a fortnight after the first Japanese bombing of the Philippines, the Japanese had landed extensive forces on the north of Luzon island and were quickly moving on Manila.

One communiqué after another flowed from Luzon—many of which were personally written by General MacArthur—telling of the heroic defence led by the one and the same General MacArthur, and he soon became known in the popular press as the 'Lion of Luzon' on the strength of it. When America most desperately needed a military hero, MacArthur came pre-packaged and continued to provide daily material to build the legend . . . whatever the reality.

In the meantime, the Japanese did not content themselves merely with the attack on Pearl Harbor and the conquest of the Philippines. With savage speed, Japanese forces were soon laying siege to Siam (now Thailand), Malaya, Hong Kong, Wake Island, the Dutch East Indies, Burma and British Borneo, where they were able to tap into the rich oil supplies. All of it was nominally to make sure everyone was ready to have 'co-prosperity' thrust upon them—not that they had a chance.

The formal Japanese declaration of war on the Allies, when it came, was at least very lyrical. The Japanese Emperor, the direct descendant of the Sun God, merely released to the ethereal ether: 'We by the grace of Heaven, Emperor of Japan, seated on the throne of a line unbroken for ages eternal, enjoin upon ye, Our loyal and brave subjects: We hereby declare war on the United States of America and the British Empire. The men and officers of Our Army and Navy shall do their utmost in prosecuting the war . . .'[20]

And so they did.

In Australia, news of the Japanese aggression in the Pacific hit like a thunderclap on an afternoon already precipitously poised with that possibility. This was not military action in some far-flung field of Europe or the Middle East well removed from their own neighbourhood—this was a brutal and hardened foe, savaging all before it and heading their way. Really. Just half an hour *before* bombing Pearl Harbor, another Japanese force had landed in northern

Malaya and was fighting its way down the Malayan Peninsula towards Britain's enormous naval base at Singapore, a site which Australians had long considered their principal source of security in the region.

Many years before, it was a couple of lines from an old English music hall song that had inspired the term jingoism:

We don't want to fight,
But by Jingo if we do,
We've got the ships,
We've got the men,
And got the money too . . .[21]

Now, Australia's situation was the exact reverse of jingoism: no ships, no men, no money. For even while Japan was rampaging over their northern neighbours, most of Australia's warships remained in the service of the British Navy in the northern hemisphere, while the might of Australian military manhood which could have provided some protection, were away in the Middle East fighting the Germans. Another division was closer to home, but it was tied up defending the Malayan Peninsula and already it was falling back before the Japanese onslaught as the invaders moved inexorably towards Singapore. At the outbreak of the distant war, there had been no hesitation in sending two divisions to the service of Mother England, yet now that decision looked foolhardy at best, suicidal at worst.

There was further irony in Australia being at war with a Japan that claimed it had taken up arms for the right to give the British Commonwealth and the United States competition in colonisation. For one of Australia's problems in preparing for war was that it still had only a tiny manufacturing base—mainly because Great Britain had encouraged its colony to provide simple raw materials and not trouble itself building factories that would provide international competition for Britain.

At least, for his part, the new Australian Prime Minister, John Curtin, reacted swiftly. He had been woken with the news of the

Pearl Harbor attack at 5.30 a.m. on 8 December 1941 in his Melbourne hotel room and responded with a simple: 'Well, it has come . . . ' before gathering himself, and moving quickly from there. He sent his beloved wife, Elsie, back to Perth so that she was safe and so he could give his every waking hour to the task without any domestic distractions. And then he got to it.

First, without waiting for Britain's lead as Menzies had done in 1939, the prime minister immediately declared war on Japan, and used strong rhetoric to underline the Australian view that this was not a mere expansion of the current war, but an entirely new war altogether. No matter that in the wake of the Pearl Harbor attack, both Germany and Italy had observed the terms of their Tripartite Treaty with Japan by declaring war on the United States, and America had returned serve.

In Curtin's view it was crucial that the Allies *not* view the possible invasion of Australia as a subordinate problem down in the bottom right-hand corner of the grander tableau, but that they view it as a key issue in its own right, requiring significant—and not subordinate—Allied resources.

In terms of trying to strengthen Australia's defences in the immediate future, the Australian War Cabinet quickly gave the nod to arm another hundred thousand Australian men and to send more troops to Darwin and Timor. The 2/21st Battalion was immediately sent to Ambon, on the eastern end of Indonesia, in part protecting the western flank of the 2/22nd Battalion, which had been in place in Rabaul since Anzac Day, 1941.

The government hastened plans to send a couple more militia battalions to Port Moresby, where the sum total of Australia's armed personnel was just 1250 poorly trained militia soldiers consisting for the most part of Queensland's 49th Battalion and three hundred natives from the Papuan Infantry Battalion—the PIB being a body of indigenous people under the leadership of Australian officers.

Beyond that, the Australian military and political leadership realised that defences in New Guinea were somewhere between 'thin' and 'non-existent'. On the entire island there were no more than seven thousand Europeans, of whom just one thousand had been formed into another loosely structured local military organisation, called the New Guinea Volunteer Rifles. Despite these admirable efforts to bolster defences, the fact remained that half of the nominally Australian territory had never even seen a white man. How did one defend a place like that?

That was what the Australian militia would have to find out . . .

As opposed to the fighting men of the AIF, the militia were soldiers who had been conscripted as the home defence force—a kind of mostly younger version of Britain's 'Dad's Army'—and before the war all these recruits had proceeded on the understanding that they would never be obliged to leave Australian shores. Because New Guinea was technically a territory of Australia at that time, though, a law change in August of 1940 meant that the militia could be sent there and still nominally be at 'home'.

It was a technicality that did not necessarily sit well with all of the men of the militia themselves, but on the other hand, who cared what they thought? On the ladder of public esteem for men in uniform, the militia was at the bottom. Derided as 'Chocos' or 'chocolate soldiers', because they would surely melt when the heat was on, the view of many—most particularly the AIF soldiers—was that the militia was naught but a shelter for those weak-kneed individuals too piss-weak to expose themselves to a real fight. Sure, before the war it had been an honourable pursuit to be in the militia, *à la* Stan and Butch Bisset, but now the war had begun, real men had long ago left the militia to join the real army. The leftovers in the militia, were considered as just one notch better than those worse-than-useless 'conscientious objectors'. So the militia would go where they were bloody well *sent*, and there was nothing more to say about it.

In the immediate aftermath of Pearl Harbor the one and only bright spot for Australia was that at least a British naval squadron, boasting the mighty battleship *Prince of Wales* and the battlecruiser *Repulse,* had arrived at the British naval base in Singapore, just six days before Japanese troops had stormed ashore on the Malayan

Peninsula to the north. This was no small measure of security, given that Singapore was famed as an 'impregnable bastion', and with firepower the like of which those two men o'war were packing, there was every reason to think it would remain so. Surely, they would at least put a serious crimp in whatever territorial ambitions the Japanese were harbouring in this part of the world.

And Mother England had, after all, made a firm promise that Australia would not be abandoned and that Singapore . . . *would . . . not . . . fall*. Certainly, all of Australia would have loved to have believed it, but under the circumstances they were a lot less confident than they had been. After all, just three months before the 'day of infamy', one of Churchill's ministers, Duff Cooper, had declared on a visit to Singapore that 'Japan is an isolated power facing overwhelming superiority in the Pacific'. And even Churchill himself had assured: 'Singapore is as far away from Japan as Southampton is from New York. The operation of moving a Japanese army with all its troopships would be forlorn.'[22]

Of all the terrible things about being in a ship with enemy bombers flying overhead, perhaps the worst is that at first flurry there is simply no way of knowing whether or not the bombs are on their way or not. You hear a searing, rising whistle and look up, but at that angle the bombs do not stand out and all you can see is sky or the bombers themselves. So all you can do is wait and hope. And that is what the men of the *Repulse* were doing at 11.18 a.m. on the morning of 10 December 1941 when they saw enemy bombers pass over, going from starboard to the port side at an altitude of 21 000 feet. With the *Prince of Wales*, the *Repulse* was just returning from a fruitless mission up the east coast of Malaya, trying to attack the Japanese invasion flotilla that had landed the soldiers when the Japs had found *them* and . . .

And they were bombs all right, and they soon sent the *Repulse* to the bottom of the ocean, followed less than an hour later by the *Prince of Wales*. When the first scattered reports of their sinking appeared in Australia, Prime Minister John Curtin refused to believe them and rushed to Sydney's ABC studios to deny them in a nationwide address. He was just about to go on air, when a producer rushed in to say, 'Prime Minister, you can't deny it for it's true—it's just been broadcast on the BBC.' Curtin's face turned ashen.[23]

The Japanese were rampant. In the land battle, each Japanese soldier had been issued with a pamphlet ordering him to take no prisoners, and with the following instruction: 'When you encounter the enemy after landing, think of yourself as an avenger coming face to face at last with his father's murderer. Here is a man whose death will lighten your heart.'

Following so closely on the shock defeat of Pearl Harbor and the Philippines, it now seemed like nothing and no one could stop the Japanese.

Well, well, well, B Company of the 39th Battalion . . . Colonel Conran looked at the report before him and gleaned enough to form at least a rough outline of what had happened. As well as training up the militia, Camp Darley also had various units of the AIF passing through—usually fresh recruits getting ready to join elements of the 6th, 7th, 8th and 9th divisions overseas as reinforcements—and there had inevitably been a lot of friction between these 'professional soldiers', and his own men of the militia. He knew that the AIF men regarded the militia as 'play-soldiers' unworthy of wearing uniforms and that they'd generally felt free to express that view. But what had started as jests, had turned to jibes, to jeers, to full-blown insults to . . . last night.

Last night, a bunch of AIF blokes had launched an all-out attack on B Company in its barracks, using fists, feet and their own steel helmets for weapons. They had been met by a B Company intent on defending their turf, using their own fists and feet, and throwing in rifle butts for good measure.

It was a curiosity of the military that while its whole raison d'etre was to fight, all fighting *within* the ranks was usually a severely punishable offence. But in this case, Colonel Conran wasn't too upset at all. There was no doubt from the report that it was the AIF who had started it, and B Company couldn't be blamed for responding in kind. The important thing was that his men had given a singularly good account of themselves, inflicting a good deal of damage on the aggressors and belying all notions that they were mere chocolate soldiers. It was, after all, a term unlikely to be used again by the attackers, once they got out of hospital, at least not within earshot of B Company.

One other thing caught Colonel Conran's eye. The whole brawl had been immediately brought under control by B Company's Lieutenant, Sam Templeton, as soon as he had arrived on the scene. This had been accomplished by Templeton uttering a few sharp words to his own men, and then personally hurling a few of the AIF men out the door as a warning to the others that they had better heed his call to withdraw.

Colonel Conran was not surprised. A big bear of a man, 'Uncle Sam' as his men called him, was a special case. At fifty-six years old, or thereabouts—Conran would not have been surprised if Templeton was older than he claimed—the lieutenant was already a vastly experienced military campaigner having served in the nascent submarine unit in the Great War, fought against the forces of Franco in the Spanish Civil War, and participated in the Irish Rebellion . . .[24]

At the outbreak of this war he had been unable to join the AIF, partly because of his advanced age and partly because he had flat feet. (The view of the Australian Army was that if you didn't have a mini Harbour Bridge between the two pads of your feet, then your fighting ability was in serious question.) So he had joined the militia and been an asset from the first day. His word among his men was law, not because they feared him, but because they respected him. He did not speak often, but when he did they listened, and no one resented him calling anyone ten years or more younger than him, 'Laddie'.

All up, Conran decided to let the whole thing slide. He would utter some gruff words, threaten holy hell if anything like this happened again, and observe the form, but he certainly wouldn't do anything to break up a group that was not only in a mood to fight but could clearly fight well. For as a group, there was no doubt that the 39th had a bit of 'mongrel' in them, and Conran and his senior officers were still laughing over another near-blue at a pub in the nearby town of Bacchus Marsh, when a rather weedy-looking private had sized up to an enormous local yokel, jabbing him in the chest and saying 'I'll *do* you mate . . . ' before adding with an encouraging nod to his mates behind, 'won't *we*, fellas . . . ?'

As it happened if the men weren't ready for a scrap then Conran didn't want them in the battalion. A short time later, the colonel was told that some men in the 39th were not happy as they felt that they'd been shanghaied into the battalion from the contributing units without having any say themselves. Calling the men into full battalion parade, Colonel Conran advised: 'I have been apprised that some of you men have come here under duress, and that is a state of affairs which is repugnant to me. Therefore, I inform you that any man who does not wish to remain a member of the battalion may say so now, and he will be returned to his previous unit, immediately . . .'[25] Some took him up on it, and were immediately replaced by men who were better disposed to fight with the 39th, should it indeed come to it. And more and more it looked like it would . . .

As December of 1941 trudged mournfully on, three American bases in the Pacific—Midway, Wake and Guam—were bombarded by Japanese planes, before the latter two were occupied by the crack Japanese troops of the South Seas Detachment, the body of the Japanese whose specific job it was to quell this part of the world. Midway was able to hold on, and then only just.

In the Philippines things were desperate, and it was not long before they became so desperate that despite the ongoing heroic communiqués coming from General MacArthur, the good general left the defence of Bataan to his less fortunate troops, and moved himself, his family and his staff to the far better provisioned island fortress of Corrigedor, where ten thousand of his best soldiers awaited. They based themselves in one of the island's many tunnels, where half a football field of solid rock lay between them and any stray bombs.

Not that this slowed down any of the heroic communiqués. In the first three months after the Philippines came under attack by the Japanese, MacArthur's headquarters released no fewer than 142 such communiqués, of which 109 were devoted exclusively to extolling the military virtues of just one person: Douglas MacArthur.[26] As MacArthur's soldiers were the only Americans engaged in serious military action anywhere in the world at that time, each communiqué was devoured by the American media, and the natural tendency under the circumstances was to follow MacArthur's lead and put progressively larger heroic haloes around his name. Anything less would have been unpatriotic, and this was no time for hard questions about whether it might have been MacArthur's ineptitude that had led the Philippines into this predicament in the first place.

Christmas of 1941 was an essentially grim affair in Australia, with many of the population worried about their loved ones fighting overseas. As well, most Australians were feeling a growing anxiety about the country's future, and were worried about how long other European outposts around the Pacific could hold out.

In Hong Kong, the answer was only hours, as the Crown colony fell to Japanese forces on Christmas morning with eleven thousand British soldiers being taken prisoner. A sign of things to come was when Japanese soldiers entered Hong Kong's principal hospital, raped many of the Chinese and British nurses, and bayoneted to death seventy of the patients.

That news would take a while to break in Australia, but in the meantime, at the Lodge, John Curtin, missing Elsie terribly, had requested that six Western Australian airmen from the local airbase join him for Christmas lunch, men equally far away from their own families.

At the 39th's Camp Darley, Christmas Day had begun with what was known as a 'Tarpaulin Muster'—a roll call for everyone from lieutenants to cooks to drivers to make sure that all were present and accounted for, and that no one had slipped away in contravention of the order Colonel Conran had made several weeks before that all leave was cancelled. It had become clear that the 39th was going to be moving out shortly, to a destination unknown. For the last few weeks the men had been regularly obliged to pack their kits, stow them in a truck and roll out, never knowing if this was just practice or the real thing. Each time they had returned to camp, but the fact that each man had been obliged to make out a will and designate a loved one to receive his pay, or part thereof, while he was away, showed that they were dinkum going to be on their way very soon.

For his part, Joe Dawson, of the 39th Battalion's B Company, had no doubt who he wanted his army pay going to—his girlfriend, Elaine Colbran. He loved her. She loved him. Joe had no doubt that, all else being equal—as in, if he didn't get himself killed in this war—he and Elaine would marry, and he wanted her in charge of their growing nest egg while he was away. When the paymaster advised that this was unwise, as girlfriends often just spent the money, Joe was uncharacteristically abrupt: 'Just do it!'

And on the subject of Elaine, Joe decided that he just couldn't stand not seeing her on Christmas Day, whatever the damn rules were. And given that they had already had one Tarpaulin Muster he figured that there was little risk of another. Quietly, he slipped away across some back paddocks, walked to Bacchus Marsh, and got a lift into Melbourne from there. There was never trouble getting a lift when you were wearing a uniform, even if it was only a militia uniform.

For one delightful afternoon Joe sat with Elaine in the front parlour of her parents' house, holding hands and talking. Goodness, she looked lovely. It was a measure of Elaine's love for Joe that she had given him three precious things. One was a silver wristwatch that she had saved up for. Even more precious was a set of rosary beads, originally from Ireland, which the nuns had assured her had been personally blessed by the Pope. Finally, a small leather case which had tiny medallions with the images of six saints on them, which he was to keep in his breast pocket at all times, over his heart, as another way of making sure that he was kept safe. Whatever else, Joe *had* to stay safe, and come back to her.

Although Joe made it back to Camp Darley before midnight, there was still hell to pay the following day when his platoon commander, Lieutenant Allan 'Kanga' Moore, hauled him up and demanded to know where the hell he had been at the second Tarpaulin Muster.

'But Sir,' Joe lied fluently. 'I just went for a run and a walk around the camp precincts. As you know, I do that quite often to keep fit. If I had known there was a "tarpaulin" on, I would have been here!'

Fortunately, there was no time for Lieutenant Moore to pursue it. Already, grumbling trucks were pulling up outside ready for the whole battalion to pile into with all their kit. This time though, there was no turning around. The trucks went straight to Bacchus Marsh railway station, where a specially commissioned train awaited them. Grumbling not a little at the weight of all their packs, as the soldiers carried their kit from the trucks to the train, they had soon boarded. Before long the Victorian countryside was rattling past them backwards, as they sat up like Jackie, crammed in 'six bums to a bench', like the sergeants said. They were on their way for real . . .

The seriousness of Australia's situation in the face of the Japanese aggression was highlighted by a New Year's message that Prime Minister John Curtin, a former journalist, penned for the Melbourne *Herald*, which appeared on 27 December 1941. In this enormously significant communication he made it clear that the times were so desperate that Australia no longer had any confidence that the traditional 'motherland', Britain, could protect them now that they were 'inside the firing lines'.

'Australia does not accept the dictum that the Pacific struggle must be treated as a subordinate segment of the general conflict . . . The Australian Government regards the Pacific struggle as primarily one in which the United States and Australia must have the fullest say in [strategy] . . . Without any inhibitions of any kind, I make it quite clear that Australia looks to America, free of any pangs as to our traditional links or kinship with the United Kingdom . . . We are determined Australia shall not go [under], and we shall exert all our energies towards the shaping of a plan, with the United States as its keystone, which will give our country some confidence of being able to hold out until the tide of battle swings against the enemy . . .

'All Australia is the stake in this war. All Australia must stand together to hold that stake. We face a powerful, ably led and unbelievably courageous foe . . .'

In Ottawa, Winston Churchill was about to give his own oration to Canada's war cabinet, when he was told of what Curtin had said. He was less than impressed. Such was Churchill's expressive way that few were left in any doubt as to his view, least of all Britain's own war cabinet, which promptly received a cable from their prime minister saying that he was 'deeply shocked', at Curtin's 'insulting speech'.[27]

Australia's need of America for its defence, and America's need of Australia as a launching pad from which they could retake the Southwest Pacific—most particularly the Philippines—had not escaped the Japanese. At that time in Imperial General Headquarters in Tokyo—the nerve centre of the Japanese military empire—the military command were deciding how best to deny the Americans any chance of using Australia in that fashion. One possibility was to simply invade the east coast cities of Australia, which were its industrial centres, while the other was to establish key bases in New Guinea and the British Solomons to Australia's immediate north. Airfields at such bases would give Japan control of the skies, while the Japanese Navy would patrol the waters between, and this would deny the Allies the same key strategic positions from which to launch counter-offensives on the Japanese, and also allow the Japanese to effectively cut the lifeline between Australia and America. If effective,

Australia would soon become all the weaker and all the more easy to absorb into the Co-Prosperity Sphere.

On the morning that Curtin's impassioned plea appeared, the good ship *Aquitania* docked at Sydney's Woolloomooloo Wharf, and began taking on board Victoria's 39th Battalion and their rough equivalent from New South Wales—the 53rd Battalion—resulting in a memorable scene.

Many of the 53rd had been taken from Sydney's Moore Park personnel depot that morning to the ship, with barely a mention as to where they were going or what they were doing. If they were lucky they had been able to get a message to loved ones that they were about to board a ship and sail away. Others had been forced on board without any chance to tell their families they were going and were of course furious and sick with worry. From waking up secure in their own beds that morning, a lot of blokes now found themselves walking the plank . . . up into the belly of the beast of a ship that would shortly depart Australian shores. What was going *on*! Therein lay something of a story . . .

The bulk of the 53rd Battalion had come into being just two months earlier when eighteen militia battalions from around New South Wales had been told to provide men to form up the new corps, with a view to them seeing service in Darwin. Some battalion commanders took the opportunity of getting rid of some of their laziest and more troublesome men, but still that wasn't the most pressing problem on this day. In the demands of the moment, Darwin was no longer the destination, replaced instead by New Guinea, and so extreme had been those demands that Christmas leave had been cancelled. Under those circumstances no fewer than one hundred of the original soldiers of the 53rd Battalion had gone AWL. Therefore, on the morning of embarkation, it was decided with some urgency that those places would simply have to be filled. So recruitment officers accompanied by military police had promptly gone round to military personnel offices and rounded up the hundred men needed to complete the battalion. Here are your papers, sonny Jim, all signed, sealed and delivered, now get on board. ON, I SAID!

A few of the wives, girlfriends and families of these unfortunates had now arrived and were screaming and crying as the ship pulled away from the dock. But the war waited for no one. As the *Aquitania* slowly turned right past Garden Island, steering towards Sydney Heads, some from the 53rd pushed to the stern of the ship, waving forlornly at their loved ones up the far end of the wharf straining for a last look as they were lost to sight . . .

On board, those who had been newly pitch-forked into the 53rd were raising a stink all right, and they were soon joined by many others in the battalion when they realised that their destination wasn't Darwin at all, but New Guinea. The plaintive cries and cursing of the 53rd kept up through much of the night, irritating the 39th no end. The mood of many of the 53rd had not been improved either, when the previous afternoon they had arrived in their bunks far below decks to find fish swimming past their portholes in the seriously overloaded ship. Sure they all knew the tub was 'chocka-block' and so she would sit heavy in the water, but what kind of bloody *nightmare* was this!

The mood on the *Aquitania*, then, was a curious mixture. For some of the men—most particularly of the 39th, many of whom had just seen Sydney for the first time and had never been on a ship before—there was a sense of adventure, while others were miserable at having left loved ones behind to head off to places unknown. Some of them imagined New Guinea as an island in the Pacific, full of swaying palms and maybe one or two hula-hula girls, with waves lapping the golden beaches. A few had even gone so far as to pack swimming costumes, golf clubs and cricket bats.

They knew they would find out soon enough, as the barely twinkling lights of Australia were left behind on the western horizon and the *Aquitania* steamed through the tropical seas to the north. To their starboard and port sides the Royal Australian Navy cruisers *Australia*, *Perth* and *Canberra* sailed as escorts. And, as an added precaution, Lieutenant Sam Templeton with a couple of others was able to put his vast military experience to good use by getting the for'ard anti-aircraft guns on the *Aquitania* into working order, and getting some of the younger laddies roughly trained in their use. (At least those laddies who were not hurling their guts up through seasickness, which certainly described a fair few of them.)

While the majority of the men in both the 39th and the 53rd were under twenty years old, there was also a good representation of soldiers in their twenties, thirties, forties and even fifties—a real collection of the young and the restless, the old and the bold. One more senior fellow with barely a tooth in his head helped to pass the time by playing 'music' on a homemade instrument consisting of a broomstick stuck through a kerosene tin, with strings attached.[28] Somehow or other, just with that, he managed to play recognisable tunes, and one or two of the young fellas of the 39th even sang along. As a general rule, the men of the 53rd Battalion did not join in.

As the voyage continued, the one hundred new recruits to the 53rd were given instruction each day before lunch out on the open deck on how to handle, fire and conduct maintenance on a .303 rifle.

It was not only, thus, mad dogs and Englishmen who were out in the midday sun . . . as the *Aquitania* continued north.

It was so cold that they reckoned the local wolves were nailing the sheep for their *wool*. The 2/14th Battalion were camped in an olive grove where they had been sent in the north of Syria to protect the border with Turkey from a possible thrust by Germans. As they shivered around their fires, the burning beach sands of Australia at this time seemed far, far away. In the midst of them all, one presence in particular stood out—Lieutenant Butch Bisset.

Butch had a very distinctive laugh, which often rang through the ranks, and his presence alone could brighten the mood of a large group of men. This lightness of being was curiously combined in Butch with a hardness of purpose that made him a rough diamond and a very fine soldier in one, the man the others instinctively looked to when the bullets began to fly . . . It was his extraordinary gregariousness, the way he knew everyone and everyone knew him; the way he kept an instinctive watch out for those on the edges of the group and was constantly encouraging them onwards. The way, all on his own, he was a binding force on the battalion.

While Stan Bisset at this point had risen higher in the hierarchy— right up to becoming the intelligence officer for the battalion—Butch's leadership was on a far more spiritual level and was every bit as valuable. Stan could not have been prouder of Butch, and in his many letters to their parents back in Victoria was constantly telling them what a fine soldier Butch had proved to be. All up they were a tough mob, and proud of it, and proud of often being known as 'Jacka's Mob' . . .

Albert Jacka had been a hardy Victorian who had served with such distinction in the 14th of World War I that the whole good name of the battalion had become associated with him. After joining up in the first few days of the war, Jacka had been one of the first Diggers to hit the beach at Gallipoli. Just a month later, when the Diggers had unsuccessfully stormed some Turks who were dug in, Jacka had volunteered for the dangerous mission of crawling around behind them. When he got there he had dived in headfirst and succeeded in shooting five Turkish soldiers dead and bayoneting two more. It was the stuff of legend that when his commanding lieutenant had finally peered over the edge of the strangely silent trench the next morning, Jacka was laconically drawing on a cigarette and said: 'Well, I managed to get the beggars, Sir.' It was the first of many extraordinarily courageous episodes for this fine Australian soldier, and he would effectively go on to win the Victoria Cross three times over. When he died in 1932 of medical problems derived from his war-wounds, his eight pallbearers were themselves each individual winners of the Victoria Cross—the only men good enough to take such a champion to his grave. Yep, they were Jacka's Mob all right, and in their Middle East campaign to date, the 2/14th had already acquitted themselves well.

After landing at Suez, they had briefly headed to Egypt to go up against Germans, who unfortunately wouldn't front for the fight. Then they had been thrown up against the traitorous Vichy French in Syria, where the 2/14th had quickly proved themselves to be disciplined, well trained, cohesive, courageous even against an ardent foe. After six weeks of vicious fighting the Vichy French had hauled up *un drapeau blanc*, read white flag.

Now that the men had fought so ferociously through such a campaign, the bonds between them were forged of blood, sweat and tears; of total dependence each on the other; of a common consciousness that only they knew what they had been through. They had lost many men, good men, great men, killed in battle and terribly wounded, and with each succeeding casualty every survivor had become increasingly conscious that their time too, might come . . .

Legends had been made both in their battalion and in their sister battalions of the 2/16th and 2/27th. Some soldiers had performed actions of such conspicuous courage that other soldiers would tell the stories again and again, and point them out to other soldiers.

'You see that bloke over there? That's Corporal Alan Haddy, from Western Australia. An amazing bloke. A couple of months ago we were going after the Vichy French, down in Syria, and you've never seen anything like it. The Froggies were dug in on one side of the Litani River, high up on the banks, and the only way we could get men across was via these canvas boats, which were literally being blown out of the water. Haddy *volunteered* to swim across the river, under fire, with a rope around his waist, and set up a kind of flying-fox to pull the boats across, meaning our blokes would be free to fire back at the turncoat Froggies instead of having to paddle.

'So, anyway, Haddy was swimming and they were firing at him, and he'd dive as deep as he could, and then come up in a different spot from the one they were expecting to get a big gulp of air, and they'd start shooting again, and he'd go under. And somehow, *somehow*—even though they dropped a mortar within three yards of him—he got to the other side. He was pretty badly wounded in the chest, with blood pissing everywhere, and was a dreadful mess, but he still tied off the ropes and the operation was a success. If he hadn't done it, the 2/16th would not have been able to get through, simple as that.'

Stan Bisset himself had gained a fair measure of notoriety for courageously leading a charge against a concrete blockhouse, where a machine gun was sending out lead as thick as lice on a mangy dog. Despite the withering fire, which had pinned down the entire Australian advance in this sector, by the time Bisset and the boys had finished the machine gun was silenced and the survivors of the defending platoon that had been manning the blockhouse were last seen running for their lives to the north.

All up, they were among Australia's finest fighting men, and as successful action succeeded successful action, their confidence continued to grow and they believed that they could face just about any enemy, any situation, and have at least a bloody good crack at besting them . . .

CHAPTER FOUR

MUD, MOSQUITOES, MALARIA AND MONOTONY

*Only seasoned men of robust bodily fitness could be depended on
to endure the rigours of even a few days marching and fighting in
these latitudes [of New Guinea], where the moist heat hangs like
an oppressive curtain and makes strenuous exertion for more than
a few hours intolerable to the white man.*

Official History of Australia in the Great War

*The natives here are known as as Coons & speak a useful language—
Pidgin English . . . The coons are rather intelligent & will do anything
for you . . .*

Salvation Army missionary, Jack Stebbings in Rabaul, 1941

As a general rule the edge of all garbage dumps around the world
have the common feature that they are stinky and blowy. The curious
feature of Port Moresby, it seemed to the newly arrived men of the

39th, was that this stinky, blowy edge looked to go clear to the core. From the moment their ship pulled into the town's harbour after six days at sea, it was hot, humid and putrid, with their chief welcoming committee composed of swarms of flies. Morale sank even further as they looked about them. Moresby's Fairfax Harbour, a wretched foreshore of dry grass mixed with indeterminate detritus, gave way to low, brooding hills on which lost little white weatherboard cottages with galvanised iron roofs clung grimly and forlornly. Many of these had their windows boarded up. The whole joint, crisscrossed by dusty little streets, just looked sad and desperate. Whatever else, it was no Pacific island paradise.

This was some kind of twentieth birthday, Joe Dawson thought, as he stared glumly to the shore. The only visual relief came by looking to their far north, where they spied something which impressed them, much as it had impressed the first European man who had given it a name. Back in 1850, British naval Captain Owen Stanley had been meandering along the southern coast of this strange land, in his ship the HMS *Rattlesnake,* when a mist which had rolled in from the south suddenly thickened to the point that nearly all was obscured. As it was clearly too dangerous to continue in such unknown territory, the second of Her Majesty's ships on this exploratory trip—HMS *Bramble,* under the command of Lieutenant Charles Yule—led the way into a bay. But late in the afternoon, the mist lifted.

'As if a curtain had been drawn up,' Stanley would later write, 'the mist and cloud suddenly lifted and the British seafarers gasped. Before them lay an extraordinary range of mountains, vaulting high to the heavens, with each of their peaks clearly shining in the last ebb of the afternoon sun.' In the captain's own honour, in the practice of the time, the peaks were named the Owen Stanley Range, and the highest of them, Mount Victoria (rising to 13 400 feet) was what the men of the 39th and 53rd could see now as they disembarked into the tiny boats which would take them into the shallow shore.

•

On terra firma again, the men stood around for some time as their nominal superiors met with the commanding authorities in New Guinea to discuss just where they would sleep for the night. Incredibly, it almost seemed as if the arrival of the *Aquitania* had been a surprise, because *nothing* had been done to prepare to receive them. Eventually it was decided that the still whining 53rd Battalion could make camp out on the Napa Napa Peninsula, right beside the mosquito-infested mangrove swamps. As to the 39th, they would have to make do with a kind of rough camping area beside the Seven Mile Airport, so named because that was its distance from Port Moresby's port, which also served as the rough centre of town. Just a few months previously the area had been the town's racecourse, until commandeered for the war.

Fall in. Move out. By the right . . . quick march!

Bit by bit as the soldiers marched, things were discarded as it became progressively clearer that this wasn't Honolulu after all. Together with the sound of *left . . . left . . . left . . . left-right-left* of their boots, came the occasional 'thump' as fishing rods, cricket bats, tennis racquets and golf clubs were hurled into the bushes, and before long the homemade cello also bit the bitter dust.

Just where the hell were they? Was this really *it*! Yup, this was pretty much it. The 39th made camp the best they could beside a small area just to the southeast of 'the camp'—and by God every sneering curl of those quotation marks was justified, because the 'camp' provided precisely no shelter or even shade of any kind. No barracks, no tents, no food, no mosquito nets, no quinine, no bloody nuthin'. There was not a single tap of fresh water, nor a single working toilet.

Sure, they had brought a lot of those things with them—some 10 000 tons of supplies in the hulls of both their own and accompanying merchant ships—but in their shambolic departure, all of the basic *matériel* had been loaded first. This meant it would be several days before it would emerge from the heavier equipment that had been loaded on top of it. Not the least of their problems was the lack of food and, for the first two days in Moresby, the newly arrived subsisted on the hardcore baked matter the men referred to as 'dog-biscuits', tins of beetroot, and gallons of tea which they boiled up in some empty kerosene tins they found on the nearby rubbish dump. Just who was the drongo running this man's army?

His name was Major General Basil Moorhouse Morris and, whatever else, he at least *looked* the part of a great military commander. He was a big man with a large brown moustache and piercing eyes; he stood ramrod straight, was always impeccably turned out, and with his ever-present sun helmet and horsetail fly-whisk, he rather came across like an antipodean Lord Kitchener who would have been perfect for a poster saying: 'I want YOU to serve in New Guinea.' The effect was completed by the fact that he adored strutting around his well-appointed Army HQ bungalow well out of town, beneath the shade of a large Union Jack flag, saying truly magnificent things such as: 'If necessary, Port Moresby must become a Tobruk of the Pacific!'[29]

For all that splendid appearance and sound, however, he was not necessarily a man born to military command. Though he had been one of his good friend General Blamey's first appointments— with Morris having been in the vanguard of Australian troops sent to the Middle East to set up facilities to receive the 6th Division— it had soon become apparent that that kind of work was not his forte. In Blamey's own words, Morris had: 'showed that he did not possess sufficient flexibility of mind to adjust himself readily to the needs of the occasion' and the apparent backwater of New Guinea had been his next port of call.[30]

Though Morris tended to specialise in dithering in most things, when it came to political infighting he proved to be very energetic indeed. And, as it turned out, at the time that the 39th and 53rd arrived, Major General Morris was never busier, engaged as he was in a bitter sectarian turf war with the man in charge of Port Moresby's civilian administration, Leonard Murray. From the time Morris had taken command of the '8th Military district' encompassing New

Guinea, on 26 May 1941, he had moved forward on all fronts, while Murray had dug in just as bitterly, fighting to his last petty official and ink-blotter to keep primary control of the day-to-day running of the colony. It was the misfortune of the newcomers of the 39th and 53rd battalions that they arrived right when the fight was achieving its climax.

For look, with one thing or another, there simply hadn't been *time* for Major General Morris to get things in shape for all the chaps arriving. When the desperate Australian Government came down heavily on the side of Major General Morris to try to resolve the dispute, it saw not only the complete withdrawal of Leonard Murray from the territory, but also the resignation of the very senior administrators and minor officials who had been keeping the wheels of government turning, however slowly. This would further worsen the situation not only for the newly arrived militia, but for all of the territory, as many native police deserted, hospitals closed down, and the rough judicial system ceased to function. As the Diggers were trying to settle in, the whole territory was teetering on the brink of anarchy with the collapse of the civil institutions.

To fill the vacuum left by the lack of civilian administrators Morris would soon create the Australian New Guinea Administrative Unit, whose job was to run the colony with a focus on native affairs and to 'marshall and lead the native peoples in support of the Allied Armed Forces.'[31] ANGAU, as it became known, was essentially the section of the army responsible for ensuring that the environment in which the Australian soldier was operating would remain as stable as possible, and that the administration of native affairs across the land would continue as before.

Which was as well, because whatever else, Major General Morris certainly had many problems to deal with in these first days of 1942, many of them medical in nature. For there was no way around it. Apart from being an infernal nuisance and irritation to all concerned, the fact that in this particular part of the world swarms of flies on the day shift gave way to clouds of mosquitoes on the night shift, exacted a terrible toll on a body of men ill-equipped to defend itself against either. (One thing that at least slightly alleviated the bloody mossies was to throw green leaves onto a fire and then sit squarely in the middle of the resultant smoke, though this was very much a case of the cure quite possibly being worse than the ailment.) As to the flies, well, the Diggers didn't like to boast, but many from Victoria's rich cattle country had innately felt that when it came to dealing with flies, there was very little you could have taught them. Here though, in this Gawd-forsaken land, they had to take their hat off, and frequently did, to the sheer number of the little buggers. And the flies which weren't buzzing around your person were always buzzing all over the food, such as it was, because in these conditions food went off in about three hours flat, sending out a siren call to every fly for miles around to come on over and buzz their filthy way all over it.

As to the mosquitoes, the problem was not the mere sting, which was as nothing, but what the sting risked leading to. If with the sting the mosquito left behind microscopic malaria parasites in the soldier's blood, then within a week that soldier would be a physical wreck, alternating between shuddering chills and burning fever as his spleen and liver become enlarged, anaemia developed, and his skin turned yellow with jaundice. If the victim was left untreated, death was a possibility, and in the short term he could do nothing but lie there and groan. Yet, despite that risk, the unsuitable khaki shorts worn by the Diggers meant that they habitually presented plenty of vulnerable flesh.

Within a week of the militia arriving, the thin resources of Moresby's medical personnel were desperately trying to cope with over 150 cases of bacillary dysentery. Shortly, there would be numerous cases of malaria, and yet another two hundred were so ill with various ailments that they were unable to do anything at all.

The one notable exception to this was Sam Templeton's B Company, which remained essentially healthy because from the beginning of their training at Camp Darley, 'Uncle Sam' had drummed into his blokes the need for cleanliness, as a way of avoiding illness. Wash your pots and pans and plates before and after eating, tend immediately to whatever minor sores or wounds you might have before they begin to suppurate, and bloody well boil any dodgy water before drinking it. He had seen too many blokes die in the Great War for simple want of taking such basic measures, and he wasn't about to see it happen again. One he didn't have to tell twice was Joe Dawson, who was fastidious about personal hygiene, most particularly when it came to teeth cleaning. Joe just had a thing about cleaning his teeth after every meal, wherever they were, whatever they were doing, something not necessarily shared by other soldiers. As a matter of fact, one of the young blokes Joe had come across early in the piece—a bumpkin from the far west of Victoria—had stared in amazement at Joe's toothbrush, and said 'What's that?'

In response to the health crisis, Major General Morris tended to storm around thrashing the side of his leg with his fly-whisk to indicate his extreme displeasure at how bad things were—and probably killing a few more flies in the process—but things continued to get worse all the same. One attempt to fix the flies around the latrines was to detail a platoon to pour petrol down into them, followed by a burning rag, as they ran for their lives. But this strategy was discontinued when it was decided that the flies posed less of a risk than petrol explosions, and what came with it. (If there had been a fan, it would have been hit.)

So as the soldiers scratched and itched and made endless trips to the latrines during the night—sometimes wearing a gas mask, if they simply couldn't stand the smell—in the daytime they were obliged to work. Most of this was of the 'hard yakka' variety. They continued to unload the ships bringing supplies from Australia, and also work on building the roads and air-raid shelters which were now being constructed all around the town. Down at Bootless Inlet on the edge of Port Moresby they constructed barbed-wire barricades and sandbag weapon pits, against the day that the Japs might try to land there. In an effort to fool the enemy into thinking there were a lot more defending troops than there actually were, they also constructed rather flimsy kinds of sheds, designed to look like major barracks from the air. There would also soon be a massive campaign underway to hack another five airfields out of the unforgiving land around Moresby, in an effort to turn the joint into a base for offensive operations.

All up, it was hot, terrible, dusty work, and there was very little time for anything so prosaic as military training. Not that they were the only ones who were suffering in that particular part of the world.

It was just the day after the 39th Battalion landed in Port Moresby, Sunday, 4 January 1942, and it happened at another Australian territory, Rabaul, some 450 miles nor' by nor'east. Twelve natives from the nearby Trobriand Islands, who had just been mercifully plucked from a stricken canoe which had been adrift in the adjacent Solomon Sea for six weeks, were sitting down to their first meal in eight days when they looked up. There was a strange rumbling coming from the skies. Within twenty seconds, twenty-two Japanese bombers were overhead at an altitude of 12 000 feet and unleashing bomb after bomb, tumbling roughly towards Rabaul's airfield below. One of the bombs crashed through the roof of the Rapindik Native Hospital just to the south of the airfield where those saved natives were having their meal . . . and killed them all. Another brace of bombs landed right on a munitions dump, and so great was the subsequent explosion that most of the valves in radio transmitters around the settlement were shattered, so as well as being attacked the town was suddenly cut off from communications with the outside world.[32]

These were the first Japanese bombs to fall on Australian territory, and this was the first signal of enemy intent in the area. By the time the raid was over—and the air-raid siren warning just then began to wail—fifteen natives were dead and another thirty were injured. The surgeon who removed shrapnel from one native counted no fewer than six types of metal in the chunk and was quick with his conclusion: 'Pig-iron Bob will find no friends in Rabaul . . .'[33] According to the *Rabaul Times* on 9 January 1942 the one saving grace: 'We are fortunate, up to the present that no casualties have occurred other than amongst natives . . .'[34] Quite.

Over the next three weeks, Japanese planes continued to soften up Rabaul's defences. In response, there was no doubting the courage displayed by many of the Australian defenders, and none more so than the pilots in the RAAF's tiny and antiquated 24 Squadron, who were sent up in Wirraways—simple, glorified advanced trainer aircraft with a couple of guns attached—to take on the infinitely superior Japanese Zeros.

While the 'Wirras' took half an hour to get to 12 000 feet and were ponderous and only lightly armed, the Zeros were something else again. Usually launched from aircraft carriers, these principal fighter planes of the Imperial Japanese Navy were fast, manoeuvrable, and were essentially a 'flying gun', coming complete with two 7.7 mm machine guns and two 20 mm cannon. The only time the Wirras could remotely approach the speed of the Zeros was, alas, while hurtling towards the ground in a trail of black smoke—and this happened painfully often.

The sanguine courage of the Australian pilots was best represented by the words of their leader, Wing Commander J. M. Lerew—he of the 'huge and bristling red moustache and a permanent grin'[35]— who managed to send a message to Royal Australian Air Force Headquarters in Townsville that proved sadly accurate for most of his men: '*Nos moriture te salutamus*'. The famous gladiatorial salute of ancient Rome, it translated to: 'We who are about to die, salute you'.[36] In the principal dogfight of the Rabaul campaign, sixteen Australian crew members in eight Wirras took off to engage in combat with no fewer than eighty bombers and forty Zeros. When the battle was over, only two Australian planes had survived while six RAAF men had been killed and just five others set foot on the ground again unscathed.

Finally, it was happening, as indicated by the thousands of propaganda leaflets that the Japanese dropped on the Rabaul citizenry, giving them a stark warning:

To the officers and men of this island. Surrender at once and we will guarantee your life treating you as war prisoners. Those who resist us will be killed, one and all. Consider seriously. You can find neither food on this island, nor way of escape and will die.
Signed,
Commander in Chief of the Japanese Forces.

The Japanese were coming all right. They were a fine body of fighting men, five thousand strong, and were black from head to toe, with black shoes, shorts and singlets, and black camouflage paint daubed all over their faces, hands, legs and arms. Nestled in hulls of an armada of twenty-five Japanese warships, they were the soldiers of the 144th Regiment. They were the pride of the elite, jungle-trained South Seas Detachment—whose principal task it was to suppress all resistance to Japanese hegemony of the Southwest Pacific.

The mood on the Japanese ship in the pre-dawn hours of 23 January 1942 was one of confidence, mixed with a holy sense of mission. After all, the core of the regiment had been together since 1937 when it had achieved its first great victory in Manchuria, before following up with equally stunning victories in other parts of China. Just in the last month, these troops had stormed the American defenders at Guam and acquitted themselves admirably, wiping out a numerically superior force which was also better armed. Against such a tough, superbly trained and totally ruthless enemy, the Americans stood little chance. The 144th were, in short, crack troops, and their destination on this day was Rabaul, with its superb natural harbour and two airstrips, nestled beneath its majestic volcano.

There, a garrison of only fourteen hundred Australian soldiers, consisting of men from the 2/22nd Battalion, plus eighty members of the New Guinea Volunteer Rifles and men from other detachments, would just have to put up the best battle they could. The truth of it, though, was that Australia was woefully ill-prepared to thwart Japanese ambitions in this part of the world, even though Rabaul was squarely in Australian territory, and it had been obvious for some time that Rabaul was a prime target. Trouble was, the few ancient guns that the foreshores of Simpson Harbour boasted were not even pointed in the direction of the invading Japanese forces.

In the end, the organised resistance of Rabaul lasted no longer than twenty-four hours, as the Australian survivors fled for their lives. As they fled, they traded stories of what they had seen, including accounts of wave after wave of Japanese soldiers hitting the shoreline and then using the dead and injured bodies of *their own men* as a kind of buffer to help get across the defensive rolls of barbed wire the Australians had put in place to stop them. Wave after wave after wave of them, and they just kept on coming.

The invaders also proved to be without mercy in their treatment of the vanquished, and were ruthless in their pursuit of the Australian soldiers trying to get back to Australia to fight another day.

Down at a place called the Tol Plantation, just fifty miles south down the coast from Rabaul, a former bank officer by the name of Captain Bill Owen had just forded a river with a couple of fellow officers to reconnoitre the lie of the land ahead for the hundred and fifty tired and wounded soldiers who had managed to escape from Rabaul when they heard the throb of motors. As Owen and his two companions took cover across the river until they knew more, five Japanese motor launches suddenly hove into view and sprayed the other shore with heavy machine-gun fire. All the Australian troops who surrendered were quickly tied up. Not long afterwards they were led one by one into the jungle, and each one was shot or bayoneted or both—their blood-curdling screams leaving no doubt in the minds of the waiting soldiers just what fate lay ahead. In the undergrowth, Bill Owen and his fellow officers wept with frustration at their inability to do anything to save their countrymen and comrades. Still, they were in no doubt as to their duty; had they tried to intervene, they too would have been cut down, which would have served no purpose. Their job really was to live to fight another day, and by God when that day came they *would*.

This horrible encounter with the Japanese became known as the 'Tol Massacre', and it would stand for decades to come as one of the lowest benchmarks of Japanese brutality.

On a day in late January 1942, Curtin was in Melbourne and just about to board a train to Perth when a journalist asked the prime minister what he made of the first attacks on Rabaul.

'Nearer, clearer, deadlier than before, the cannon's opening roar . . . ' Curtin replied, drawing from one of the famous passages from Byron's 'The Eve of Waterloo'. 'Anybody who fails to perceive the immediate menace which this attack constitutes for Australia, must be lost to all reality . . .'[37]

As it turned out, very few were lost to that reality and the view that things had definitively changed was confirmed with intelligence reports that the initial invasion force of five thousand had quickly been joined by another twenty thousand Japanese soldiers and endless shiploads of supplies, weaponry and ammunition.

This still did not prevent, however, Australia's Deputy Prime Minister and Army Minister, Francis Michael Forde, shortly afterwards expressing his disappointment at the way some Australians had behaved in the face of the Japanese aggression. 'The civilians who took to the bush at Rabaul,' he said, 'should have stayed at their civil posts or plantations . . .'[38]

Despite this official insensitivity and ignorance in Australia as to just what the people on the ground in the northern climes were up against, the upshot was that in short 25 000 frontline Japanese soldiers had been installed in a secure harbour with ample stores. Put together with the newly secured airfields that Rabaul boasted, the Land of the Rising Sun was now better placed than ever to reach out even further into the Southwest Pacific.

To emphasise this dominance, a pack of sixty Japanese planes had dropped bombs on the settlements of Bulolo, Lae and Salamaua on the north coast of New Guinea at around noon on 21 January, destroying some twenty-two Allied military and civil aircraft in the process. (The sum total of defences ranged against the planes was one ancient Lewis Gun from the Great War at Salamaua, three at Bulolo and one at Lae.[39]) The only fortunate thing in the whole disaster was that there had been few casualties, with only one man killed, a pilot by the name of Kevin Parer who, among other things, was Damien Parer's first cousin. He had been killed while trying to scramble skywards.[40]

Affirming the obvious, that Moresby itself was now in grave peril and that the situation was desperate, Major General Morris did two key things. The first was to pass an edict that every able-bodied man in the Territory under forty-five years of age had to present himself for military service. The second was to issue a message on the morning of 27 January 1942 to all commanding officers of the various units making up the Moresby Garrison: 'No position is to be given up without permission; outflanked positions must continue to resist; even the smallest units must make provision for counterattack . . . We have the honour of being the front line defence of Australia. Let us show ourselves worthy of that honour.'[41]

For starters, most of the men of the 39th were simply trying to show themselves worthy by not drowning in the monsoonal rains that had just arrived; but still they did what they could to strengthen their defences.

And sure enough, proof positive that Moresby's new neighbours, the Japanese in Rabaul, were seriously interested in paying a kind of courtesy call came at three o'clock on the morning of 3 February 1942, when the shrieking sound of air-raid sirens suddenly filled the air in Moresby. Only a short time later, the roar of plane engines arrived with exploding bombs. No one was killed in that particular raid, but when it was followed by another one two days later, the city as a whole was so shaken up by the certainty that the Japanese were on their way that panic was widespread. Many of the native police simply abandoned their posts and headed back to the hilltop villages whence they came. Among some of the Australian forces there was a sudden massive breakdown in discipline, which manifested itself most damagingly in widespread looting of government stores. There was a sense that you might as well help yourself to anything you wanted because, after all, there was no point in leaving it for the Japs!

An Australian bloke by the name of Tom Grahamslaw watched all the stealing with disgust. He'd lived in these parts for many years—mostly on the nearby island of Samarai as a customs agent—and had returned to Moresby in response to Major General Morris's edict that all able-bodied men make themselves available to serve with the armed forces.

But did Grahamslaw *want* to serve with such men?

Every evening at sundown now, he sat with his mate, Wardrop, on his verandah, and watched first the RAAF blokes and then the army boys trudge down the street in front of them, carrying empty sacks. An hour later they would trudge back with sacks full to bursting, courtesy of the looted stores or homes that were being hurriedly abandoned. The troops considered themselves *really* lucky if they could stagger back drunk, as the most prized loot of all was liquor and they usually ripped into it straightaway.

For more durable loot, the great advantage for the RAAF blokes was that they had a way of smuggling their ill-gotten gains out because they were there to maintain the air-link to Australia. It wasn't just the soldiers and airmen who were doing the looting, though. No less than an RAAF padre arrived in Australia carrying, of all things, '12 volumes of the *Encyclopaedia of Religion and Ethics* to the value of Pound 25', which he had obviously stolen. When asked why, the padre acknowledged that it had been a difficult decision, but a chat with the Bishop of New Guinea had revealed that 'His Lordship' had 'no objection'.[42]

Only through severe disciplinary action could Major General Morris restore order, and all the while the Japanese raids continued on an almost daily basis. The Diggers dug their slit trenches all the deeper and built walls of sand bags around their key armaments. Under such sustained bombardment, the centre of the town was effectively abandoned as a place to live and in typical Digger humour, it soon became known as 'Bomb Decoy no. 1'.[43]

More factually, it was probably 'no. 2', as the bombers seemed to concentrate on Seven Mile Airfield, the town and the port in that order. As the bombers appeared, the soldiers and few remaining civilians sheltered in their slit trenches, while the anti-aircraft artillery known as 'Ack-Ack guns'—in this case not much more than a couple of heavy old naval guns with a minor supporting choir—sent up useless volleys of fire which exploded and turned into picturesque puffs well below the altitude of the thundering behemoths.

After the bombers had mercifully left, everyone would then emerge from the trenches, do their best to clean up whatever damage had been done, and settle back to what they had been doing in the first place—sweltering. The only good thing that came out of the raids was that when the bombs hit the harbour near the foreshores, which they often did, the explosions would sometimes throw fish up on to the wharves providing some much-needed variation to the soldiers' diet. Such fortuitous fare was highly prized.

Unable to strike a blow at the Japanese so many thousands of feet above them—and there were certainly no Australian planes doing them any damage—the men of the 39th had continued to work like navvies, doing hard labour. For there was a lot to do, from digging ever-more trenches, to clearing away rubble from the bombing, to building roads around the defensive perimeter of Moresby, to constantly unloading the ships which came from Australia . . . too far away. It was bloody hard yakka, and the dullness of it! The sheer brute boredom of hours hanging heavy in the tropical torpor, as they dragged their way through the day. Men joked about their lives being ruled by the four 'M's: 'Mud, mosquitoes, malaria and monotony.'

As the Diggers worked, little by little they came to know something of the New Guinea natives who populated the town and its outskirts, a little of their customs and beliefs, and most crucially the curious language in which they conversed called 'pidgin English'. This last had developed over the previous sixty years of English-speaking occupation of the island, initially as a kind of bastardised version of the King's English with which the natives could talk to the colonists, and even more importantly over time, as a language that the disparate tribes could use to converse with each other.

The structure of the language was very simple. As an example, 'him' was 'EM'; 'he' was 'E'; 'party' was 'SINGSING'; and the possessive sense was indicated by 'BILONG'. Put together then with joiner words, if you wanted to say of a particular Digger that 'he is fond of parties', you said 'EM I MAN BILONG SINGSING TRU . . . ' In a similar vein 'whose book is this?' became 'BUK BILONG HUSAIT?' and 'a long time ago' was 'LONGTAIM BIFOR'. A 'fella' was a 'PELA' and 'one, two, three, four . . . ' became 'WANPELA, TUPELA, TRIPELA, FORPELA . . . ' and so on. In the view of the usually diminutive natives, the Diggers were all 'STRONGPELA', strong fellas, and mostly 'GUTPELAS', good fellas, too.

Generally the Australians and the natives got on well, the more so when some of the more affluent of the soldiers and the non-commissioned officers would give a couple of shillings to hire a native as a servant to make their beds, shine their shoes for parades, prepare their meals and all the rest. It was through such constant contact that some of the Diggers began to understand a few of the natives' customs and ways. While their extended families were important to them, the most identifying grouping was their 'WONTOKS', 'one-talks', as in their own tribe who spoke their own language. They had no concept of the 'nation' of New Guinea although they were aware of the 'BIK WOR', 'big war', going on between the 'white man', 'WITMAN', and 'Japanese', 'JAPUN'.

Something that amused the Diggers greatly was the natives' idea of the human body. According to them, the most important organ of all was the 'LIVA', liver, and it was from here that all thoughts, emotions and life force was generated. 'EM I ASKIM LIVA BILONG EM', 'he asks liver his', meant 'he is searching his memory'. 'ASKIM GUT LIVA BILONG YU', as in 'ask well liver of you', meant 'examine your conscience'. One word specific to the local tribe's Motu language the Diggers learnt was 'DEHORI', which meant 'wait awhile', and this was the standard answer whenever anything was required of any of them.[44] The Diggers repeatedly tried the imperative 'KARAHARAGA', meaning 'hurry up', but it never really seemed to help much.

For all that, the general consensus was that while the natives were clearly a very primitive people, they were generally 'not bad Joes', and many of the Diggers formed a rough affection for the 'boongs', as they were all but universally known from the start. There were more than a few strange things though . . .

Tits. Everywhere. Women's breasts. Big ones. Little ones. *Really* big ones. Swaying freely, coming this way, as the native women walked down the streets. They really were everywhere, and it would take the newly arrived Australians some time to get used to seeing breasts at least every time they went into town, and often around and about their encampment. Curiously, few found it at all sexually appealing, even though back in Melbourne more than a few had parted with a day's wages just to see naked breasts in a St Kilda strip joint.

In any case, there was little to no fraternisation between the Diggers and the native women, it having been made clear to them by old hands that, on the odd occasion it had happened in the past, the usual form was for the native bloke who had been cuckolded to simply take a knife and redeem his honour by wearing the white fella's balls for earrings thereafter. Under those circumstances the young soldiers didn't need to be told twice and, one way or another, it wasn't long before they didn't even blink an eye at a native woman's bare breasts anyway.

That potentially delicate issue settled, the natives in turn formed their own impression of the Diggers, their machinery, their guns and their industrious activities. These soldiers in the street had doubled the white population of Port Moresby, strange aircraft were landing at the new airfield at Seven Mile and Catalina flying boats were churning up Fairfax Harbour.

From the tiny speck of urban settlement that was Port Moresby in all the vastness of New Guinea proper, the word went out. From the natives working in the town, who had some interaction with the tribes on the fringe, who talked to the tribes in the hills above the town, who themselves had been observing more and more planes overhead and white faces all around and big guns being installed on terrain overlooking the harbour . . . the news spread.

'PLUNDI WAITMAN E CUM LONG HELPIM YU E RUSIM MAN BILONG JAPON. MIK BIK WOR.' 'Lots of white men have come and want us to help get rid of the Japanese. There is going to be a big war.'

The situation in Singapore was grim and getting grimmer. After a long and devastating march down the Malayan Peninsula, the Allies resolutely focused their defences on the few roads; but the Japanese constantly outflanked and choked them by moving through thick jungle previously thought impenetrable. It seemed that the end was near. By late January, the Japanese had pushed all Allied defence back to the island of Singapore itself and were storming it from the direction of the Malayan jungle just a few hundred yards across the narrow causeway to the north. This meant that most of Singapore's much-vaunted fixed defences, with guns pointing to the sea in preparation for a seaborne invasion, were worse than useless.

By 10 February 1942 still no serious support had arrived from Britain despite Singapore's pleas. Instead, Winston Churchill sent a stirring cable to his commanding officer, General Archibald Wavell, a man whom he had, just seven months before, removed from command in North Africa when it became apparent that Wavell couldn't match it with General Rommel. In the kind of language that gave the word 'Churchillian' its punch, the British Prime Minister essayed to give mettle to his men from afar, asserting that Wavell and his officers should abandon any 'thought of saving the troops or sparing the population. The battle must be fought to the bitter end at all costs. The 18th Division has a chance to make its name in history. Commanders and senior officers should die with their troops. The honour of the British Empire and of the British Army is at stake.'

It was one thing to be magnificent enough to send such a cable, and quite another of course for the recipients to be magnificent enough to live up to its dictates. Because, on balance, the besieged officers and their troops decided they'd rather live. And on 15 February 1942, they made that decision. General Arthur E. Percival, the famously buck-toothed commanding officer of the Allied forces defending Singapore, walked purposefully, if sorrowfully, out from the Allied lines. One of his aides carried a Union Jack, while another carried a white flag, generating the famous picture symbolising the death of the British Empire in the Far East. It was over.

The 'impregnable bastion' of Singapore—or '*Syonan-to*', or Light of the South, as it was promptly renamed by the victors—had fallen to the marauding Imperial Japanese Army, despite the attackers being outnumbered two to one and almost out of ammunition. Never more would the European have the right to a superior swagger in those parts.

Almost eighteen hundred Australians were killed, while the remaining fifteen thousand were captured and sent to either the infamous Changi prison camp or worse, to labour on the Thai–Burma railway. All up, thirty thousand Japanese soldiers had routed a hundred thousand armed defenders, at a loss of only 3500 of their own. Prime Minister Curtin issued a statement from Sydney's St Vincent Hospital where he was being treated for a bad attack of gastritis. While he described the fall of Singapore as 'Australia's Dunkirk'[45] and the future as 'the Battle for Australia', the clear difference was that while the glory of Dunkirk was more than 300 000 Allied soldiers escaping to fight another day, for the most part the captured Australian soldiers were out of commission for the rest of the war, if not all eternity.

Not least of this disaster was that most of those Australian officers experienced in jungle warfare were either dead or locked away as prisoners of war unable to impart their crucial experience. The same did not apply to the Japanese, whose victorious officers were quickly assigned new horizons to conquer.

With the fall of Singapore, the strategic importance of Australia in Japan's Greater East Asia Co-Prosperity Sphere came into sharper focus. The key point of resistance for Japanese hegemony in the Pacific was the great South Land and Curtin himself warned his fellow citizens that the 'Battle for Australia' was just beginning. But, in the absence of so much of her military manpower, who would defend Australia against an enemy which in the previous nine weeks had notched up comprehensive victories against the best the British, Americans and Dutch could throw at them? Certainly not Britain.

In a strongly worded cable, Winston Churchill made it clear to John Curtin that whatever meagre resources the mother country could garner in that part of the world would be devoted to defending India, Britain's 'Jewel in the Crown'. Australia would have to sort itself out. No matter that Australia had lost sixty thousand men in World War I in the service of Britain, and that at the outbreak of this war Australia had promptly sent two full divisions of men to fight beside Britain in the Middle East to defend British interests. Now, it seemed to Curtin, when Australia was in need, Britain simply wasn't there.

Curtin replied with an equally direct cable, which was typical of the tightening tension between the two wartime leaders. The previous month Curtin had cabled to his wife Elsie in Perth that the 'War goes very badly and I have a cable fight with Churchill almost daily. He has been in Africa and India and they count before Australia and New Zealand. The truth is that Britain never thought Japan would fight and made no preparations to meet that eventuality. But enough, I love you, and that is all there is to say . . . '[46]

Churchill was less than impressed with such cable sparring and, as only he could, took umbrage at Curtin's colossal presumption in demanding that Britain support Australia, just as Australia had previously supported the mother country. While in cables to Curtin the British Prime Minister did not mince words assuring him that Australia was in minimal danger, in private he was scathing, claiming that the Australians were 'jumpy about invasion' because they came from 'bad stock'.[47]

Australia's sudden sense of isolation and vulnerability was dramatically affirmed on the morning of 19 February 1942. The general shock at what was to happen is personified in the young sailors congregated on the deck of the minesweeper HMAS *Gunbar* in Darwin Harbour when they noted a neat formation of planes approaching. They were just commenting on the skill of the pilots in retaining a tight formation, when they noticed the planes releasing tiny silver objects . . . and then all hell broke loose. Before their very eyes, it seemed like half of Darwin exploded. The sound of bursting bombs rolled to them over the water, plumes of flame and smoke shot skywards and whole buildings fell to the ground.

These were the very Japanese bombers with escort Zeros—188 planes in all—from the aircraft carrier fleet that had destroyed Pearl Harbor, and they were doing much the same thing over Darwin: unleashing death and destruction from a clear blue sky.

By the time the planes had vanished, eight Allied ships lay at the bottom of the harbour, Darwin's principal RAAF airfield had been damaged, twenty-three planes and numerous buildings were destroyed, 243 Australians were dead and some three hundred were wounded.

Australians in the Territory panicked, convinced that the bombing was simply the classic Japanese softening up of defences before an imminent invasion. The roads leading out of Darwin were clogged with refugees, some of whom were deserting soldiers. Such was the certainty that an invasion was occurring that, before fleeing, many people burnt their houses and sheds to deny the Japanese any succour, and the mood was beyond grim.

Very little of this reality showed up in the public pronouncement of Prime Minister John Curtin, when he said: 'In this first battle on Australian soil it will be a source of pride to the public to know that the armed forces and the civilians comported themselves with the gallantry that is traditional in the people of our stock.'

It was a pronouncement to allay panic in the country's main population centres, and Curtin could get away with it because Darwin was so distant and a fairly basic form of wartime censorship applied; but privately his government was worried as day by day the bombing on Darwin continued.

Japan recognised that Darwin was a base for naval and air operations against them, and that it was also an important conduit for transporting *matériel* to Allied troops across Southeast Asia trying to thwart them. Clearly, Darwin had to be destroyed. With its virtual destruction, the situation of the Allied troops became more desperate and the spectre of Japan more threatening.

The day after the bombing, Curtin was even stronger in his resolve, and was quoted in the *Sydney Morning Herald* saying that there was to be 'no more looking away now. Fate has willed our position in this war. From now until victory, fate and war are the total words. We accept the issue and follow our destiny.'[48]

In Port Moresby, the Diggers did what they did most nights and gathered around whatever radio was available to get every bit of news they could. This was grim stuff indeed, for if the Japs were hitting Darwin, there were only two possibilities—either they would cop it next, or their families at home would . . .

More than ever, Prime Minister Curtin was now clear in his mind that it was time to bring the boys home. At that time, both Australia's 6th and 7th divisions were on their way east across the Indian Ocean, but the issue was their destination. In very broad terms, Britain wanted the Australians to help thwart Japan's push to the west towards India, while Australia wanted its finest sons to help thwart Japan's thrust south towards Australia.

Winston Churchill took the view that all Commonwealth countries must do their bit to help further British Commonwealth interests, under British direction, and he had been insistent that the Australian troops be split between bolstering British defence of Burma, and putting garrisons in both Ceylon and Java. In an effort to convince Curtin, Churchill had even engaged the support of President Roosevelt, who sent cables to the Australian leader agreeing with the British prime minister's line of reasoning.

Curtin was equally insistent that the Australian troops be brought immediately to Australia to defend Australian soil, and even two days before Darwin was bombed, had cabled Churchill to that effect. It was a big step for the prime minister of a country firmly within the British realm to insist on the primacy of his own country's needs against the demands of a British prime minister, let alone against such a key ally as President Roosevelt, but Curtin had done it, even if the stress of it had been one of the factors that led to his hospitalisation.

What dismayed Curtin as he left hospital and again took over the reins of government, was that his cable had not altered the course of the troopships. At least one part of the problem was that Australia's representative to the United Kingdom, Earle Page, had told Churchill that he would endeavour to change Curtin's mind, and indeed tried to do so. Curtin's reported comment in response to Page's recommendation was one for the ages: 'There are numerous geographical centres where an AIF or any other Division would be useful,' he said, but from the viewpoint of Australia, 'there is none east of Suez of greater importance than Australia [itself].'[49]

Curtin, in short, stuck to his guns, insisting that the boys come home to an Australian people who were clearly expecting them.

Churchill was equally insistent. His views had been set in stone when, back on 22 November 1940, he had sent a memo to his First Sea Lord, insisting that there be a concentration of 'all possible naval and military aid in the European field, to the exclusion of any other interest . . . ' If this was followed, Churchill maintained, 'the defeat of Germany was ensured with certainty, and if subsequently it was in the American interest to deal with Japan, requisite steps would be possible.'[50] And the implication of this was that if it wasn't in the American interest, then countries like Australia would be on their own. The needs of Britain still came first.

The Japanese were now just forty miles from the Burmese capital, Rangoon, and the British prime minister wanted the Australian troops between the two, if only he could get them on site. Thus, in a display of extraordinary arrogance—even for the time—Churchill gave orders that instead of returning to Australia, the troopships were to alter their destination to Burma. It was only after he gave the order that he informed Curtin of what he had done—a full twenty-four hours after the event.

Curtin, shocked that it had come to this, needed time to think. So he went for a walk around Canberra's Mount Ainslie. A long one. It was in fact so long that his key adviser on defence issues, Frederick Shedden, organised for messages to be put up on screens in the city's theatres around Canberra, asking that Prime Minister Curtin return to his office or at least contact it. He did return, just after midnight, and sent the cable which fully affirmed Australia's right as a sovereign nation to determine where its own troops would be sent.

'[Indonesia] faces imminent invasion,' he wrote flatly to Churchill. 'Australia's outer defences are now quickly vanishing and our vulnerability is completely exposed. With AIF troops we sought to save Malaya and Singapore, falling back on the Dutch East Indies. All these northern defences are gone or going. Now you contemplate using the AIF to save Burma. All this has been done, as in Greece, without adequate air support. We feel a primary obligation to save Australia . . . as a base for the development of the war against Japan.'

Churchill replied with a cable saying that because of the change in direction he had ordered, the ships would have to stop at Ceylon anyway for refuelling, which would give the Australian government three or four days to consider its position. Curtin replied immediately, informing Churchill in no uncertain terms that there would be no change of heart.

Churchill did the only thing he could do under the circumstances. He acceded to Curtin's insistence. With the exception of two brigades of the 6th Division that Curtin allowed to stay in Ceylon as a temporary garrison, the rest of the convoys headed home to Australia, to the manifest relief of the troops themselves. Many of them had been away from family and loved ones for as long as eighteen months, and not only were they desperate to see them again, but if the homeland really was going to be under threat of invasion, then there was no doubt where the rightful place of its fighting men was. Crank the engines up, Huey, steer sou' by sou'east, and let's get these tubs home!

None were quite sure what their immediate future held, though it was at least a fair bet that it would involve fighting directly to defend home, either in Australia or at least in the region, as opposed to fighting for Britain in some far-flung destination.

As to the prospect of fighting side by side with 'the Chocos'— the militia—that was a far less thrilling prospect. Everyone knew the militia were pathetic jokes with no guts or gumption, and no one wanted to go into battle with blokes like that guarding your rear or protecting your left flank. You needed blokes you could *rely* on, the *serious* soldiers, blokes like themselves.

This view was so widespread, and so often spoken about by the men, that one military commander, General Ned Herring—the Commander of the 6th Division—decided to address his troops on the subject. Gathering them in front of the bridge as the ship steamed through the Indian Ocean, Herring gave it to them straight.

'In this fight,' he said, 'we are going to be alongside the AMF. I shall be quite honest with you. Perhaps I have said as many rude things as you about the militia. But we must forget about that now. We must help them. We must be a united people in this hour of crisis. We must not only put away all recrimination but we must help them in every way, in battle and out of battle. We have to show what an Australian should look like and how he should behave. You fellows have to remember that you have something to be proud of in the AIF and have to make the best of ourselves and not the worst. If we set the right example, people will stand firm, there will be no panic, and Australia will be safe. If we do not, then God help Australia.'[51]

Yes Sir, sure Sir, whatever you say, Sir. No one was going to have themselves up on insubordination charges by laughing out loud or cat-calling, but not one took it seriously either. It would take a bit more than a few words from a general to make them change their view about the Chocos.

During the six-week trip home on the Australian troopship *City of Paris*, Stan Bisset, in his role as Intelligence Officer of the 2/14th Battalion, helped pass the time in a useful manner. He taught the attentive soldiers such things as how to use your watch as a compass. If they were in the southern hemisphere, then when you pointed 12 o'clock to the sun, then halfway between 12 o'clock and the hour hand was north. In the northern hemisphere, you used the same method, but halfway between 12 o'clock and your hour hand would show south. You could also find your bearings by using the stars of the mighty Southern Cross, see, drawing imaginary lines in the sky between 'The Pointers' and the two principal axes of the cross, and . . . so on.

All the while, the troops ships kept heading home, home to Australia . . .

On another Australian troopship heading east was photographer Damien Parer. All the Australian troops had viewed the Japanese landing at Rabaul with alarm, but in the photographer's case it was more so. For who could doubt that one of the most obvious places for the Japanese to next land would be on the north coast of New Guinea, which was precisely where his parents, John and Teresa Parer, had settled with some other members of his family. They were running a hotel at Wau, a place where the temptations of gambling didn't just jump out and grab you. Despite the trials of Damien's youth, and his father's problems, Damien had remained close to his parents and now feared for their fate if they were caught in Japanese clutches.

When it had become clear that the Australians were pulling out of the Middle East, Parer's boss, Captain Frank Hurley, had told him that he was himself intending to join the British Ministry of Information, so as to be able to stay there, and why didn't Damien make the same move? Damien's response was clear: 'I don't want to photograph the bloody English,' he said. 'I want to photograph Australians.'[52]

And even on the ship home, Damien was doing exactly that, capturing them sweltering in the midday sun, doing the odd calisthenics, eating, drilling, waiting, waiting, waiting—waiting to be off the ocean and home again . . .

CHAPTER FIVE

SWEATING IT OUT

You can have no idea just how hostile aircraft can be until they come to your area . . .

Aircraft which strafe or bomb your positions should be regarded with suspicion, if not deep mistrust. Aircraft which bomb and strafe your position and wear a red circle should certainly be regarded with deep mistrust. In fact, the deeper the better. A six-foot-deep slit trench is an ideal place from which to mistrust them . . .

Australian soldier VX116124[53]

Softly, softly now.

Frank Green, the clerk of the House of Representatives, had heard from John Curtin's long-time driver—who resided at the Lodge—that the prime minister was getting very little sleep. With that in mind, Green, who was very close to Curtin, dropped into the Lodge late one night to have a chat, to see if perhaps he could calm the prime minister's troubled spirit. (And that it was seriously troubled there was no doubt. At one point, Curtin's senior Labor colleague Ben Chifley had returned to his room at the capital's famed Kurrajong Hotel to find a message from Curtin. It was begging

Chifley to come to the Lodge, however late it was, as Curtin felt he was 'spiritually bankrupt'.[54])

But now Green was standing at the portals of the Lodge, when, away to his left, he spied an ethereal figure standing in the moonlit garden.

'Prime Minister . . . ?' he called out softly.

The ghost-like apparition turned and moved just a few feet forward before stopping. John Curtin did not look well, his rather deathly pallor being the only thing that reflected the moon's little light. He had had a terrible run of ill-health in recent times, but still that was not the only reason for the pallor.

'Is there anything wrong?' Green enquired gently.

'Can't sleep,' the PM replied.

'Why can't you sleep?'

For more than a minute, Curtin did not reply and simply remained standing there, as if he were turning the question over and over before making reply.

'How can I sleep,' he said, 'when I know that our men are out there on transports on the Indian Ocean, with all those Japanese submarines looking for them . . . ? How *can* I sleep?'

It was a question for which there was no easy answer. And it was an all too real possibility. Just three months earlier, the light cruiser HMAS *Sydney* had been sunk by a German raider off the West Australian coast, taking 645 Australian lives with it. Green led the PM back inside and, in an attempt at the classic Australian cure-all, they had a chat over a cuppa tea. One of Curtin's many other worries was the preparedness of the Australian militia men in Moresby, should there ever be a Japanese attack in those parts.

Others were also forming their views about the likely fighting capabilities of the Chocos . . . or lack thereof.

One was Osmar White, a fine Australian journalist, accredited by the Australian Government to cover the war, and providing most of his output for Melbourne's *Sun* newspaper. He was in his early thirties, and for the past ten years he had been knocking around the world as a freelance journalist, most particularly between the

Tropics of Capricorn and Cancer. Noted for his encyclopaedic knowledge of tropical conditions, no one in the Australian press corps was better equipped to cover potential military action in New Guinea. He had been to many places in his journalistic career, one of them the Japanese jungle training school in Formosa, where he was impressed by the Japanese soldiers' thorough preparation for jungle warfare.

On an afternoon in late February 1942, just a week or so after he had arrived in Moresby, White was surveying the 'battle stations' set up by the 39th, 53rd and 44th battalions—essentially the defensive perimeter of Moresby, where the soldiers and artillery were dug in against the best that the Japanese could throw at them. While he watched, the soldiers continued a little desultory digging and wheeling of soil to places unknown. The heat was high and their hearts were low.

Though fighting hard against his own response, White was far from impressed. Was this really *all* that stood between the advancing Japanese army and Australia? *These* blokes?

'Most of them,' he wrote later, 'were youngsters between nineteen and twenty-three. They had lost an average of twenty pounds in weight. They were scrawny, yellow, wild-eyed, and listless in their movements. Their skins were pocked by infected insect bites.'

This impression of their general inadequacy was compounded when, having seen what he could of the newly constructed defensive ramparts, he made his way back to town in the back of an army truck that stopped to pick up a sorry excuse for a soldier who was thumbing a ride. This fellow's face was so badly bitten he had been unable to shave for a week, and the sores oozing puss on his knees and lower legs were so bad that Osmar could barely look at them.

'You must have been scratching yourself, son,' one of the other men in the back of the truck said to him.

'I don't when I'm awake,' the man muttered in miserable reply, 'but a man can't help himself when he's asleep.'[55]

Bloody hell. Fair dinkum. What chance were these blokes going to have if they went up against hardened Japanese battle veterans?

Osmar White was certainly not the only one asking the question. In the view of the men of the small AIF garrison that had already been in Moresby for many months—and who had observed the shenanigans of the new arrivals with growing dismay—the answer was just about none. The AIF men could barely believe that the Australian Government could have sent these blokes north. And while these AIF men were careful to keep their distance from the amateurs, that certainly didn't prevent them having fun at the militia's expense.

In one famous incident, described by another notable war correspondent, George H. Johnston, a platoon of militiamen were travelling in an army truck out in the open when the skies were filled with Japanese bombers and their escorting fighters. No sooner had the first bomb dropped and the machine-gun bullets started spurting up the dust in an angry line down the road, then the truck screeched to a halt and the militiamen piled out to take shelter under the bulk of the vehicle. Alas, so keen had the driver been to get out that he had neglected to put the handbrake on, and in the instant that the militiamen were under the truck it had commenced slowly rolling forward. Still desperate to keep under their shelter, the men were obliged to frantically move forward with the truck while remaining on all fours, as the AIF men secure in their trenches cheered them to the echo and sang: 'Git along, little dogies, git along, git along!'[56]

And just possibly the men of the 39th might have laughed too, once they'd got over the shock of bombs dropping on them, but there was simply too much work to do to spend much time being jocular. There were ships to be unloaded, runways to be extended, roads to be built and latrines to be dug; they were still trying to build a war base more or less from scratch. The way it seemed to the men of the 39th, just about every activity involved a shovel—funny, they thought they were going to be fighting this war with rifles.

One of the biggest earthwork projects was building enormous, horseshoe-shaped earthen mounds, called revetments, to protect planes on the ground from bombs. Nothing would save the planes from a direct hit, but a bomb going off twenty yards away wouldn't do any damage at all, as long as there was an earthen wall between the plane and the explosion. They had been proven to work magnificently well, but it was back-breaking, gut-busting work to construct them and it wasn't long before the same men who'd hid under the truck would almost look forward to the Japanese bombing runs as a break from the tedium of it all.

Still, on one occasion when the Japanese appeared overhead Osmar White was there when an Ack-Ack gunner had just had e-bloody-nough. Straight after the bombers had dropped their deadly load, the Digger jumped from his pit, shook his fists and roared at the departing planes: 'Why don't you come down, you dirty little yellow bastards, and let us have a crack at you!'[57]

Making the Japanese bombing even more frustrating for the men was the fact that they had no aerial resistance to put up against them. For months the defending forces had been promised their own squadron of Australian Kittyhawks, all to no avail. The planes had so often been promised for a 'tomorrow', which never came, that they became known as 'Tomorrowhawks'.

By the end of February 1942, the sum total of Port Moresby's aerial defence consisted of two tired Catalinas and a Hudson held together with bandaids, fencing wire and constant prayer. It was pathetic, and the running gag among the soldiers was that they were all cross-eyed, because they spent their time simultaneously digging below and looking up for what they now called 'Betties', the Jap bombers.

While they were busting to have a go at the bloody Japanese—fired up by an unending stream of horror stories coming from refugees straggling in from Rabaul—there was also a serious streak of realism among the Diggers about how long they could hold out if the Japs really landed. In Rabaul, they knew, resistance had lasted no more than twenty-four hours. And there were also intelligence reports that the original five thousand Japanese soldiers had now been joined by another two thousand as Rabaul had become their major launching base.

If then, the Japs really did land a full-blown invasion force on Moresby, it was clear that after the Australians had given the brutes merry hell they would need a fall-back position so they could hopefully be evacuated back to Australia. There was only one possibility for that—the small settlement of Daru. Four hundred miles west of Moresby on the southern New Guinea coastline, and just a hundred miles from the tip of Australia's Cape York, it was their only chance of retreat. It was for this reason that, as White walked around and got to know the Diggers a little better, he kept hearing talk of the 'Daru Derby'.

Upon inquiry, he found that most soldiers had formed themselves into informal small groups and had made actual route and supply plans for making their way to Daru. Many soldiers kept a bag with essential supplies—iron rations, waterproof cape, mosquito tent, 140 rounds of ammunition—constantly on hand for that purpose.

None of this indicated an unwillingness to fight, even though in self-mockery another running gag was that after the war was over they would all have the 'Cross of Papua' pinned to their chests, replete with its yellow ribbon, and they sometimes referred to themselves as the 'Mice of Moresby', as opposed to the famous and revered 'Rats of Tobruk'. Rather, it was a realistic assessment that after they had given whatever they could to the Japs, shooting through to Daru would be the best thing for both themselves and Australia, which would then be in even more urgent need of them. Between times, they kept preparing for the invasion that they knew was close, as frustration rose that they couldn't give the Japs a bit of what-for themselves.

Tom Grahamslaw had a problem. Like many of his ilk who had lived in New Guinea long before the war and understood the native culture, he had been recruited by the Australian Army to work in civil administration (soon to become ANGAU) and found himself working as a senior officer—he was now Captain Grahamslaw—

based in the village of Awala, just inland from Buna on the north coast of New Guinea. The problem was that a part of his function was to oversee the administration of justice, and his first case was a potentially explosive one.

At least the facts were fairly straightforward. Shortly after Rabaul had fallen, a group of fleeing Europeans had been escorted from the north coast along the treacherous track to the nearest airfield, Kokoda—well inland—by a native village constable, named Kenneth. The constable had looked after them impeccably, seeing to their porters, accommodation and food. He had done it so well that one of the Europeans had given him a glittering ring as a token of appreciation—which is where the problem had arisen.

In the course of the journey, Constable Kenneth listened closely to the conversation of the refugees and decided that the Japanese simply couldn't be stopped, and that they would shortly reign supreme. He now returned to his village and announced that no less than the King of Japan had made him, Kenneth, the king of the whole region, as proved by the glittering ring he now showed them. To display fealty to both himself and the King of Japan, Kenneth announced that he now required the village—under orders from the 'captains' he'd appointed from among his friends—to build an airfield and barracks, ready for the Japanese troops when they arrived. And they had begun to do just that when one of Tom Grahamslaw's colleagues arrested Kenneth.

The only thing to do with him, Tom decided, was to put Kenneth behind bars in Moresby—well away from any possible Japanese landings. The natives had to be shown that it was the Australian Government that still ran things in these parts, and that anyone who cooperated with the enemy Japanese would be dealt with *severely*. For it really was a situation that had to be watched closely. In the Great War of three decades earlier, the first Australians killed had died at the hands of New Guinea natives working for the Germans.

That wasn't going to happen this time.

•

As it happened, though, it began to look more and more like Constable Kenneth was prescient. The net amount of resistance Australia had offered to this point in, most notably, Malaya, Singapore and Rabaul had been minimal, and the first discussion among the Japanese leadership about invading the great southern continent had, by early March of 1942, evolved into fully detailed plans. The view that such an invasion should be prioritised was put most cogently by Admiral Isoroku Yamamoto of the Japanese Naval General Staff—an extremely influential man as he was credited with being the driving force behind the stunningly successful Pearl Harbor raid. The admiral asserted in strong terms that the way forward was to establish a major naval base on the east coast of Australia, which could be used to put a stranglehold on the nation's economic centres, and also thwart all attempts to use the island continent as a base from which the Americans could relaunch a campaign on the Philippines.

The Chief of the Naval General Staff, Admiral Osami Nagano, fully supported this contention and noted that by the estimation of the First (Operations) Section of the Naval General Staff, just three divisions of the Japanese Army would be capable of occupying key population centres in Australia. After all, on this very day, 7 March 1942, the news had just come through that the Imperial Japanese Army had notched up another important conquest with the fall of Batavia in the Dutch East Indies.

So now, with all the newly gained territories, the Japanese war machine was also blessed with a sure supply of the resources, raw materials and manpower it needed to move into overdrive. Prime Minister Tojo himself had recently boasted to the Japanese parliament that when Japanese forces had invaded Borneo they had secured seventy of the hundred and fifty oil wells in working condition and with the half a million barrels they could deliver in the next year, there would be no further problems with oil supply.

Against this, the Japanese Army itself was a lot less sure. It was still engaged in the war in China, as well as in holding the perimeters of the new Japanese Pacific empire which extended over almost two million square miles and, even more crucially, in defending their own homeland against possible Russian attacks. The Japanese Army had been surprised at how quickly Singapore, Malaya and Burma had fallen, and its leaders were still gathering themselves.

One other thing that gave them pause was their view of how the Australian population would react. A Japanese Army document written at this time, called the General Outline of Policy on Future War Guidance, noted that 'if the invasion is attempted, the Australians, in view of their national character, would resist to the end . . . '[58]

In sum, the Imperial Japanese Army felt that they would need ten divisions to satisfactorily quell Australia and, as their manpower was already stretched thinly across most of the Pacific, this was not feasible at this time.

As a compromise—and keeping the possibility of invading Australia open—a preliminary plan was decided to secure Port Moresby. The central plank of the plan was to launch a seaborne invasion from the east, by way of the Coral Sea which curled around the eastern tip of New Guinea. With a Japanese base then securely entrenched at Moresby, the Land of the Rising Sun would be well placed to launch an invasion on Australia, as their planes could now easily bomb Darwin and North Queensland. The Japanese would also be in a relatively secure position to rebuff any Australian incursions against Japan's newly established empire in the Pacific, which now stretched from Tokyo, through the Philippines and all the way to Singapore and then Burma. With the successful invasion of Port Moresby, the boundary fences of the Greater East Asia Co-Prosperity Sphere would be secured.

A preliminary invasion of New Guinea, on a much smaller scale, had already been planned for some time. On 8 March 1942—at around the same time as Rangoon fell—Japanese forces totalling some three thousand troops landed at Lae and Salamaua, on New Guinea's north coast. These two settlements stood on opposite sides of the bay through which the Markham River flowed to the sea, on terrain suitable for airfields near the newly established beachheads. The Japanese intended to be there for the long haul, with the soldiers coming complete with their own specially printed 'occupation money', which they intended to use to purchase the natives' produce and labour, just as they had been doing in Rabaul. It was the same money they planned to use when later they occupied Australia and New Zealand.[59]

The Japanese secured the landings at Lae and Salamaua with so little resistance, that just a few days later Imperial General Headquarters formally embraced another plan put forward by the Japanese Navy to capture not only Port Moresby by seaborne invasion, but also the ring of islands formed by Samoa, Fiji, New Caledonia, the New Hebrides and the Solomon Islands. This desire to take over islands was a hallmark of the Japanese campaign. While Britain still took the view that when Britannia ruled the waves, the rest would naturally follow, Japan regarded the water merely as a thoroughfare to get to the next bit of land, and while a strong navy was important, it was not an end in itself. And occupying islands and establishing airfields ensured air-cover for the next step forward.

These minor Japanese landings on the north coast did not overly worry the Australian military authorities at Port Moresby, even though the Japs were now just 170 miles away. They felt secure knowing that while the enemy was settling in on the other side of the island, the impassable Owen Stanley Range would separate them from the Australian forces. As Major General Morris told the correspondents who asked, while there was apparently some kind of track which led over the mountains, it was only a rare white man who had made it across, and there was no chance that an entire battalion of Japs could get through to the other side intact. It was, as they described it, a *boong* track, and nothing else.

Up north, nearer the landings, the natives weren't so sanguine. News of the Japanese arrival on the coast travelled quickly from village to village and from plantation to plantation throughout much of that part of the island. The general view of the natives seemed to be that the heavily armed newcomers were 'invaders', and this perception was encouraged by the white plantation owners and ANGAU officers.

'JAPUN MUN E CUM LONG STILIM GROUN BILONG YU.' 'The Japanese men are here to steal your land,' Tom Grahamslaw told the natives as he moved among them, his eyes flashing angrily on their behalf, 'and will stop at nothing to get it. MUN NOGUT. They are a terrible people who will burn your villages, KILIM OL MUN, kill all the men, and rape the women. But do not be afraid. If the Japanese invaders come, they will get a very big surprise. I, and many of the other BIKPELA PAPA BILONG GROUN land-owners, will go to Port Moresby and come back with many, many soldiers, who will drive the Japanese back to the beaches and back onto the big boats they came in on.' Generally, in the face of such speeches, the native labourers would listen fearfully at this extraordinary and upsetting news. A new force was indeed unleashed in the land . . .

Despite Tom Grahamslaw's warning that the Japanese would rape the native women, that was not the situation in Rabaul, where strict punishment was meted out to any Japanese soldier who interfered with a local woman. For even the more brutal of the Japanese authorities had realised that what had occurred during the likes of the 'Rape of Nanking' had gone too far, and had since taken measures to ensure that it didn't happen again.

So, as well as taking severe disciplinary measures against any soldier who transgressed, they introduced a new idea—*jugun ianfu*—which translated to 'military comfort women'. In essence, they were women taken from Japan's occupied territories who were forced to work as sexual labourers for the Japanese troops, to keep their morale high and ensure that they remained well behaved among the locals. Later estimates calculated that there were between 80 000 and 200 000 comfort women scattered around the Co-Prosperity Sphere serving the needs of the six million soldiers, sailors and airmen that Japan had under arms. The 'comfort', however, certainly didn't extend to the women as they were forced to submit to an average of twenty to thirty soldiers a day, seven days a week, with Sunday always the busiest.

In Rabaul, the comfort women worked in the old Cosmopolitan Hotel, on the edge of Chinatown, but now converted into a military brothel. It had water on three sides with Japanese Military Police situated outside, ensuring that order was maintained. Inside, Japanese doctors worked hard to ensure that the women did not succumb to any venereal disease, as this would have subsequently affected the fighting ability of the soldiers.

For a young woman by the name of Okryon Park, however, who originally hailed from the small town of Muju in the newly established Japanese colony of Korea, the thought occurred that if she got a venereal disease, at least she would be able to get some relief, as the doctors always gave a week's break to any woman showing symptoms. As it was, Okryon's vagina was swollen and bleeding from constant, systematised rape. Generally, the men were meant to use condoms, but Okryon found that some simply refused and beat her if she dared complain. Pregnancies that resulted were terminated by the doctors.

This was of little concern to the Japanese military men who kept arriving. The soldiers arrived in trucks from the early morning until four o'clock in the afternoon, whereupon the non-commissioned officers took over until seven o'clock in the evening, and then commissioned officers until ten o'clock at night, though sometimes the very senior officers stayed all night.

A ticket system operated. Regular soldiers purchased a white ticket, the non-commissioned officers blue and the higher officers red tickets. Like the other women, Okryon collected the tickets and handed them in at the end of the shift, so the authorities could keep track of how many men she had 'comforted'. The only break in the routine was on Japanese national holidays when high-ranking officers who had not been before were allowed to visit, and all the comfort women had to stand together to sing the Japanese national anthem.

How had Okryon come to this? It was the question she kept reflecting on as the wretched weeks and then months went by. She had been born the third child of a loving family, with parents who never scolded her, or even demanded that she worked in the rice paddies with them, preferring that as a happy child she enjoyed herself by playing. But a bad marriage, followed by two other disastrous relationships, estranged her from her family and their simple life, and she had found herself in the big city with an infant son, constantly struggling to get the money necessary to survive. At the age of twenty-three, with the Japanese occupying Korea, she finally heard of a way out of her woes. Apparently the Japanese needed women like her to go to the battlefields and work doing domestic duties, washing clothes and so forth for the senior officers. The pay was so good she would be able to pay her debts quickly, and then return to reclaim her boy from the friends she'd left him with.

But no sooner had she arrived in this building in Rabaul with thirty other women than the soldiers had stormed in and raped them. The women had fought with all their strength, but there was no escape and they simply had to try to survive. Of all the many brutal indignities she was obliged to submit to, the one she found most appalling was having to say *'Iratsyaimase'* to every successive soldier and officer. It translated to welcome.[60]

Crying herself to sleep most nights, the one thing that kept Okryon going was the hope that her son was okay and she would one day be able to see him again . . .

Up in the Philippines the 'Lion of Luzon', General Douglas MacArthur, remained ensconced in his heavily fortified tunnel of Corregidor. His troops continued to do it tough upstairs, and also on the adjacent Bataan Peninsula, where, since retreating to Corregidor, MacArthur had returned only once, and then only for a couple of hours. It did not sit well with his troops and gave rise to two popular ditties. The first focused on the soldiers' predicament:

We're the battling bastards of Bataan,
No mama, no papa, no Uncle Sam.

No aunts, no uncles, no nephews, no nieces,
No rifles, no planes, no artillery pieces,
And nobody gives a damn.[61]

And the other on MacArthur himself:

Dugout Doug MacArthur lies ashakin' on The Rock,
Safe from all the bombers and from any sudden shock,
Dugout Doug is eating of the best food on Bataan,
And his troops go starvin' on.

Chorus:
Dugout Doug, come out from hiding,
Dugout Doug, come out from hiding,
Send to Franklin the glad tidings
That his troops go starving on.[62]

While the troops were not happy, neither was Washington. MacArthur's extraordinary popularity across America meant that he was effectively untouchable and they certainly couldn't relieve him of his command. For one thing, the effect on public morale would have been devastating—but there were other ways. In early February, the US Army Chief of Staff, General George C. Marshall, had sounded out MacArthur about leaving the Philippines with his family and taking up a new command. MacArthur was still considering it. One thing that appealed about the offer—going to Australia had been mentioned—was that it was becoming obvious that the Americans were not going to hold out much longer. MacArthur would not contemplate being captured by the Japanese, and he was less than keen to have his name on the bottom right-hand corner of a whole tableau of defeat. Maybe the answer *was* to go to Australia and use that as the launching pad to storm back to the Philippines when American strength was greater . . .

The news of the Japanese landings on the north coast of New Guinea, as small in scale as they were, did not sit well in Australia. Though it had taken some time for details to emerge, on 14 March,

John Curtin lifted the tone of his language one more notch in a radio address that was also broadcast to America.

'The Anzac breed will trade punches with the Japanese, until we rock the enemy back on his heels,' he said in his typically passionate tones. And no matter which way the battle turned, 'there will still be Australians fighting on Australian soil until the turning point be reached, and we will advance over blackened ruins through blasted and fire-swept cities, across scorched plains, until we drive the enemy into the sea . . .'

But, and this was the whole point, American assistance was paramount.

'Australia is the last bastion between the west coast of America and the Japanese,' he said with great emphasis. 'If Australia goes, the Americas are wide open . . .'[63]

Though some might claim that the prime minister's sense of geography placed the continent of Australia somewhere in the region of Hawaii, his point was not missed, either by the Americans or his fellow Australians.

Right up until the bombing of Darwin, most Australians still viewed the war as a distant problem. Sure, the population had had to suffer things like petrol rationing and enforced blackouts, and quite a few people had taken the possibilities of bombing seriously enough to dig slit trenches in their backyards, yet to this point there had been no universal view that the Japs were coming.

But now things had changed. With the fall of Singapore, bombing of Darwin and the Japanese landing in New Guinea, there came the real possibility that Australia would soon be a country under occupation, just as France was under the occupation of Germany. Things were grim. Vance Palmer, writer and social commentator of the time, reflected the mood.

'The next few months,' he wrote, 'may decide not only whether we are to survive as a nation, but whether we *deserve* to survive. As yet none of our achievements prove it, at any rate in the sight of the outer world. We have no monuments to speak of, no dreams in stone, no *Guernica*, no sacred places. We could vanish and leave singularly few signs that, for some generations, there had lived a people who had made a homeland of this Australian earth.'[64]

Dawn. Darwin ahead, and beyond it, stretched mile after endless mile of Australia. At the first sighting of the great southern continent, 62-year-old General Douglas MacArthur who was by his own estimation, 'the best General that the United States possesses,'[65] had moved up into the cockpit of the B-17 Flying Fortress.

Two days earlier MacArthur had left the Philippines and the mass of his troops to their common fate under the command of Major General Jonathan M. Wainwright. Accompanied by his wife, Jeannie, infant son Arthur and thirteen of his most senior and loyal staff, MacArthur had arrived in Australia to take up his new post as Supreme Commander of all the Allied troops in the Southwest Pacific. Starting with a fast torpedo boat to get him off Corregidor, and then transferring to a series of planes flying through enemy territory, it had been a hairy trip.

Before leaving, MacArthur sent a message to his troops that while he was going, *they* must hold on as reinforcements were on their way and would shortly relieve them. Many subsequent historians have been at a loss to understand why MacArthur said this, because there was no such thing, and it seemed cruel at best to promise his besieged American troops that the cavalry was coming when he knew that not to be true. As it happened, the total dominance of the Imperial Japanese Navy in the Southwestern Pacific—after it had invaded and secured all American bases on islands between the Philippines and Hawaii—meant that it was impossible to get American troops through to Bataan and Corregidor from the direction of the west coast of America, and the only hope was to use Australia as their launching pad.

The four B-17s landed at Batchelor Airfield, some forty miles south of Darwin, and right in the middle of . . .

Nowhere. There was nothing there, and no sign of anything in the horizons shimmering all around them. A few tents, a lot of flies, some 44-gallon drums of aviation fuel, and that was pretty much it, not counting the limitless sand and scrub that surrounded them. The impression that they were right at the very back of beyond— and maybe even further back than that—was strengthened when MacArthur inspected the American honour guard that had been called out to greet him. A single rag-tag platoon of American GIs from the 102nd Anti-Aircraft Artillery Battalion was all that could be managed.[66]

MacArthur was appalled, but consoled himself with the knowledge that they were, after all, right up in the northern reaches of Australia, in a very isolated spot. At the conclusion of the inspection MacArthur took aside the Commanding Officer of the 102nd and asked him precisely where in Australia the American troops were based. The officer looked back with some confusion.

'So far as I know, Sir,' he replied, 'there are few troops here . . .'

How could this be? US Army Chief of Staff General George C. Marshall had cabled MacArthur back in January, and he understood that there were no fewer than forty thousand troops waiting for him to command, even as 'every available vessel' was steaming towards Australia. How could it be?

He would have to wrestle with it some time soon, but the most pressing thing was to get to civilisation. His good wife Jeannie refused to fly *one more mile*, and MacArthur wasn't too unhappy to hear it. Still, advised by the bemused Australians that the nearest train was to be found at Alice Springs, some seven hundred miles south, MacArthur reluctantly agreed to get back on the plane, but only as far as the Alice, where he expected a train to be provided forthwith.

Sure enough, a train was dispatched from Adelaide to go and pick him up, and on 18 March, MacArthur and his entourage boarded it: one engine, one passenger car and two freight cars.

There is something in even the slight lurch of a train when it slows from *clickety-clack-clickety-clack-clickety-clack* to *clickety . . . clack . . . clickety . . . clack* which tends to wake passengers and so it proved on this occasion. Somewhere in that vast ocean of nowhere, MacArthur's train slowed for seemingly no reason, waking him, and he was shortly told that they were being flagged down by a group of sheep ranchers who knew he was on the train. Not unnaturally MacArthur presumed the ranchers were there to greet him or see him or somesuch, and he quickly rehearsed a few magnificent, magnanimous phrases. Alas, they simply wanted to see MacArthur's doctor as one of them had a steel splinter in his eye. Once that doctor had removed the sliver, the train rumbled on, albeit with one now slightly deflated American general.[67]

Not that MacArthur let too much of that disappointment show when he shortly afterwards performed for the press, who had gathered at Terowie Station, north of Adelaide, to greet him. It was time to be frank with them and tell them exactly how heroic and crucial he was going to be to the outcome of the war.

'The President of the United States ordered me to break through the Japanese lines,' he announced in his magnificently commanding tones, while they scribbled furiously, 'and proceed from Corregidor to Australia for the purpose, as I understand it, of organising the American offensive against Japan, a primary objective of which is the relief of the Philippines. I came through and I shall return.'

Yes, yes, yes, MacArthur was certainly here to defend Australia, and the people needn't worry, but within America's framework, the defence of Australia was not an end in itself, so much as a platform from which the Philippines could be re-taken.

Of the grandiloquent 'I shall return' line, a later biography, *General MacArthur and President Truman* by Richard H. Rovere and Arthur M. Schlesinger summed it up rather pointedly, noting that his 'Caesaresque words . . . left rather an ashen taste in the mouths of the men who knew they would be called on to return somewhat in advance of him.'[68]

Quite.

As to his 'breaking through Japanese lines', there too MacArthur had an amazing story about what a close-run thing it had been. MacArthur's claim was that on the way into Australia their planes had been buzzed by Japanese fighters. Oddly though there was no record of Japanese fighters in the area on that day, but that would have been a detail overlooked in the excitement of the great man arriving. (And for the record, the wireless operator on MacArthur's flight, Master Sergeant Dick Graf, went on the record after the war to say that there had been no Japanese planes *at all*, and the flight had been purely routine.)

Never mind. MacArthur continued south. By the time he was getting close to Adelaide, although he had confirmed that he had been appointed Commander of all American forces in the Southwest Pacific Area, he was appalled to find that it didn't actually mean much. Such American forces as there were in Australia were mostly engineers and airmen. From Perth to Parramatta, from the Great Australian Bight to Birdsville, there was not one American infantryman with a rifle that the great commander could command, nor was there any artillery. As to Australian forces, their four divisions remained overseas, on duty in North Africa, while their home forces of militia might have boasted 170 000, but only one-third of these were on duty at any given time as they still held down their regular jobs, and even then they were reportedly of very poor quality indeed.

As the train continued to clatter through the South Australian night, MacArthur paced up and down the corridor, muttering, 'God have mercy on us!'[69] It was something that he simply didn't understand. The Japanese had brought America into the war and had attacked him in the Philippines, but President Roosevelt had quickly come to an agreement with Winston Churchill that eighty per cent of America's manpower and resources would go to the European theatre of operations, and only twenty per cent towards stopping the Japanese.

The strange thing, Joe Dawson sometimes reflected, was how quickly you got close to blokes . . .

Just a few months ago, he had never even met Ray Phillips and Wally Gratz, but now they were his best mates. He could identify the deep voice of Ray or the easy laugh of Wally among a hundred other babbling voices on the parade ground, just as he could pick the silhouette of Ray's jutting jawline or Wally's nose on sentry duty fifty yards away in the sudden gloom of dusk. As a matter of fact he could do the same for most of the fellas in B Company. It just came from being around the same blokes, hour after hour, day after day, month after month. And you got to know, of course, not just their physical form and the timbre of their voices, but what kind of men they were inside. You saw them under pressure and letting loose—when they were up, when they were down, when they got a good letter from home and when they were told that their mum had been a bit poorly lately—just as they saw you in all the same situations. It made for very strong bonds, and Joe had none stronger than those he had with Ray and Wally, who very quickly became like brothers to him. For whatever reason, they just formed a natural trio, looking out for each other, looking after each other, sharing things they might not necessarily share with others.

Ray and Wally, for example, were the only two Joe really opened up to about his girlfriend Elaine, what she was like, what she did, how much he missed her and how he had decided he wanted to marry her. Wally in turn confided his love for his girlfriend in Maidstone. Other blokes were already starting to get what were called 'Dear John' letters from their girlfriends telling them they'd found someone else and had decided they didn't want to go on with it, but both Joe and Wally just knew that wouldn't happen to them, and quietly told each other as much.

All over the battalion, there were similar duos and trios which had formed up, and small bunches of friends. It just felt better to know that if anything ever did happen there'd be a couple of mates you could count on to cover you, just as you would cover them.

Sometimes, very rarely, Joe and Ray and Wally could get away for an all-too-rare drink at a Moresby pub. Local legend had it that the Australian-born Hollywood star Errol Flynn had been passing through just before the war started, and got involved in a fight with another bloke that had started at the bar and continued all the way down to the wharf about 150 yards away. The fight was not surprising, in one way. For the way they heard it, Flynn was a mongrel who left town without paying his debts.

But moving right along. Most often the conversation would inevitably turn to the Japs. It didn't really sound like they were going to be *too* much of a problem. The way the Australians heard it, they were mostly small, bucktoothed, shortsighted little coots without too much grunt about them . . .

There is no hold so tight as that of a loving mother embracing a beloved son who has just returned safely from a war, and for what seemed like ten minutes, Olive Bisset, weeping, held both strapping sons to her, refusing to let them go. Her many prayers had been answered, and her boys were now home safe.

There, there, Mum, we're here now, and we'll be here for the next few days. Still, this good woman held on as the pressure of holding her agonised emotions in check for the previous eighteen months was now released and she could let it all go. Their father George was more restrained in his own expressed emotions, giving both his boys very firm handshakes and quick, manly embraces; but for all that it seemed he just couldn't take his eyes off these two fine men, his sons, now Australian Army *officers*, who had returned safely to home and hearth. Yes, they were back only for a few days, but it was something all right.

Back in New Guinea, the war in Europe seemed far, far away. Private 'Smoky' Howson of the 39th Battalion's C Company was just finishing a fairly unpleasant stint as cook's offsider—which essentially meant doing an enormous amount of washing up in a huge vat—when an idea came to him. Why waste all that hot water? He was a man in desperate need of a relaxing soak and here was a vat of hot water. A bit greasy and scungy, sure, but beggars couldn't be choosers.

No sooner thought of than done, and there he was soaking with his knees tucked up under his chin, sitting out in the open and just starting to relax, when he heard them . . . and then saw them. Zeros. A dozen of them, coming his way and strafing all before them.

'They were literally strafing the shit out of us,' he later told author and fellow 39th Battalion soldier Victor Austin, 'and that is what I was doing, shitting while scrambling out of the tub, and running like hell, "starkers".

'I ran until I came to a big trench, and in I dive. The planes turned and came in from the opposite direction, so low you could see the whites of the pilot's eyes, and down I crouch. After a few sweeps there was a lull and I decided to leave the trench and go to the gunpit up the hill for greater safety. But just afterwards the Zeros zoomed in for another sweep. I started to run, but head over turkey I go, tripped by a big stone. Someone yells out, "They've got Smoky!" . . . But they hadn't, and as soon as the strafing stopped I got up and dived into the gunpit, panting like a billy-goat which had just finished a lap of Flemington Racecourse . . .

'After everything finally quietened down I realised that I was covered in shit—and it wasn't all mine, because that first trench I dived into was the platoon latrine!'[70]

Some days later, in the wee hours of 20 March, a radio transmission from Australia informed the garrison at Port Moresby that, this time, the Kittyhawks were definitely on their way and should be arriving at Seven Mile Airfield just after 7.00 a.m. The aerodrome would need to be whipped into shape to receive them.

Just as promised, at a quarter past seven the following morning, a drone in the distance signalled that the planes had arrived and all the Australians on duty charged out of their slit trenches, abandoned their Ack-Ack guns and began cheering, scrambling forward to give a wonderful greeting to the long awaited planes.

But that was funny, those four planes didn't seem to have the classic shark-nosed shapes of Kittyhawks. As a matter of fact they rather looked like . . . like . . .

ZEROS!

Just what the Japanese pilots thought when they came over the low hills at the northern end of the runway to find that instead of flak and gunfire there were crowds of cheering Australians waving them in and inviting them to land will never be known, but the moment they opened fire and started shooting up the whole aerodrome the Australians reverted to type and charged straight back to their slit trenches and Ack-Ack guns. A strange, strange people, these Australians.

And of course it had to happen. Had to! That was just the way things were in Moresby at that time. If things could go wrong, they would go wrong.

Bang on a quarter past seven the following morning, again there was the rumbling of aircraft in the distance, but this time the boys on the Ack-Ack were not going to be fooled. From the moment they saw the red and white insignia on the side of the plane they recognised the symbol of the Japanese Rising Sun flag and they let the bastards have it until . . . oh . . . shit!

They're Kittyhawks! The red and white were the roundels of the RAAF. It was too late though, and two of the arriving planes were hit, including that of the squadron leader, John Jackson. This time they knew exactly what the incoming pilots thought of the reception they received because they were very quick to express it, and expressed it at such volume that soldiers some distance away were also privy to their thoughts. Still, at least no one was killed, and Jackson proved to be a nice kind of bloke anyway, reportedly saying to Colonel Conran 'Congratulate your blokes on their shootin'. I've been over in the Middle East and that's the heaviest ground fire I've ever been through!'[71] In any case, spirits rose because that afternoon thirteen more Kittyhawks arrived to complete the No. 75 RAAF Fighter Squadron.

And still the best was to come when, shortly afterwards, a big Jap bomber trundled over the mountain, insolently sure that it could take its time to do whatever it wanted to do. But no . . .

At a point where the bomber was well away from the airfield, and so couldn't see him taking off, one of the newly arrived Kittyhawk pilots went after it. As the thousands of men around Moresby watched, the bomber was on its return run back to the port, when out of the clouds the Kitty suddenly swooped down, its guns chattering something that sounded close to the Australian national anthem. In seconds the bomber was trailing smoke and screaming earthwards, crashing into the reef.

The men cheered, the men laughed, the men fell all over each other in celebration. You bloody beauty! Get that up yer, Tojo![72]

And this was just the beginning. In next to no time at all, those magnificent men in their flying machines were going out after the Japs on regular sorties. Soon after arriving, Jackson led a raid on the Japanese airbase at Lae, flying in from the north across the sea and destroying a dozen Zeros, with five more reported damaged. *Now* it would be a fairer fight against those bloody Japs. And it wasn't a bad effort from a squadron that had had just one week's training back in Townsville.

Certainly, the war in the air was unequal. There remained the problem that Kittyhawks operated poorly above 12 000 feet and just about not at all above 20 000—meaning that the Japanese bombers only had to remain above that level to stay relatively safe—but it was still a whole lot more firepower than Moresby had had before.

You beauty. Tom Grahamslaw was on patrol less than an hour's walk from the government outpost of Kokoda when he saw a fine sight. A group of Japanese bombers were returning from a raid on Moresby when two Kittyhawks dived at them out of the clouds, shot the front bomber out of the sky, and then disappeared back into the cloud cover before the furious escorting Zeros could exact retribution. Before Tom's eyes the Japanese bomber hurtled towards a mountain behind Kokoda station, trailing smoke all the way, and he could just see plumes from the wonderful explosion when it hit. That was one more for the good guys.

As the government's man on the ground in that area, he searched for the crashed bomber and located it, and the remains of its crew, a day later at an altitude of 7000 feet on Mount Bellamy. Each dead Japanese crew member had a little cotton bag of sand with him, presumably as a memento of the home town in Japan they would now never return to.

Two other things took Tom's interest, and he wasted no time in passing them on to Army Intelligence. One was a Japanese code book. And the second was an accurate map of New Guinea and North Queensland, with notations on the latter, possibly targets.

Meanwhile, back at Moresby.

'Now, let's try it again . . . ' Captain Merritt said to the attentive men of the 39th Battalion's C Company encamped at Port Moresby, enjoying a rare day off from working as labourers, and receiving instructions about the newly issued Thompson sub-machine guns.

'You take an aggressive stance, like so,' Captain Merritt said, holding the Tommy gun before him in a fierce manner. 'An expression of pugnacity and determination on your face . . . '

'Begging your pardon, Sir . . . ' a voice called out from the back, 'but are we supposed to *frighten* the bastards to death, Sir?'[73]

All the men fell about laughing, and even Captain Merritt, after he'd calmed down, saw the funny side. It was to be a rare moment of levity in the otherwise serious business of getting ready for the Japs, who were expected to fall on Moresby at any moment. And at least they were doing some much-needed military training, which had tended to get lost in the recent flurry of work details. It was a lot more than the still worrying 53rd had managed.

CHAPTER SIX

THE DYNAMIC DUO

*'What is the truth about MacArthur?' his son Tom once asked him.
'The best and the worst things you hear about him are both true,'
Blamey replied.*

Hetherington, *Blamey*[74]

Way to the south General Douglas MacArthur masterfully hid the
despair he had been feeling about the lack of troops at his disposal.
He alighted at Spencer Street Station in Melbourne just before noon
on 21 March 1942, greeted by some five thousand citizens, sixty
reporters, an honour guard 360 strong, and Australia's Minister
for the Army, Francis M. Forde.

Stepping imperiously from the train, MacArthur looked every
inch the conquering hero, and was greeted as the same. Nevertheless,
he took the opportunity to note to the press (and so bring to the
attention of both the Australian and American governments) that
his genius alone could not win the war.

'I have every confidence in the ultimate success of our joint
cause,' he stated, 'but success in modern war requires something

more than courage and a willingness to die: it requires careful preparation. That means the furnishing of sufficient troops and sufficient material to meet the known strength of the enemy. No general can make something out of nothing. My success or failure will depend primarily on the resources which the respective governments place at my disposal . . . '[75]

The following day, General Sir Thomas Blamey returned from the Middle East, making his first landing at Fremantle, and on the dock he was officially given a letter from Prime Minister John Curtin, advising that he had been appointed Commander in Chief of the Australian Military Forces, concurrent with his present position as Commander in Chief Allied Armies in Australia. In essence, this meant that while Douglas MacArthur was the Supreme Commander of all the Allies in the Southwest Pacific Area, Blamey was the top Australian dog of the Army, Navy and RAAF. While still on the ship bringing him back to Australia Blamey had been informed of MacArthur's arrival in Australia and appointment to the supreme commander position, he remarked: 'This is the best thing that could have happened. MacArthur will be so far from his government that he will not receive any interference, and as for our own government he will take no notice of it.'[76]

Which was as may be, but MacArthur was at least reasonably diplomatic with the Australian Government when in public. Just three days after arriving in Melbourne and now, along with his family, a little more settled, MacArthur flew to Canberra to have his first personal meeting with John Curtin and also with the prime minister's bi-partisan Advisory War Council. It was an important meeting and came at a time when President Roosevelt was exerting pressure on the Australian Prime Minister to put MacArthur in charge of all Australian forces in the Southwest Pacific Area. (Curtin was of a mind to do exactly that, though had held back formal approval until he had met MacArthur and had been able to agree on the many details such an appointment would entail.)

Prima facie, MacArthur and Curtin were not a natural fit. MacArthur was a rich and highly educated Protestant patrician of abstemious nature, a born-to-rule man'o'war with right-wing politics and a detestation of journalists. Curtin, meanwhile, was all of the above in exact reverse. The son of a Catholic policeman and sometime publican and prison warder, the West Australian had left school at thirteen and educated himself thereafter. He had risen to prominence through a combination of his leadership of a trade union, his anti-conscription activism during World War I—which had led to him being briefly jailed—and his political representation of the socialist left, suffering a severe bout of alcoholism along the way.

Nevertheless, the two got on remarkably well, and when they emerged from their meeting in Curtin's prime ministerial office, MacArthur was comfortable enough, and presumptuous enough, to place a protective arm around Curtin's shoulders and tell him: 'You take care of the rear, and I will handle the front.'[77]

In the short term, however, MacArthur decided to handle that front in Melbourne itself, some 4000 miles from the nearest Japanese base, by settling into the best suite of the exceedingly plush Menzies Hotel, which as it turned out, still wasn't quite plush enough for the MacArthurs.

Indeed, one of the general's first instructions was that a piano be installed immediately. Jeannie MacArthur would often play while their son, Arthur MacArthur IV, bounced around, and the general gazed benignly upon the hundreds of Australians who gathered outside hoping to catch sight of their saviour.

MacArthur's office was set up in an old insurance building at 401 Collins Street in downtown Melbourne and was officially known as GHQ, General Headquarters. Indicative of his primary focus of returning to the Philippines in triumph, the phone at GHQ was always answered with a single word—'Bataan' and his immediate staff continued to refer to themselves as the 'Bataan Gang'.

And a very tight clique they were, a kind of military Manchu Court, devoted to the advancement of their emperor, General Douglas MacArthur. He was, after all, the one who had found space for them on his flight from the Philippines, despite the fact that Washington had given authorisation for only one of them, Chief of

Staff General Richard Sutherland. The rest of his retinue had been meant to stay there with the troops.

Despite another command from Washington on 3 April 1942 that MacArthur was to include Australian officers on his senior staff, the Lion of Luzon had refused to do so. The general disregarded the fact that the high command of the Australian troops in the most crucial year of WWII would be peopled by Americans with little or no combat experience and absolutely no knowledge of the ways of the Australian soldier or the conditions the men were fighting in.

In short order, the details of MacArthur's command had been worked out. On 17 April, he was formally appointed the supreme Commander of the Southwest Pacific Area—incorporating all Allied Army, Navy and Air Forces in that geographic area, encompassing the likes of the Dutch East Indies, the Philippines, New Guinea and Australia.

Within the now formalised framework, Thomas Blamey became the Commander of the Allied Land Forces. This meant that he would nominally have authority over American forces as well, though effectively all orders of significance to them continued to come via MacArthur himself, or his Bataan Gang. Far more important than the fact that Blamey would have some nominal say over American forces, was that MacArthur had very real authority over Australian soldiers. Given that the Australian Prime Minister, John Curtin, had so recently asserted the primacy of Australia's need to defend itself over and above that of its need to defend Britain, it may have seemed a curious move to hand control of Australian forces to an American.

But at this stage Curtin really did feel that there was no choice. His line that 'Australia looks to America' was not a ploy.

And MacArthur's view? He never made any bones about it, and spelt it out to Curtin very clearly. As Australia was a member of the British Commonwealth, the American maintained it was *Britain's* responsibility to defend Australia. America was there in Australia, yes, and this would add to their defensive capacity. But the USA 'had no sovereign interest in the integrity of Australia' and would only support the 'Ossies' insofar as it was in their own interests to do so.[78] Happily indeed, this was the present position, as the USA needed Australia as their launching pad to retake the Philippines, but however much Australia might look to America, the overall responsibility for Australia's defence remained with *Britain* . . .

In late March 1942, at MacArthur's Melbourne headquarters, the American general and Thomas Blamey met and talked for the first time. MacArthur, whatever else, certainly looked the part of a great military commander, and it wasn't just the gleaming black boots, pristine pants and stars. Far more than that, observers noted his impeccable bearing and born-to-rule air, his deep tan, dark glasses and corn-cob pipe, the whole topped by his field marshal cap placed rakishly aslant. If Hollywood had sent to central casting for someone who looked like a great American general, it couldn't have done better than MacArthur. Just as another famous American military commander, General George S. Patton, had silver pistols as his signature, MacArthur nurtured his own idiosyncratic appearance almost as a statement that because there was no one higher than him on the military food chain, he could wear whatever he damn well pleased, and did so.

Blamey, on the other hand, was as short as he was rotund as he was perpetually rumpled, and even on a good day was no more outlandish in his dress sense than a minor government clerk. As a matter of fact, he took the view that it would be highly improper of him, as the Commanding Officer of the Australian Army, to wear anything other than strict regulation military dress. With this in mind, he had turned up for the meeting with MacArthur dressed in the same Bombay bloomers he had been wearing in the heat of the Middle East. With his wide-brimmed hat, the effect was peculiar in chilly Melbourne, so much so that at first sight, a senior American officer had remarked, 'What do we have here . . . the Boy Scouts of Australia?'[79]

For Blamey it indicated the kind of patronising pomposity he would have to deal with in coming months and years whenever he was around Douglas MacArthur and his senior staff.

As one part of their wide-ranging discussions Blamey and MacArthur covered the situation in New Guinea, where the Japanese had already made two landings on the north coast and established two small bases. The obvious danger was that these landings were a mere prelude to a far greater invasion force, and the choice for MacArthur and Blamey was clear. Either hold back the prime Australian troops to the Australian mainland, or take the battle right to the enemy in New Guinea.

Something of a compromise was reached whereby, for the moment, the militia would provide the key defence of New Guinea, while the best units of the AIF forces that were available—the 7th Division, including the men of the 2/14th, 2/16th and 2/27th battalions who had just returned to Australian shores—would remain based in Southwest Queensland in the area around Nambour and Yandina. The AIF would thus be in place to defend against any invasion of the Australian mainland—at least south of what was later known as the 'Brisbane Line', which marked the northernmost point of Australia the AIF considered defensible—and also be available to be deployed in nearby New Guinea should they be needed.

Beyond defending Australia, MacArthur had many other things to keep him busy, including trying to run the ongoing defence of the Philippines all the way from comfy Melbourne. The Japanese had now lifted their offensive on the Bataan Peninsula and were bombing with greater force every day and shooting the survivors—nearly all of whom hadn't eaten properly for three months. Surrender seemed the only way to ensure survival for the masses of American troops and their officers, but MacArthur would have none of it.

'I am utterly opposed,' his message to General Wainwright went, 'under any circumstances or conditions to the ultimate capitulation of this command [the Philippines]. If food fails, you will prepare and execute an attack upon the enemy.'[80]

This message was ignored and, on 9 April, the troops on the Bataan Peninsula surrendered, leaving the fortress island of Corregidor as the only remaining point of effective resistance. Once more, MacArthur was disgusted.

Just north of Brisbane, the men of the 21st Brigade, now returned from home leave and getting back into it, were leading a far more comfortable existence, though they were still very busy in a multitude of tasks. In short order they would be making their way to Queensland, where they had a dual role.

The first role was to strengthen the defensive lines to the north of Australia's principal industrial centres, against the day that the Japanese might land somewhere on Australia's northeast coast, which was always a fear. Just to their south, the small city of Brisbane was filling with both 'For Sale' signs and American troops, as remaining residents dug slit trenches in their backyards and shops were sandbagged. At night, there was a 'brown-out' with no outside lighting allowed for fear of bombing, and the certainty grew that the end was nigh.

Under those circumstances, the decision to place the 2/14th, 2/16th and 2/27th just to Brisbane's north was a politically popular move for the Australian Government, the more so because the troops would also put a lot of time and energy into digging trenches and building roads and barricades on the beach, and familiarising themselves with the landscape and the likeliest lines of enemy attack.

The second focus of the AIF troops was to keep in top condition— with their fighting capacity honed to a sharp edge—by engaging in a variety of battalion and brigade exercises against each other. A lot of the exercises were conducted at night, where they often simulated guerilla ambushes in the jungle, which frequently involved a lot of climbing rough tracks around the Blackall Ranges, just inland from a tiny beachside village by the name of Noosa. As well, they would go out one platoon at a time to try their hand at living off the land for as long as five days, shooting kangaroos and birds, milking a

AWM 027006

A view of Imita Range and Ioribaiwa near the start of the Kokoda Track,
showing range after range of jungle terrain.

AWM 128400

The small village of Kokoda sits on a plateau in the Owen Stanley Range.
It was the key strategic possession for both the Japanese and Australians,
with the only airfield within four days march in any direction.

JOE DAWSON

Members of 12 Platoon, B Company, 39th Battalion, gather for a meal.
The young men of B Company were the first Australian troops to set off on the
Kokoda Track.

JOE DAWSON

'Uncle Sam'—Captain Sam Templeton, the Commanding Officer of 39th's B company.

JOE DAWSON

Members of the 39th Battalion prepare for action, including Joe Dawson's mate, Ray Phillips, at the front. The 39th were a militia battalion with little training and no real fighting experience.

JOE DAWSON

Joe Dawson and his girlfriend, Elaine, at Camp Darley, the 39th's training ground in Australia.

AWM 026821

These steep stairs, known as the 'golden stairs', were made after the first troops
had departed. For the 39th, there was no help up the track.

AWM 013288

'The bloody track.'
Members of the 39th Battalion trudge through mud and slush up part of the track.
(Negatives by Damien Parer.)

AWM 013290

AWM 027031

A patrol from the 39th looks over the Uberi valley at the beginning of the track.

AWM 027010

Major Cameron, who was initially displeased with the performance of
the 39th Battalion, discusses tactics with them.

AWM F01212

Due to the difficult terrain of the track, supplies were delivered by 'biscuit bombing': planes flew low over the ground at Myola and dropped supplies out, often resulting in mini explosions, like the flour bag to the right. (From Damien Parer's *Kokoda Front Line* footage.)

AWM 013254

Even with biscuit bombing, food was still extremely scarce—these soldiers are making what they can out of flour, egg and sugar. (Photograph by Damien Parer.)

AWM 013469

Eventually the 39th Battalion was reinforced with experienced AIF troops like these boys who had already served in the Western Desert and Syria. (Photograph by Damien Parer.)

AWM 013285

Bren guns were popular with the Australians, partly because they could be fired from the hip while charging forward. (Photograph by Damien Parer.)

few stray cows, making it up as they went along, but learning how to *survive*.

It was not certain yet where they would fight their next campaign, but with the Japanese running amok in the South Pacific, it was a fair bet that when it began it would involve battling the brutes in the jungle somewhere, and that is what the Australians began to prepare for. (At least the best they could without a jungle to train in.) As it happened the AIF men had only the foggiest idea of just how the campaign was faring in New Guinea, but at least they knew that fighting was taking place there and it was their most likely next destination.

Under the guidance of the Commander of the 7th Division, Major General Tubby Allen—himself a distinguished veteran of Gallipoli—senior officers studied the lessons that had been learnt from combating the Japanese in Malaya.

The fact that America had now entered the war meant that for those in Moresby resources began to flow, and at last US Army Air Force bombers turned up, together with a few fighters, as well as some army engineers and two units of American 'Negro' labour units, whose job was to establish aerodrome construction. (For nearly all of the Australians, this was the first time they had ever seen a black American.)

With them, more Australians arrived too, most of them from AIF anti-aircraft units who had been seconded to the militia battalions as reinforcements. Typically, many of the AIF men bitterly resented serving beside the 'chocolate soldiers'—so much so that they outright refused to wear the 39th Battalion's Mud Over Blood patch, instead secreting their own true AIF patch of grey safe inside their hatbands. Yes, they might nominally be among the militia, but they were not *of* them.

Meantime, however, the aerial attacks on Port Moresby continued. A particularly notable raid occurred on Tuesday 28 April. On that day eight Japanese bombers escorted by fifteen fighters swooped in and unleashed their usual cargo of catastrophe aimed at destroying the runway, planes and hangars. When the bombers had finally gone and the clean-up crews were moving in to assess the damage and get the runways back into shape as quickly as possible, they noticed that something odd had been left behind. There were three bulky packages wrapped in brown paper, sitting on a grassy verge near one of the runways, and well away from where the other bombs had hit.

What the hell was this? Some kind of booby-trap, surely. Making that all the more likely was a note attached to one of the packages which said, in impeccable English and copperplate handwriting: 'Any person who has received this package is cordially requested to send it over to Army Headquarters in Port Moresby.'

There was discussion for a good hour about just what to do with the bundles until finally a courageous engineer decided to take matters into his own hands and, after the packages were carefully moved to a dry creekbed, he gingerly . . . slowly . . . slowly . . . took his penknife to them. Out tumbled hundreds of envelopes—letters for home from the many Australian soldiers and civilians who had been taken prisoner by the Japanese in Rabaul. Here were the Japs trying to bomb them out of existence on a daily basis, and yet somewhere in the soldierly soul of Nippon there was still enough humanity to think of organising and doing something like that! Who would have thought it?

Across Australia, then, shortly afterwards, joyous news came in their letterboxes. Not only were their loved ones still alive, but there was an actual letter from them! In the absence of having them safe back home, or out of the clutches of the Japanese, it was close to the next best thing and gladdened many a heart.

The course of battle was not going well for the last American defenders on the island fortress of Corregidor, in the Philippines. Once the Bataan Peninsula had been abandoned by the Americans, the Japanese had been free to concentrate their attentions on that tiny patch of ground and, from that point on, were nothing if not energetic. Around twelve thousand shells a day were falling upon

Corregidor—more than one for every American defender. It was so comprehensive that for most of the men the only way to survive was to remain in the tunnels well beneath the surface. So, when one thousand Japanese soldiers landed to establish a beachhead on the afternoon of 5 May, followed up by tanks, there was little resistance from the starved soldiers. In just under a day, all resistance ceased, and General Wainwright gave the command for the American flag to be lowered as a sign of their surrender. Bar for a tiny fragment of that flag, which General Wainwright wanted preserved as a commemoration of his men's heroic defence, the rest of the flag was burned.

From Melbourne, General MacArthur was *triply* disgusted at the news, the more so as he had explicitly sent an order countermanding Wainwright's command to his troops to surrender, and still the soldiers did not again take up arms. What was *wrong* with them?

The fall of the Philippines clearly had repercussions across the rest of the Southwest Pacific theatre, as all those Japanese troops that had been focused on its defeat were now free to fight elsewhere, and among other tasks they would now reinforce the base at Rabaul. As well, just two days earlier, the Japanese had notched up a new conquest when, against the claims of a small British–Australian garrison, they seized Tulagi in the southern Solomons. With its superb harbour, Tulagi perfectly provided for a Japanese naval base, and its strategic value was all the greater for being just seventeen miles away from the plains of the island of Guadalcanal, which would be perfect for building an airbase. In the South Pacific, the Japanese presence was just getting stronger.

And hell, in one way or another, so were Smoky Howson and the boys. In this man's army, where everything was undersupplied except flies and mosquitoes, the only way to get by, Smoky had decided, was to carefully pilfer what you needed and share it with the blokes in your platoon. Listen, as a bloke who was raised as one of nineteen kids with never enough to go round, Smoky knew there wasn't a lot you could teach him about pilfering, okay? No worries, he had soon organised a few of the lads unloading at the docks to be on the lookout for stuff heading to the Officers' Mess and the like. This was so the common soldiers, too, could get some grog and goodies such as there were. It only seemed fair, after all.

This habit of making do with what you could get your hands on wasn't limited to just alcohol and food though. For Smoky and some of the boys soon realised that while they were desperate for more arms and ammo, which just never came, many of the wrecks of the aircraft that littered Seven Mile Airfield had *just* the guns they were looking for. It was sad that each of those wrecks mostly represented a pilot and crew that had been killed, including Squadron Leader Jackson who, though valiant, hadn't lasted long. But you couldn't think like that. You had to concentrate on getting what you needed, come what may.

With all the blokes helping, it didn't take long to get down to the 'drome, grab the guns out of the planes, and set them up. In a jiffy, Smoky's platoon, which had started with two old Lewis guns from the Great War, now had a *serious* machine gun, .303s and a 50-calibre gun for every man.

No one in authority told them to do it; it just seemed the obvious thing to do when they were copping it from the Japs and nothing was being done to support the boys on the ground. It was up to *them*, so they just got on with it.

In the air, meanwhile, on the bright beautiful morning of 6 May 1942, in his Hudson A16–160 of 32 Squadron, RAAF Pilot Officer Pennycuick was conducting a reconnaissance flight around the eastern tip of New Guinea when his eye was caught by the tiniest speck of something ahead in the vast blue nothingness. Nosing towards the speck, which he estimated to be some ten miles north by northeast, he soon saw another speck beside it, with each one showing wisps of smoke coming from on top and a wake of white water behind. Going only close enough to confirm, he was quickly on the radio to report the sighting.

'Moresby Control, this is Pilot Officer Peter Pennycuick of 32 Squadron, there is a Japanese convoy heading south by southwest, approximate position ten miles west of Misima. There appears to be at least one aircraft carrier with many more ships around it, do you copy? Over . . .'

And things moved quickly from there. This, it seemed, was the Japanese invasion force headed for Moresby, just four hundred miles from it, which had been half-expected since the previous month when codebreakers had intercepted a signal indicating that there would be an invasion force launched from Rabaul.

Although Port Moresby was not designated by the Japanese command as the target area, it was the obvious choice, and the sighting of the convoy confirmed it. The codebreakers had given the Allies crucial time to assemble the forces necessary to thwart the Japanese action, and from his Land Force Headquarters in Brisbane, General Blamey signalled Major General Basil Morris: 'A serious attack against you and the troops under your command will develop in the immediate future. All possible forces are being assembled to deal with the enemy. Do not doubt that you and your command, which includes troops of our great ally, the United States of America, supported by Allied Air Forces, will show the Japanese that Australian territory cannot be invaded without meeting a most determined and successful resistance. Australia looks to you to maintain her outposts, and is confident that the task is in good hands . . .'[81]

Morris replied: 'Grateful your inspiring message . . . We are determined not to let Australia down.'

And now those American forces—including the aircraft carriers USS *Lexington* and USS *Yorktown*—under the command of US Admiral Frank Jack Fletcher, were thrown into the fray.

From their positions all around Seven Mile Airfield, the soldiers of the 39th Battalion saw aeroplane activity like never before, as reconnaissance planes and other planes from the respective aircraft carriers engaged in actual battle. The soldiers and citizens of Port Moresby watched the constant landings and launching of aircraft with enormous interest and no little trepidation, even as the soldiers themselves scrambled to defensive positions around the town's beaches, steeling themselves. For if those Allied planes failed to do their job, then Moresby had perhaps less than twenty-four hours before the Japanese would be storming ashore.

While this 'Battle of the Coral Sea', as it became known, continued, the invading Japanese troops of the *Nankai Shitai* (the South Seas Detached Force) heading towards Port Moresby—including the 144th Regiment drawn from Shikoku—sweated impotently in the bellies of their nautical beasts. At any moment they could be torn apart by a bomb or torpedo. There was nothing for them to do but wait it out. As they had already proved across the devastated Pacific, on land they could fight like demons, yet on water they were at the merciless whim of the battle gods.

On the afternoon of 8 May, though, the keenly trained senses of the soldiers picked up a change of rhythm and movement. Their troopships were turning around. The Japanese invasion had been routed.

In the final balance of the Battle of the Coral Sea the Japanese had lost a light carrier, a destroyer and three smaller ships, together with seventy-seven planes shot down and over one thousand men killed or wounded, while the US had lost one aircraft carrier, the *Lexington*, as well as another carrier severely damaged, an oil tanker and destroyer sunk, sixty-six planes shot down and over five hundred men killed.

While the losses of the two sides were roughly comparable, there was no doubt that it was an American victory, given that the industrial resources of the United States were so much greater than Japan's and the only way Japan could win the war was to have a series of rapid and overwhelming victories. More important still, perhaps, for American and Australian morale was the fact that the Japanese invasion force had been obliged to turn around and this marked the first time that the relentless Japanese expansion in the Pacific had been checked. The result of the Battle of the Coral Sea was that Japan had lost the capacity to launch a seaborne invasion of Moresby.

Still, luckily for Japan, their troopships, carrying thousands of crack soldiers, had emerged from the battle unscathed, and they would just have to find another way to get them there.

Perhaps they could do once again what they had recently done so successfully in Singapore, which was to attack overland from a direction that the defenders were not prepared for. As the Japanese military leadership saw it, it might be possible to land on the north coast of the island, around Buna and Gona, and then march across a track which went all the way through to the central government station situated at Kokoda, on the northern foothills of the Owen Stanleys, and proceed from there to Port Moresby. Of this track, the Japanese knew little, other than that it was clearly marked on the map as the sole thoroughfare between the north and south coasts of the eastern end of the island; but it stood to reason that being in constant use it would have to be in fairly good condition . . .

In the meantime, the narrow escape from the Japanese seaborne invasion galvanised the 'Mice of Moresby'. During the days when the battle hung in the balance, and it really seemed as if the Japs would soon be arriving, the garrison had put its grand defensive plan into operation, with massive movements of men and munitions heading off on their pre-ordained routes. The result, with traffic jams, mayhem, lost platoons and bungled communications, made a dropped bowl of spaghetti look organised, and it was clear that if the Japs really did come then the Australians were a long way from battle ready. But the 'dry-run' had helped to highlight the weaknesses, and afforded the Diggers opportunities to correct them.

In Australia proper, the news of the victory in the Coral Sea also had a bracing effect. At the height of the battle John Curtin made a speech broadcast nationwide in which he said: 'A battle of crucial importance to the whole conduct of the war in this theatre is going on,' and the people awaited the outcome impatiently.

While good news would come, any thought that the Japanese danger had receded was countered just a short time later when, on the night of 31 May 1942, three Japanese midget submarines—launched from a pod of mother submarines just off the coast—made their way into Sydney Harbour. Fire torpedo one sent the HMAS *Kuttabul*, an RAN barracks ship, to the bottom, killing nineteen sailors. Fire torpedo two and three: missed. By this time the alarm was raised and two of the submarines, trapped by special submarine nets, were destroyed by depth charges, but one escaped.

And this was just the beginning. Over ensuing weeks, Japanese submarines sank Australian ships up and down the east coast of Australia, while shells were also lobbed into Sydney and Newcastle—ensuring as a side effect that the price of harbourside homes plummeted. You practically couldn't *give* them away.

While the physical damage to Sydney was not great, the effect on Australian morale was enormous. An American official in Australia at the time wrote a report for Washington and noted: 'There is a fatalistic depression that is almost solid, and if the Japs landed tomorrow, the great majority of Australians would just turn over and play dead.'[82] It was precisely this kind of fatalistic attitude that John Curtin had to expend much of his energy fighting, something that drained him dry.

And certainly, the Japanese tried to capitalise on this low morale—sometimes at the expense of the truth—even with the Australians who were already under lock and key. Up at the infamous Changi prison camp in Singapore, for example, thousands of Australian soldiers were told to form up as the Japanese Commanding Officer would be making a very important announcement.

Standing on a rough platform above them, the officer shouted the news of the bombings on the Australian mainland, relishing the impact it would surely have upon these roughshod enemy prisoners.

'Sydney. One thousand bombers. BOOM, BOOM, BOOM—all gone.'

Sure enough, there was consternation in the ranks and a whispering wail of despair among the Australians, even as the Japanese officer followed up.

'Melbourne. One thousand bombers. BOOM, BOOM, BOOM—all gone.'

Same result, and the officer drove it home one last time.

'Brisbane. One thousand bombers. BOOM, BOOM, BOOM—all gone.'[83]

A momentary stunned silence fell upon the Australians as they contemplated the horror of what had just been announced and the officer stood there preening. The silence was only broken when one Digger by the name of Kelly Davidson drawled an enquiry about his own tiny town, situated just north of Glen Innes in the New South Wales hinterland.

'What about Llangothlin . . . ?'

The officer drew himself up and one more time shouted the grim tidings: 'Rrrangothrin. One thousand bombers. BOOM, BOOM, BOOM—all gone.'

This time there was a different quality to the momentary stunned silence that followed the pronouncement as the tide suddenly turned from rising gloom to runaway merriment.

'Bullshit!' Kelly Davidson called out. 'Bullshit your one thousand bombers!'

The cry was taken up among the ranks—'Bullshit! Bullshit! Bullshit!'—as the Australians fell about laughing and the Japanese officer perhaps realised his mistake. Kelly was severely flogged for his trouble, but for the rest of his days he'd maintain it had been worth it.

MacArthur had had enough. Certainly enough of Australian newspapers printing what was going on in his domain—he was definitely not happy about it. He wanted total control of the flow of information emanating from his area, and censorship of anything that didn't meet with his approval. As he explained to Australia's Advisory War Council—defined by Curtin as a body 'representative of all parties and empowered to investigate, advise and assist the government in all its war efforts'—it was the only way to ensure proper security over all sensitive military matters. It was a measure of MacArthur's dominance that the Advisory War Council promptly acceded to his request.

From the middle of May 1942, MacArthur was the *sole* source of information about MacArthur, MacArthur's operations, and anything with which MacArthur was remotely associated. For a man who had once made his way in the Public Relations Division of the US Army, this was manna from heaven; he could construct any image of himself and his operations that he damn well pleased and choke off any information that he didn't like. He did not miss either opportunity. For the journalists in the field who were ill-disposed to form part of the MacArthur machine, it became virtually impossible to do their jobs properly, which was to report and comment without fear or favour.

As an infuriated Osmar White would write of how these edicts affected his own work reporting from New Guinea: 'Once news sources are officially controlled by censorships, no individual writer can deflect by as much as a hair's breadth the impact upon the public mind of the tale wartime leadership wants to tell. But history may judge the relationship of dead facts . . . '[84]

Up in Japan, Prime Minister Hideki Tojo had introduced similar restrictions through the Ministry of Home Affairs. Not only was he upset about newspapers printing stories which contained what he considered sensitive military information, but he had also become concerned about the effect on the Japanese public of hearing stories of Japanese soldiers being killed. He wanted it stopped, and it was.

Too early to be sure. Way too early. But on 18 May the Allied codebreakers were all but positive that one of the intercepted Japanese messages mentioned a land route leading from the north coast of New Guinea across the Owen Stanley Range into Port Moresby—a plan known as Operation MO. What made the codebreakers and their superiors so unsure was that it seemed so unlikely. Yes,

THE DYNAMIC DUO · 133

nominally, there was some kind of track there, but very little was known about it, and what little knowledge there was indicated that it would be impassable for an invading army. Still, the information was passed on and it was reviewed by both MacArthur and the Bataan Gang, and General Blamey with his senior staff. On balance the combined Allied military leadership decided to ignore it. Many years later, one of the codebreakers concerned related how, after they had passed on their tip to the nation's highest military leaders, 'They said: "Nobody in their right senses would land there!" We told them this was going to happen. Blamey couldn't have cared less.'[85]

It was simply inconceivable that the Japanese would try to invade Port Moresby overland through New Guinea's dark heart. Or was it? As the Japanese continued to make their own provisional plans, they decided that they would take hundreds of bicycles stored in the holds of their invading ships to better facilitate troop movement. And if they went ahead with it, those bicycles would be as much mechanical force as the troops had. The Japanese might not have known much about New Guinea—few from the outside world did— but they at least knew that it was a conquest which would be won or lost on manpower alone, and not mechanised power as it had been in the theatres of Europe and the Middle East.

Their greatest asset in such a venture would be the fine fighting men of the 144th Regiment of the *Nankai Shitai* (the South Seas Detached Force), men who had been trained for precisely this kind of venture. If they indeed decided to execute the plan, the 144th's Commanding Officer, Major General Tomitaro Horii, estimated that his men could be at the gates of Moresby in just over a week.

It was late May 1942, and Tom Grahamslaw was not happy. He had just received a report from a colleague that a launch with a few Japanese troops on board had arrived at the tiny coastal village of Morobe. The Japs had landed and, with the aid of interpreters, were apparently asking questions about Buna—the little native village and government post just a little further east along the coast—

and about the track that led from Buna to Kokoda and then Port
Moresby. Tom passed the information on to Moresby immediately,
though it must be said they hadn't seemed particularly interested.
At the least, they hadn't followed it up with a flurry of enquiries
pressing him for more information and the like. His report seemed
to have just disappeared into the gaping maw of New Guinea Force
Headquarters and was never heard from again.

It became known as the Battle of Midway, and in some respects it
was not unlike the Battle of the Coral Sea. Situated right at the
north of the Hawaiian chain of islands, the tiny atoll of Midway,
which had slumbered there for millennia, suddenly burst into life.
Eager to establish a base where they could launch aircraft, ships
and submarines at the American flotillas in the central Pacific, the
Japanese military leadership had decided to seize the highly strategic
islands. Launching on 3 June 1942, a flotilla of four Japanese aircraft
carriers, five cruisers, twelve destroyers and 250 planes moved on
Midway from the west. With that level of naval firepower, the
Americans would *have* to respond, and it was hoped that in the
subsequent decisive battle, the American carriers would be destroyed
once and for all.

This time, however, because of the work of the Allied codebreakers,
warnings had been heeded, so the Americans knew the Japanese
were coming and placed their forces accordingly. No sooner had
the Japanese fleet steamed over the horizon near Midway than the
Americans attacked with three carriers, eight cruisers, fifteen destroyers
and, most importantly, 330 planes, many of them land-based from
Midway itself. When the smoke had cleared, four of the six Japanese
aircraft carriers which had attacked Pearl Harbor were sunk side
by side with a heavy cruiser, three destroyers and approximately 150
planes, while many of Japan's most experienced pilots and navigators
had been among the 4800 men killed. Although America lost the
carrier *Yorktown*, a destroyer, 150 planes and 307 men, it was a
wonderful follow-up counter-offensive to the Battle of the Coral

Sea and meant, in the short term, that all Japanese plans to invade New Caledonia, Samoa and Fiji were put on hold.

Instead, Japan now reluctantly came to the view that America would have to be more efficiently choked off, with far-flung bases and areas of support being taken out one by one.

On 14 June 1942, Lieutenant General Hyakutake, the commander of the 17th Army in Rabaul, was given a formal order to proceed with the plans to send troops overland to Moresby.

In the meantime, training for the 2/14th, 2/16th and 2/27th battalions went on in southwestern Queensland. More manoeuvres, more living off the land, more night marches, more tests of their endurance. In one test, one of the 2/16th's companies managed to march 65 miles in two days, while a platoon of the 2/14th managed to march 120 miles in four days and nine hours. It was good training as far as it went, but most seemed conscious that it didn't go far enough. After what they had been able to accomplish in the Middle East, it just didn't make any sense to leave them here festering in inaction. Why couldn't they be at least moved closer to where the action was most likely to occur?

And they were not the only ones who felt it, then or afterwards. To have, as the closest Australian force to the Japanese invaders, mere wet-behind-the-ears militiamen who had for the most part done only a few weeks training, and who were in no way equipped to deal with the unique conditions that New Guinea would place upon them—and all while far more experienced troops were ready, willing and able to be deployed—was regarded by many as nothing short of insane.

But MacArthur, for one, wouldn't hear of it. After the successes of the battles of the Coral Sea and Midway, he told Australia's Advisory War Council that there was no further risk of an invasion of Australia. And what MacArthur said went. Insanity dressed up in military orders, black on white . . . *by the right . . . quick-march!* . . . had a momentum all its own, and quickly routed all quibbles on the grounds that they were in the first place unpatriotic, and in the second place insubordinate.

At much the same time, a high ranking American military officer by the name of Major General Robert C. Richardson visited Australia. He had been sent by US Army Chief of Staff, General George C. Marshall, to do a report on how the relationship between American and Australian officers was working in the Southwest Pacific Command.

For a true American patriot, the report that Richardson prepared did not make for pretty reading, most particularly for the fact that in some cases Australian officers were *in charge of American soldiers*. Scandalised, the major general reported in scathing terms to Marshall that 'the present organization was an affront to national pride and to the dignity of the American Army'.[86] In short, while it was no more than General MacArthur's due to be in charge of the Australian Army, Navy and Air Force, it was an *outrage* for an Australian to pull rank on an American at any level. Richardson saved his most scathing language of all for General Thomas Blamey, who still retained nominal control over the American Army in the Southwest Pacific Area. Blamey, Richardson reported to his Washington masters, was a 'non-professional Australian drunk'.[87] (Others within the Bataan Gang, it should be noted, demurred and maintained that Blamey was actually a professional drunk.)

Though Osmar White briefly returned to Australia in May—because in his view MacArthur's censorship restrictions were simply making it impossible for him to function effectively as a journalist—he nevertheless returned to Moresby in early June. Something told him that this was where the next major Japanese action would take place, so it was the place he had to be. All was as before. Hot, horrible, harrowing. There was a sense of foreboding, a sense that bad things were moving towards them, though for the moment the spectre lacked specific form and structure.

The only possible antidote to all the gloom and doom in the air was laughter, and, as it happened, a fellow came into Osmar White's orbit at this time, a fellow who was always a sure source of a laugh. His name was Damien Parer and he was one of the hottest documentary-makers in Australia at the time, and of his many distinctive features it was his loud hooting laugh that White would treasure longest. Of those other distinctive features, there were many and, as White later described Damien: 'He was young, tough, keen and unshakably courageous . . . The more I saw of the man, the more I liked and admired him. He was long, stooped, black-headed, sallow-faced, smiling. He had great piston legs covered by a fuzz of black hair and ending in size 12 feet that looked as if they could crush the skull of a python.'[88]

Instinctively, both men liked each other from the start, and they became a common sight around the military installations of Port Moresby, Parer's rather dark and aquiline Spanish features somehow managing to make Osmar White and his strong jaw look more than ever as if they had been carved out of granite.

With still nothing happening in the environs of Moresby that was 'news', White and Parer decided to use their time by making an overland journey across New Guinea to get some idea of the real country. They might even get some stories and footage of the guerillas code-named Kanga Force—a combination of AIF commandos from Major T. P. Kneen's 2/5th Independent Company, and a detachment of New Guinea Volunteer Rifles—who were making hit and run raids on the Japanese along the north coast around Lae and Salamaua. The guerillas were known widely for their daring raids on the Japanese, and personally for their exotic uniform which included beautiful bird of paradise plumes emerging from their felt hats. A whole load of supplies were about to be delivered to the guerillas by a gruelling circuitous route, and White and Parer received permission to accompany the native supply-bearers.

While they were still organising this trip north, Damien kept shooting. On the afternoon of 17 June 1942 he had his best camera set up above Port Moresby's Fairfax Harbour and was capturing the essential New Guinea experience for so many diggers at that time—the unloading of a ship. This was the *Macdhui*, and if Damien had a particular interest in the ship it was because he recognised it as the ship that had brought his parents and brothers and cousins to New Guinea several years before.

Down on the deck of the ship at that time, Joe Dawson was in charge of the detail hauling the cargo of tinned food and boxes of ammunition out of the hold and onto the flat boat called a 'Lighter' that nestled nearby, like a baby chick next to its mother hen. It was this boat that would take the cargo to shore.

There were one or two of Joe's superior officers also there, but they had gone below to the ship's saloon to get out of the heat and have a drink with the *Macdhui*'s captain, James Campbell. Joe kept to his post in all the stinking, dripping oppressive humidity, but then suddenly heard an air-raid siren in the distance. In an instant he saw them—an angry flock of Jap bombers, protected by Zeros, was approaching the harbour from the east. In an instant the captain of the Lighter told Joe to get his soldiers back onto the *Macdhui*, because it would be safer for them there, and in any case the bombers would in all likelihood be going for the harbour's one massive T-wharf. If that wharf was taken out, the problems of supply for Moresby would become critical.

Only marginally relieved, Joe ordered his soldiers to get back onto the ship, which was very quickly underway as, with great skill, Captain Campbell tried to move the ship out of harm's way. But as Damien Parer's cameras faithfully recorded it, the bombers had no interest in the T-wharf. They had eyes for one thing: this prize fat ship lumbering around in pathetic zig-zags on the pearly waters beneath them. Of course the Ack-Ack guns did their best, as did the 'pom-pom' guns—so-called because of the *pom-pom-pom-pom* sound they made—but the bombers were too high to be affected.

Thus, all around the *Macdhui*, bombs began to drop, with the subsequent waves of concussion constituting an absolute physical force. Still on the deck, Joe had just turned away from the explosion of one bomb while holding onto the rail, when another bomb dropped even closer. The force of it lifted him up—he had the momentary sensation of an enormous hand grabbing him by the trousers and hauling him high, causing enormous pressure on his groin area—and then his whole body smashed into the ship's superstructure below the bridge, before he fell to the deck again, an all but broken rag doll. When he roused himself to get up and moving again, strangely the ongoing roar of the battle sounded like it was coming to him through the bottom of a barrel packed with cottonwool. The *Macdhui* had a terrible list as it took on water amidships, but it was at least still under way. Most upsetting for Joe in that first instant was that somehow the explosion that had knocked him over had also blown his wristwatch off and into oblivion. That wristwatch was a present from his beloved Elaine and it near killed him that it was lost.

Far more tragically as Joe soon discovered, six members of the 39th, including the two officers below, really had been killed by one of the bombs which had penetrated the decks before exploding in the saloon bar. Six men dead. Good men. *Dead*. In an instant, Joe Dawson's sense of appalling unreality was compounded when he spied, on the deck of the ship, a whole human leg, the dead owner of which could only be identified by the name written on the inside of the leg's puttees. Horrified, but mesmerised, Joe kept looking at the leg and two or three thoughts kept reverberating through him: 'This is really a *war*. Blokes are going to get *killed*. *I* might get killed.'

The *Macdhui* survived for that day, when the Japanese were chased away by predominantly American planes twenty minutes after the bombing had begun, but nothing would bring those dead men back. A dreadful pall fell over the entire 39th Battalion, as they came face to face with the dreadful realities of war for the first time.

Though Damien Parer still had his cameras with him as the ship came to the wharf and they evacuated the dead and dreadfully wounded, he turned the cameras off. Somehow, it just seemed disrespectful to the dead and frivolous to the wounded. They were dead and there were missing limbs, and he wanted to make a film about it? No thank you.

One of the soldiers who'd been with Damien up on the hill, but had sheltered in a slit trench as bombs exploded all around, couldn't contain himself.

'Christ, how did you stay up there? Didn't you hear the bombs?' he asked.

'I didn't hear any bombs,' Damien replied, 'I was filming.'[89]

And he was still filming the following day when the Japanese returned to finish the job. Again the *Macdhui* made a run for it, but this time it took three bombs through the deck and it quickly ran aground, with thirteen killed and ten wounded.

As John Curtin had so aptly quoted: 'Nearer, clearer, deadlier than before, the cannon's opening roar . . .'

CHAPTER SEVEN

UP THE BLOODY TRACK

I remember Ted or I stating the idea that fighting in this would be like fighting in a fog. We thought about this as we went along. You wouldn't be able to see much. Your bullets would go through all the bushes, just like in a fog, you wouldn't know whether you were hitting anything. And if somebody shot at you, you wouldn't know whether he had hit you.

Report from Lieutenant William Alec Palmer and Lieutenant William Edward Young[90]

Read this alone—and the war can be won. It is an historical fact that in all tropical campaigns since ancient times far more have died through disease than have been killed in battle . . . To fall in a hail of bullets is to meet a hero's death, but there is no glory in dying of disease or accident through inattention to hygiene or carelessness.

Colonel Masanobu Tsuji[91]

New blood. At the end of June 1942, 30th Brigade, comprising the 39th, 49th and 53rd battalions, was reinforced by thirty-six officers snaffled for the most part from the 7th Division, which had just returned from the Middle East. Major General Sir Thomas Blamey's view was that it would help to strengthen the fighting power of the militia units if their leadership ranks could be leavened with experienced officers. The 39th took half of these officers and the other two battalions divided the rest, though the 39th approached the new officers differently from the 53rd. A key difference in the approach taken by the 39th Battalion, was that the 39th posted the new officers to battlefield command positions. The 53rd Battalion, meanwhile, did not give command of a single company to one of these men most experienced in running a company on the battlefield, and instead used theirs back at headquarters as staff officers.

In sum, the 39th got one major, six captains and eight lieutenants. And while New Guinea had at that time a fair number of what was known in military parlance as 'Snarlers', short for 'Services No Longer Required'—which was what a number of incompetent AIF officers in the Middle East had their papers stamped with—the experienced AIF officers who joined the 39th now proved to be first class.

As a rule there was an immediate respect, if not awe, for these new officers who had actually been in the thick of battles. These men had a presence about them, an authority, quite unlike most of the officers they had replaced. From the beginning of their tenure, there was a sudden surge of voltage through a battalion life that had tended towards lassitude in recent months since their commanding officer Colonel Conran had spent so much time in hospital with various illnesses.

It was a surge of power that was desperately needed. The newcomers were nothing less than shocked by what they'd found with their new charges. They'd heard that the Chocos were bad, but had never imagined it could be *this* bad. The officers had come from serious military outfits, where reveille was at 5.30 a.m. and not a minute later; where men shaved, polished their boots and presented for inspection; where they knew how to strip and assemble a Lewis gun in ninety seconds flat and reassemble it; where there was a basic understanding of military techniques and tactics. Here, though, despite the fact that the men seemed willing enough, there was a general laziness and slovenliness that seeped into most things, and a complete lack of understanding that THEY WERE IN THE ARMY NOW!

And it wasn't just the officers' imagination. Five weeks before, back in Australia, the Deputy Chief of the General Staff, Major General George Vasey, had written to all Australian Army commanders asking them to submit their estimation of the combat efficiency of brigades under their command, with the highest rating being an A for 'Efficient and experienced for mobile operations', down to 'F' for 'Unit Training is not yet complete'.[92]

The 39th, together with the 49th and 53rd battalions, had been classified with an 'F' grading. (The 49th Battalion had not moved one jot from the estimation of Blamey's Chief of the General Staff, Lieutenant General Sturdee, the previous July that it was 'quite the worst battalion in Australia'.[93])

And yet here, with the Japanese right at their door, was 'F Troop', while back in the calm of Queensland, the 'A Team'—the 7th Division, which these officers had just left—was being held in reserve. To the bewildered new officers it just didn't seem to make sense. What was the army *thinking*? Rumours among the officers just might be true: that high command had taken the view that New Guinea might be a hopeless case, like Singapore. And if that was so, then it didn't make sense to lose your frontline troops to the Japanese, as had happened in that tragedy, and it was a much better idea to keep them safe for the main game, which was to defend the Australian mainland.

Dismay at the decision to keep the prime troops back from one of the likely frontlines went into the highest reaches of the Australian Army, with Lieutenant General Sydney Rowell, then Commander of the 1st Corps, later noting that the decision not to send the AIF made his 'headquarters weep at the time',[94] In his memoirs, Rowell called it a 'cardinal error'.[95]

Whatever they thought of the decision at the time, however, the newly arrived simply had to do what they were sent to do: whip their new charges into shape. From the moment the new officers arrived there was an imposition of genuine army discipline; an insistence that soldiers rise at reveille, immediately shave and get themselves presentable; that they do physical fitness activities; that they genuinely engage in at least basic military training, including drill, route marching and night work, instead of digging ditches and the like all day long.

There was resistance initially from some members of the 39th, but even these men could see that if they went into battle they really needed to be in better shape and, besides, it was much better to work with rifles any day of the week than shovels every day of the week.

While there was some relief among the older officers of the 39th that they'd been replaced and were now free to return to Australia, there was also relief among one or two of the older men who were allowed to remain. Chief among these was Captain Sam Templeton, the Commanding Officer of the 39th's B Company, who had continued to grow in the battalion's estimation as the weeks had passed. With all of his experience and senior years, Sam Templeton projected confidence and a can-do spirit to a group of mostly much younger men who were in need of precisely those qualities. It was also likely that a lot of them were missing their fathers, from whom they had so suddenly been separated for the first time in their lives.

Others of more mature years had already attached themselves to the 39th. One notable fellow was Father Norbert 'Nobby' Earl, a refugee from Sacred Heart Mission near Samarai, which had been evacuated to Moresby. Looking to make himself useful, Nobby turned up at the HQ of 39th Battalion one afternoon, and an account of his arrival would later be written in 39th Battalion veteran Victor Austin's book *To Kokoda and Beyond*.

Nobby: 'I am Father Earl. I have just been appointed Chaplain of the 39th Battalion.'

Commanding Officer: 'That's news to me. I haven't been informed. (*Pause.*) Where's your uniform?'

Nobby: 'They didn't have any uniform to give me.'

C.O.: 'Do you mean to tell me you haven't got a uniform! What clothes have you got?'

Nobby: 'All I stand in—a shirt, singlet, pair of shorts, pair of long socks, a pair of shoes.'

C.O.: 'Where did you join the army?'

Nobby: 'In Port Moresby, half an hour ago.'

C.O.: 'Have you a pay book?'

Nobby: 'Oh yes, I have a pay book!'

C.O.: 'That means all you have is a pay book and the clothes you stand up in?'

Nobby: 'No! I have something else.'

C.O.: 'Well man, tell me what it is.'

Nobby: 'Four cases of whiskey.'

C.O.: 'Come in, Padre. Come in. What are you standing out there for?'[96]

Meanwhile, Damien Parer and Osmar White were now well on their way. They had begun their trip to the north coast of New Guinea on 2 July 1942 by embarking on the schooner *Royal Endeavour*, which took them along the south coast of the island, west of Port Moresby, until they joined a convoy of canoes going up the Lakekamu River. From there they began the gruelling process of foot-slogging their way across the mountains with the porters taking the supplies to Kanga Force.

Though nothing would stem the deepening friendship between the writer and the photographer, one thing that confounded Osmar White now that they were together twenty-four hours a day was Parer's insistence on saying his prayers every morning and every night, no matter where they were, no matter the circumstances. At a later point in their travels together, they found themselves sharing a hut with fifty of the roughest, toughest and perhaps most

God-forsaken soldiers in the territory as all were turning in for the night to sleep.

But not yet they weren't. Damien Parer fell to his knees, and began praying, rather loudly. One soldier took mild umbrage and called out: 'I say, Parer . . . '⁹⁷

Forgive him, Father, for the soldier knew not who he was dealing with on this subject. Damien had always been more than merely serious when it came to praying. Back in Sydney he had asked his sweetheart Marie how she prayed and when Marie had told him she prayed in bed, he had told her very firmly that that just wasn't good enough. The only way to pray, he told her, was on your *knees*, and he had been so persuasive she had done it ever after. It was like when Damien had told her he didn't want to do any 'parking', because it could be the 'occasion for sin'. It wasn't simply what he said, it was the way he said it . . . ⁹⁸

Just like Marie, the troops in the hut sensed equal sincerity in Damien. For as soon as the soldier said, 'I say, Parer . . .' the documentary-maker looked up and said, in a clear, penetrating, entirely unembarrassed voice, 'Just a minute. I am saying my prayers.'

As Osmar White recorded: 'There was silence until he had finished—and no word of comment.'⁹⁹

He was a strange cove all right but, by Jove, Osmar White liked Damien an awful lot. And Parer returned the affection in kind. One thing he noted about Ossie was that, as an experienced traveller in these parts, he was practically obsessed with staying as clean and hygienic as possible. It was not vanity: it was survival. Every night before turning in, White washed his whole body, before putting powder under his armpits, on his groin and his feet. Even the tiniest scratch was immediately covered with iodine before he carefully put adhesive plaster . . .¹⁰⁰ In these parts, the writer explained to the photographer, such measures could mean the difference between life and death.

They continued north, Ossie with his enormous Mountie hat atop and large revolver by his side, Damien ever and always jingle-jangling his way forward, with cameras, lenses and tripods seeming to grow out of his very person.

In the wake of the Allied successes in the Battle of the Coral Sea and at Midway, General MacArthur's firm desire was now to gather his forces and launch a massive simultaneous attack on all of the Japanese forces now entrenched in Rabaul, at Tulagi, on Guadalcanal and at Lae and Salamaua. This would be a mere prelude to his stated main goal all along: returning to the Philippines in triumph.

MacArthur's masters in Washington, however, would have none of it. To begin with, such places as Tulagi and Guadalcanal were not designated as being within MacArthur's zone of responsibility and, in any case, the command in Washington had already decided on a more measured attack in stages. Their orders were for, first, Admiral Ghormley's forces to take back Guadalcanal, and then for MacArthur's men to launch on the Japanese in Lae and Salamaua. Then, and only then, would MacArthur be allowed to move on Rabaul. It was a decision which was well received by a US Navy highly reluctant to provide ships for what it saw as General MacArthur's adventurism.

For his part, the good general was furious that his own daring plan was being rejected. It seemed crazy that *they* could presume to know what was the best way for *him* to proceed militarily when they were ten thousand miles away from the front!

Still, as June 1942 progressed, MacArthur focused on how best to achieve the tasks that the joint chiefs of staff had set him. He came to the view that, for the purposes of both launching future attacks and defending against further Japanese encroachments, the tiny settlements of Milne Bay on the eastern tip of New Guinea, and Buna on the north coast of New Guinea, would be key. Milne Bay could offer a strategically important Allied airbase, as from there they would be able to harass all Japanese ships around the Coral Sea and also defend the key water passage to Port Moresby.

As to Buna, an airfield for American bombers could also be easily constructed on the flat, grassy terrain just inland from the seaside village, which would be useful when the time came to retake Rabaul. Another crucial reason to establish a force in Buna was that all New Guinea maps showed that the one thoroughfare between the north and south coasts of the island started at Buna and meandered across the Owen Stanley Range, via a government settlement called Kokoda before coming out at Port Moresby. Kokoda was important, also, as it had an airfield, native hospital, police house, officers' houses and surrounding rubber plantations. MacArthur had some slight concern because, as he told Blamey, 'There is increasing evidence of Japanese interest in developing a route from Buna through Kokoda to Port Moresby and that minor forces might try to use this route to attack Moresby . . . '[101]

The track had been formed by the feet of natives over centuries as they went from village to village for trade and tyranny, love and war. In the early years of Europeans in New Guinea, this track had been considered as being almost exclusively for the natives, on the grounds that 'white fellas' simply wouldn't be able to make it across. Despite the fact that a few white men and indeed one white woman had successfully traversed the track in those early years of European settlement, the view about the inherent difficulty of it as a thoroughfare remained, even when gold had been discovered not far from Kokoda. Two large parties set out from Moresby to get to the goldfields and were never seen again. At least not by Europeans.

Certainly MacArthur concurred with the previously expressed view of General Morris that it seemed only a remote chance that the Japanese would launch a land-based attack on Moresby by way of this track—in the same fashion as they had overwhelmed Singapore—but if they did, then Buna was the obvious place for the Japanese to establish a beachhead. For MacArthur to consolidate forces at Buna, therefore, would serve both offensive and defensive purposes. Once it was secured, a regiment of American engineers and a labour force would come in by sea and build the airfield and base, from which the wider Allied forces could then launch raids on Japanese positions.

After due consultations, MacArthur issued an order in the third week of June for Major General Morris to send out forces to first secure Kokoda and thence proceed to Buna. MacArthur's rough timetable called for the force to cross the mountains, secure the Kokoda airfield by the middle of July and then Buna by early August when the American engineers would arrive.

Reluctantly, as he did not like to denude Port Moresby of its already thin defences, Major General Morris in turn gave the orders for his men to make rapid preparations to do exactly that. But he was never a believer, writing at the time: 'Even if the Japanese do make this very difficult and impracticable move, let us meet them on ground of our own choosing and as close as possible to our base. Let us merely help their own supply problems to strangle them, while reducing our own supply difficulties to a minimum.'[102]

It was decided that Captain Templeton's B Company of the 39th Battalion, which was without doubt the best of what was available, would be given the duty of following MacArthur's orders. They would be joined by some platoons from the Papuan Infantry Battalion, and supply and medical detachments which, put together, would be called 'Maroubra Force'. Other companies of the 39th would follow them thereafter.

Generally, the men of the 39th greeted the news with great excitement. After months and months of digging ditches, fixing roads and constructing shelters, it was a chance to throw down the shovel, get out of stinking Moresby and maybe even have a go at the bloody Japanese. In the frenzy of activity that resulted from the order being given, a key figure came into the orbit of Maroubra Force and it became his role to organise 'supply' and ensure that they would always have sufficient rations and munitions no matter where they were on the track.

His name was Bert Kienzle, and though his nominal position was as a lieutenant with ANGAU, his value was that he was a capable and charismatic man who'd lived in New Guinea for many years, actually since the days of the 1927 gold rush, and knew the territory backwards. Though Kienzle hadn't found gold in those early days, he was one of the very few Europeans to prosper in the country, and had in fact established a thriving rubber plantation at Kokoda, which was so successful he'd been obliged to build an all-weather airfield to service the plantation. So Kienzle, a mountain of a man who was well over six foot tall for his eighteen stone, brought to Maroubra Force three notable attributes: he'd already traversed the Owen Stanleys, spoke fluent pidgin English and was familiar with the ways of the six hundred native porters who would carry supplies forward in the absence of even one available transport plane.

Also, there was a *humanity* about Bert, borne of no little suffering. He'd seen his mother die on the day his youngest brother was born, had not only seen his German-born father interned in Australia during the Great War, but had been interned himself with his three brothers and sisters and stepmother. Such suffering had given him an empathy for those who suffered too, and one of his first moves was to improve the appalling conditions that the very restive porters were being kept in.

Kienzle's facility with the natives was crucial because their ways were indeed particular and they would provide the key manpower to set up the 'staging camps' at ten-mile intervals along the course of the track. At each staging camp there would be a dump of supplies that the porters would carry in, and each camp would have its own platoon to dole out whatever was needed to the passing soldiers. To run each post, Kienzle was also training up a group of specially selected staff officers.

The other mission for the strapping Kienzle, at the behest of Major General Morris, was to build a road along the length of the Kokoda Track, and by 26 August of that year at that. Kienzle knew that such a road could never be built over such terrain and certainly not in that amount of time, but it was one of those things that Major General Morris just didn't want to hear. So after a little argy-bargy the senior man had pulled rank and *ordered* Kienzle, as a bare minimum, to evaluate it. (Strangely, despite having been in charge of military matters for the previous eighteen months, Morris had never had the Kokoda Track reconnoitred by competent military officers, or anyone for that matter. Its contours and form remained an impenetrable mystery to the higher echelons of the military.) Kienzle said he would do as he had been ordered, *Suh,* and continued his preparations, the key one of which was rounding up the porters for the urgent task of getting supplies in place for the 39th and for subsequent troops that might be crossing the track.

Overseeing the health of the porters was one of Kienzle's friends from the pre-war days in New Guinea, ol' Doc Vernon, an elderly Australian who, after attending the Shore school in Sydney and then Sydney University, had briefly worked as a doctor in the dusty Queensland town of Winton before joining the 11th Light Horse Regiment as the Regimental Medical Officer in the Great War. After being awarded a Military Cross for 'conspicuous gallantry' he'd returned to settle in the New Guinea highlands. He was so old and deaf, courtesy of an exploding shell at Gallipoli, that the Australian Government had tried to forcibly evacuate him from New Guinea with all the other civilians the previous December; but Doc had enthusiastically refused to go, knowing that he might be useful.

And now this sixty-year-old man had found his calling, as *Captain* Doctor Geoffrey Vernon, if you please, of ANGAU, looking after the health of the native porters, initially from his base at Ilolo at the beginning of the track. Like Bert Kienzle, Doc Vernon's command of pidgin English was superb, and his caring way with the natives over such a long period of time meant that they had an enormous amount of respect for this skinny man who had wrinkles on his wrinkles on his wrinkles—the face of a man who had lived hard and long. Kienzle knew him to be a good man to have beside him in such a venture.

It was in the early hours of 1 July 1942. In the tropical waters off Cape Bojidoru in the Philippines, Lieutenant Commander 'Bull' Wright, the captain of the ultra-modern American submarine USS *Sturgeon* felt alive as never before. They called him 'Bull' because of his love of whiskey and telling tall stories, but he sensed now that he might be about to have a story to beat them all.

Just a few minutes earlier he had been awoken from the half-sleep only a submarine commander knows by a sudden change in the sub's course, which could mean one of two things: either the *Sturgeon* had found a target, or they suddenly *were* one. With a deferential knock on the door a few seconds later his executive officer told him, praise the Lord and pass the torpedoes, it was the former. The *Sturgeon's* SJ radar—a state-of-the-art system capable of communicating the compass bearing of a target to the sub's targeting system—had picked up a ship, a big ship, speeding from the Japanese controlled Philippines northeast into the South China Sea.

As speed was crucial, 'the Exec' had already begun the hunt, taking the sub to the surface to take its speed from nine knots to twenty knots, and embarking on a closing course. Bull Wright's orders in this case were clear. He was to attack all targets in his area of patrol, as part of the overall American effort to isolate and weaken the Japanese aggressors.

Unbeknown to him, though, while this target was indeed Japanese shipping, the 7267-ton *Montevideo Maru* was bearing unusual cargo. Manacled and asleep well below decks were 1035 Australians, most of whom were survivors of the Japanese invasion of Rabaul. Roughly 850 were soldiers, while the rest were civilians and missionaries. These were the very prisoners whose letters home had been dropped on Seven Mile Airfield back in March by the Japanese, causing such relief in Australia that they were still alive. There were also thirty-six Norwegian sailors rescued from the cargo ship *Herstein* when the Japanese bombed them while they were loading copra in Matupi Harbour. Now they all slept as their prison ship ploughed on . . . and the *Sturgeon* edged even nearer.

Tension in the submarine was high. There was little noise in the conning tower as officers and men went systematically about their work, apart from the strained hum of the sub's engines on full power. Bull Wright and the Exec soon selected a salvo of four torpedoes for the pursuit attack, two aimed at the target and one on either side, in case the ship sighted the inbound torpedoes and altered its course to port or starboard. By twenty past two in the morning, the *Sturgeon* had closed the gap to the point where it was just possible to fire a torpedo at the *Montevideo Maru* and dispatch it to where, in Bull Wright's view, all Japanese shipping belonged: the bottom of the ocean. Perhaps he could have got closer still, but he wasn't prepared to take the chance that the brutes would get away.

The final settings were applied to the torpedoes and then Bull gave the commands in his authoritative, calm voice: 'Fire one'. This was immediately repeated by the Exec—'Fire one'—and the whole submarine shuddered and shimmied as the first torpedo went on its way. Bull Wright and the Exec clicked their stopwatches simultaneously and then continued.

'Fire two . . . ' 'Fire two . . . '
'Fire three . . . ' 'Fire three . . . '
'Fire four . . . ' 'Fire four . . . '

It was exactly 02.25 hours as the crew of the *Sturgeon* felt the last of their four torpedoes discharge, firing out at a range of just under 4000 yards from the target. Now the submarine commander and his number two looked at their stopwatches. The 'time to run' of the torpedo was critical if they were to know whether the torpedo had exploded prematurely or had run past the target. The second hands of the watches slowly clicked by as the seconds to run were counted down aloud by the Exec. There was a hollowness in everyone's stomach in the conning tower as the impact time of the first torpedo passed, with no sound. Bull Wright ordered the periscope up to observe the target. Just as he located it in his periscope's field of view, the *Montevideo Maru* seemed to alter course and, almost instantaneously, they heard two loud explosions. The submarine had done its job, and two torpedoes had found their mark.

The aquatic missiles had exploded in the bowels of the ship near its stern quarters and almost instantly the ship began to list to starboard as wild panic broke out on board. For the many prisoners below there was no chance, though several of the Japanese crew managed to launch a couple of lifeboats. Then, at 02.40 hours, stern first, the *Montevideo Maru* sank to the bottom of the ocean with over one thousand Australians still aboard.

Bull Wright didn't wait to watch the ship sink. He ordered the *Sturgeon* to a depth of two hundred feet and to rig for counterattack, just in case there were any enemy combatants nearby, and ordered a course to establish maximum distance from their target. As the submarine serenely glided into the deep, the final noises of the ship breaking apart could be heard. Like a spring unwinding, the tension of the pursuit and attack drifted rapidly from Bull Wright's mind as he applied his thoughts to the safety of his submarine and his men. In Wright's and his crews' minds, was the grim satisfaction that they had done their jobs well.

On the morning of 7 July 1942 the men of the 39th Battalion's B Company were gathered right beside where the track began, at McDonald's homestead just near the village of Ilolo. (Ol' McDonald had a farm, a rubber tree plantation and—as a veteran of Gallipoli— had put it entirely at the disposal of the Australian Army so they could use it as a base for stockpiling supplies and launching their men along the track.)

At that point, to the north of B Company there was only a scattering of Western civilisation comprising a thin confetti of plantations, missions and seven ANGAU posts dotted along the north coast of New Guinea specifically looking out for Japanese shipping and planes. Somewhere out there too was a 35-strong brigade of the Papuan Infantry Battalion, commanded by a Major Bill Watson—a decorated veteran of the Great War—with five Australian officers. The PIB had set out two weeks before to reconnoitre the northern side of the Owen Stanley Range. Despite this advance guard, the men of B Company still had a sense that they were heading off into the wilderness on their own and would have to stick together. They talked about what might lay ahead and discussed a feature called the 'Kokoda Gap', which they would have to pass through, a gap so narrow you had to turn sideways to get through it in some parts. The way they told it, if you had just a few men with enough ammo, you could hold off an entire army at the gap.

Most of the B Company men carried their personal belongings, machetes and .303 Lee Enfield rifles themselves. They secured everything they were carrying tightly to their upper torso, to prevent it from swinging and making a noise, just the way 'Uncle Sam' Templeton had shown them.

The reason they were travelling so lightly was twofold. A lot of the heavier equipment they would need to help secure Buna was being brought around to Buna by the Thursday Island lugger *Gili Gili*, while Bert Kienzle had set off the day before with his porters to set up the staging camps along the way and, apart from supplies, those porters were also carrying the company's tents and ammunition.

The men of B Company were not quite footloose and fancy free, but it certainly showed how little they knew of what awaited them that there was a certain impatience to get going on their adventure, to start marching across the green hills far away, which awaited them.

At last, at around eight o'clock in the morning, Captain Sam Templeton gave the order: 'Move out!'

With Templeton in the lead, as was his wont, B Company of the 39th Battalion was soon swallowed whole by the jungle. And at the back, filling his new role as B Company's Acting Company Sergeant Major, was Joe Dawson. Had he had the position of CSM back at camp it would have involved a lot of dreadful paperwork, but on the track it effectively meant he was responsible for such practical things as discipline, mail-drops, liaising with the platoon sergeants, ensuring that everyone had sufficient ammunition *and* seeing that no one was straggling.

Joe's temporary promotion had occurred because the official CSM was deemed too old to make the trip to Kokoda. Joe himself wasn't too happy about it, as he would have much preferred to have stayed with Wally and Ray and the 'family' of his platoon, but Sam had asked him to do it and, when Sam asked, you never said no. (As a matter of fact, Joe always felt an affinity with Sam, because just as Joe had put his age up a year to join the army, he was just about positive that Sam had knocked a few years off his own age to be able to do the same.)

That same morning, back in Port Moresby, Lieutenant Colonel Bill Owen formally took over the post as Commanding Officer of the 39th from Colonel Conran and the rejuvenation of the 39th leadership was complete. The outgoing colonel, who had departed well before the newly promoted Colonel Owen arrived, had not felt good about formally leaving his men and battalion but, on the other hand, like many of the older officers of the 39th, he had become so ill over previous months running a battalion in such conditions, that he was no longer effectively commanding them, not from a hospital bed anyway.

For his part, the far younger and more energetic Bill Owen was pleased to take command, not simply because it was the highest post he had achieved in the army, but because he was the same Bill Owen who, six months earlier, had led the escape of 150 refugee soldiers from Rabaul and then witnessed most of them being killed in the Tol Massacre. The horror of that was with him every day and, though not a vengeful man by nature, it was certainly his hope to have some back at the Japs.

There was a lot of activity around Port Moresby that morning, and for good reason. For not only were the forward elements of the 39th on the march, but at MacArthur's request, Australia's 7th Militia Brigade were also on the move, on that day receiving orders to embark on troop-carriers to be transported to Milne Bay on the eastern tip of New Guinea. There the men would add their elbow grease to the construction of more airfields and also help to defend the whole area, along with the two squadrons of Kittyhawks the RAAF had based on the one operational airfield, ready in case the Japanese decided to attack.

The Japanese were certainly in the mood for doing exactly that. Just the day before at Guadalcanal, on the southern end of the Solomon Islands, some two thousand crack Japanese troops sent from the garrison at Rabaul, together with labourers and engineers, had begun constructing their own airfield. Yet one more front in the Japanese war to control the Southwest Pacific had been opened and so, too, the Emperor's forces were stretched ever thinner, even as their supply line stretched just over 3000 miles from Yokohama, via Saipan, Truk and Rabaul to Guadalcanal.

Under the command and care of Bert Kienzle and Doc Vernon— the latter a recurring vision of khaki clothes and long brown limbs moving up and down the line—the native porters, many of whom were Koiari tribesmen, were going well. In small groups of between eight and a dozen men, bound by the fact that they were WONTOKS coming from the same tribal area, the porters murmured their way forward across the mountains. There was no system at all in the way they carried their loads, or even what they wore. One man in a lap-lap, another in shorts, the other in something akin to a dress salvaged from somewhere because he liked the colours. The first carried his load in a sugar bag that he simply slung across his back; the next had tied a vine between two smaller fully-laden bags and then used his head as the point from which to suspend them, thus leaving his hands free; still another was doing it 'Chinese-coolie' style, with two bags hanging from either end of a strong staff placed horizontally across his shoulders.

Who were these porters and why were they chosen? There were a variety of reasons, not all of them pleasant. Under the provisions of the National Security (Emergency Control) Regulations, many of the porters had been conscripted by the field officers of ANGAU, who had authority over the villages in their region. These officers, together with some of the native policemen still in their service, were extremely insistent with the natives—in several unfortunate cases to the point of brutality—saying that the 'GAUMAN', 'government', had made a 'LO', 'law', that the men had to provide their services or they and their village would face severe penalties. Many of the native porters in that situation had, thus, left behind weeping families, and been brought to this place virtually under guard.[103]

For many ANGAU officers like Tom Grahamslaw, though his own methods of persuasion remained civilised, this kind of forced recruitment did not sit well. The traditional role of Australian field officers in the villages had been as a kind of paternal government protector. But now the needs of war had converted them practically into mini-dictators, having them demand that the natives do what they were told to. At least Grahamslaw was personally instrumental in ensuring that the native porters recruited from his own region would get not the six shillings a month the government had offered, but the figure he *insisted* upon, which was ten shillings.

Together with this still minimal salary though, the natives received something else, which they highly coveted—the tobacco sticks they got as part of rations. In many parts of New Guinea these tobacco sticks were practically currency in itself. Just one stick could get you a good bunch of beetlenut, a whole basket of sweet potatoes or a couple of coconuts. You could gamble with them and, of course, you could smoke them, which the porters did, more or less constantly, in between chewing beetlenut and mumbling softly to each other, and moving forward to they knew not what . . .

The men of the 39th's B Company had no maps. They had simply been told that if they headed off up the track and followed their feet they would eventually come to Kokoda, and they were doing their best to do exactly that. Finding their way wasn't the problem. *Making* their way was, for while they were carrying light packs, the going was beyond tough. After walking for a mile alongside the Goldie River, the track suddenly reared up at them rather like an angry snake—with a bite more or less the same—as it went straight up a spur on the Imita Range. Gasping for air, shocked at the strain, the men wondered how on earth Bert Kienzle's native porters had managed to get up there the previous day, barefoot and laden down with at least three times the weight they were carrying. And it wasn't as if the agony was over once they reached the top of the Imita Range. For, as they bested it, before them was range after range of similar topography, and there was nothing they could do but stagger forward. They soon learned that it was better for each Digger to leave at one minute intervals rather than all together, so that time would not be wasted for all those clogged up behind the weakest link in the chain.

How far were they travelling? That was entirely beside the point. On such a track as this, distance was not measured in anything so prosaic as yards or miles, it was all a matter of time and how many days march remained before a particular destination was reached. The usual answer was 'more than you'll be able to bear', for as they marched on, their feet became blister farms and the straps of their rucksacks chafed the skin of their straining shoulders red raw. One of the most infuriating things about the bloody track was that so much of it just didn't make *sense*! Never did it take the shortest route between two points, but instead meandered up the very steepest of the hills, plunged into the deepest valley and then detoured right to the edge of disaster above a killer cliff-face before heading for the swamp.

The Diggers of the 39th, struggling up and over these God-forsaken mountains, tried in vain to come to terms with their new surroundings. This was like no place they had ever been before, or even heard of. For many of them, particularly those from the often long, low, featureless plains of western Victoria, it was beyond their imagination. The mountains and ranges continued to the far horizons. To all points of the compass, valleys, crevasses and creases sprayed out seemingly at random, many of them filled with thick mist and most of them, the men knew, entirely uncharted by Europeans.

Through it all somehow, the track, the bloody track, poked and prodded its way roughly northward, sometimes gripping grimly to the side of a mountain above a raging torrent, sometimes going from rock to rock in that torrent for as long as a mile, sometimes glugging along beneath four feet of marsh, often going up a slope which was just a few degrees off vertical to an absolute height at the top of the ranges of over 7000 feet. Then, it wasn't just the gut-wrenching agony of reaching the top only to find that a dozen more hills exactly like it lay between them and sundown, it was the bone-jarring agony of the equally steep descent, torturing knees that had never been subjected to such punishment, and all the while risking falls that could maim a man for life. Before half a day had passed, nearly all of the Diggers had used their machetes to good effect by hacking a walking stick out of the jungle, which seemed to help marginally. At least it eased the ache in their knees as they descended by taking some of the strain. Plus, for many of them, a walking stick somehow felt appropriate, as they were suddenly feeling very, very old.

As the day wore on, it was all that the company medic, Warrant Officer Jack Wilkinson, could do to keep them moving as a body of men. When they made camp on that first night in the small village atop Ioribaiwa Ridge, most of Wilkinson's time was spent strapping up twisted ankles, handing out salt tablets and trying to ease blisters, chafe and fevers. For all his ministrations, and liberal lashings of the old hardy potash permanganate on the worst of the blisters, some of the men were suffering so badly that they had to be immediately sent back because they were obviously not going to make it. Wilkinson was vastly experienced in patching up soldiers, having previously served with the AIF in the Middle East before joining ANGAU, yet he could barely believe how quickly the jungle had taken its toll on these men.

The men slept like the dead despite the moisture and mosquitoes, and, always in the morning, the track, the bloody track, lazily ribboned out in front of them and the survivors of the trek thus far had to push themselves to follow wherever it led. If only the track would just go away! Sometimes it did, all but disappearing when the ever-pressing jungle occasionally succeeded and seemingly squeezed it out of existence altogether.

Man might find it hard to long endure such conditions, but just about every other life form seemed to prosper there as nowhere else. Particularly in the marshy lowlands, the hot blanket of throbbing, humid, fetid air covering the track was thick with gases and mists and teemed with enormous insects of infinite variety but universal sting, the like of which would have done the new genre of the Hollywood horror movie proud. Amid the vines, trees, wild orchids, palms, ferns, staghorns and all the rest, snakes, spiders and leeches slithered and sheltered together, competing for space. It was the classic Darwinian environment, where only the strongest survived, and that strength was measured either by the force of the individual organism or, failing that, by having enough numbers of weaker organisms to prevail anyway.

But this was simply the start of nature's array of horrors. There was also the weather. The usual way of rain is that it consists of so many separate droplets. But the men discovered that New Guinea rain—which on most days started at around noon and continued for hours—wasn't like that at all. There were no drops. Instead, it sort of gushed, rather like a tap turned on just above your head. Sometimes as much as ten inches of rain fell in a single day as part of an average annual rainfall of *16 feet*. Buckets of rain from the outside, buckets of sweat from the inside, and such humidity all around that none of it evaporated.

Put together it meant that clothes were permanently wet, as were the contents of your rucksack. All too often, zealously guarded cigarette papers or letters were just turned to mush, and remaining scraps of toilet paper into a kind of horrible puree.

How did a soldier survive in such conditions? Only just. For apart from the sheer life-sapping exhaustion of it all, the troops soon became aware that even the slightest medical matter—a blister, a scratch, an ulcer—quickly turned serious and continued on its way from there, as the body's natural defences were overwhelmed by what grander nature had in store for all who ventured into the jungle.

Among these conditions, still the thing the men found most soul-destroying of all was the false crests. Often, after labouring for hours to get to the top of a ridge that steepened as it rose, they would begin to see the hoped-for lightening in the jungle foliage ahead, maybe even a patch of blue sky. It was a sign that the summit might have been reached at last. Yet, all too often, another three minutes climb revealed that it was merely a spur, and the true summit remained, upward, ever upward. And then another and another, till the soldiers developed what they called 'laughing legs' or 'happy knees', where the leg muscles became so exhausted and spasm-ridden you couldn't stop your agonised knees from shaking even when you were standing still.

Sometimes the men would throw themselves to the ground and gulp in vain for enough air to ease their tortured lungs, gasping for all the world like the stunned fish that used to be thrown up on to the wharves at Port Moresby after a Jap bombing. Moresby . . . it seemed so far away, and a virtual Shangri-la of urban sophistication compared to the wilds they were in now.

Weighed down as Bert Kienzle's porters were, it wasn't long before the 39th caught up with them, and from that point they all continued together. Of all of them, none was stronger up and down the hills, oddly enough, than the ol' fella, 'Uncle Sam' Templeton. It was for good reason that the admiring native porters said of him: 'IM E WOKABAUT STRONG' as in, 'he walks very vigorously . . .' He was a big bear of a man and the heavy haversack on his back seemed as nothing to him. Many a youngster struggling up a hill looked up to see Templeton's hand reaching down to pull him up a difficult rockface, or offering to take his rifle or pack to the top of the hill so he could get his breath back. Sometimes Templeton ended up carrying five rifles at a time, together with a couple of rucksacks. The porters would look at Templeton carrying the five rifles in amazement and recount it to the other porters: 'IM E KARIM FAIPELA MUSKETS!'

Like a supremely masculine version of a mother hen, Templeton was constantly moving back and forth along the line to make sure that everyone was coping with the strain, and ensuring that those who weren't were given the helping hand they needed. That was

Sam all over, constantly moving around on his own, while still somehow being solicitous of everyone.

After camping the first night at the top of Ioribaiwa Ridge, they had made their way the next day to the village of Nauro, which lay on the far side of the awesome Maguli Range. Then it was another day's trek to the village of Menari, then to Efogi up at the shivering altitude of 5000 feet, before the descent to Eora Creek.

Now the scenery is changing . . . we are entering a moss forest. We have climbed up into the 8000-feet belt of timber. Be careful here, the eternal mists and dripping mosses have rotted the very earth you walk upon. Step from root to root. Feel how the green-coated earth pulses like a drum beneath your weight—you can sink to your height in rotting vegetation here.

Stop for a moment. The silence of death is in this forest. The trees themselves are dead . . . rotted with the moss which drapes twigs, branches, and trunks with a dripping green beard . . . it is a fantastic picture from a Grimm's fairy tale . . . and over all drips a perpetual mist . . .[104]

Back in Port Moresby, there was a sudden stirring in the tropical torpor of military administration. On 13 July, General MacArthur's man on the ground, Major General Charles A. Willoughby—MacArthur's eyes and ears and the nerve centre for Allied Intelligence in New Guinea—made a formal recommendation that both Milne Bay and Buna prepare themselves to repel Japanese landings, and be closely watched in the meantime. Just three days later, though, Willoughby changed his mind and 'declared that the Japanese purpose was to consolidate areas they already held, not to invade new ones . . .'[105] This came as a great relief to all concerned.

Finally, when the men of the 39th's B Company staggered into the village of Kagi, the first lot of porters was sent back to the beginning of the track to bring up the next lot of supplies. Lieutenant Peter Brewer, the patrol officer from the government station at Kokoda, then greeted B Company with fresh porters to take them the rest of the way. In the fog of the men's exhaustion, swirling aptly with the billowing green clouds of the endless ranges, the village of Isurava came and went and most gave it barely a glance.

Generally, these tiny villages were little more than small outposts with a tenuous hold against the encroaching jungle, but they did help to afford some shelter from the driving rain. It gave the men pause to think that they were from a supposedly more sophisticated nation, yet here they were dragging themselves like mangy dogs out of the rain and into skilfully constructed bone-dry huts made in two days flat by a so-called 'primitive' villager who had neither hammer nor nail. The men would rest for a night and hope that their clothes would partially dry over the fires that perpetually smouldered in the breezy constructions.[106]

Most importantly, the villages always had market gardens, which would help to alleviate the soldiers' strictly rationed and monotonous diet of tinned bully beef, biscuits and 'goldfish' (army-issue canned herrings, which the men detested).

The villagers tended to be shy but friendly, especially in these early stages of the war. True, many of the younger children had never seen anything as strange as a white man in their lives, and would sometimes burst into tears at the sight, but it usually didn't take them too long to get used to the soldiers' pasty complexions and red, puffing faces. In no time the children would be laughing and carrying on, running to get the exhausted soldiers paw-paw and water. It was a part of tribal culture to share whatever food they had with visitors. And in the face of such joyousness one or two of the older men would suddenly fall quiet as they were reminded of their own children waiting for them at home.

By 15 July, some eight days after B Company had begun its journey, the soldiers were camped in the village of Deniki, within cooee of their first destination, the government station outpost of Kokoda. With its landing strip, magistrate's house, native hospital, station gardens, police station, officers' houses and surrounding rubber plantations, Kokoda was the only outpost that resembled 'civilisation' in these parts.

By the time they got to Deniki, Templeton and Kienzle realised how exhausted both the soldiers and the porters were. They gave them a day's rest in the small nondescript village perched in the foothills on the northern side of the Owen Stanleys, while they went forward to have a look at Kokoda on their own. Kienzle was particularly keen to get back to the homestead at his rubber plantation to see how it was faring. As they walked on the rare and pleasant flatlands that separated Deniki from Kokoda, he and Templeton talked. There was an easy relationship between these two old hands and each had come to respect the other's ability enormously over the previous difficult days.

Naturally enough, they discussed those difficulties. The real problem was that when you were sending out that many natives on such long a trek, a huge proportion of what they were carrying had to be consumed by the porters themselves—about half the provision for an eight-day walk. It made it almost impossible to carry any of the other many necessities of war. And even allowing for luggers like the *Gili Gili*, bringing 20 tons of ammunition and general supplies to Buna, it was still a massive operation to get any of that stuff inland. The only way to do the job properly was to bring things in by air. In just twenty minutes flying time, one full cargo plane could land as many supplies at Kokoda as 160 porters could manage in eight days. And though cargo planes were precious commodities at Moresby, Templeton agreed that when he made his report to the higher authorities he would make the point forcefully that they must have aerial supply.

Arriving at Kokoda, both men had to get busy. After checking on his plantation homestead, the next day Kienzle said his goodbyes to Templeton and B Company—who had now moved forward to Kokoda—and headed off back to Moresby to organise the next lot of native porters to bring up supplies for the next company of the 39th, which was shortly due to embark on the track . . .

Templeton took one of his best men with him and headed the other way, north towards Buna where, in the nearby small and inconspicuous harbour of Oro Bay, the *Gili Gili* and three men of the 39th had landed with all their heavy stores. To shift them, ANGAU officer Tom Grahamslaw had assembled another large group of native porters.

In Kokoda, B Company spent their time recuperating and doing a few patrols in the immediate area. Joe Dawson, for his part, spent a lot of time distributing ammunition to the men, and one of his key jobs was to prime the boxes of Mills 36 hand grenades the porters had carried forward to get them ready for battle. This involved carefully—oh . . . so . . . *carefully*—unscrewing the base plug of each grenade, which the men called 'pineapples' because of their distinctive surface, and putting in the fuse and cap, before screwing the base back on. *And any slip . . . meant death*. That done, the men of B Company at least were now better equipped in case there was any action.

Up at Buna on 20 July, now that the *Gili Gili* had been unloaded, Templeton and his officers and the native porters headed back towards the small village of Awala, just a short distance inland where they could take a brief break at a government station there before making their way back towards the main body of B Company at Kokoda.

Unbeknown to Templeton, at that very moment just under two thousand Japanese soldiers, composed largely of men from the crack 144th Regiment and a company of marines from the elite 5th Sasebo Naval Landing Force, were on a convoy of ships leaving Rabaul. They, too, were intent on making their way to Kokoda and beyond. For this was the beginning of the planned land invasion of Port Moresby, starting on the north coast of New Guinea, and pushing across the Owen Stanley Range via Kokoda and down to the New Guinea capital. The other key component of this expedition was the 15th Independent Engineer Regiment whose job was to ease the passage of the massed forces by widening the track into a road, building light bridges, cutting steps into possibly difficult sections of the track and establishing a series of staging posts where supplies could be stockpiled. Everything had to be done to facilitate the passage south for the Imperial Japanese Army.

An indication of the priority placed on this mission was that the whole force was under the command of the highly regarded and accomplished Colonel Yosuke Yokoyama, an engineer. Only after his men had established the beachhead and pushed the passage through to Kokoda itself, would he hand his command to Major General Tomitaro Horii, whose South Seas Force was built strongly around the 144th Regiment. The main body of the South Seas Force was due to land on 7 August. It would then be Horii's role to take them all the way through to Moresby.

The morale of the Japanese soldiers on this night of 20 July as they headed south on their ships was high. This was simply to be the latest in a long string of victories for the Imperial Japanese Army. They had learnt the finer points of jungle fighting in their way down the Malayan Peninsula, had defeated many of Britain, Australia and India's finest in the siege of Singapore, destroyed a lot of the American resistance in the Philippines, laid havoc through the rest of Southeast Asia and were yet to taste defeat. It was unlikely that whatever Australians or natives they might encounter in New Guinea would give them too much trouble.

Still, always at times like this, on the eve of the next battle, thoughts inevitably turned to home and the loved ones left behind. Since time immemorial preludes to battle have generated in men thoughts of just what the battle was for, and where they had come from to get to this point . . .

In this instance, there was no doubt what these soldiers were fighting for. While the natives of New Guinea might be loyal to their families, their village and their WONTOKS in that order; and the Australians loyal to their flag, their country and their mates; the Japanese soldiers were fierce in their devotion to the holy Japanese Emperor, the most divine flower of the Chrysanthemum Court.

The famous Japanese battle-cry of '*Banzai!*'—frequently screamed just before a soldier charges straight into enemy fire—translated roughly as 'Long live the Emperor!' and from a young age most of these young men had been taught that there could be no higher calling than to be killed in battle in the service of the Emperor. Reinforcing that point for each of them were words in the Imperial Japanese Army Instruction Manual, which they carried with them at all times.

If one were to be captured in battle, the manual stated: 'Upon release one should return to duty with the will to wipe out the humiliation and to seek death with the courage of the will to die. However, if an officer of high principle, usually the only course is to commit suicide.'[107]

There was no excuse for being captured if wounded, as the manual also made clear: 'Under no circumstances should you cling to life by accepting defeat, nor should you forget the dignity of our Imperial forces to the extent of enduring the disgrace of being taken prisoner.'

The convoy of Japanese ships ploughed on through the night, the marine life scattering at their first vibration . . .

CHAPTER EIGHT

ATTACK!

The ingenuity required on the frontier, which Australians call the 'convict mentality', was very real. There was also a genuine ruggedness to the national character. Physical courage was highly prized. A broken nose was easy enough to come by in pre-war Australia . . . It is, I think, safe to say that somewhere along the line the 'Protestant work ethic' lost some of its intensity in Australia. An Australian infantryman who served [in New Guinea] told me they were glad to hear of the Japanese attack because that freed them from an ugly road building detail in the mud. Soldiers who would rather fight crack Japanese assault troops than build roads, win wars.

Eric Bergerud, *Touched With Fire.*[108]

His name was Nik, and he was a young native of the Orokaiva tribe living in the village of Buna. In the humming late-afternoon sun of 21 July 1942, he was walking along the sands of the nearby Basabua beach when he chanced to look seawards and saw something that would remain with him for the rest of his days. It was a ship, perhaps a mile offshore, and hovering around it were smaller craft onto which many soldiers were climbing. The little boats were flat-nosed barges about ten yards long, powered by quiet motors. Now only a few hundred yards off the shore, one of those landing craft was coming over the breakers. A just-discernible white flag with a red spot in the middle and red rays coming out of it indicated where they were coming from. When Nik looked to the part of the beach it was heading to, he could see hundreds of soldiers had already landed. Nik ran back to the village proper . . . 'JAPON E CUM! JAPON E CUM!'

Some of the curious villagers accompanied him back to the shore to see for themselves, but they had no sooner gained the soft sand than some shots rang out. The low drone of a plane close overhead told them they were observed and it was clear that they were no longer welcome on their own shore where, coming off three troop transport ships—protected by cruisers and destroyers—were some eighteen hundred Japanese soldiers ready to establish their beachhead. With them, in boats behind, came twelve hundred Rabaul natives and fifty packhorses, there to do a lot of the hard work of hauling the Japanese supplies forward. A new power had arrived in the land bringing in its wake the worst feature of the twentieth century—war on a massive scale . . .

In the nearby village of Gona, just one mile to the west of Buna, the news arrived quickly and caused immediate action. The picturesque village—perched between the dark jungle on one side and the shining Solomon Sea on the other—had a red-roofed Anglican mission with church and schoolhouse, headed by Father James Benson with two other priests and two sisters, Sister May Hayman and Sister Mavis Parkinson. In this tranquil place by the sea, the two sisters were doing their mending and listening to some wonderful gramophone music in the lovely cooling shade of the mission's verandah amidst the wonderful fragrance of the hibiscus and frangipani flowers, when the news reached them.

'O JAPON MUN E CUM!'

Suspecting only too well what could happen if the Japanese caught them, they quickly gathered a bare minimum of personal possessions and, with a few other mission staff, took off down the track towards the small settlement of Kokoda where they hoped they would be able to catch a plane to the safety of Port Moresby.

As they took their first hurried steps up the track, one of the Japanese ships fired a few shots of artillery towards an unknown target—more than likely just as a warning to whatever minimal resistance there might be on shore.

At Awala, Sam Templeton and his men heard the distant rumbling coming from the cloud-lined coast and put it down to the thunder one frequently heard in New Guinea.

Damien Parer and Osmar White, on the other hand, were then far to the west with Kanga Force, camped high on Mount Tambu. Guessing what the rumbling signalled, they immediately made plans to trek to the nearest airfield and return to Moresby to file their copy and photographs, and make reports on the war hotting up in New Guinea.

Most importantly, however, the booming of the guns attracted the attention of both Lieutenant Alan Champion and Sergeant Barry Harper where they were working at the administrative outpost of the Buna government station. Harper had arrived in New Guinea as a member of the 39th, but had quickly transferred to the Air Warning Wireless Company as a spotter, and had now no sooner heard the sound than he climbed up to his lookout point to see the shore. Quickly scurrying back to his radio, he flicked it to the emergency frequency and furiously began intoning: 'Moresby this is Sergeant Harper. A Japanese warship is shelling Buna apparently to cover a landing at Gona or Sanananda. Acknowledge, Moresby. Over . . .'

'Moresby this is Sergeant Harper. A Japanese warship is shelling Buna apparently to cover a landing at Gona or Sanananda. Acknowledge, Moresby. Over . . .'

And on and on he tried, greeted only by silence and static. Still he kept going.

'Moresby, this is Sergeant Harper, do you read me? Over . . . Moresby, this is Harper, do you read me, over? Moresby, this is Sergeant Harper, if you read me a Japanese warship is shelling Buna. Possible cover for a landing at Gona or Sanananda. Over . . . '

Unfortunately, such were the vagaries of radio communication in New Guinea that Sergeant Harper received no response from Port Moresby because his message was not received. It *was* picked up, however, by another government station, Ambasi, to the west of Gona, which was manned by three soldiers also formerly of the 39th, Sergeants Holyoke, Hanna and Palmer, and later that afternoon they succeeded in getting the urgent message through, before tearing off into the jungle on their own account desperately trying to outrun the Japanese.

All up, it was a comfortable trip. A neat four months after Douglas MacArthur had arrived in Melbourne, he set off for Brisbane with his entire entourage to establish his new headquarters a little closer to the action. His wife, Jeannie, still refused to fly, so the Australian Government had provided them with a train. But not just any train. It was a train replete with plush carpets, mahogany furnishing and the royal coat of arms, as it had been constructed for the Prince of Wales for his state visit several years before. An appropriately regal conveyance for such as the American general and, as the MacArthurs moved north, crowds of Australians formed up on platforms, overpasses and simply by the track just to see them go past.

The good general had just pulled into Sydney, though, when a top priority urgent dispatch reached him. The Japanese had landed at Buna and were already in control of the immediate area. The Japs had, in short, beaten him to it.

Clearly, there seemed to be an urgent need to get Allied soldiers between Buna and Kokoda to thwart any Japanese attempts to move inland. Still, MacArthur wasn't too worried. By the time he had conferred with his two experts on this part of the campaign—his former Chief of Staff, General Richard Sutherland, and Major General Charles A. Willoughby—they had assured him that the Japanese landing at Buna was likely a minor incursion, much as it had been at Lae. Certainly, the codebreakers had warned them two months before that the Japs might try to invade in force across the Owen Stanley Range and all the way to Moresby, but MacArthur and his team still viewed this as impossible.

With this judgment, there seemed to be no need to send the men of the 7th Division to New Guinea. The AIF men could be safely kept in Australia for the main game, which was to retake Rabaul as a stepping-stone to the Philippines. Certainly, Allied aircraft had been quickly sent over the ranges in New Guinea to strafe and bomb the Japanese landing craft at Buna and had achieved some limited success. But it was the nature of the terrain that once the Japanese soldiers were on the ground it was really only other soldiers that could effectively counter them. So, at least as a nod of recognition to the fact that the situation had changed, and after discussions with MacArthur, General Blamey ordered General Morris in Moresby to send the rest of the 39th Battalion over the Owen Stanley Range to parry whatever minor thrusts the Japanese might make.

Well, he'd be blowed. Bert Kienzle had just arrived in the village of Nauro on the ridge overlooking the distant village of Ioribaiwa, while on his way back to Moresby for more supplies, when who should he spy sitting under a tree—sheltering from the infernal pelting rain and having a cup of soup—but ol' Doc Vernon. The two greeted each other warmly and compared notes.

Kienzle told Doc how they had fared on the TREK with all the PORTERS and how very TOUGH it had BEEN!—speaking very loudly to compensate for Doc's near profound deafness. Doc replied that he was moving up the track to check out the medical facilities at each of the staging posts that Kienzle had set up. Doc had been a very keen walker all his life and was coping admirably with the hills. But he was also gaining insight as to how badly the terrain would knock around both porters and soldiers carrying heavy loads.

He had already taken copious notes on the medical wear and tear he had witnessed so far—from blisters to badly twisted ankles and knees, to terrible respiratory infections brought on by the mountain air. But no time to tarry. Each had his work to do and they headed off in opposite directions. There was a war to be won and they had to get on with it.

Was his life jinxed? The 55-year-old English-born Father James Benson could be forgiven for thinking just that with every step, as he continued along the track heading south with Sister May and Sister Mavis and others from Gona mission. As they tried to escape the Japanese, who they knew were in hot pursuit, several things worked at Father Benson's spirit.[109]

One was the conversations he'd had with a young ANGAU officer by the name of Tom Grahamslaw. That young man had implored him to send Sister May and Sister Mavis back to Australia out of harm's way. If the Japanese landed, he had said, it wasn't just those beautiful young women who'd be in trouble, but also the ANGAU personnel who would be sent out to save them. He'd been so convincing that Father Benson had proposed the idea to his Bishop, but it had been the view of that good man that it was the Sisters' duty to remain. And, dedicated young women that they were, remain they had. And now here they all were in the middle of a war in a jungle.

And the other thing that worked at Father Benson was the same thing that had pressed at him every day of his life, as his mind turned to the events of many, many years before when his life had all been so different. Then, he'd been a supremely happy rector on the south coast of New South Wales, living in Bodalla with his darling wife and three young children. One dark night he'd been driving the whole family home when up ahead he saw the light of the car ferry pulled into the siding to take them across the Clyde River.

Taking the car straight on to the ferry he had only realised at the last instant that the light was in fact simply a lantern left there by a workman as a warning of work they had been doing on the siding . . . but by then it was too late. The car had plunged into the waters. Time and again after bursting to the surface he had dived back into the waters trying to get his family out, but nothing. When they were retrieved the following morning they were all blue and swollen. Why were *they* the ones to die, while *he* was the one to survive? Could there have been anything crueller than to have to live with the knowledge that because of his mistake the four people most precious to him in the world had died a terrible death? Nothing had tested his faith more, and after a long unsettled period he had moved up to the north coast of New Guinea where he had done fine work in educating and improving the health of the natives. But now this.

When the Japanese had started shelling Buna and sending their boats into the shore, the missionaries had gathered essential supplies in barely five minutes and started trekking to another mission some thirty miles inland where they could both warn of the approaching danger and get some immediate refuge. Just two hours later, though, while resting briefly in a small clearing off the track, they had heard approaching voices and looked through the tall, razor-sharp kunai grass to see a Japanese patrol moving forward. Where to now? Japanese soldiers behind, Japanese soldiers ahead. There was only one way. Through the jungle. With Father Benson and his compass in the lead, they'd stumbled and staggered through the night, trying to make their way to another mission, this one on the Lower Kumusi River.

Sam Templeton moved quickly when he realised that the 'thunder' they'd heard the previous evening was nothing of the sort as it continued the following morning through blue skies. The Japs were obviously attacking, and this was confirmed shortly afterwards by a runner coming from the coast.

On the morning of 22 July Templeton was also able to get the radio message through to one of his best men, Lieutenant Seekamp, who was in charge of 11 Platoon, then positioned at Kokoda. The soldiers were to come forward urgently, he instructed, and be prepared to engage the Japanese. Just near Awala, they would find a small force of Major Watson's Papuan Infantry Battalion set up in defensive positions, and they were to reinforce them. Templeton also instructed 12 Platoon to move down about halfway to Awala, to the village of Gorari, and provide a fall-back position, while 10 Platoon under Lieutenant Gough 'Judy' Garland was to hold the fort at Kokoda and set up for the massive reinforcements that should be arriving shortly. Templeton, meanwhile, headed back to Kokoda to receive the 39th's Commanding Officer, Lieutenant Colonel Owen who, he had just been informed, was being urgently flown in.

Completely exhausted, 11 Platoon marched through the day and night, and were getting near Awala just as the forward scout of a PIB patrol led by Lieutenant Chalk sent a signal that a Japanese patrol was on its way and would shortly be upon them. The Japs were many. They were few.

But, despite the disparity, these young Australians were not without confidence as they waited for the Japanese to walk into their trap. After all, everyone knew that one on one the Japs were not formidable foes. Popular legend had them as short-sighted brutes of minimal intelligence and tiny stature, no more than five foot three or four. Yes, the Japs had registered some impressive victories in recent time, but that was no doubt due to their sheer weight of numbers more than anything and . . .

And here they come now. It was slightly before four o'clock on the afternoon of 23 July, at a time when the searing quality of the day was starting to be replaced by a certain sleepiness. Through the tips of the kunai grass on this rare long straight stretch of track, they could just see the caps on the heads of the Japanese bob-bob-bobbing along towards them. Funny, that was pretty high grass, so it seemed odd that they should be seeing their heads already . . .

JESUS! These Japs were monsters! Around the corner, into full view, came enormous Japanese soldiers, six foot two if they were an inch, and of all things they were wheeling *bicycles*. What was going on? As they came even closer, clearly visible on their vests were two crossed silver anchors above a chrysanthemum, indicating that these blokes were marines, and not mere soldiers as they'd expected.

But to business. Steady now. The key to an ambush was to hit the enemy while they were close enough for you to do maximum damage, but still far enough away that you could make good your own escape once the enemy had recovered from the initial onslaught. Also, everyone had to strike at precisely the same instant to achieve the greatest effect.

So it was that the Australians remained crouched, barely daring to breathe, waiting as the Japanese came closer . . . closer . . . closer . . . closer . . . waiting for their commanding officer, Lieutenant Chalk of PIB, to fire the first shot.

Now!

The *thud-thud-thud-thud* of the heavy machine guns rang out first, followed by the faster staccato of the automatic weapons carried by the individual soldiers. The first Japanese soldiers were mown down like grass, and the air was filled with their screams, though just behind them the other Japanese soldiers had quickly gone to ground and were already returning heavy, accurate fire. Sweet Jesus, these guys were good. And they had hardware. Mixed with the sound of the heavy machine guns was the relentless boom of mortars and soon whole clumps of jungle around the entrenched Australians began to explode as the heavy artillery hit. Many of the natives from the Papuan Infantry Battalion simply ran away, never to be seen again.

The Australians held their positions while the Japanese quickly put into operation the method of advance they had so effectively refined over the previous five years of war. That is, at the first shot all went to ground as they tried to pinpoint where the shooting was coming from. Then, while the forward contingent kept up fire to pin down this key danger point, other soldiers would work in flanking pincer movements to curve around to the left and right and ensure that the danger point was choked from both sides. If these pincer movements could meet up behind that initial point of fire then all the better, as once the principal attack point had been cut off from its support it was always easier to destroy.

After only a short time, it was obvious to the Australians that they were in danger of being encircled and, as quickly as they could, they withdrew along their planned routes of escape. Taking their wounded with them, they joined up with each other further down the track, where another platoon had made ready to cover their withdrawal and had set up the next ambush for the Japanese.

The mood of the men, even as they pulled back, was very positive, almost exuberant. Now that they had been 'blooded' in action, they felt stronger—as trite as it might sound—like a bloke who has lost his virginity might suddenly feel more of a man and comport himself more confidently thereafter. It wasn't that they now swaggered back down the track, but there was certainly a consciousness that as a group they had seen action, had put 'up a good show', and had given the Japanese at least as good as they got—and probably a bloody sight better! The wounding of fellow soldiers was upsetting, certainly, but somehow in the hurly-burly of all the action and scrambling to get to the new position, a bloke didn't really have time to focus on that. There would come a time for tears and overwhelming emotions over what had happened to mates, but that time was not now. Now was the time to check ammunition belts, get a feed, grab some sleep and get ready because those little bastards would surely be coming swarming again.

Back at the site of that first contact, a special unit of the Imperial Japanese Army was now, with great ritual and solemnity, gathering their dead to burn their now holy bodies on funeral pyres and ensure that their ashes were soon returned to Japan. A Nazi officer who was in Japan at this time to study Germany's new allies in depth and prepare a report for the Third Reich's military leadership, related the importance of such ceremony.

'No one knows Japan,' he wrote, 'who has not seen how the ashes of fallen heroes are received. Hundreds stand in rows in solemn silence, members of national associations, veterans, the national women's league and school children. They bow solemnly as soldiers, usually comrades of the fallen, carry the urns of ashes as if they were carrying something holy. The urns are delivered to the family members and brought to their distant villages. They sit in the trains in silence, holding the urns on their knees. Each who enters the train takes his hat off and bows deeply before the heroic spirit of the fallen and burns a small candle as a sacrifice. This is how the homeland honours its soldiers who have died on distant battlefields.'[110]

Back in New Guinea with the Japanese forces there was sadness for the dead, but also a renewed reverence, for in a nation that worshipped its ancestors as deities, these fallen soldiers were now to be worshipped.

After that first thrilling attack on the Japanese, it would never be that easy for the Australians again. From this point on, the invaders were perpetually on their guard for ambushes, and only risked one or two scouts at the front at any given time—together with ever more natives as a screen—with the main body of Japanese soldiers well back from the point of contact. As the Australians soon found out, they were up against a superbly prepared fighting force.

Not only had the Japanese Army refined their jungle tactics—and practised those tactics for years at their Formosa Jungle Training School—but it had also developed a superb range of equipment specifically designed to operate in such conditions. It included mortar guns and ammunition that could be carried by just one man; a mountain gun that could be dismantled, with each piece being alternately carried by men in a platoon; haversacks that were strong but light and waterproof and the same colour as the jungle; sulphur ointments to treat wounds, mosquito repellent and vitamin tablets that could help keep a soldier going even when his food supply was low. Endless research and work in camouflage now meant that, almost literally, the Japanese soldiers disappeared into the foliage.

They not only wore jungle greens, which blended in superbly with their surroundings, they also covered their faces and extremities in a greasy green paint, and were proficient besides at covering their bodies with parts of bushes and vines to make them blend in to the background even further. Their helmets were also green with a kind of netting over them, extending over their face, which helped keep the mosquitoes at bay and also muffled any ringing sound a twig might make when hitting the metal helmet.

Sometimes the Australians would finally have some Japs in their sights and then, fair dinkum, it would seem that they would just vanish before their very eyes! For their part, the Japanese had no such problem with spotting the Australians. This was in large part because these strange round-eyed men from the south were not dressed in jungle greens, but were kitted out in the same khaki uniforms that had been so useful and appropriate for fighting in the Middle East. They were simply the spare uniforms available at the time, so that is what the men were dressed in. Their bare arms and legs were exposed to mosquitoes, leeches, the cold and Japanese eyes. General Blamey did not consider camouflage important and had insisted that it was not worth the trouble. If there was an irony in the situation it was that in the Middle East the Australians had long laughed at the ludicrousness of the Germans wearing their heavy dark-grey uniforms—perhaps perfect for Berlin, but hopelessly hot and visible in the desert sands—and yet here in the jungle highlands of New Guinea the Australian military command had made an equally elementary mistake. Not that many of the Australians on the ground had any time to complain about army fashion.

As the Japanese continued to advance, now more tentatively, the Australians fell back and crossed the fast-flowing Kumusi River on the Wairopi Bridge—so-called in pidgin English because it was made of wire rope. It was while on that western side of the Kumusi River, on the morning of 24 July, that the commander of the Papuan Infantry Battalion, Major Watson, got a message from Sam Templeton, which for the first time gave some clue about just what they were up against: 'Reported on radio broadcast that fifteen hundred to two thousand Japs landed at Gona Mission Station. I think that is near to correct and in view of the numbers I recommend that your action be contact and rearguard only—no do-or-die stunts. Close back on Kokoda.'[111]

Thus, Major Watson's contact with the Japanese from this point should only be in the form of a rearguard, executing a couple of quick ambushes to slow the brutes down, but they should avoid toe-to-toe donnybrooks.

In one skirmish, Joe Dawson found himself with Company Head-quarters on a bank of the Kumusi River when a force of Japs appeared on the other side and a fire-fight broke out across the fast flowing waters. The Japs had mortars while Joe's blokes had none. For the first time Joe heard the cough of the mortar on the far bank, followed by an explosion a few seconds later, practically on top of them.

In the middle of all this, a runner slithered in beside Acting Company Sergeant Major Joe Dawson and, by way of greeting, said 'What's the state of your underpants, Sarge?' The short answer was 'not good', the same as everyone else's, but anyway. The one thing that gave Joe comfort in such difficult moments was fingering his rosary beads and the silver shield of protective saints that Elaine had given him to put over his heart. Still, the runner's message on this occasion at least provided additional relief. Sam Templeton's Second-in-Command, Captain Stevenson, wanted them to move back to join 12 Platoon at Gorari. Joe gave the orders . . .

Before pulling out, the Australians took some delight in cutting the cable that held up the bridge and sending it into the rushing waters below. *That* would give the little yellow bastards something to think about, at least for the day or so it would take them to rig up a rough alternative. In those parts, where engineered infrastructure was primitive at best, there was very little to blow up to gain great advantage, but at least that bridge was something.

Under the overall command of Major Watson they fell back, but even then it wasn't easy. There were no fewer than fifty river and creek crossings between their position and Kokoda, and each one presented its own difficulties. Mostly, the way over was nothing more than a couple of logs held together by vines. This was fine if you were a New Guinea native-born, and had been going across such 'constructions' all your life, but it was more than a bit hairy for blokes who were conscious that a single slip might mean their death. Still, it was worse where there were none, so each log crossing got the same treatment as the Wairopi Bridge. Gone to the depths below. Anything to slow the Japs down and give the Australian forces some breathing space to get themselves organised.

The Australians set up their next ambush just eight hundred yards to the east of Gorari where Major Watson saw that the track would force the Japanese soldiers into nice groups with little place for shelter from the Australians' shooting. Bill Watson was a good man to have in such a situation. In down-time this son of a Tasmanian blacksmith was always smoking a pipe, and somehow—even in the middle of battle—exuded such 'unruffledness' and confidence that the soldiers around him felt that everything would be all right. A former rugby union player of great distinction, Major Bill had played five tests in the front row for Australia before the Great War. He had about him the air of one who had seen a battle or two in his time and had always come through, just as he would no doubt come through this one. Which was as well, in this instance, because all the soldiers knew that they were going to be up against it.

But the other great thing about the major was that he really *was* pretty much at home up in these New Guinea highlands. The journalist George H. Johnston called him: 'one of the most picturesque characters of New Guinea . . . For years he was one of the best known soldiers of fortune in New Guinea. He recruited native labour (in a period he still refers to as his "blackbirding days"); traded around the island in crazy schooners; tried cattle ranching; worked as trader, beachcomber, plantation manager, and then as a gold prospector in the then practically unknown Owen Stanley Range. Several times he struck it rich, and always the money seemed to run away . . .'[112]

For better or worse, New Guinea was in his blood. He spoke the language of the natives, understood them, and they in turn respected him immensely. There could nary have been a better man in the whole territory to have in charge, and the men felt it.

Now that they had doubled their strength with 12 Platoon, the confidence of the Australian soldiers had grown at least a little. If the boys on the concealed Lewis gun did their job properly, there might be some happy carnage.

That night, the Australians dug into their ambush positions and through the wee hours strained both eyes and ears to determine whether the Japanese were still coming at them. Even the tiniest sound of another soldier moving restlessly, or the bow of a tree creaking in the wind, could make an entire platoon grip their rifles more tightly. And is that just another shadow in the thin moonlight, or is it the silhouette of a Japanese soldier? Whither the dawn. Where are they?

'They' were still camped on the north side of the Kumusi River, waiting for some engineers to come forward and rig up another kind of bridge across the deep, fast-flowing torrent. At first light this was done in under an hour and the Japanese soldiers swarmed across.

They were a curious mix these men of the South Seas Force. On the one hand there were ruthless killers of the dreaded Sasebo Fifth Special Landing Force and the 144th Regiment, who were expert at intimidating local populations who resisted and wiping out their defenders; while with them were the rather more gentle engineers, who were superbly educated and deeply intelligent. Their expertise was in building bases from which the soldiers could launch their attacks, and bridges for them to cross rivers, ravines and the like. In New Guinea, Tokyo had hoped that the engineers might even have been able to build—using the many labourers they had brought with them from Rabaul—a fully-fledged road from Buna to Kokoda and thence to Imita Ridge just outside Moresby. But already that plan was looking unlikely.

Over the previous few days, the commanding officer of the men on the ground in New Guinea, Colonel Yosuke Yokoyama, had sent rather gloomy reports back to Rabaul that building a road was going to take a lot more resources and forces than had been planned. A later report of the campaign, which was secured and translated by a special section of the Australian Army, also indicated some dismay from the Japanese military commanders on the ground that things were not quite as they had expected . . .

'As the rivers shown on aerial photographs were narrow, it was estimated that they would be easily crossed. However, these mountainous areas have steep inclines and generally speaking, in this locality the velocity of a stream is surprisingly great. Although the surface appears calm, drowning will occur in the rapid undercurrent.'

And again . . . 'Although New Guinea is listed as a place with little water, the fact is that there is such a large quantity of water that it causes trouble.'[113]

But despite the unexpected difficulties, the Japanese kept pushing south.

So this was Kokoda. And he was on the ground at last, after an aborted landing attempt the previous day. Commanding Officer of the 39th Battalion, Lieutenant Colonel Owen, stepped out of the flimsy aircraft on the late afternoon of 24 July 1942 with a great sense of relief. He had been following scattered reports about his men and the Japanese incursions and been excruciatingly aware that there was nothing he could do for them back in Moresby. His rightful place as commanding officer, he had quickly decided, was to be commanding them in *battle*. On the track. So let's get to it.

When the Lieutenant Colonel stepped down from the plane, Sam Templeton was waiting for him and within minutes the two were making their way forward to the Gorari ambush site, Templeton briefing Owen as they went. Neither man was in any doubt that this small outpost of Kokoda, with the only airfield within four days march in any direction, would be the key strategic possession in this campaign.

Nestled in the Yodda Valley beside the Mambare River, the village itself was perched on a neat plateau that was surrounded by the rubber trees of a large plantation. The plateau sat some forty feet higher than the valley floor in the break in the mountains known as the 'Kokoda Gap', and therein lay something of a story . . .

For on both the Australian and Japanese sides of the campaign there had been great confusion as to just what kind of topography would be described by the name 'Kokoda Gap'. Initially, it was thought that to be a gap, as opposed to, say, a valley, it would have to be a singularly narrow aperture in an otherwise solid wall of mountains. For the more educated of soldiers, and more particularly some of the officers back at GHQ, there was talk of the Kokoda Gap perhaps being like the famous battle of ancient Greece which occurred at Thermopylae in 480 BC, where in a very tight mountain pass a small, heavily outnumbered Greek force was able to hold off the enormous invading Persian army. On a battle-field where there could be no flanking movements, all that counted was that your frontline troops be more powerful than the men they faced and there could be no limit to the number that they would kill.

But could the Kokoda Gap really be like that? Not one little bit. For when Lieutenant Colonel Owen looked around he was amazed—just as all new arrivals are amazed—to find that the famed Kokoda Gap was ten miles wide! If this was a mere gap, they'd hate to see what one of New Guinea's wide valleys looked like. Maybe the gap was on the other side of the first hill, into the Owen Stanley Range proper. Somehow, because of the name bestowed on this geographical feature, they had all felt it must be in at least rough proximity to Kokoda village itself. For now though, Lieutenant Colonel Owen kept walking in the opposite direction, eager to be with his men as they set up for the next crucial confrontation.

It was a mark of Owen's stamina that after he and Templeton arrived in Gorari at 2.00 a.m., the Lieutenant Colonel spent a couple of hours reconnoitring the terrain in the moonlight and consulting his commanders. And then, after he had rearranged their defences to his satisfaction—with his best men taking the brunt of the likely fire and the native battalions protecting the flanks—he set off immediately back to Kokoda to organise the small force there in similar fashion and hopefully receive fresh troops by air.

•

With the sun high in the sky on 25 July, the Japanese were suddenly sighted on the approaches to the Australian ambush position at Gorari.

Sssssssssssssst. The Australians knew that the thing with an ambush was of course to effect total surprise, but on this occasion it was a close-run thing. For just as the first of the Japanese troops were moving into the desired position, one of them saw a bush move ahead and shouted a warning to his comrades. Within a second the Japanese troops had dived for cover, expecting a volley of shots.

On the Australian side, however, there was no movement. Total discipline. While their every strained breath in the stillness sounded to their own ears like the shrill whistle of a steam train, their best hope remained that the Japs would regain confidence that there was no one waiting for them and would then move back on to the track.

And so it proved. From behind the thick foliage, the Australian troops kept their guns trained and through their sights they saw the Japs slowly get back on the track, led by the sheepish scout who had shouted the first warning and was now gazing right at the bush he had seen move. Within a minute a whole column of Japanese soldiers was making its way forward until it was almost on top of the Australians.

The man behind the Lewis gun, Arthur Swords, was sweating more than most. He was in a forward position and the Japanese lead scout was right upon him, looking, it seemed, right at him— much as Arthur was looking right down the barrel of the Jap's gun—and it was all he could do to follow the order not to fire.

Hail Mary, full of grace, the Lord is with thee.

Blessed art thou among women, and blessed is the fruit of thy womb, Jesus. Holy Mary, mother of God, pray for us sinners now and at the hour of our death . . .

NOW! Lieutenant Harry Mortimore effectively gave the order by firing the first shot and, as one, the Australian troops opened up, killing or at least seriously wounding some fifteen Japanese soldiers before the rest had recovered themselves and were returning withering fire. Because the ambush site had been so well chosen, the Australians kept the Japanese pinned down for four hours. But from the moment the Japs began their flanking movements, all knew that every minute the Australians remained was another minute to their disadvantage, so Lieutenant Mortimore gave the order to retreat. In mere minutes the men born beneath the Southern Cross melted away to the next prepared ambush site at Oivi, some two hours walk towards Kokoda.

That night, apprised by radio of what had happened, Lieutenant Colonel Owen managed to get a message to Moresby: 'Clashed at Gorari, and inflicted approx 15 casualties at noon. 5 p.m. our position was heavily engaged, and tired platoons are now at Oivi. Third platoon now at Kokoda is moving to Oivi at 6 a.m. Must have more troops, otherwise there is nobody between Oivi and Dean, who is three days out of Ilolo. Must have two fresh companies to avoid being outflanked at Oivi. Advise me before 3 a.m. if airborne troops not available.'

At the time that Owen's message was received at Port Moresby, there was only one troop-carrying plane available—a Douglas DC3—but at least it was cranked up. Alas, there simply weren't 'two fresh companies' able to go at such short notice, and the best that could be managed was 16 Platoon, comprising some thirty men, commanded by Lieutenant Doug McClean. Given that the maximum the plane could carry at a time was just fifteen men, McClean went forward with the first half of the platoon. As they crossed the Owen Stanley Range, many of the soldiers were caught between wonder at their first time in an aeroplane, relief that they did not have to cover on foot the thickly covered ridges and valleys, and great trepidation at what might await them when they landed. Though they had been told very little, the speed with which they had been called up told them that their boys were in trouble up ahead . . .

And there was the airfield beneath them, not surprisingly blocked with many oil drums and logs to ensure that a Japanese plane carrying troops couldn't simply land any time it liked and take the place by storm. The pilot went low a few times to waggle his wings and show the blokes on the ground that he was of the realm, but even then it seemed a long time before ant-like figures below stole out of the jungle to remove the obstacles and clear the runway. Even then, it wasn't easy. As the plane descended it was buffeted by the hot winds coming up from the valley and many of the soldiers lost their breakfast into their tin hats.

Colonel Owen was waiting for them as they alighted, and just as he had done two days earlier, within minutes of landing they were heading down the track to Oivi, four hours march away.

Back down the track, Doc Vernon had just finished trying to reorganise the medical staging post there and was resuming his journey northwards in the company of Sergeant Jarrett of ANGAU when a young police boy overtook them and handed Sergeant Jarrett a note. Without a word Jarrett read it and passed it over to Doc. There was news. The Japs had landed at Gona and were already moving inland towards Kokoda.

Doc, the senior man, took over. 'I'll go on. There's no medical officer with those 39th youngsters and they will likely be needing one. You go back to Efogi and get them ready for casualties.'

With which they parted.

Two days march behind the good doctor, Captain Dean's C Company of the 39th struggled their own way forward, doing it every bit as tough as Sam Templeton's B Company had found it two weeks earlier. If there was inspiration for the men in the middle of all the agony, it was Father Nobby Earl who, though not physically fit and clearly suffering with every step, never breathed a word of complaint. Not a single one. Men didn't like to whinge when Father Nobby could do what he had done.

Five hours after the first half of the platoon had disembarked at Kokoda, in the mid-afternoon the DC3 returned, bringing the second half of the platoon, under the command of Sergeant Ted 'Pinhead' Morrison. These men had been so rushed into action that on the plane they unloaded the newly issued Bren guns, fresh from the boxes packed by their manufacturers at the arms factory in Lithgow. Again, Colonel Owen was the first man they saw at the foot of the plane stairs, looking relieved to see them. As it happened the colonel knew Sergeant Morrison quite well from having served with him in a militia battalion before the war, and he hailed him with warmth . . .

'What the Devil are you doing here, Pinhead?'

'Getting ready to fight for you, Sir. What's the plan?'

'You'll have to get straight on down to Oivi and join Lieutenant McClean there.'

'Oivi . . . Where's that?'[114]

In response, Colonel Owen pointed in a roughly northerly direction to the end of the airfield where the beginning of a small track was just visible, disappearing into the thick kunai grass. He said: 'Just keep going down that track and you'll get there . . . '

So off they went. At this point, the newly arrived Australians took the total number of Maroubra Force to 480 men, most of whom had never fired a shot in anger. Ranged against them somewhere between Kokoda and Buna were some fifteen hundred crack Japanese troops, with ten thousand more soon to reinforce them.

By the time Lieutenant McClean had arrived with his men at Oivi, late on the afternoon of 26 July, there was barely time to settle before the Japanese attacked. There would be no ambush this time and, just after three o'clock, the Australians suddenly came under extraordinarily heavy fire from their front and right. In a bizarre strategy, the Japanese interrupted their assault of massive firepower with attempts to coax the Australians from their cover by calling out such things as—and this one particularly would stay in Joe Dawson's memory—'Come forward, Corporal White!'[115] (Did they *really* believe that among these several hundred Australian soldiers there would be a corporal named White who would then stand up and walk forward when he heard his name . . . only to be cut down by their guns?)

As ever, it wasn't easy to see the Japanese soldiers, but their bullets and mortars and heavy shells were all too apparent. With mortars and shells, particularly, the Japanese were much better equipped for this fight than the Australians. Not only had all of the Japanese equipment been designed for use in jungle and mountain conditions, but in addition to their individual heavy machine guns and mortars, the Japanese troops were supported by mountain artillery units. The light mountain guns could be dismantled for movement along narrow mountain tracks, and quickly reassembled when required for combat. These mountain guns, mortars and heavy machine guns would give the Japanese a deadly edge over the relatively lightly armed Australians.

Returning fire the best they could, it was still apparent after two hours of fighting that the surviving Australian B Company force was in danger of being surrounded. Sam Templeton knew that if that happened, then the reinforcements who were heading their way might be heading straight towards an ambush. To forestall that possibility, at just before five o'clock in the afternoon, the captain took quick leave of his men and headed back down the track to warn the newcomers. He went on his 'Pat Malone', which was bloody well typical of him, always heading off somewhere with no accompaniment. On this occasion he was very quickly lost to sight as a combination of the jungle and the fading light swallowed him whole. Alas, alas . . .

Only minutes later, in a brief lull in the battle all around, his men heard a single burst of fire coming from the direction he had headed. They waited in vain—please dear God, *no*—for him to reappear. Joe Dawson kept straining his eyes in the direction where Sam had disappeared, *willing* him to come back into view, but he never did. He never did. Four men of B Company went out after him, vainly hoping to rescue him, but although they killed two Japanese soldiers, they had to turn back in the face of the swarming enemy. Against all odds, B Company continued to hold on to the hope that Sam Templeton might still be alive, but with him or without him they were obviously surrounded.

Again, they looked to one man—Major Watson. Without 'Uncle Sam', the major was the senior officer, and it was he who was then and there assessing their situation and working out the angles. What was obvious was that they were going to do no more real damage to the Japanese and the best thing they could do was to live to fight another day. Fortunately, it would be dark before long, which might facilitate their escape. Moreover, they had something the Japanese didn't—a guide who knew the area backwards at midnight, which was useful under the circumstances. Lance Corporal Sanopa, a former police constable, was one of the Papuan Infantry Battalion's finest. A massive man by any standards—well over six feet tall and strong enough to hold and fire a rifle one-handed as if it was a pistol—Sanopa had been with Watson from the beginning of the formation of the Papuan Infantry Battalion and had stuck to him throughout while others had run or drifted away. Now Watson addressed him.

'SANOPA MIPELA MUS LUSIM DISPELA PLES.' 'Sanopa, we've got to lose this place and get away. Which way do we go?'

'MI SARWAY ROT LONG GO.' 'I know a way we can go.' 'BEHINIM MI.' 'Follow me.' As Sanopa spoke, the leaves he had in his hair for camouflage *rustled*, heightening the impression that this man was a force of nature right at home in this part of the world. If anyone could get them out, Sanopa could.

They chose their moment of exit well. Lieutenant McClean and Corporal Pyke crawled some thirty yards towards a group of Japanese soldiers without being detected, and were able to launch a grenade attack that appeared to do serious damage, judging from the screams. It also provided exactly the kind of cover needed for all of their men to follow Sanopa into the jungle. He quickly guided them in a southerly direction away from the track and in a circuitous route towards, hopefully, Kokoda. In the confusion out on one far flank, six soldiers of Maroubra Force, under the informal command of Private Arthur Swords, were left behind.

Jesus Christ. If there was ever a feeling more lonely than finding yourself just six Australian blokes up in the New Guinea jungle surrounded by half the bloody Japanese Army, then none of them had felt it, but at least they kept their heads. For together with the darkness, a pounding rain had now reduced visibility to the point where, unless they bumped right into some Japanese soldiers, they had to have a fair chance of getting through. And while Major Watson and his men had set off in one direction behind Sanopa, Arthur Swords and his men went in the other, intent on hooking up in the dawn.

For both groups, it was pure bloody murder to be travelling in the jungle in the night. With visibility practically nil, the only way forward was for the lead man to poke and prod for obstacles and take one tentative step at a time, while each man behind held the bayonet scabbard of the man in front, so forming a kind of carefully creeping conga line. Inevitably, you sometimes had to let go in order to climb down the ravines, and then contact was kept by the fact that each man attached some of the luminous fungus that abounded on trees in those parts on to the back of their hats and helmets. You knew then that the little blob moving just ahead was your mate.

Sanopa led his group down towards Oivi Creek, and when they got there a good hour was spent wading waist-deep through its freezing waters before Sanopa somehow instinctively knew the best point to get out. For Swords's group the night was equally filled with silent terror in the darkness as they tried to make their escape, but the upshot was that both groups successfully evaded the Japanese clutches and had the deep satisfaction of hearing at the precious dawn a massive Japanese attack being launched on what was now an abandoned position. With any luck the bastards'd end up shooting each other.

Shortly afterwards, Sanopa had his men on a track which led to Deniki, where the major dump of the 39th's forward supplies were situated. Arthur Swords's group, meanwhile, found its way back to the track leading to Kokoda and eventually arrived there late on the afternoon of 27 July, only to find that it had been abandoned by Colonel Owen and the rest of their comrades . . .

This was a decision that hadn't come easily to Colonel Owen. But having received the devastating news the previous day that Oivi was surrounded and Templeton likely killed, Owen had reluctantly decided that with a battalion of Japs in full flood and rolling their way, discretion was the better part of valour and it would be more prudent to pull back with his remaining fifty men to the far more defensible position of Deniki. So, after torching all the supplies at Kokoda that they couldn't carry, they'd done exactly that.

Which was fine for them. But when Arthur Swords's men got to Kokoda late that afternoon they were too exhausted to take another step, Japanese or no Japanese. So, rustling through the still glowing coals of what had been burnt, they managed to find some tinned stuff that looked a lot like dinner—and that was already cooked at that!—before turning in for the night.

And this was luxury on a massive scale, at least, the very best luxury that Brisbane could offer in 1942. At much the same time as the troops were fighting at Oivi, Douglas MacArthur was savouring the pleasures of Brisbane's finest establishment, Lennon's Hotel, where he had settled in with his family and entourage. The hotel's penthouse suite on the fourth floor was not quite as fine as the purpose-built penthouse the general had only four months previously been occupying in Manila's best hotel, but it wasn't bad all the same. It was in fact four adjoining suites. MacArthur and his wife took one, his son and nanny took another, his doctor went into the third, while the fourth served as an office and library. The hotel also kindly constructed a theatrette where the general and his family could watch the westerns that he so adored. In the hotel's driveway, two chauffeur-driven limousines were always on call, one for Jean MacArthur, the other for the general to take him daily to the AMP Insurance Building on the corner of Queen and Edward streets, just five blocks away, where the new GHQ had been set up. The numberplate on MacArthur's black Cadillac read 'USA–1' with the four stars of his generalship embossed above, while Jean had 'USA–2'—the first personalised plates in Australia. (War was hell.)

General Blamey, meantime, had taken over a section of the new Queensland University campus in the leafy Brisbane suburb of St Lucia for his Allied Land Forces Headquarters. He had meetings with MacArthur or one of several of the Bataan Gang, on average, four times a week and was in phone contact at least daily. The conversations were far more a case of the Americans telling the Australian what was going to happen, rather than sounding him out as to what *should* happen, but they were at least always able to achieve something that could safely be called 'consensus'.

In the case of the Japanese landings at Buna and subsequent incursions inland, while they had been viewed with great interest and discussed at great length, still neither Blamey nor MacArthur was particularly alarmed. After all, the Japanese had already made two landings on the north coast of New Guinea that year—at Lae and Salamaua—and had been content to effectively 'sit on their blot' from that point, making no serious drive to the south. MacArthur's view was that there was every indication that they would do the same at Buna. Blamey concurred, so they saw no reason to send fresh reinforcements to New Guinea. Historians have since speculated on another possible reason. While MacArthur wanted to keep the top-notch 7th Division troops fresh for the main game—island-hopping their way back to the Philippines, starting with Rabaul—Blamey's desire was probably for them to be on hand in Australia, against a possible Japanese invasion of the Australian mainland.

Either way, the upshot was the same. While Stan and Butch Bisset and their comrades continued their training up on the coast and hinterland just north of Brisbane, the Japanese were set to develop their strength at the Buna–Gona beachhead, where they would continue to pour men, mules, machinery and munitions. They did not do this entirely without resistance as Allied planes continued to bomb them sporadically, just as Japanese planes returned serve on Seven Mile Airfield—with both sides achieving mixed success. But in this particular battle theatre both sides were conscious that the day would neither be won in the air, nor on the sea, but instead by soldiers in the muck . . .

And there they were. When Doc Vernon walked over the ridge and into the picturesque village of Deniki at eight o'clock on the morning of 28 July, it was to a scene that caused him some concern. Exhausted men lay everywhere; some of them had simply sunk into the sucking mud and not moved since, while others were badly wounded and awaiting attention.

Doc didn't waste time and said immediately to the paramedic Jack Wilkinson: 'Jack, I heard there was some action up here and thought you may need some assistance. Where do I start?'[116]

God bless you, Doc, and you can start just about anywhere. Though as deaf as ever, Doc was still able to pick up most of the conversation after he had personally received all the 'hail-fellow-well-mets' from an exhausted group of soldiers who really were very glad to see him—despite the fact that many there were hoping against hope that the mysterious figure emerging out of the mist would prove to be the still missing 'Uncle Sam' Templeton.

Doc Vernon picked up the thread of what happened, as he tended wounds and handed out the few painkillers he had. Private Arthur Swords, who had just returned from Kokoda with five others, reported in that the government station had not only *not* been stormed by the Japanese, it was entirely empty just three hours ago when they had left it. Colonel Owen, while staggered to hear it, was eager to capitalise on the unexpected opportunity and now that his force had built up a little from his position of forty-eight hours before, he decided to re-occupy.

He didn't expect that the seventy-seven men he could now muster would be able to hold off the Japanese if they struck in force, but, with luck, if they could control the Kokoda airfield, Moresby might be able to at last fly in the companies of reinforcements they needed. Quickly he gave his orders. They would move out in ten minutes, with each man taking as much ammunition and food as he could carry. And Doc Vernon, he could set up a medical post for the wounded evacuees who might well soon be coming back once they got to grips with the Japs.

Doc Vernon did what he always did on such occasions. He nodded his head as if he understood the orders entirely and would carry them out to the letter, but in fact made his own plans. He could always claim afterwards—as he often did—that he must have misheard the orders. What he did know was that if there was going to be fighting on a massive scale, he knew where he should be. And after all, what good were all the army regulations in a situation like this? So what if he was deaf? He knew for a fact that there was barely one man in the whole 39th Battalion, or the rest of Maroubra Force, he had seen who would have had *any* chance of passing an army medical physical; and yet there they were heading off to fight for their lives! In war, you adapted. Trailing the bulk of the men, at the safe distance of a couple of hours behind, Doc Vernon moved forward one more time.

To the east of them at this time, Father James Benson and Sister May and Sister Mavis had continued to push on through the jungle, together with other assorted refugees, and had found the mission they were looking for, enabling them to rest up for a few days safe, they thought, from the Japanese. That illusion would be shattered soon enough. Not long after a native appeared telling them that the Japanese were on the approach, a group of Australian soldiers hurriedly arrived. They included the three former members of the 39th Battalion, Sergeants Holyoke, Hanna and Palmer who had succeeded in getting the message out from their wireless station at Ambasi that the Japanese had landed. Also there were five Americans who had been shot down while on a bombing raid over Gona and were now trying to get back to Moresby. Father Benson and the two Sisters, with the few native staff from the mission who were still with them, decided to travel on with the soldiers in the slim hope that together they might be able to get through. One of the Americans was on crutches from a bad leg injury and both Sisters were poorly, so the going was slow.

As they travelled, the villagers they came across everywhere looked at them completely stunned. In their whole lives they had never seen white fellas and natives walking together like this. Blacks and whites simply did not travel together, and white fellas *never* travelled these tracks. The natives instinctively knew that there must be a big disruption in the land, and the stories told them by the black fellas confirmed it.

'JAPUN MUN I CUM. BIKPELA GUN. BIKPELA BOM. PLUNTI MUN E DI. JAPUN MUN NO GUT. WITMUN NA BLUKMUN MUS FAIT WUNTIM.' 'The Japanese have come with big guns and lots of bombs. Lots of men have been killed. Now the white man and black man must fight together.'

The natives would see a lot more of such things in the weeks ahead, as all over the north coast the white fellas burnt to the ground just about everything they had spent years building up, gathered whatever servants had remained loyal to them, loaded them with everything they could carry and tried to make their way south—*away* from the swarming Japs.

It was at last light on the day after the two groups of missionaries and soldiers had joined that the worst happened. Bullets from a Japanese patrol started whistling around them and the group did the only thing they could, which was to rush into the jungle and keep hurtling through as far as they could, the vines tearing at them and the undergrowth and roots constantly tripping them. In the madness of it all Father Benson became separated from the main group. Two days later, the group were just outside the village of Manugulasi, when again a Japanese patrol opened fire from a distance and again they dived every which way. This time though, they would not escape unscathed. Three soldiers were hit and killed on the spot, while another three were wounded and quickly bayoneted to death.

Two others got away, but were captured shortly afterwards and executed by the Japanese, one after brutal interrogation. The two Sisters, meanwhile, continued to wander through the jungle, as did Father Benson on another track. The Sisters were both relieved when they came out at the village of Dobodura, which they knew of and thought to be friendly. But they were mistaken, for in no time a village councillor by the name of Embogi, who was in the employ of the nearby Japanese, had betrayed their presence and they were captured and interrogated.

Shortly afterwards, the two Sisters were taken by four Japanese soldiers into the jungle. Two of the soldiers were carrying shovels. Sister Mavis had on a tattered red, white and yellow dress, while Sister May was in green.[117] They went off the jungle track into a small clearing. The soldiers dug a hole in the soft jungle floor about three feet deep, which to the two Sisters looked a great deal like a shallow grave. Please, Dear God, oh merciful Jesus, son of the Father and the Holy Ghost, NO.

Sister Mavis made a sudden attempt to run, but was grabbed by a Japanese soldier who plunged a bayonet deep into her side. She fell screaming and died almost instantly. Sister May, praying to her Lord and Saviour, was ordered in a kind of sign language to put a towel over her head. The instant she tremblingly did so, a soldier cut her throat. Without ceremony, their bodies were thrown into the hole and covered as, unseen, a native lad witnessed the whole scene from behind the bushes.

The murders of the two Sisters left Father James Benson as the sole white-fella survivor of those who had originally set out to escape from the Japanese. Although he was yet to find out that Sister Mavis and Sister May were dead, he was all too aware of their likely fate and the fates of many of his other friends and colleagues on the north coast of New Guinea. Again, he could not understand that somehow he had survived while others close to him had died. For some time as he stumbled through the jungle, Father Benson contemplated suicide. At the precise moment he was looking at a promising vine to see whether it would hold his weight, he spied a Japanese patrol some distance away. He surrendered. If they killed him on the spot he would be no worse off. Putting on his priestly garb to indicate he was a non-combatant, he walked towards them with his hands in the air and asked if any of them spoke English.

At least one soldier had a basic grasp of it because he stepped up and roared 'Spy!' and punched him in the face. Two soldiers with bayonets drawn came at him giving him just enough time to make the sign of the cross before they . . .

. . . grabbed him and led him away. With that, his three years of imprisonment had just begun.

Many of the scattered Australians along the north coast were not so fortunate and met similar fates to Sister Mavis and Sister May. Often, after the Japanese had captured the Europeans they would be interrogated and then dealt with summarily. On one occasion nine captives from Sangara rubber plantation and a nearby mission—including two priests, two female missionaries, a young woman and a young child—were taken on to Buna beach as the villagers and Japanese troops gathered around. The Japanese soldiers from this most brutal of units, the Sasebo Landing Force might have known what was coming, but the gentle villagers of Buna did not.

One by one the captives, including a male plantation assistant, were made to kneel. Then, drawing a massive samurai sword, an enormous Japanese officer with the rank and name of Sub-Lieutenant Komai, shouted something unintelligible in his own language, raised the sword high above his head and brought it down hard on the back of each individual's neck, smiting their head off with one clean blow.

In all the screams of horror, none was more frightened than those coming from the six-year-old son of the plantation assistant. This youngster was obliged to stand there as his kneeling and weeping father told him that he loved him, just before the Japanese officer brought down his sword. Immediately afterwards, the same officer took the weeping child, obliged him also to kneel and then took his head off too. In terms of the Kokoda campaign, it was the first piece of barbarous savagery done publicly, but by no means the last. To the villagers of Buna, it served as a warning: the invaders were here for a purpose and would brook no resistance whatsoever. Those who resisted in any fashion whatsoever would be dealt with equally summarily.

As it happened, however, the Japanese would not themselves escape from much the same barbarity. On their trek through the mountain ranges, Osmar White and Damien Parer had met an Australian soldier known as 'Paddles', who was travelling with—as

White later described him—'a small, pot-black native about four feet nine inches tall, nicknamed Lik-Lik, a cheerful-looking creature with a grin that spread right around his head. Paddles said that Lik-Lik was being sent back in disgrace and told us about his offence . . .'[118]

It seems that when Lik-Lik had accompanied an Australian patrol in a raid on Salamaua a short time earlier, the native had begged for permission to carry the ammunition bag for one of the sergeants. This he had done with great alacrity during the raid, and had even proved himself to the point of personally killing two Japanese soldiers with his bush knife. But immediately after the raid, as Paddles told them, Lik-Lik had suddenly disappeared.

At last though, as White wrote: 'Lik-Lik arrived, exhausted, dragging a bulging copra sack. It contained 13 Japanese heads. He then had the effrontery to ask for leave so that he could take them back to his village in the hills and hang them on the pole of the *darimus* (men's club-house). When it was pointed out to him that very little credit would devolve on him for cutting off the heads of men killed by other warriors, he replied simply: "But they were not dead [when I found them], boss. They were only wounded".'

CHAPTER NINE
STRIKE-BACK!

Securing the daily 3 tonne supply for the Force would require approximately 230 carriers per day reaching the front line. This amounts in total, given the 20 day round trip, to a requirement for approximately 4600 carriers. If the front were to advance to Port Moresby, some 360 km distant from Buna, then to supply food alone would require 32 000 carriers.

General Horii before the campaign began[119]

It was an experience I would not have cared to miss, and among the impressions of that exciting night, none stands out more clearly than the weirdness of the natural conditions—the thick white mist dimming the moonlight, the mysterious veiling of trees, houses and men, the drip of moisture from the foliage, and at the last, the almost complete silence, as if the rubber groves of Kokoda were sleeping as usual in the depths of the night, and men had not brought disturbance.

Diary entry of Doc Vernon, when the 39th left Kokoda[120]

Colonel Owen left a skeleton crew of men at Deniki—almost literally, as constant marching and fighting and lack of proper food had had its effect—and took eighty men of the 39th forward to reclaim possession of Kokoda late on the morning of 28 July 1942. As the weary Australians marched into the village, the feel in the air was eerily still, as if a big storm was brewing on the horizon. There was no sign of the villagers who continued to make themselves scarce while all the fighting was on and, more bizarrely still, there was still no sign of the Japanese even though the crucial Kokoda airfield had been left unguarded for over twenty-four hours. What the men of the 39th felt instinctively, though, was that the Japs were not far away. As far as the Australians knew, none of their own forces were north of this point, meaning that there was nothing between the Japs who had been at Oivi and them in Kokoda, so why wouldn't the Japanese now be at least on the edge of the jungle, only two hundred yards away?

Just before noon, after having assessed the situation, Colonel Owen got a radio message through to General Morris in Moresby: 'Re-occupied Kokoda. Fly reinforcements, including 2 Platoon and four detachments of mortars. Drome opened.'

Ahhh, the sheer relief of it! For just three hours later, Colonel Owen and the men of the 39th felt their spirits soar as they could hear the drone of approaching aircraft from the direction of Moresby. Up there! In a small break in the cloud cover, they suddenly saw two American Douglas transport aircraft. Though the men on the ground didn't dance around, that was certainly the mood. Once the planes had landed and disgorged soldiers and supplies they *really* might be able to give the Japs a workover and . . .

And, slowly, almost imperceptibly at first, but then you couldn't mistake it, the sound of the aircraft *receded* again, ebbing away to nothing but the sudden roar of the flies all around. How could this *be* . . . ?

Up above the thick cloud cover, the Allied pilots had caught sight of Japanese Zeros in the distance and quickly hightailed it for home. In their view, it was not merely their lives at stake, but those of the soldiers each plane had on board. They were even keen to save the life of one of the brutes in the back of one of the planes who, with his brand new Bren gun, had smashed a hole in a window of the brand new aircraft and was poking his gun out ready to fire on the first Zero that came within range.

Unbeknown to the frustrated Owen below, the fact that the planes wouldn't land was not for want of remonstrations by one Australian, Captain Max Bidstrup, who begged the American pilot to land as the troops below were in desperate need of reinforcements and it was worth the risk. The pilot refused.

Upon returning to Moresby, General Morris sent for Bidstrup and a key conversation took place.

General Morris. 'I believe you flew over?'

Captain Bidstrup: 'Yes, Sir.'

General Morris: 'What's the track like?'

Captain Bidstrup: 'I was quite surprised. It has very thick cover in most places, but there were quite a few open spaces where I believe we could use mortars on the Japs.'

General Morris: 'Rot, boy! Bloody rot! The mortars would burst in the treetops!'[121]

Interview over.

So mortars were not provided. No matter that Colonel Owen had specifically requested them, and Bidstrup had affirmed that they would be useful. It was yet one more example of the military mindset in this New Guinea war where the leadership had extremely set ideas of what the situation was and what needed to be done, and held fast to that view whatever information was provided to the contrary. Regrettably, there would be many more occasions to come.

In the then and there, though, the net result of the plane's failure to land was that what would have been a mere twenty-minute trip for the men on board, became a six-day slog to get there the hard way. Only a short time after returning to Seven Mile Airfield, the remainder of the 39th Battalion headed off on Shanks's pony—their own two legs—to once again try to get to their comrades at Kokoda. Time and again over the next few days as they pushed their exhausted way forward, these troops would think of how very close they had got, of how easy it would have been; but now they had to face this . . .

The only break these unfortunates got on the way up was, sometimes, when they arrived at a clearing and the lieutenant would call a halt and they were allowed ten minutes or so of practice-firing with the Thompson sub-machine guns they had been issued the day before leaving. Most of the men had never fired a machine gun of any description in training and the lieutenant thought it best that they have a rough idea of what it was like before facing the Japanese. What they learnt too, soon enough, was that while the Thompson had received rave reviews from the AIF who had used it in the Middle East, here in the jungle with all the humidity and mud, it all too frequently jammed up. D Company, under Captain Bidstrup, were the only ones to have the far more highly prized Bren guns, and then only by a stroke of good fortune.

On the eve of departure—right after his frustrating conversation with General Morris—the good captain had been at Company Headquarters when a bloke with a truck had pulled up asking where Brigade Headquarters were.

'Why do you want Brigade?' the captain asked.

'I've got six Bren guns for them.'

'This is Brigade Headquarters,' Bidstrup told him, and scribbled an unintelligible signature for authorisation. Of course the officer risked almost certain court martial if caught, but given that they were leaving at sunrise the following day and were about to get to grips with the Japanese, it seemed reasonable that they were going to need the Brens much more than Brigade Headquarters would.[122]

The Bren, he knew, was a bloody beauty. The gun was a Czech invention that came with 28-round magazines, which you could empty in fifteen seconds or fire as individual shots, depending on which switch you hit. While the usual fashion of firing was to set the gun up on the bipod that was part of the weapon, it was also possible for a strong man to lift it and fire from the hip, even as he charged forward. It was a lethal bit of weaponry, and squarely in the frame of what General MacArthur was referring to when he had remarked: 'Whoever said the pen is mightier than the sword obviously never encountered automatic weapons.' Brens were going to be important up there, and would maybe help to even the odds a little.

Back at Kokoda, Colonel Owen decided he just had to make the best of what he had and prepared to defend the village with his eighty good men and true. He told the soldiers to dig in atop the tiny natural plateau on which the outpost was based—a small lump on the valley floor and at least forming a natural defensive position. At this point, the level of confidence among the young Australian soldiers was not particularly high. More than a few Diggers would later acknowledge to looking around at their young comrades, and thinking that things were pretty grim when only the likes of them stood between the Japs and Moresby, which in turn stood as the gateway to Australia. But there was naught to do, for most of them at least, but to keep on keeping on; pack up your troubles in your old kitbag and smile boys, that's the style.

One of their number, Lieutenant Peter Brewer, had been posted by ANGAU at the Kokoda Government Station before the Japanese had landed and, when he had received orders telling him to return to Moresby, had buried his supply of grog in a back garden, for the day . . . And *this* was that day! Now returned to his home he dug it up on the sly, and doled out some much prized whiskey to his mates. One of the recipients was Jack Wilkinson, who put a good whack of it in his canteen and mixed it with water. On the one hand Jack was thrilled to have some grog right there whenever he wanted it, but on the other hand, he decided he daren't risk having even a sip. They were in a game of life and death here, the Japanese might attack at any time, and he was all too conscious that the tiniest slip on his part might be the difference between eternal blackness and ongoing light, for both him and his mates. Better to keep the lid on, and be safe, as they stayed in their defensive positions and peered into the encroaching jungle for signs of movement.

This sobriety was as well, for about an hour before dusk, one of the soldiers reported seeing what he thought was some suspicious movement at a distance of about 150 yards to their north. There was a palpable tightening of the tension, as their eyes squinted and strained, searching the distant shadows for signs of malevolence. Bayonets were fixed, and ammunition supplies were checked one more time. The men softly murmured to each other. It looked like it was going to be *on*, and more than one man wondered as the sun went down whether it was to be his last.

Just after dusk fell, mortar fire with scattered machine-gun bursts gave the first indication that the Japanese were indeed on the Australians' northern perimeters. Some of the mortar fire exploded on impact with the rubber trees, spraying shrapnel over a wide, and even more dangerous, area. With each '*cough*' in the distance to signify a mortar was on the way, all the Australians could do was to hug tighter into the embrace of Mother Earth and pray that not even a tiny part of the incoming shell had their number on it. In his own trench, with Wally and Ray tight beside him, Joe Dawson fingered his rosary beads furiously, thought of Elaine waiting for him at home, *focused* on her and felt calmer. Something just told him that he and Elaine were meant to be and that he was destined to live. Christ, he hoped so, anyway. The mortars kept falling, amid the odd call from the Japanese now that they had crawled closer. 'Corporal White' still did not move forward, however . . .

The sole Australian on the whole plateau who didn't hear the mortar barrage and gunfire was deaf Doc Vernon who, exhausted, had arrived in the late afternoon and a short time later—after ensuring that the Regimental Aid Post was up to scratch—had gone for a kip in one of the old houses that stood on the edge of the government station. He had left instructions that he be woken at the first casualty and, because no one had been hurt in the first skirmish, they let him sleep on, reckoning all too grimly that he really would likely be needing all his energies when the attack did come. Though at one point in the early evening he woke briefly from the vibrations of Japanese machine-gun bullets hitting the far wall from where he was sleeping on the lounge with a large ginger cat, the good doctor was never a man for panic and, when the bullets stopped, went back to sleep. For he, too, sensed that the night ahead would be tiring.

By midnight the firing between the two sides was almost continuous, though to that point the Japanese officers had not sent their soldiers on any full-throated charges. Rather, the Australian soldiers were simply being softened up for the charge to come, and the hope was that some might turn and flee.

Not bloody likely, mate. Maroubra Force held their positions and kept firing, even as those who'd drawn the shortest straw of all scurried in the darkness, head down, to keep the ammunition up to their brothers in arms.

Just before 2.00 a.m. though, a force of four hundred Japanese soldiers indeed laid siege to the Australians' defences with devastatingly accurate mortar fire. They were aided in no small part by a moonlight so strong it would not have put the earliest hour of the day to shame. Platoons of Japanese infantry began to probe close to the Australian positions and the battle for Kokoda was on in earnest.

In one of the most oft-recounted episodes of the American Civil War, during the Battle of Spotsylvania, the Union General John Sedgwick was prancing up and down behind his soldiers, exhorting them to ever greater efforts, when one of his aides ventured to say: 'Sir, don't you think it would be a good idea if you were to present a less obvious target to those damn Rebels?' 'Don't be ridiculous!' boomed the fearless general. 'They couldn't hit an elephant at this dist . . . ' The fullstop to his sentence was a single shot from a Confederate soldier, and the general had breathed his last.

Whatever the truth of the story, it is certain that since war began military leaders have taken it as bad form to take cover as the missiles begin to fly, and there is equally no doubt that Colonel Owen was of their number. For, sure enough, as the action became thicker and the Japanese got closer—even as just a few of the Australians suddenly did disappear from their frontline positions—

Owen not only constantly exhorted his men to greater efforts, but was singularly active himself with both grenade and gun, right at the front of the frontline, much of it while standing fully upright.

To Colonel Owen's left, about ten along from him in the defensive position on the perimeter, Sergeant Joe Dawson was firing hard in the direction of the fire-flashes of the Japanese guns in the jungle. Other blokes used to aim just a little to the right of those flashes, thinking that was the best chance of scoring a hit on a Japanese soldier's body, but Joe aimed directly *at* the flash, reasoning there had to be a Japanese head in direct line behind it. The Japanese themselves, of course, were doing much the same in the direction of the fire-flashes generated by the Australians, and bullets were whistling around them all the while as they tried the impossible task of keeping their heads and bodies out of harm's way while still aiming effectively at the approaching swarm of jungle Japs.

Only Colonel Owen seemed to have no fear at all. There was no doubt he was 'as game as Ned Kelly'—as the men referred to the type—but one who could barely stand the unnecessary risk he was taking was Lieutenant Gough 'Judy' Garland.

'Sir,' he said carefully, 'I think you're taking an unnecessary risk walking around among the troops like that.'

'Well,' Owen replied equably, 'I've got to do it.' Alas, just before 3.00 a.m., while Lieutenant Colonel Owen was in the process of hurling a grenade at one of the scurrying figures in the darkness, a Japanese bullet hit him just above the right eye and dropped him cold as a spud.

Doc Vernon was woken partly by the hand on his shoulder, and partly by the ginger cat, which had suddenly bounded off the couch in alarm at the sight of the intruder in the moonlight. It was Lieutenant Peter Brewer.

'Colonel Owen's been hit,' Brewer said. 'You'd better come.'

Under heavy fire, Doc Vernon, Major Watson and Jack Wilkinson got to the severely wounded officer—now regularly shuddering with seizures—and managed to drag him back from the frontline. But in fact, it wouldn't have mattered if he had been taken straight into the best Sydney hospital. From the first moment that Doc Vernon got a look at him in some decent light and established that not only was there no exit wound, but brain tissue was visible around the edge of the entry wound, it was obvious that Owen had taken a bullet with his number on it and there remained only the barest breath of life in him.

Even while they were treating him, and trying to ascertain whether he was still breathing, the Japanese fire around them was as thick as mosquitoes in a swamp and getting thicker still. At one point, Major Watson was holding a lantern for Doc to see by, and every time he raised it above the level of the window, a burst of bullets from a distant machine gun hit the building all around. Courageous defence was one thing, but mass suicide quite another. With Colonel Owen now only twitching there was no doubt he would die within minutes, so the surviving Australians took advantage of a propitious deathly white mist which had suddenly rolled in and, under the command of Major Watson once more, began to withdraw. Doc Vernon reluctantly followed the order to leave the colonel where he lay and joined the others, after moistening the colonel's lips and making him as comfortable as possible. Only a short time after the doctor left, Daisy Owen, sleeping restlessly at her home in Moonee Ponds as she waited for her husband William to return to her, became a widow.

Getting out now. So thick was the mist on the Kokoda plateau, it was like languorously pushing through a cottonwool too light to feel other than by its moisture. Just two members of the 39th disobeyed the direct order to retreat. Deciding that the opportunity was too good to miss, Private 'Snowy' Parr and his offsider, 'Rusty' Hollow, hid on the edge of the main clearing in the village and waited, with a Bren gun between them. Among the other soldiers Snowy was known as a bit of a ratbag; he was always getting into scrapes and never cared what anyone wanted him to do, and this was a case in point.

Sure enough, not long after the chatter of gunfire had ceased, the first flitting figure in the darkness appeared ahead, followed by other Japanese soldiers who were soon in the mood for celebrating the victory. In no time at all, in the ethereal light of the pre-dawn, a group of them was raising a Japanese flag up Kokoda's one flagpole and dancing a kind of jig around it.

Steady, steady, steady . . . NOW! Snowy opened up with his Bren gun on the Japs, while Rusty kept the ammo up to him. Both had the grim satisfaction of seeing as many as fifteen of the brutes fall to the ground, and the air was rent by their screams. Take that you bastards. That was for Colonel Owen and the six men of the 39th who'd been killed in the previous actions. It felt good to shoot straight into a massed bunch of mongrels who'd killed their mates and they kept firing at the now writhing figures on the ground. At that distance each Bren bullet made a hole as big as a Jap's bloody head every time it hit a body.

In no time at all, taking advantage of all the confusion and fear, the two Australians had hightailed it into the mist themselves. Yes, they knew they would no doubt catch hell for disobeying orders, but it was worth it to get some revenge. Before long both soldiers were well into the rubber trees. Somehow, the early light through the scattered mist and branches made such crazy shadows, and alternating shades of light and darkness, that it formed something like the haze between life and death that many men from both sides had just passed through.

It was well after daylight before the last remnants of the 39th got back to Deniki where the two sections of D Company had set up the defensive position. It was time to regroup. Again, even though they were retreating in front of the advancing Japanese, there was a strong sense among the men that they were going all right and, at the very bloody least, were letting the Japs know they had a dinkum fight on their hands.

On the one hand it went against the grain to be constantly moving backwards, but on the other there was really no choice because to make a firm stand against such a far superior enemy could only result in their own quick annihilation. And, by constantly making hit and run attacks, the Australians had the added advantage that they could keep the Japanese off-balance, always uncertain about just how many soldiers they had ranged against them. This proved to be an effective tactic, because even though at this early stage of the fight the Australians had never added up to more than 110 soldiers, at a much later point, documents recovered from the Japanese Battalion Headquarters showed that the Japanese thought they had a body of no fewer than six thousand Australians against them.

Of the specific action at Kokoda, the diary of Second Lieutenant Noda Hidetaka, of the 3rd Battalion, 144th Japanese Infantry, when it was later found and translated, had an entry that was illustrative of how well the Australians must have fought, confusing the Japanese as to their true numbers.

> *1 August, Saturday. Overcast, occasionally fine.*
>
> *Last night when the soldiers were chatting together I heard them say that Lt Ogawa, Yukio, Commander of no.1 Company, had been killed in action. I told them with a smile, not to spread rumours but this morning, when I was walking on the North Side of the command group who were reading out the Imperial Rescript, 2nd Lt Hamaguchi confirmed that Lt Ogawa had been killed.*
>
> *Being very surprised I hurried to the office and looking at the report found that in the Kokoda area our advance force who have been engaged in battle . . . had suffered unexpectedly heavy casualties.*[123]

At least the survivors of B Company managed to get a message through to Port Moresby on the morning of 29 July: 'Kokoda lost from this morning. Blow the [aero-]drome and road east of Oivi. Owen mortally wounded and captured. Templeton missing.'[124]

Fortunately for the Australians there was no immediate compulsion on the part of the enemy to pursue them down the track. Though the Japanese were slightly behind schedule at this point, and the Australians had provided far more resistance than had been expected, the key thing was that the objective of securing Kokoda had now been accomplished. It was now time to make a decision about whether to push on or not.

Communications between Rabaul and Tokyo had flown back and forth, exchanging information and views, but on the morning of 28 July, General Haruyoshi Hyakutake, the Commander of the 17th Army in Rabaul, received the coded cable from Imperial General Headquarters in Tokyo he'd been waiting for, and he in turn passed the orders on to Colonel Yokoyama in New Guinea. They had been given clearance to proceed to Port Moresby, which they estimated could be achieved in just eight days march from Kokoda, including fighting.

In Rabaul, General Horii would organise for more men and more supplies to be landed at the Buna beachhead, and push on down the track, which was now being widened and improved by the native labourers brought from Rabaul.

Back in Brisbane on that same afternoon, a key new American general had been welcomed by General MacArthur's staff. General Thomas Kenney was to take over MacArthur's air wing, and in the course of his welcome Major General Richard K. Sutherland thought it best to lay on the line just what kind of a situation the Bataan Gang were dealing with. He thought it important that the new general know that the Australians fighting up in New Guinea were 'undisciplined, untrained, over-advertised and useless'.[125]

At least this low opinion of the 39th Battalion served for one thing. With the fall of Kokoda, it was more than ever clear that Port Moresby really was at risk if this southern thrust by the Japanese was not thwarted. So, finally, the wheels were set in motion for the Australian 7th Division who'd earnt their spurs in the Middle East, to get to New Guinea immediately. It had taken a great deal of time, but at last, on 3 August 1942, the orders were given for the 7th Division to move. Within hours, the likes of Stan and Butch Bisset and Alan Haddy and all the soldiers from the 2/14th and 2/16th were packing up their kitbags and making ready.

Still, everything wasn't as smooth as it might have been. When the time came to embark on the awaiting ships, although their destination was nominally still top secret—though some in the ranks had been told they were heading to a new base in North Queensland—it was clearly not a secret to all. For there on the dock at Townsville were their munitions in huge wooden boxes about to be loaded into the hull of the ship and each clearly marked 'King's Harbour Master, Port Moresby'.[126] Against that, was the good news that the munitions were even being loaded at all as the wharfies had recently gone on strike and been successful in their insistence that they receive danger money for handling them!

Stan was just heading up the gangplank to go into the 2/14th's ship, the *James Fenimore*, when the man just a little way ahead of him suddenly pulled out of the queue. It was Captain Phil Rhoden, the Second-in-Command of the 2/14th and a great friend of Stan and Butch's from their days with the Powerhouse Club back in Melbourne, where Rhoden had been a strapping sportsman in his own right and also Second-in-Command of the Powerhouse Militia Battalion. Now though, he had just grabbed a wharfie and was speaking to him with some urgency. Be blowed if, in the hurly-burly of departure, Phil hadn't nearly forgotten the most important thing of all!

'Mate,' the army captain said to the wharfie, 'would you mind posting this for me?'

'No worries, mate,' the wharfie replied, tucking the envelope into a greasy pocket, clearly with no idea of just how important it was to the Australian officer. For in the letter Phil Rhoden had poured his heart out to his girlfriend in Melbourne, Pat Hamilton, telling how much the events of the previous two years had made him realise the depth of his love for her and . . . would she marry him? Captain Rhoden's task achieved, he hoped, he got back in the line and, together with the Bisset boys and all the rest, not long afterwards the ship departed.

North.

•

North, way north, as the numbers of Australian soldiers on the Kokoda Track increased—and the loss of the Kokoda airfield meant that nothing more could be flown in—the problem of supply became excruciating. Bert Kienzle and his porters did the best they could, but the situation lurched from one crisis to the next. If the men weren't desperate for more munitions, it was that the food supply had dwindled to nearly nothing. If it wasn't medical supplies which had run out, it was blankets.

In desperation, the army had tried what became known as 'biscuit bombing', which was low-flying aircraft dropping supplies in crates, or packed tightly inside bags, right beside assembled troops; but that had many problems. One of the main ones was that in the endless green acres of the highlands it was hard for pilots to find the designated drop sites. Another was that when they *did* find the site, it was no easy task to get the crates on target, and even then the crates frequently burst on contact with the ground, while others careened into the jungle where they could never be found. Time and again bags of rice, particularly, hit the ground and burst in the manner of mini-bombs, with the individual grains of rice-shrapnel being spread out over an area as large as fifty square yards. Other bags and boxes disappeared so far into undergrowth that they were simply impossible to find. Biscuits in tins were smashed into crumbs from the impact and tins of bully beef were punctured, meaning their certain ruination in a matter of hours. Some heavy weaponry was dropped and disappeared so deeply into the mud it couldn't be retrieved. A rough estimation was that sixty per cent of what was dropped was not recovered—at least not by the Australian soldiers, for yet one more problem was when precious supplies fell into the hands of the Japanese . . .

Finally though, something twigged with Bert Kienzle. Just vaguely, he remembered that on one of his many flights from Kokoda to Port Moresby he had deviated from the most direct route and noted that rarest of all things in the New Guinea highlands—a valley with a fairly large flat piece of ground at the bottom, somewhere between Efogi and Eora. The fact that the area didn't show up on any maps was perfect as it meant that the Japanese wouldn't know anything about it. Kienzle left the porter lines in the hands of his offsiders and, taking his two most trusted natives with him, plunged into the jungle at a point where the track crossed a river. Two terribly difficult days later, at last . . . bingo! There it lay, in the valley below. Exactly the flat area he needed. When Kienzle started down for a closer inspection, however, his porters jacked up.

'PLES E TAMBU. MEPELA E NOKEN GO LONG DISPELA PLES.' 'This place is taboo, and we ain't going there, sport.'

Kienzle, though, insisted. 'YU MUS I GO. MI BIKMAN. MI TOK. YU HURIM. MIPELA MUS GO NUW.' 'You must go. I am the bigman boss, and when I talk, you hear and obey. We're going. Get going!'

Reluctantly they accompanied him, and together they were soon at the bottom of an ancient volcano and able to establish that as a drop zone it was perfect. For not only would the place be easy enough to find from the air, but the relatively flat and open terrain— with rough contours of 2000 yards by 600 yards, positioned at an altitude of 6000 feet above sea level—would indeed permit fairly easy recovery in an area close enough to the battlelines that the porters would be spared a week's walk.

On the spot Kienzle christened the place 'Myola' after the wife of his Company Commander at ANGAU, Major Syd Elliott-Smith—the word meant 'dawn'—and formed up plans to make it the major supply depot for all the subsequent Australian fighting in the area. On the morning of 4 August, he and his porters set off from Myola, blazing a new track along a ridge in a northeasterly direction, to force as direct a route as possible through to the main track leading to Kokoda. The new junction that was formed, thus, was at a flat spot where the track crossed Eora Creek, and Kienzle named it Templeton's Crossing, in honour of Sam Templeton who, it was now accepted, was not coming back. The main thing was, the job was done. The Australians now had a place to establish an advance supply depot until such times as they re-conquered the Kokoda airfield, which would make everything easier still.

And on that subject, there were already plans afoot . . .

In the first days of August 1942, the battle-wearied veterans of the 39th who had seen action at Awala, Wairopi, Gorari and Kokoda were joined by the rest of the exhausted 39th Battalion who had made their way forward to the picturesque village of Deniki, which overlooked the Yodda Valley leading to Kokoda. Together as a battalion for the first time in the highlands, there were some 460 members gathered. Together with the remnants of the Papuan Infantry Battalion, and a few soldiers from the ANGAU force and some native policemen, Maroubra Force now numbered five hundred. The 'veterans'—for that is what they now were—were pleased to see the new arrivals for more reason than that they were friends and reinforcements. Far more urgently they had some *food*, which the veterans lacked. Though it was putting it too high to say that those who had been on the track for the last month were outright starving, the fact was that their supplies were pitifully low. Fortunately the new fellas had no hesitation in sharing what few rations they had left after their own long trek. As they shared the food, and the stories, the spirit of the men seemed to lift. This wasn't like being a lost battalion in the backblocks of Port Moresby counting the hours of every stinking day till it was done and they were closer to home. This was like being a full body of fighting men together for the first time on the battlefront up against a ruthless enemy, and aware that from here on in they would be depending on each other.

The fresh arrivals—though fresh was hardly the word for them, given their six-day trek to get there—included Major Alan Cameron, who walked into Deniki on 4 August to take provisional command of the 39th after the death of the valiant Colonel Owen. Major Cameron was a no-nonsense military officer complete with bushy moustache and fired up by what he had witnessed in the fall of Rabaul in much the same manner as Colonel Owen had been. He had served with the 2/22nd Battalion there, and also witnessed the

Japanese barbarity, before managing to flee in an open boat with twelve others. Very much of the 'take-charge-and-then-chaaarge!' school of military thinking—as he had first learned with the cadets at Melbourne's elite Scotch College—Major Cameron was frank in his first meeting with the 39th's officers, where he laid it on the line.

First up, he was not well pleased with the performance of the 39th thus far. With very little idea of what had gone on to this point, and seemingly no cognisance of the fact that these wet-behind-the-ears young men from Victoria had taken on hardened Japanese veterans and acquitted themselves well, Major Cameron was brutal. He focused on his view that there had been some Australian soldiers from B Company who had shot through in the thick of defending Kokoda, some of whom he had been appalled to meet on the track as he was walking to get to the front. And he was also appalled that as a company they had continued to fall back in the face of the Japanese. Put together, it meant that the name of the 39th was forever sullied. His comments did not sit well with his exhausted but now outraged officers, who, despite everything, knew that the men had bloody well done *all right* and for that matter weren't aware of anyone who had shot through. As for falling back, they knew there had been no choice if they were to live to fight another day. But they continued to listen as Cameron told them what the men of the 39th were going to do now to redeem themselves.

They were going to retake Kokoda, *that* was what they were going to do! With Kokoda came the airfield, and with the airfield came the potential to get both immediate supplies and reinforcements in, plus a way of quickly evacuating their wounded. And it would also be a good way of getting the new arrivals 'blooded' quickly, making them all the better for it as soldiers.

It didn't take long for the purport of Major Cameron's remarks to filter through to the lower ranks of B Company, who were collectively angry. The veterans of B Company, including Joe Dawson, Ray Phillips and Wally Gratz, looked at each other with hollow eyes. After everything they had been through, *this* was their reward? To have their name maligned by a bloke who didn't have the first clue about what had happened but was prepared to crucify them anyway? Who the hell did he think he was? For the moment, alas, there was nothing they could do but wear it.

Strike two. After their success in the Battle of Midway, on the morning of 7 August the Americans launched their next strike-back at the Japanese. Always the American way had been 'when in doubt, send in the marines', and this is precisely what they did. Under cover of darkness, some six thousand US marines of the 1st Marine Division landed on Guadalcanal and successfully attacked the two thousand Japanese soldiers defending the newly constructed airfield. By dusk the following day, the Americans were the new defenders of the airfield, the many captured Japanese supplies that came with it and the crucial port facilities.

In Imperial General Headquarters in Tokyo, the American move was viewed with alarm, and as soon as the next night, 8 August, the Imperial Japanese Navy arrived with such force that the American Navy—after losing four cruisers—had to abandon its marines there. The stage was set for the massive battle of Guadalcanal, with both the Americans and Japanese continuing to pour in more and more men in a bid to control the crucial airfield.

For the first time, Japan's resources in the Southwest Pacific were stretched to almost breaking point. It didn't mean that the Japanese military leadership would abandon their plans in New Guinea, but it certainly shifted their focus from the island.

Contact. On the morning of 8 August 1942, for the first time Major Cameron at Deniki was able to get a message through to Port Moresby along a landline to tell them the state of play. Communication along the Kokoda Track to this point had been extremely difficult for the Australians. While, typically, the Japanese had long before developed a special lightweight radio that worked perfectly in jungle conditions, the Diggers were not so blessed.

At the beginning of the campaign, the same backpack radios weighing around thirty-five pounds that had worked so well in the

BASIL BUTLER

The men who tried to make sure Australians back home knew what their soldiers were facing in New Guinea: *above*, photographers George Silk and Damien Parer, taken in the Western Desert; *below*, journalists Osmar White from the Melbourne *Sun* and Chester Wilmot from the ABC, at the Kokoda front.

AWM 013472

AWM P00525.006

Officers of the 2/14th Battalion on the Kokoda Track, they include Lieutenant Bisset *(second from left)* and Captain Nye *(third from left)*. Together with the 39th Battalion, the 2/14th would play a major role in the campaign.

AWM 026716

(Left) Brigadier Arnold Potts, Commanding Officer of the 21st Brigade, which included the 2/14th, at a forward post on the track.

AWM P01637.001

Private Bruce Kingsbury of the 2/14th Battalion played a heroic role in the Battle of Isurava and was awarded a Victoria Cross for his extraordinary courage. His grave is located at the Kokoda War Cemetery *(below)*.

AWM 072431

AWM 013260

(Above and right) Eora Creek, a base for the Australians close to the front, was a heaving mass of wounded soldiers, native porters and mud at the end of August 1942, during intense fighting. (Photographs by Damien Parer.)

AWM 013257

Australians prepare for a battle at Eora Creek village. The native village huts often provided a good spot for the wounded to rest away from the incessant rain. (Photograph by Damien Parer.)

AWM 013250

AWM FO1212

Two stills of wounded soldiers from Damien Parer's *Kokoda Front Line* film.
The soldier below, from the 2/14th, is on a stretcher, with a native stretcher bearer—
a Fuzzy Wuzzy Angel—behind him waiting to carry him back down the track.

AWM 013287

AWM 026320

The wounded who could manage to walk back down the track often formed 'conga lines' to support each other. These men from the 39th had a six-day trek to reach a hospital.

AWM 027003

A welcome sight for soldiers heading back from the front:
the Salvos moved up the track offering relief for the wounded.

AWM F01212

Colonel Ralph Honner proudly addresses his 39th Battalion at Menari. The 39th had long been considered an inferior force, but after weeks of intense fighting on the track they proved themselves to be 'ragged bloody heroes'. Damien Parer was there to capture the bedraggled 39th's moment of redemption.

AWM 013289

Middle East were issued and then lugged by porters up hill and down ravine for mile after wretched mile. Alas, once in place in the jungle it was discovered that they really didn't work for ranges beyond a mile and a half anywhere other than in the relatively flatter country to the north of the Owen Stanleys and, even then, only when the wind was blowing in the right direction! The high humidity affected the efficient functioning of the radio, as did the hilly terrain of most of the track. Unless there was 'line-of-sight' between the transmitter and receiver, it simply didn't work. So, as part of an enormous exercise of logistics conducted by the Signals Brigade, a cable of telephone wire was laid all the way from Port Moresby to Deniki, and this now worked . . . at least reasonably well.

Because human speech could be transmitted on the cable for only ten miles or so, signal stations were set up along the track roughly along those intervals. And, to avoid the classic case of Chinese Whispers changing the original message entirely, each signalman would not only receive the message, but check that he had it exactly right before passing it on. In such a laborious fashion did Port Moresby command keep in vague contact with its men in the field.

On this morning, Major Cameron sent the message that his three companies were moving out with the objective of retaking Kokoda in a surprise attack by nightfall. At the head of C Company, Captain Cyril Dean would head carefully north along the main track back into Kokoda, while Captain Noel Symington and A Company would make a circular flanking movement to come at the plateau from a little-known side track, which had been suggested by Bert Kienzle. Captain Bidstrup with D Company would go all the way around on another track which went in a northeasterly direction, and come out at a spot on the track between Oivi and Kokoda, which would enable them to cut the Japs' supply line. They could then fall back on Kokoda, where A and C Companies would, they hoped, already be in possession. Two other companies, including the 'disgraced' B Company, would man the fall-back positions at Deniki and further back at Eora Creek, and Major Cameron would stay with them.

(As they said among the common folk of the privates: 'RHIP', Rank Hath Its Privileges.)

By his own men, Major Cameron's orders had been greeted with something less than enthusiasm, most particularly by the officers who had been put in charge of each assigned section, and who understood the tactical dubiousness of what their commander was proposing. Dean, Symington and Bidstrup were all fresh to the 39th, having come as the reinforcement officers from the AIF a couple of months previously. Dean and Symington had seen action in Syria, while Bidstrup had fought in Tobruk, and all three of these officers— vastly more experienced than Cameron in matters of battle—were quietly of the view that Cameron was something of a 'gung-ho merchant'.

It was the older and bolder Captain Symington who voiced these concerns.[127] There is a particular kind of military language where, without risking a court martial, a subordinate can put the view to a senior officer that the orders he has just given might possibly be construed, just possibly, as *insane*, and Symington used that language now. Peppering his remarks with many a 'Sir' and 'is it possible that?', he noted that it seemed, perhaps, a trifle risky to send small forces of men into an area where the strength of the enemy was all but entirely unknown. Did Major Cameron have, perhaps, any information that he, Captain Symington, was not privy to, as to the strength of the Japanese around Kokoda, or even back at their beachhead? Major Cameron did not, but he still insisted that his orders be followed to the letter, right down to his order that Captain Symington fire off a Verey flare as soon as he and his men were *in situ* at Kokoda, despite Symington's expressed view that the flare would only be visible to every Japanese soldier within ten miles, but remain unseen to the men of the 39th it was meant to alert back at Deniki.

'Do exactly as I have asked, Captain Symington, is that clear?'

'Yes, *Suh*.'

Another who felt trepidation about the orders was Captain Dean, whose task it was to go right down the main track towards Kokoda with his men until such times as they encountered resistance—despite the fact that they had precisely *no* information about what strength that resistance would be and where they would find it. Such an order meant that it was all but guaranteed that he would lose at least some of his men when they came to the Japanese ambush which was sure to be set up. By way of temperament and personality, however, Captain Dean was not like Captain Symington and did not remonstrate with Major Cameron. He accepted that he had been given an order and, however unwise he thought it, however much in his heart of hearts he might have wanted to tell him to go to billy-o, he decided that it was his duty to follow it.

The companies moved out as ordered, separating as they went along their assigned tracks.

Unfortunately for Dean, C Company had only proceeded a short way towards their objective before the encroaching Japanese indeed ambushed them. In the ensuing fire-fight, Captain Dean was hit by a sniper's bullet.

'Through the stomach, too,' he managed to get out, as he put his hands over the wound, and then fell down and died almost immediately. He was a good, brave man, popular among his men, and somehow the sight of him there, dead at their feet, galvanised them as one. His enraged men charged straight at the Japanese positions, firing as they went, and bayoneting those few Japanese who stood their ground. Operating less in the realms of conscious thought than a collective rage that had built to bloodlust, they kept pursuing the fleeing Japanese, and when the battle was over a great number of Japanese soldiers had been killed for the loss of only a few Australians.

But that was still a few too many, and the one who was lamented most was the brave Captain Dean. In his absence, a doctor from Brisbane, Captain John Shera, took command and called a halt to pursuing the Japanese further. With the certainty that there would be another ambush at the Japanese fall-back position that would surely be waiting for them over the next hill, he told the men that C Company would go no further. Instead, with the assistance of the omnipresent Father Nobby Earl, they buried their dead, gathered their wounded and—helped to calm just a little by the cigarettes they had pilfered from the dead Japanese soldiers—turned back. In such difficult situations, the presence of Father Nobby Earl, always with his long stick in one hand and his rosary beads in the other, provided great spiritual succour. Even for the men who had not a religious bone in their bodies, the sense of care and goodness he projected was a comfort. For the rest of the day, C Company slowly limped and staggered back to Deniki, fighting a rearguard action all the way.

The 39th Battalion's D Company, meanwhile, was hit by another Japanese ambush at the tiny village of Pirivi, but they also fought back well. In savage hand-to-hand fighting, where the bayonet did at least as much damage as the bullet, the Australians had the best of the notably bloody fighting. At the conclusion of the second engagement of the morning, the Japanese had been especially badly hit and it was they who'd withdrawn and the Australians who were momentarily masters of this bloody section of the track. So hurried was the Japanese withdrawal that they left behind their dead and some of their immobile wounded, including one Japanese soldier who had been hit in the upper thighs. He was still conscious, lying sprawled on the track, his own machine gun out of his reach as the Australians tentatively approached.

The sergeant took one look at him and gave an order: 'Smoky, finish him orf,' he said to one of his men, 'Smoky' Joe Howson.

Stillness on the track. Heavy air, with insects buzzing . . . *roaring.* Every ounce of the Japanese soldier's terrified consciousness was now focused, staring up at the pure blackness of the muzzle that the Australian soldier was pointing at his forehead. Pointing, not moving . . .

'Smoky, finish him orf,' the sergeant had said. Smoky knew it was obvious that the bloke could live, but he asked himself what else could he do?

'With that I looked down,' Smoky would recount after, 'and he looked back at me. And I've been looking at those eyes ever since . . .'[128]

It was indeed going to be a long and savage fight, with no room for mercy from either side. Taking prisoners was out of the question for both the Japanese and the Australians. Not only were there no cells or secure enclosures handy in the jungle, but as the fight for domination of the track progressed it would be too dangerous and draining to assign much-needed soldiers to escort prisoners back to secure lines. Perhaps even more important than both these factors, however, was that taking prisoners would mean more mouths to feed and greater strain placed on supply lines that were always under severe pressure.

With the two fighting forces operating as much as ten days march from their bases, through extremely difficult terrain, lack of food and ammunition would be a constant source of angst. Both sides knew it, and acted accordingly. No prisoners. No mercy.

After a day of bloody fighting, the survivors of D Company were able to achieve their objective and regain the track between Kokoda and Oivi, arriving just in time to ambush a platoon of Japanese who were marching double-quick time to what they thought was a battlefront way ahead of them. It was one thing to have cut the Japanese supply line to Kokoda, but quite another to hold it, as D Company now came under attack from both directions.[129]

With so much Japanese resistance out along the main tracks defending Kokoda from the main Deniki thrust, there were precious few soldiers left in the main garrison near the airfield itself and, by just after one o'clock, A Company—with the former 'local' Lieutenant Peter Brewer and the ever-faithful Lance Corporal Sanopa of the Papuan Infantry Battalion guiding them—was right on the outskirts of Kokoda. Ahead of the men was the thick rubber plantation, and just peeking over the tops of the trees they could see the roofs of the village. But no Japs! Were they about to enter a trap? Was their next step going to be their last? Could it really be *this* easy to re-take a key position on which so much blood had already been spilt by both sides? Almost . . .

Indeed, as A Company proceeded with great caution through the plantation, the men did see a few Japanese soldiers in the distance and had a few shots fired in their direction. None of the Japs were in it for a real fight though and, by half-past one in the early afternoon, the Australians were in total control of the plateau once more and manning the defensive positions.

There, they made two significant discoveries. In one of the station houses they unearthed Japanese documents clearly noting the track through Kokoda as the planned route to Port Moresby, and the level of detail the map showed about the topography that remained was staggering. Clearly the Japanese intelligence was first class and Captain Symington wasted no time in giving the maps to Lance Corporal Sanopa with instructions to break through enemy lines and get them to Major Cameron. He was also to inform the Major that they were in possession of the airfield and needed Moresby reinforcements urgently.

The other discovery was rather more grisly. It was Colonel Owen's bloated and decomposing body lying like a piece of forgotten rubbish beneath a tree not too far from where he had been left by Doc Vernon ten days before. A small crew remained to man the defensive trenches while the rest gathered to respectfully bury the battalion's courageous commander on a section of the plateau with a wonderful vista overlooking the terrain he had died to defend. A soldier's grave, they buried him as he would have wanted—with his boots on—and then got back to it. Always in this war, whatever the circumstances, you had to quickly get back to it, but at least there was no doubt that, because of the intense experience they had all been through, this was an entirely different bunch of men to the ones who had set off from Ower's Corner those few short weeks ago.

For by this time the men of the 39th were, if not exactly comfortable with their surroundings, at least beginning to adapt to them and maximise their chances of surviving. One thing they had all learnt in the previous weeks was to abandon everything in their haversacks that wasn't absolutely essential. Lifting that weight up and down the mountains was near killing them, so every ounce saved was a precious ounce of energy that wasn't wasted. Did you really need, for example, a whole towel, when you barely ever got to wash anyway? Towels were cut in half and sometimes even shared between two mates who were particularly close. Did you really need the whole shaving kit when all you really wanted was the razor and a tiny bit of soap? Out it went. Many others abandoned shaving altogether, not just for the weight, but for the fact that a thick beard gave them one tiny bit of flesh protected from the little brute insects that continued to pester them. Close mates decided that by the simple expedient of sharing their mess tins, one could have the luxury of throwing his own away. Finally, all sets of underwear had been abandoned, including the ones you wore, for the simple reason that wearing underwear meant trapping heat in the groin area, which meant even more humidity, which in short order meant horrible and infuriating rashes that near drove a man *mad*.

They had also learnt a few more skills that were on display this particularly wet afternoon. One of the most crucial they had learnt was how to get a fire going even in a downpour that would kill a brown dog. In such conditions the only way to get dry wood was to do what the natives did: get a huge log and with a machete hack away the pulpy wet outside of the log and get to the tinderbox dry wood inside. Then, while your mate held the groundsheet above you, you got a precious dry match to the tinder and, hey . . . presto . . . fire. Once the fire was going all the other wood could dry and you were away. A cooking pot? Why not your helmet, or 'panic hat' as the soldiers called them? First one bloke had tried it, then another, then the whole battalion had taken to using their helmets for saucepans, or perhaps they'd been using their saucepans for helmets, it didn't really matter. Admittedly, their first few meals tasted remarkably like burnt paint, as the insides of their helmets seared, but you could get used to that too.

The Diggers were adapting to their circumstances the best they could, and one who had taken particular satisfaction in the way they'd done it, because he'd seen much the same thing happen in the last war, was Staff Sergeant Jim Cowey. He was perhaps the oldest soldier there, now that Sam Templeton was no more, and a distinguished one at that, having won a Military Cross in the Great War while serving with the 46th Battalion.

Right on dusk, as per Major Cameron's plan, and Captain Symington's reluctant order, Sergeant Jim Cowey let off a Verey flare that exploded with a burst of green on the night sky to signal that they were indeed in possession of Kokoda. In return . . . stone cold nothing. Not a cheery answering flare to indicate that they'd got the message and would soon be on their way, not even a good ol' rifle shot from the Japanese to let them know that *they* at least were nearby and A Company weren't the last survivors left on the planet. Nevertheless, they still hoped that either their flare message would have got through to Deniki, or at least Lance Corporal Sanopa had.[130] One way or another, the important thing was that Port Moresby get the news that Kokoda was theirs once again. This would hopefully mean that planes could land on the morrow with supplies and, more crucially, reinforcements.

As it happened, Major Cameron indeed had received the news from Sanopa, and in turn got the message through to Moresby. He was promised in return by General Morris that a plane *would* arrive the following day on the Kokoda airfield.

Captain Symington's men spent the night practically with one eye open and one finger on the trigger, ready to move into action in a second, and still scarcely believing that the Japanese weren't out there, close and getting closer.

Indeed they were, but they were being careful. Lieutenant Colonel Tsukamoto was seriously aggrieved that the airfield that he had been responsible for holding was now in the hands of the enemy, and he was very eager to reclaim Kokoda. But the experience of the previous three weeks had taught the Japanese not to underestimate these Australian soldiers, most particularly when they were demonstrating confidence enough to let off signal flares to let the whole world know precisely where they were. Just after ten o'clock the following morning, after as much surveillance as they could muster, Tsukamoto carefully moved his men forward on the Australian positions, hoping to get as close as possible before beginning their assault.

The first of the Japanese soldiers were about two hundred yards away from the advance Australian positions, in the middle of a thick grove of rubber trees, when they heard one of the round-eyes shout something unintelligible in their strange language. In fact, it was: 'Here comes C Company through the rubber!', with the Australians having mistaken the attackers for their own men, coming from Deniki, as had been half expected.

Whatever it was they'd shouted, the Japanese didn't care, the point was they'd been spotted, so they immediately opened fire. A bullet came and drilled and killed Private 'Bluey' Williams clean. Frank McLeod reckoned he could see the Jap who got him and dropped to one knee to fire a shot at the sniper. Somewhere about 150 yards forward the bullet missed, giving the sniper the half-second he needed. For just as Frank was pulling back the bolt to fire his second shot, a Japanese bullet pierced his temple and he was gone too. Two mothers' sons from Australia, and good men too, had gone down, dead, in twenty seconds. But at least that would be the last of the Jap's easy kills, for within seconds the rest of the Australian force were in their trenches and returning heavy fire. Five times through the course of the day, the Japanese tried sustained assaults on what they judged to be Australian weak points, but each time they were hurled back.[131]

Out on the western flank of the Australian perimeter, and cut off from their main attacking force, a company of Japanese soldiers led by Second Lieutenant Hirano decided to make their own full-blooded attack as soon as dusk fell. After all, there had to be a limit to how long the Australians could hold out, and they had fired so much during the day that surely their supplies of ammunition had to be running low. Creeping low in the stinking mud that was made even more slippery by the driving rain, the platoon got to within seventy yards of the Australian perimeter before they were spotted, at which point a furious fire-fight ensued, which was so intense that Lieutenant Hirano had no choice but to withdraw his men to relative safety.

They would wait till full darkness, he told his panting desperate men and then, *then* they would take the Australians. Somehow, though, in the pitch black and the still pouring rain, it was well after ten o'clock before they moved on the enemy again . . . and then it was even worse.

On their hands and knees, one Japanese soldier's head pressing against the next soldier's buttocks, they snaked forward in the stinking blackness until they got to the forward outpost. The burst of machine-gun fire was like so many chattering flashes of torch light at five yards. Men were screaming and it wasn't clear who was who, as your own men—or was it the enemy?—fired back and there was the flash of bayonet silhouetted against three more flashes of fire-light and still more screaming and grunting and groaning and was the shadow ahead enemy or friend, or just a shadow, and you had less than one second to decide and then it chattered too and the man beside you died and . . .

And suddenly Hirano himself was in a fight for his very life and was grappling with an enormous round-eyed man and each of them was trying to bring their bayonets to bear when Corporal Hamada, who had just killed an Australian, threw a grenade that exploded not five yards away. Suddenly the Australian groaned and Hirano could feel a slick wetness from the soldier's back as he staggered, clearly hit and . . .

And in all the madness, Lieutenant Hirano gave the order to fall back. But where to? In the thick jungle, with the night so heavily black upon them, it seemed the sun would never rise again—which for several Japanese soldiers of Hirano's company was the truth. It just wasn't possible to form up the men. Hirano wandered, bleeding, hissing out names, looking for them, occasionally falling, but at least finding two of them. And then suddenly, there were explosions all around as the three inadvertently wandered to within forty yards of the Australian lines, where soldiers were now throwing grenades at them, and it was all they could do to break contact and crawl away.

Finally, at three o'clock in the morning, Lieutenant Hirano could go on no longer. It had been a terrible day and a worse night, here in the highland hell of New Guinea, so far from his home, fighting an infernal enemy that simply wouldn't quit. As unaccustomed as he was, he began to cry tears of rage and bitterness.[132] He was hungry, cold, and devastated at the loss of so many of his men, as well as the pure futility of the exercise they had just been engaged in. A heartbeat in the jungle, when so many hearts around had grown cold, he awaited the dawn, thinking of his home and his mother and father and wishing he could be with them, safe.

His name was Brigadier Arnold Potts and he was the Commanding Officer of the 21st Brigade—made up of the 2/27th, 2/14th and 2/16th battalions—and he had flown into Moresby ahead of his troops to get the lie of the land. This thorough approach was typical of him.

In civilian life, Potts was a grazier from Kojonup in Western Australia, but had also fought with distinction with the 1st AIF, and had the supreme badge of honour among the Australian fighting men of the time in that he, too, had stormed the shores of Gallipoli. He had also served on the Western Front in France, where he had been awarded the Military Cross for his gallantry in action. Indeed, he had finished that war with the rank of captain. At the outbreak of World War II he'd again joined up, and by the conclusion of the campaign in Syria he had not only become the Commanding Officer of the 2/16th Battalion, but had won a Distinguished Service Order for valour under fire.

The 45-year-old was, in short, a vastly experienced soldier and military commander of great capacity, and this had been recognised when, after commanding the 2/16th in the Middle East, he was promoted to Commander of the 21st Brigade.

Now at the beginning of his next important campaign, getting any solid information about the Kokoda Track was proving extremely

difficult. Shortly after arriving in Moresby, Potts had gone to New
Guinea Force Headquarters hoping they might be able to hand over
a document or dossier or some such detailing information on such
things as the military positions, native food sources, difficult terrain,
and so forth. In response, there was a fair amount of head scratching
and some nervous coughing, the upshot of which was that no such
document existed![133]

Despite the fact that the 49th Battalion had been in Moresby
for nigh on eighteen months by this time, they had never set *foot*
on the track leading to Kokoda. And no one had thought to collate
any of the information that had come back with the refugees from
the north coast who had made their way down the track, nor from
the medical evacuees from the 39th who had been out there on the
track for well over six weeks. There was no sense at all of a military
organisation that was, well, *organised*, and Potts left in high dudgeon.
In sheer desperation, he himself ventured a small way up the Kokoda
Track to the Imita Range, just to get some idea of what his men
faced.

CHAPTER TEN

HOLDING ON

Yes, you knew them well, the bank clerks, farmers and school-teachers; the factory workers, jackaroos and mechanics who go to make up 'our patrols'. But they have changed in some indefinable way since you last saw them . . . The evil vapours of the jungle, and feverish fires of malaria, have sapped the sun-bronze from their faces, have drawn their muscular bodies to sinew and whipcord: their faded green shirts and slacks are continuously mud-bespattered, clammy with sweat and rain.

The jungle stamps an indelible imprint on those who fight in it. But guts, endurance, self-sacrifice and initiative, all stretched to breaking point many a time, have left their imprint, too, so that a less war-weary age could say, 'These men have the look of great fighting men . . . '

Jungle Trail, 1943[134]

It had been another terrible day on the plateau at Kokoda, this tenth day of August 1942, with still no sign of the hoped-for reinforcements. Even though early in the morning an Allied plane had flown low over the valley, and a few of the Australians waved their hats and helmets, the plane just as quickly disappeared, somehow managing to give the impression that it really didn't care. And that was it. No more planes. No messages. No *nothin'*.

Back in Moresby, the reconnaissance plane reported that while there were a few Australians in possession of Kokoda, it was equally clear that the Japanese were pressing in on all sides. On the strength of this report, tentative plans to fly in men of the 49th Battalion to Kokoda were cancelled.

Once again the men of A Company felt abandoned, and more than a few felt that—in the vernacular of the times—they were 'up shit creek in a barbed wire canoe'. Down on the Japanese lines, however, the appearance of the plane hastened their soldiers to action once more. Though that plane hadn't landed, there was nothing to say a dozen of them might not suddenly appear and land with massive reinforcements, in which case all would be lost, and the need to dislodge the defenders became ever more urgent. After desultory pot shots during the day, in the last hour of light the Japanese began a collective cacophony of wailing, screaming and chanting, like ancient tribesmen whipping each other into a frenzy for the attack they were about to launch.

Then, at a sudden break in the chant, a thickly accented voice called out to the Australians: 'You don't like that, do you?'[135] As a matter of fact, Tojo was pretty right about that, because none of the Australians *were* too crazy about it. But seeing as this particular Jap spoke English and therefore probably understood it, many of the Diggers took the opportunity to express their own thoughts on the matter and to tell him just where he could stick his bloody bayonet and, while he was at it, to tell the murderous bastards he was with that they were gonna get their own throats slit before long! And so it went.

Really though, what the hell? In a choice between them screaming or shooting at you, the Australians would take screaming any day. The main thing was that Captain Symington had passed the word that, once it was dark, they were going to pull out anyway and get back to Deniki. Symington's reckoning was that while they had lost men and had not been reinforced, the likelihood was that the Japanese would have massed for a big attack that night and there was no point in getting themselves massacred. Besides that, they had no food left, bugger-all ammunition and their guns were beginning to jam for lack of oil. They had held the airfield for two days now without Moresby flying anything in to them, so what was the bloody point?

No point, cobber. Saddle up. We're out as soon as the captain gives the word.

At seven o'clock in the evening the captain gave the word. They moved out in three groups, with Lieutenant Brewer taking the front group with most of the firepower necessary to fight their way out if they had to. The middle group would have the wounded and Battalion Headquarters, and Sergeant Jim Cowey would take a few good volunteers with him to act as the rearguard and beat the beggars back if they tried to follow too closely behind.

Down in Melbourne at that very moment General Blamey was preparing for dinner. It had been a long day and had included a meeting with the prime minister and all six state premiers. They had discussed both the war effort in Australia and how Australian troops were faring overseas. Among other things, General Blamey had reported that the fighting around Kokoda was not particularly significant, nor important.[136]

The Australian soldiers got off the Kokoda plateau just in time. No sooner had the first two groups moved out just after seven o'clock than the Japs attacked the plateau like a bloody bunch of banzai banshees, charging all at once from every angle and firing as they came, screaming all the while. In the middle of it, Jim Cowey was with his rearguard and by this time they had also picked up a few stragglers who had become separated from the main group and were all dead on their feet.[137] With hell breaking out all around, it looked like they were dead, but ol' Jim didn't see it like that. Realising that in the limited light of the moon everyone was just a silhouette, and that the only way the Japs would know they were Australians would be if they started firing at them, he ordered his men to hold their fire and, get this, 'walk out'. And he was serious! Jim said that if they just kept their heads about them and acted like they had no fear, then the figures in the near distance scurrying hither and thither around the trenches the Australians had just abandoned would think they were Japs.

The men looked at him. Jim looked back at them. He really was serious. But given that no one had a better idea and it really was apparent that if they fired one shot in the direction of the invaders then the full might of Tojo would come down upon them, they really had no choice. So when Jim suddenly stepped out into the open from behind the rubber trees where they were sheltering and sauntered down the track, they quickly followed, waiting . . . waiting . . . waiting . . .

Waiting for the sound of a rifle shot and then searing pain somewhere on them before they died, they walked—with even those who were wounded in the legs trying to do so without a limp—their spines tingling for the shot, the shot, the shot . . . which never came. In no time at all they had crossed the airfield and were safe in the jungle, while the shouts of the Japs receded in the distance. Ol' Jim had known what he was about and when, a little while later, he told the men they would stop here for the night to try to recover, he didn't have to say it twice. In a small clearing just off the track they sank to the mud and were asleep within minutes. Jim, though, sat up through the night, keeping guard.

Some blokes called it a 'dingo's breakfast'—a bit of a scratch, a bit of a stretch, a bit of a fart and a bit of a look around. And that is pretty much what all three separated groups of A Company had on the morning of 11 August as they woke from a bitter night and continued to straggle by differing routes towards Deniki. There was nothing at all to eat and a hell of a long way to go so they just got on with it.

But jeez things could be a bugger sometimes. As the second group of A Company, with its wounded, was still on the hills looking back to Kokoda, they heard, and then saw something in the sky—planes. Two of them, coming in low over the valley without attempting to land, suddenly opened their doors and out rushed plentiful quantities of the very supplies they had been begging for, for days, but which were now tumbling into the grateful hands of the Japanese.

Back at Kokoda, Lieutenant Colonel Tsukamoto was mightily relieved, and not just for the manna which was suddenly so propitiously tumbling from the heavens. Given that, after everything, Buna had proved to be an unsuitable place for an airfield and the strategic value of Kokoda had thus increased hugely, in this man's army the loss of Kokoda would have left Lieutenant Colonel Tsukamoto with only one option: to commit harakiri. That would have involved him taking his bayonet, or an equally sharp knife, and plunging it into the left-hand side of his stomach before pulling it across to the right and then dragging it upwards. If he was still strong enough, he would then have to stab himself again just beneath the sternum, and drag it down to the first lateral cut, before slitting his own throat. All of it, as the samurai creed demanded, without uttering a cry . . .

But now that Kokoda was back in Japanese hands the need for such an extreme form of self-criticism had been averted.[138]

Yes, the Australian's counterattack had cost the Japanese two days on their schedule of advance, but that could be made up. And now, with their loss of the airstrip, the Australians' line of supply once again stretched all the way over the range to Port Moresby. The Japanese officers judged that if that tiny force of Australians was the best they could muster for such an important objective as the Kokoda airfield, then clearly their overall forces could not be too strong. In short, Tsukamoto was able to report to his superior back in Rabaul, General Horii, that there was no further impediment to sending the remaining forces of the South Seas Force down the track.

Not that he underestimated the fighting capacity of the individual Australian soldiers. Now that the Japanese were in possession of the terrain they had fought so hard for, he still found it hard to believe that such a small number of soldiers had been able to mount such a strong resistance. He was not alone. That night, in his small diary, a Lieutenant Onogawa of the 144th Regiment noted: 'Though the Australians are our enemies, they must be admired.'[139]

Halt.

The night after leaving Kokoda, and after a full day's trek and one battle with pursuing Japanese, Jim Cowey's rearguard group joined up with Captain Symington's group in the tiny village of Naro, to the west of the main track between Deniki and Kokoda. Captain Symington did not want to take the wounded men they were carrying to Deniki immediately, as it was likely that the Japanese would shortly attack there as well and he also wanted to give his men some respite.

Wonder of all wonders, though the Naro villagers had all disappeared with the sound of the gunfire nearby, they weren't far away, and when some of the braver souls decided the Australians weren't dangerous, and returned with no ill effect, it wasn't long before they all returned. That night, the exhausted Australian soldiers dined on vegetables from the village gardens and slept in huts—it was far and away the most comfortable night they had had in the past three weeks. The following morning a villager was sent to Deniki to pass the message to the rest of A Company that they were safe in Naro, but that they would need help to move the wounded any further.

It was far and away the most uncomfortable night he had spent for many a long time. Back in Port Moresby, Lieutenant General Sydney Rowell—Thomas Blamey's former chief of staff—had just arrived to take command of all forces in New Guinea. And just what had he let himself in for? Tossing and turning all night long in the wretched heat, he kept thinking back to early February, when he had personally signalled Major General Morris with a distinct warning:

'Japanese in all operations have shown inclination to land some distance from ultimate objective rather than make a direct assault. This probably because of need to gain airbases as well as desire to catch defences facing wrong way. You will probably have already considered possibility of landing New Guinea mainland and advance across mountains but think it advisable to warn you of this enemy course . . .'[140]

And so it had proved, and yet as far as he could see, Morris had done just about *nothing* to prevent exactly that taking place! What kind of mess had he inherited here?

With Rowell came General Tubby Allen, the commander of the 7th Division, whose men would shortly be arriving. It all meant that General Morris was now free to take over ANGAU, thus removing him from the frontline of military operations and leaving him in a far more administrative position.

On 13 August, these three military leaders, Rowell, Allen and Morris, had a meeting with Brigadier Arnold Potts to work out the next step. And that step was clear. It would be the job of the 21st Brigade—composed of the 2/14th, 2/16th and 2/27th battalions—to recapture the Kokoda airfield, which could then be used as a supply base and from which they would push the Japs all the way to the sea. The 53rd Battalion were already heading on their way up the track to try to help out, though they remained such a rag-tag bunch, with so little training, that—apart from a few genuinely good men and officers—there seemed little hope they would be able to make much difference. General Allen was forced to allow Potts only two of his three 21st Brigade battalions: the 2/14th and 2/16th. He required the 2/27th to stay in Port Moresby as the divisional reserve, pending events on the Kokoda Track and at Milne Bay.

There was, from that point, a great deal of discussion about the logistics of the operation, though the level of ignorance that still flourished about the Kokoda Track at this highest level of military command in New Guinea was staggering. Even after six weeks of having Australian soldiers in the field, seeing for themselves the lie of the land, General Tubby Allen continued to push the view that just one well-equipped and courageous platoon with enough grenades could hold the Kokoda Gap. And nor was his view singular. General MacArthur's chief of staff, for example, General Richard Sutherland, had sent word that the track to Kokoda passed through such a deep ravine that in one spot it might be 'blocked by demolition'. Genius![141]

Still, Potts thought to himself, if it were as simple as that, why hadn't it happened? He knew Australia had competent commanders in the field and courageous men. It seemed to him that if it had been possible to hold the Japanese at a point like that, Moresby would have already heard about it from the men in situ. He also didn't put a lot of store by Tubby Allen's view that the 'the Owen Stanleys are impassable'. It certainly hadn't seemed impassable to the Japanese, who had already made massive inroads into the range, and though he knew from his own venture up there that it was singularly difficult terrain, he set no confidence in the view that geography alone would beat the invaders. The whole track record of the Japs in the war to date had proven that they didn't regard anything as a physical obstacle and had been able to use that kind of thinking to their advantage.

For now, though, there was nothing for it but to get down to tintacks. By far the greatest problem with ensuring that his men would be an effective fighting force by the time they got to the Japanese was rectifying the supply problem. Sending close to one thousand men to the front meant that the demands on supply would be enormous, which was where Basil Morris came in. In his new role as the head of the ANGAU it would be his job and overall responsibility to ensure that, as the men of the 2/14th and 2/16th made their way forward, at least two planeloads of supplies would be dropped at Myola every day.

Potts was happy to hear it. But just in case there were any mishaps—and notwithstanding the fact that his men would be without porters to do a lot of the heavy lifting, as the 39th had been blessed with—Potts insisted that his men carry a fair measure of extra supplies. Experience told him the only way to be sure that

a soldier had the bare basics necessary for survival was for the
soldier to have them on his person.

Up at Eora Creek, just a day's march back from the Australian
frontlines, Doc Vernon had his hands full as never before. He was
trying to patch up the wounded well enough that they could continue
walking back to Moresby, while also looking after the porters, many
of whom were now breaking down. Time and again the porters
would reluctantly say to Doc, 'MI FILIM NOGUT, MI TUMAS
KOLT', they did not feel well and were very cold, and it was never
difficult to see why. Underfed, overworked, going without rest for
days on end, and often in the high climes that the lowlanders were
simply not used to, they were simply breaking down under the
strain.

It was usually the wounded soldiers who required the most urgent
attention, though, and with another orderly in the rough tent that
had been set up as their frontline 'hospital', the old doctor worked
eighteen to twenty hours a day, removing shrapnel and bullets,
cleaning wounds and sewing them up, fixing splints and trying to
deal with the endless cases of malaria that continued to blight the
fighting men. Even in the middle of the night he was not off duty.
One of the soldiers with him at this point, Sergeant Jack Sim of the
Signals Platoon, later told of being in a similar situation with Doc
at Efogi, sharing a hut built on stilts with him. It was a freezing
night up there in the highlands, and around three o'clock in the
morning Doc briefly disappeared, carrying his blanket, only to
return without it. Bert Kienzle was there too.

'Where's your BLANKET?' Bert shouted at him.

'Wrapped a carrier in it,' Doc replied matter-of-factly. 'Poor
devil, dying of pneumonia. All I can do is make him warm for his
last hours.'[142]

Bloody hell. Where's all the green? Where was the jungle? From
the decks of the ships *James Fenimore* and *James Wilson*, the first
view of New Guinea looked nothing like what the men of the 2/14th

and 2/16th had been expecting. It was now the height of the dry season and, from the deck, Moresby appeared brown and dusty, hot and listless, as they spied it across the skeletons of sunken ships that dotted the shore. It looked, frankly, about as welcoming as a German with a toothache in a bunker, and as the troops of the 2/14th made ready to disembark, the mood blackened a little.

For all that, Osmar White was there on the morning of 12 August when the ships pulled into Port Moresby Harbour, and was immediately impressed as the men of the 2/14th disembarked. As he would later describe it: 'These troops were tested and selected by war. They were scrawny, muscled and burned to the colour of leather by desert winds. There were no weeds among them. They betrayed no enthusiasm. They did not cheer and catcall. They knew what fighting meant and they were going to fight.'

By God they were. And they didn't really care what stories they heard from wild-eyed wounded shortly after arriving, stories about six-foot Japanese as strong as mallee bulls, who were also like snakes creeping silently on you in the night and slitting your throat in such a way that you wouldn't even cry out . . .

Yeah . . . bullshit. Maybe the Nips could do those kind of things to the Chocos, but not them. Now Australia had sent in *the men*. And how tough could the Japs really be if only the likes of the Chocos had held them up as long as they had?

By nightfall the battalions had been trucked to a camp at Itiki, at a spot about thirty miles northeast of Moresby. Potts had especially selected the site as a place where his men would have the best chance of staying clear of the nightmare of Moresby and its surrounding malarial swamps, while also being close to the beginning of the track leading to Kokoda.

In a strange kind of way, it was almost worse than a surprise attack. Back at Deniki, the troops with Major Cameron could see Kokoda with the naked eye in the distance, and the columns of tiny ant-like figures filing out, clearly heading their way. The weird thing was that even at that distance, those ants kinda looked *angry* and intent on doing them damage. It looked very much like the Japs were building for a major attack on their position and the Australian preparations for digging in became feverish. True, there were not a lot of them to defend their position, but they would simply have to make do. At least Deniki was on relatively high ground and marginally easier to defend than the Kokoda plateau; though the Australians were a much depleted and weaker force than they had been just four days previously before embarking on Major Cameron's foolhardy plan to retake Kokoda. Through the night, every sound, every creaking branch or broken twig, sounded to the soldiers like the Japanese Army massing on their perimeters. Maybe it was, and maybe it wasn't, but few got much sleep that night.

The following morning, they all waited for the attack to begin. Though they couldn't see them yet, they just knew the Japs were there. Among the defenders, Smoky Howson kept playing over and over in his head a scene that had occurred just a couple of months before he'd joined the 39th. He'd been with the 52nd Battalion for only a short time when they'd called for volunteers to join the 39th and go overseas, and he'd put his hand up. Then, just before he was about to depart, the word came through that the government had decided that because he grew vegetables, he was classified as being a part of 'essential services' and would have to return to the market gardens. Well, Smoky had kicked up such a stink that the officer in charge of placements had spat back at him, 'Oh, if you want to go and get yerself bloody well killed, well we won't stop you. Off you go then!'[143] And off he'd gone. And now here he was. Jammed into a hole in the ground, while the Japs came ever closer. It was the waiting which killed him most, because it gave a bloke time to think, and once you started thinking you realised you were shit scared.

But now, and here was the strangest thing of all, once the Japs started firing there was never any time to be frightened. When the attack started it was almost a relief. Like now . . .

The first mortars started coming in, someone yelled 'Take cover!' and Smoky felt an immediate calm come over him.

In this early morning of 13 August, the Japanese were hitting Deniki with force, peppering the Australians with sniper fire, pounding them with mortars and constantly probing their perimeters, looking to exploit any weakness. Now experienced in the ways of the Japanese, though, the Australians followed orders and held their fire until such times as they had an absolute bead on a Japanese soldier. Earlier in the campaign they had learnt that one of the key Japanese tactics in such situations was to put out a heavy blanket of fire with the sole purpose of drawing Australian fire in return, which would allow the Japs to determine their position. But not this time, Tojo. Conscious that even one shot in retaliation risked bringing a mortar on their heads, the Australians simply gritted their teeth and lay doggo, waiting for the Japs to get to close enough quarters that mortars were useless and it no longer mattered that the Australians were giving away their positions. Still, if the opportunity to fire before that was too good to miss, they at least moved quick smart away from the point they fired from, for fear of the mortar which would likely soon be heading their way. Another thing the Australians had learned was to paste mud over their gun barrels so that no stray ray of sunlight could shine off the barrel and needlessly give away their position.

When the Japs really were close it was on for young and old, and no one was seen to be sending more lead their way than Smoky Howson. Though remaining absolutely dead calm inside, he just kept firing, all the time firing, pausing only to reload, and had gone through twenty magazines before his position became too hot and he had to move back momentarily. He must'a killed *dozens* of them.

Another all but on the spot, and one of the few officers Smoky really liked, was a former AIF bloke by the name of 'Tubby' Jacobs who had witnessed it all and promoted Smoky to corporal, adding that he was going to nominate him for the Military Medal.

For the 39th's B Company in this engagement there would be no such nominations for medals as, still in disgrace—at least in Major Cameron's eyes—they were kept well back from the front line of the Deniki battle in nominal reserve.

To the north of Deniki at that time, still at Naro, Captain Symington's A Company heard the fighting and wisely decided to detour around Deniki. Not only were they exhausted and laden down with their wounded, but they were unlikely to have been able to make any impact against the attacking Japanese, who would most certainly have set up ambushes against any Australian force coming from their direction. By an alternative track, they pushed on to the next village back down the track, Isurava.

Back at Deniki the Diggers fought on, with surely the most extraordinary episode occurring around noon. After a furious fire-fight, some quiet had suddenly descended and for the life of him, Lieutenant Don Simonson, in a far forward position on the eastern flank, swore he could hear Japanese happily chatting somewhere nearby. Carefully, oh so carefully, he inched his way forward, slowly lifted his head above a bluff of rock and saw a dozen Japanese soldiers having lunch! For dessert he gave them two lobbed grenades before scurrying back to his position . . . and it was on again. (Lieutenant Simonson would later be awarded the Military Cross for his bravery in action on this occasion.)

By the morning of 14 August, Major Cameron knew there was no way his men could hold on to Deniki for another day. The Japanese now controlled the high ground overlooking the Australians' defensive positions and were beginning to push through the perimeters. Staying there meant certain annihilation. One more time, they would have to withdraw, and get back to Isurava. The major managed to get a brief message to Port Moresby advising them of his decision, concluding with the heartfelt words: 'We have done our best.'[144]

Quickly, almost in a scramble, the Australians moved back, taking as much food and ammo as they could carry—Smoky set the record by carrying 1100 rounds in bandoliers around his neck— but unfortunately they were still obliged to leave a lot of their equipment and ammunition behind. Also, some of their number became isolated from the main body of retreating troops and would have to fight their way both through the jungle and against Japanese patrols to reach Isurava. But the job was done. For the most part the Australians had survived, and lived to fight another battle. Even for those who were still relatively strong though, it was a long haul. Isurava was well up into the highlands, thousands of feet above Deniki and perched on the steep side of the first of the Owen Stanley Range when approaching from the north—getting there was one hell of a climb.

Back in General MacArthur's Headquarters in Brisbane, the mood was grim when the news got through. On the situation map, the tiny little flag indicating the furthest reaches of the Japanese forces moved half an inch closer to Moresby, while the Australian flag moved half an inch backwards, always backwards. What was wrong with these Australians? Why didn't they fight like men? If only, thought, MacArthur if *only* he had some marines, some American fighting men ready to go, he really would be able to turn the situation around.

Happily though, that moment was not far off. Even then, two divisions of American infantry were training in Queensland, and MacArthur was waiting for the right moment to throw them into the fray and really show these *'Ossies'* how to fight. If all went according to MacArthur's plans once the Australians had stopped the Japanese advance down the track, the Americans could counter-attack and chase them all the way back to the sea whence they came. And *that* would provide some choice raw material for absolutely stunning communiqués from the good general . . .

A small parenthesis here. Among Australia's leading politicians and military officers, there was an equal impatience to see American troops thrown into the fray. Shortly after MacArthur had arrived in Australia, he had journeyed to Canberra and, in his address to the assembled politicians, had declared that, 'as a soldier on a great crusade we shall win or we shall die, and to this end I pledge you all the resources of all the mighty power of my country and all the blood of my countrymen . . . '[145]

To this point though, however much American resources had been appreciated, in terms of Australia's key military action in New Guinea, it had really only been Australian blood that had been spilled. And way too much of it. Close parenthesis.

Now the Australian forces gathered at Isurava and began to dig in for the next, inevitable, Japanese assault. To give the Australians more time, Captain Max Bidstrup, with two platoons of his D Company, set up an ambush on the track to Deniki one hour's march north of Isurava to knock over the first of the Japanese who came their way. They did not have to wait long. On the morning of 15 August, D Company's ambush accounted for some eight Japanese deaths. The Japanese fell back to regroup. Captain Bidstrup called his own men back to set up another ambush. So it went. Simply slowing the Japanese advance and blunting their thrust with their every probe forward was, as ever, a victory in itself.

It was the question that Osmar White simply couldn't hold in any longer. What the hell was the 21st Brigade doing going all the way up there anyway? Why take them on so far from Moresby when it had to be obvious that the advantage would be with the Australians if they chose a battlefield far from the Japanese beachhead and close to the Allied supply dumps?

Lieutenant General Sydney Rowell, the new commander of the New Guinea Force was, whatever else, an honest, straightforward man who never beat about the bloody bush and he told it to the journalist straight: 'As far as I'm concerned, I'm willing to fight and let the enemy have the rough stuff if he wants it. I'm willing to present the Jap with the supply headaches I've got. But there are those who think otherwise. We need a victory in the Pacific and a lot of poor bastards have got to get killed to provide it.'[146]

Nor did Rowell try to hide from the fresh troops just what kind of battle they had in front of them. For Damien Parer's great friend from Tobruk, the ABC correspondent Chester Wilmot, had now arrived in New Guinea and was present a couple of days later when

Rowell addressed the assembled troops, in more or less their own vernacular.

'You're going to have a tough walk in,' he told them. 'You'll need to be fit and you should be. But you'll have to walk hard so don't think you're in for an easy time. Yes, I know what you're thinking, "That's all right for the old bastard, he hasn't got to do it himself." That is as it may be but I know you'll do the job well. Don't overestimate this little man. Whenever we've met him on equal terms we've cracked him hard. You've seen these Japs before the war—if you met him in a pub, you'd kick the bottoms off the little buggers—go and do that now.'[147]

Potts himself also had a word with a combined gathering of the 2/14th and 2/16th before they left, to give them a better idea of just what they would be facing. As a rule, the men loved Potts and his quiet but effective way of going about things, sprinkled liberally with his very good sense of humour. In a way he was an *Australian's* Australian Army officer in that he depended less on the pips on his shoulder to have his men's respect and more on his manner and presence. When Potts talked you listened, not because you had to but because he was worth listening to. On this occasion Potts took the men into his confidence.

He acknowledged that the issue of supply was difficult, but expressed his confidence that it would all be sorted out by the time they got to Myola. What he wanted them to know was their overall goal: they were personally going to relieve the 39th, counterattack the Japs, retake Kokoda itself and then keep going so hard they would push all the way back down the track and 'drive the Japs into the sea at Buna and Gona'.

The latest intelligence assessments at GHQ had the number of Japs on site as 1500 which, while considerable, was far from insurmountable. Pound for pound, Potts knew the Australians were better fighters than the invaders and he felt great confidence that they would do themselves and their country proud.

And yet one more bloke talked to the Australian soldiers before they departed. His name was Tom Grahamslaw and he was apparently some local cove, vastly experienced in the territory they would be travelling to, and would be attached henceforth to Brigade Headquarters as a kind of adviser.

In the early evening, the young ANGAU officer spoke knowledgeably about what the track would be like, how best to traverse it while conserving as much of your energy as possible, and how to maximise your chances of survival in the jungle. If there was a point Tom particularly emphasised, it was that the terrain they were heading into was nothing like what they were used to in Greece and Syria, and they had to be prepared for that. And whatever else, the soldiers had to make sure they treated both the natives they came across in the highlands, and the porters, with *respect*. The natives were good people, and deserved to be so treated, but they were also people that the Australians were relying on and it would be damaging on all fronts to get their backs up.

Maybe his speech helped, maybe it didn't. But what Tom saw as he looked out was a bunch of blokes who exuded, above all, confidence. They clearly felt that whatever the track could throw at them, they were up to it.

Dismissed.

Ugh. The news was bad. An officer from the New Guinea Force Headquarters came up and gravely informed Brigadier Potts that, as it turned out, his men might be facing many more than the 1500 Japanese soldiers they'd estimated. Some last-minute intelligence reports had come in putting the original number considerably higher and adding that the coastwatchers had just reported that the Japs might have landed as many as four thousand extra fresh troops. Potts took it on board, but did not alter his essential plan. If there were more Japs on their way, it was all the more urgent for the Australians to get to the front quickly and get started, claiming as much valuable terrain as possible. And besides, Potts counted on having his third battalion, the 2/27th up there soon. It was just a question of more Japs to kill than he'd thought.

That night, the final night before the 2/14th headed off to they knew not what, Brigadier Potts did what most of the men, whatever their rank, did. He wrote to his wife back in Perth, and it was the last letter she received for some time. In his careful copperplate that night he started.

Sweetheart,

Can just squeeze in a line before it gets dark and the lamps are frowsy in any case . . .

Such lots and lots of things I see and want to share with you, marvellous views, colours, groups of people and thousand and one things that delight the eye, and I try and tell you at the time but it isn't quite, not quite as nice as a squeeze of the hand and 'It's lovely, Bill.' You darling . . .

We're on our toes, in the chocks and aching to go . . . My dear delight. I've only odd waking moments to dream of you and worship the memory of you.

At night I sleep so solidly that I just don't dream and when I wake it is too late. Oh yes, I know if you were near it would be different. Did you ever work out what a nuisance you were to an early rising cocky?

Has shearing been started at Percy's yet? Don't overdo things Belovedest. There is only one of you in the world. How are the bairns and Dad? Has he kept fairly fit or slipped back again? Can't see the paper so goodnight Valiant Heart.

I love you,

Bill [148]

Sealing it up, he kissed the envelope, put it aside for his orderly to post and turned in for the night. Tomorrow was going to be a big day.

He couldn't believe his eyes. In the early morning, General Rowell had just been driving past Seven Mile Airfield when he saw the most extraordinary thing. American transport aircraft. All together.

Neatly lined up, side by side in two rows with each wing-tip almost touching the wing of the plane next to it. In peacetime it would have been perfect, an indication of a well-run operation with an emphasis on order and neatness. In wartime, especially given the recent experience at Clark Airfield in the Philippines, it was insanity! Here they were, presenting a neat target for enemy bombers. With twenty planes sufficiently spread out, and put in the revetments that the Diggers had so laboriously built, it would take twenty bombs to destroy. But all put together like this it would take just one well-placed bomb and the whole lot would go up. It was for this reason that the generally mild-mannered Rowell was unusually forceful when speaking to the American Commanding Officer, General Ennis Whitehead, later in the morning. Though it went against the grain to be just about taking orders from an *Australian*, Whitehead gradually took his point and promised that the planes would be immediately dispersed.

Osmar White and Damien Parer were among a group of correspondents who went up to watch the departure of the 2/14th up the 'Kokoda Track', as it was becoming known. They arrived in the back of a truck about an hour after first light on Sunday 16 August—an unusually lovely day, with barely a cloud in the sky, as if all were right with the world.

And sure enough there they all were. An entire acre of a beautiful green meadow flanked by rubber trees was filled with Australian soldiers, each making final preparations for the long haul ahead. As White noted, 'their shirts were off and their backs were sun-tanned, rippling with muscle. They had set up Bren guns against surprise strafing—an automatic precaution that marked them as veterans. Some were singing, some writing letters home. One group had borrowed a small grindstone from the plantation house and were sharpening their bayonets, slouch hats pulled rakishly down and their eyes bright and reflective.'[149]

It was an impressive scene and White had no doubt that he was looking at one of the finest bodies of fighting men in the world.

The men looked every inch the epitome of bronzed Australian manhood that morning. Strong, tall, straight of back, clear of eye, purposeful. There was a bloody tough job to do and they were the men to do it. They had trained for this campaign and they were ready for it. But still . . .

But still, for the first time Osmar had a few doubts. Yes, these blokes were strong, but they were carrying packs filled with bedding, clothing, mess tins, half dixie, groundsheet, ammunition, five days' worth of biscuits and bully beef—and all of it put together, with the steel helmets perched atop their heads, weighing sixty-five pounds! That very morning, each man had been issued with an extra bandolier of fifty rounds of ammunition, just on the off-chance that there was some problem with supplies at Myola. And some men, besides, were also obliged to carry either mortars or mortar ammunition, while still others were laden down with signals equipment.

Having himself experienced the kind of track they were about to travel, Osmar White wondered whether they could travel it and still be in shape for the fight when they arrived. And while they really were accomplished veterans of battle in the Middle East, the fact that they had their shirts off showed they were neophytes in New Guinea where the tiniest sting of a mosquito could bring the same result as a bullet from a Japanese Juki machine gun. And of those Japanese guns, White already knew, there would be many, and they would be manned by ruthless veterans in their own right.

There was no way around it. As he gazed out upon the assembled soldiery he could not escape the thought, as he later recounted, 'of how many of them would never again see this quiet grove, the trees tinged with red with brief winter, or feel the caress of the coarse grass, or lie on their backs watching the trade-wind clouds race over a sunny sky.'[150]

Certainly White wasn't alone in wondering exactly that. And the army itself had already taken some precautions. Each soldier about to head off into the 'Jaws of Hell' had two identity discs hanging around his neck; these were known to the soldiers themselves as 'dead meat tickets'. If a man was killed, one of the discs would be left in his mouth to allow the clean-up brigade to identify his name, army number and religion, while the other would be handed to the commanding officer as proof of the death. It also bore a man's blood group, as an aid to the medical corps if he was so badly injured that he couldn't speak for himself.

On that same morning, some four hundred miles to the northwest, there was a lot of action down at the principal pier of Rabaul's magnificent Simpson Harbour. Yet *more* crack Japanese troops of the South Seas Force—these ones entirely unknown to Australian Intelligence or the coastwatchers—were being loaded onto ships for the short trip to Gona. Just before filing up the gangplank, each Japanese soldier turned and made a deep ritual bow in the direction of the Emperor's palace in Tokyo, then turned and walked up into the hot, humid holds of the ship.

These reinforcements, ordered by General Horii, were soon ready and, shortly, two full battalions of the 41st Regiment would be on their way south to mop up what was left of the Australian resistance. They would sail fully laden with 230 horses and 175 Rabaul natives to help move supplies and construct roads.

Most nervous were the natives. Never in their lives had they left the environs of their island, and now they were being herded on to some kind of massive vessel, taken to an unknown fate, by these evil men who had so recently invaded their tranquillity. Not even the point of a bayonet could make them go into the hold of the ship, so they were left on the deck in the charge of Second Lieutenant Noda Hidetaka. He knew he shouldn't, but Hidetaka looked upon the whimpering, fearful natives with some sympathy. What was *wrong* with him? Why did he get these feelings of concern for others, when it was against everything he had been trained for? It was like what happened at a recent sick parade, as he had recently confided to his diary:

'Today the Medical inspection of those weakened by sickness was carried out to determine whether or not they are sufficiently fit for battle. The leaders of our company were present . . . I myself am inclined to leave behind many of those who are not really fit. Can it be that I am not sufficiently ruthless? It is a matter regarding which some self examination is necessary. I am worried because I cannot unconcernedly overlook another's troubles . . . I feel that I am becoming detached from my comrades through insufficient mental discipline. Diligent people talk of their hopes. Lazy people bemoan their misfortunes. I will rectify my lack of mental discipline by diligence and industry.'[151]

Just like he had been taught. But for now there was nothing for it but to settle in with the nervous natives and hope that he could summon the required ruthlessness once they landed and started the campaign proper against the Australians.

The ship ploughed through the night, heading south—south to the coast of New Guinea.

CHAPTER ELEVEN

A WEARY WAY TO GO . . .

Kono kuso ame!

> While the Japanese language has no real equivalent to the western notion of swearing, this phrase loosely translates to 'this shitty rain!'

I remember from the time I met Ralph Honner I felt a new course of blood. I thought he was the best battalion commander I ever had the privilege to serve under. He was just a man who knew where he was going and what he was doing, and never had to put on any airs and graces . . .

Lieutenant Hugh Dalby, MC, 39th Battalion[152]

Heading north, north to the highlands of New Guinea, there was no doubt that the men of the 2/14th were far more prepared than the 39th who had ventured up this same track six weeks earlier. At least the 2/14th departed *knowing* that there was a serious battle ahead. More than that, some of the experience gained by the 39th had been passed on, including the fact that the Japanese snipers seemed to focus on officers. As a countermeasure, it was deemed prudent that officers should remove any identifying insignia of their rank, that they forbear to wear pistols and instead carry rifles like the ordinary soldiers, and furthermore that they no longer be addressed as 'Captain', 'Lieutenant', 'Major' etc, but instead be called by their nicknames.[153]

Finally, letters written, guns checked, prayers said, packs hoisted. Time to move out. With which, platoon by platoon, 554 men of the 2/14th began their trek, leaving Ilolo at 9.00 a.m. on Sunday 16 August 1942. They were under the direct command of Colonel Arthur Key, who had assumed command just after their return from the Middle East. He was a very softly spoken, very efficient officer of the old school, who worked well with Potts. Whatever the new orders about calling officers by their nicknames, with Key it would never stick. He was not a 'one-of-the-boys'-type officer and didn't want to be, and the men who served under him did not mind.

He was a good cove and they were happy to serve under him, none more so than Stan Bisset who was both the intelligence and quartermaster officer, and was responsible for reconnoitring ahead of the main body of men and establishing facilities at each staging post. Given that Stan was also among the physically fittest of the 2/14th, he had no trouble pushing well ahead to ensure that all was in order, that the campsites were marked out, that each staging post had plenty of salt tablets ready for when the men arrived, and so forth. This meant, of course, that in the first instance, he had no idea of just what scenes were occurring behind him with both the 2/14th, and those who set off the following day, the 2/16th . . .

For whatever their physical fitness and innate strength, the AIF men were doing it tough, and no mistake—in many ways even tougher than had the 39th. Without porters, the experienced army men were—to use their own expression—'boonging' it, carrying their own supplies. As Osmar White had feared, some were weighed down with as much as seventy pounds of extras. It was a wonder they could move at all, let alone climb and descend a jungle track that, at its highest, reached some 6000 feet.

And when the 39th had crossed the Owen Stanleys, there hadn't been enough of them to really chew up the ground. But now, with upwards of a thousand men trudging along the same narrow wet track, the roots and undergrowth that had once held the path together had been broken apart. This meant that the wet ground in the lower sections soon became mud, mud soon became quagmire, and quagmire soon became something that their boots would sink into up to the ankles, requiring them to suck their feet out again to take the next step, before the whole process was repeated once more.

Also, their boots, which had been so well designed for the Syrian desert, lacked sufficient tread to grip the slippery slopes of the muddy track, and time and again men would use their last resources of energy to conquer a particular bluff only to slip and slide back down the slope to start again. The worst of it was when one man fell and took out the man behind him, who 'dominoed' into the one behind him, and so on. Those who tried to get a little off the beaten track where it was possible to escape the mud, soon found a mass of spiderwebs and enormous spiders waiting right at face height. More than one soldier would 'lose it', falling screaming to the ground trying to scrabble the spider from his face.

Maybe in the stress of it all, some of the soldiers cried, but no one could ever tell. The infernal, eternal, rain kept falling. It joined the sweat from their bodies to ensure that their clothing was completely soaked through all the time, making them even heavier and meaning they sweated even more.

Arnold Potts—carrying his own fully laden pack—started with the 2/16th, but quickly moved ahead, as he was keen to get to Myola before the main body of men and ensure that everything was in order with the crucial supplies. As he moved forward he saw scenes that both amazed and depressed him. Time after time, he would come to a tough part of the climb and see ashen-faced men lying down and gasping for air. Certainly they would straighten up at his sight and try to regain their feet, but there was no doubt that some were simply incapable of it.

Men had become so exhausted that not even the great Australian cure-all of a good cuppa tea did anything for them. Many would vomit it up, on the grounds that their bodies were entirely rejecting anything except lying rigid on the ground and not moving one wretched muscle.

Potts shook his head time and again, wondering in just what state the men would be when they finally got to the front. He pushed on, though at one point on the morning after he set off, he looked up after hearing the distinctive buzz of Japanese planes high overhead. The sound receded to the south in the direction of Moresby, and not long afterwards they heard the sounds of distant explosions . . .

Major General Morris had a serious temper going. Since suffering the recent humiliation of having his command effectively taken away and handed to General Rowell, he pretty much always had a temper going, just on principle. Then he heard them. Plane engines, and not just *any* plane engines. This was not the reassuring and rather thrilling throb of the Kittyhawks as they returned from their missions, it was the infernal high-pitched screaming of Japanese bombers and Zeros making one more raid on Seven Mile Airfield.

It was ten o'clock on the morning of 17 August, and if any of the thirty-five Japanese bomber pilots coming out of the high clouds had had the pleasure and privilege of taking out Clark Airfield in the Philippines eight months ago, they surely would have felt a sense of déjà vu . . . *Unbelievably*, right down there on the tarmac, neatly lined up in two tight rows almost as if they were begging to be bombed were no fewer than twenty-seven planes. In one line were the Dakota C47 'biscuit bombers', while right next to them were the famed Flying Fortresses, laden with fuel and bombs.

For the skilled Japanese pilots, it took just one quick, clean run to drop every bomb they had on, or within damaging distance of, the target, and by the time they were gone three Flying Fortresses had been entirely destroyed, as had all the Dakota C47 transports, while ten other planes of the same stripes had been so badly damaged that they were out of commission well into the immediate future.

When Osmar White and Damien Parer screamed to a halt in a commandeered jeep just ten minutes later, the whole airfield was a chaotic scene of billowing black smoke rising above reddish-yellow dust, ongoing explosions, panic, flames, and trucks and men going every which way trying to regain control of a situation which was approximating hell on earth. Somehow, General Rowell's earlier order that all planes be placed at a considerable distance from each other simply hadn't been followed.

Cometh the hour, cometh the man. The hour was one o'clock, on this hot August day, and the man was Lieutenant Colonel Ralph Honner. A softly spoken but highly accomplished AIF officer from Perth, he had worked as a schoolteacher, solicitor and barrister before distinguishing himself in the Middle East, Greece and Crete.

Straight of back, clear of eye, fit as a trout, he walked into the village of Isurava—where the 39th were then preparing to make their stand—and went straight up to a group of officers. They looked at him. He looked at them. It was a friendly appraisal from both sides, though the group was entirely ignorant of who he was or what he was about. The main thing they noted about this neat, fit-looking fellow was that he was a high-ranking officer, and thus their deference was automatic.

'Can I help you in any way?' Lieutenant Keith Lovett asked the newcomer pleasantly.

'Yes, I'm Lieutenant Colonel Honner, and I'm your new commanding officer . . .'[154]

There was a stir among the men, as to this point there had been no warning that Major Cameron was about to be relieved of his command of the 39th—not that they were particularly sad to hear it as Cameron had never quite 'taken' as their leader. This new chappie, though, was one of those rare birds who gave out an air of friendly knockabout competence even before he had said a word, while still having a commanding presence. All up, he made a very good impression from the first. He'd arrived with no large retinue of staff, no bugles, no hoopla, just one aide and a very engaging presence.

Colonel Honner, *Sir*, it was then. Lieutenant Lovett introduced himself more formally and asked how the colonel would like to get started.

'Well, I'd like you to take me around and introduce me to the company commanders and we'll settle down and start our business . . . '

That business, Honner quickly made clear, was to follow his orders—orders that they halt the Japanese advance to Isurava until such times as the AIF could arrive and push the enemy back down the track all the way to Gona.

And so it began. Lovett showed Honner around, and while the battalion seemed to take a shine to him immediately, Colonel Honner's own views about *them* were not quite as admiring. Quietly, and privately, he was appalled.[155] The men he was surveying were ragtag, physically exhausted, and weakened by weeks of fighting without sufficient sleep or food, and by merely existing in appalling conditions.

By burning day and freezing night these boys—for that was pretty much what most of them seemed to be—had been lashed by rains, stunned by sun, shot at, bombed, starved and bitten by bugs unknown. They had hollow eyes, rotting boots and foul, ragged uniforms, most of which had not been washed for the full forty days since they had last seen Port Moresby. Compared with the AIF men he'd commanded in the Middle East, the men of the 39th also seemed amazingly small physically, somehow as if their stature had been diminished by living in a jungle where everything else grew with such abundance. Aces were high, dysentery low, gangrene was trumps and death had a reserved seat at the table.[156]

The one saving grace was that these fellows of the 39th still seemed plucky. They did not have anything of the beaten-dog look about them, even though they clearly had a right to it. The colonel still heard plenty of talk of having 'another crack at the Japs', and 'giving it to those yellow bastards this time'.

In a way they were reminiscent of some of the final lines of the great Australian poem, 'The Man From Snowy River', concerning the mount which had done so well tearing up and down the mountains, but was now very much the worse for wear:

> But his hardy mountain pony he could scarcely raise a trot,
> He was blood from hip to shoulder from the spur;
> But his pluck was still undaunted, and his courage fiery hot,
> For never yet was mountain horse a cur.

Colonel Honner woke the next morning—on his thirty-eighth birthday, 17 August—feeling better after a good night's sleep and welcomed by a moment of rare, benign sunshine. It looked like a good day to begin doing what had to be done: preparing to defend Isurava against the inevitable Japanese attack which would shortly be coming their way.

On that same morning, some thirty miles to the north, General Horii was setting foot on New Guinea soil for the first time, landing at Buna with the remaining two battalions of the 144th Infantry Regiment, as well as ancillary units of mountain artillery, signals, munitions and Ack-Ack guns—some three thousand fresh troops in all.

And yet, despite these fresh supplies, General Horii was not without his own problems. Though all around him at that moment he had everything a fighting man could need, from fresh ammunition and clothing to bountiful food, he too faced the problem of getting those supplies to his men at the front. When the first of his troops had embarked up the track almost a month before, they had been issued with just ten days' rations on the reckoning that that would be more than sufficient to get them through to Moresby. But now, the extraordinary Australian resistance meant that they were way behind schedule and it was now clear that the Japanese had to either crush the Australians quickly and force their way through or . . . or, he wasn't sure what. Failure to achieve the objective had never even been considered. There was nothing for it but to get his men off the ships as quickly as possible and move them up the track. As to his own means of transport, well, that was being unloaded before his eyes—a superb white stallion that he had brought all the way from Japan and which had become his signature with the troops.

Dawn. The high ranges of New Guinea, just north of the village of Menari. The first strains of light reveal slightly stirring clumps on the jungle floor. They are the men of the 2/14th, who, at last light of the previous day, had more or less dropped exhausted where they fell, with barely enough strength to pull their ground sheets and half-blankets around their bodies as some protection from the endless rain.

Now, a piercing whistle reverberates through the clearing. It is a whipbird, just warming up for what will soon be an endless cacophony of calls throughout the day, but still that does not wake the exhausted men. What does, is the sergeant major, moving quietly from bundle to bundle, giving them a quiet shake to indicate that the day has begun and that they will shortly move out. As the men emerge from their bundles one by one to head off to nearby trees to perform their ablutions, they look like nothing so much as baby giraffes, tottering uncertainly on legs they are not at all sure of, as their whole bodies rebel against any instruction to move again. But move they do, bit by bit, murmuring the odd 'g'morning' to each other. The company now has the fire going, the billy is soon boiling, and their breakfast biscuit will soon be washed down with scalding black tea as the first of the men move out. Before they know it, it's on again, all the slithering and sliding and sucking it up, just to try to keep going. Somehow, through it all, the men of the AIF kept moving along the track, towards their goal of relieving the 39th and their own task of sending the Japs back to the sea.

Amid the exhaustion of it all, one thing among many particularly worried the Australians—their khaki clothing. It had been perfect for the desert sands of Syria where they blended into the background, but it was hopeless for the dark green jungle where they stood out from as much as a mile away. As one lot of Diggers got to the top of a hill, they could look across a valley and clearly see the bunch of Diggers ahead of them on the next hill, shining like lighthouses on a dark night. They presented, in short, perfect targets. And on top of all that, such lightweight fabric did not protect them from the cold nights, which at the high altitude of the highlands could get very chilly indeed.

While the men of the 39th had experienced exactly the same problems, and simply accepted it, neither the 2/14th nor the 2/16th were so disposed. Something had to be done before they got into action and, typically, something *was* done. At night, after their meagre dinner was eaten, the massive cooking pots were commandeered and water boiled up in them. When it had come to a rolling boil, large chunks of jungle foliage were thrown in, and the khakis thereafter. It worked, a little. At the least the uniforms' khaki colour was dulled to a more greenish hue, and as the 2/14th pressed on day after day they began to blend in a little more with the jungle around.

Every battlefield, every topographical feature on the earth's surface, comes replete with its own natural defences, shelters, avenues of attack, escape and so forth. Ralph Honner liked to expend considerable energy examining the battlefield for such features before configuring and placing his troops for strategic advantage. This is why he spent most of the morning of 18 August walking around with his senior officers, looking things over.

The village of Isurava had some two hundred natives in times of peace, but as was consistent in the whole Kokoda campaign, they had simply disappeared the moment the fighting and soldiers had got close. The grass huts they left behind would have absolutely no chance of stopping any bullets, but they were useful for obscuring the enemy's vision along certain sightlines and for providing a place for the severely wounded to shelter from the incessant rain.

The warpath that was the Kokoda Track ran in the north/south direction, right on the western side of the village, which was in itself perched on the side of a hill. On the northern perimeter of Isurava there was a large vegetable garden which then gave way to dense rainforest. On the southern perimeter the forest came right to the village edge. Two creeks, which became known to the soldiers as 'front creek' and 'rear creek'—with front creek on the northern side, closest to the Japanese—ran roughly along the northern and southern perimeters in an easterly direction down into the Eora Valley, providing additional obstacles for any invading force to get across. On the eastern side of the village the ground was thickly wooded, with a very steep slope also leading to the valley floor below.

The Australians expected that the Japanese would attack from the western side of the village, where the ground was higher and the forest more sparse. An expanse of relatively open ground between the forest and the perimeter would also allow the Japanese to mass their troops before sending them charging at the Australian defences across easier ground.

Which company of the 39th to put on this, then, the battalion's most vulnerable front? Honner had no doubt. When he had taken over command of the 39th the previous day, he had had a brief meeting with the outgoing Major Cameron, who had once more been scathing in his assessment of B Company who, in his view, had so woefully failed at Oivi and Kokoda. His strong recommendation was that B Company be broken up and scattered into the other companies as reinforcements.[157]

Honner had listened carefully and considered the recommendation, but now, after consultations with his senior officers and some deep thought on his own part, decided to do quite the opposite. Instead of obliterating B Company, he would give them the position of greatest honour and responsibility—he would give them the western perimeter of Isurava, the position which would be guaranteed to take the most heat and the one which had to be held at all costs.

Honner's view was not only that Major Cameron's assessment might have been a bit harsh from the outset—the bulk of B Company had acquitted themselves well—but also that he simply couldn't afford to have one company cease to exist in a situation where the

Australians were already likely to be outnumbered by a factor of five to one. He had to make the most of what he had, trust in the men, and ask them to put their best foot forward. To bolster B Company further he put Lieutenant Bevan French at their command, in place of Sam Templeton. Honner had met French only the day before, but already liked the cut of his jib, and that was that.

From the first, the decision to give B Company the hardest but most crucial assignment looked to be inspired. For, from the moment Honner explained to them that they were the ones upon whom the whole battalion was relying, it seemed like the men of B Company grew another foot taller.

As to the other areas of the perimeter, E Company was allocated the northern side to the left, which fronted onto both the village garden and the track which went towards Deniki, while C Company took over the northern side on the right, D Company took the southern side facing the exceptionally dense rainforest, and A Company had the eastern flank above the steep slope. The area to be defended by the whole battalion was no more than five hundred yards across in any direction, and against the possibility that the Japanese were able to break through in any sector, Honner organised for a reserve of two platoons to be on standby to immediately move to stem the breach.

On the frontlines the men had to be spread widely enough to cover the whole perimeter, but still close enough that the arcs of fire from their guns interlocked each other. It was all about setting up a defensive structure so that each man supported the one next to him, and that each section, platoon and company did the same. Again and again and again over the ensuing days, Honner made the 39th practise manoeuvres designed to plug any holes in the perimeter. With one group pretending to be the storming Japanese, each company had to work out precisely what its men would do if that happened; how they would fire to cut down the infiltrators and precisely whose responsibility it would be to hurl them back.

Honner further drilled into his men the necessity of understanding that whenever the Japs probed one position and were stopped, they always sent out flanking movements, and if you were prepared for that, you could be there waiting for them. And what if this section was in danger of being wiped out altogether? How would his mobile unit be contacted? Where would they go once they arrived? Was this unit familiar with the terrain? No. Well let's get them here so they can work things out.

Little by little as they practised, Honner could feel the confidence growing and was satisfied. In his view confidence was everything, as with it men would fight and support each other, whereas without it, the battle was already lost.

As part of the same program, Honner ensured that, apart from the foxholes the 39th had dug and were manning, they also had fall-back foxholes to retreat to should the Japanese fire become too withering. And one other thing. He wanted all their foxholes to be dug *deep*. Just one look at the way they had been constructed to this point told him they were too shallow and he wouldn't have it.

The difference between being able to hold a position and having to abandon it, the likely difference between life and death itself, may well be the simple extra effort to get the thing done right in the first place, and that is what they were going to do. They don't call you blokes 'Diggers' for nothing, so keep digging. They kept digging using, in the regrettable absence of appropriate tools that had never been issued, helmets, bayonets, bully-beef tins and their bare hands. And no matter that in those wet climes a combination of the high water table and high rainfall meant that as often as not the bottom two feet of their foxholes were filled with water. In a choice between wet feet below, or a bullet above, wet feet won every time. *More* digging!

Happily, as he moved around among the men, Honner himself seemed to inspire even further confidence. As a student at the University of Western Australia he had played rugby for the First XV and captained the university's athletics team, and he was if not strictly speaking a man's man—in the slightly overbearing blokey sense of the word—he was still certainly a man's officer, always projecting an air of great competence and resolution, mixed with compassion for how the men were faring. A word here, a question there, it was clear to them that the bloke actually *cared* that they were getting as much sleep as possible, that their food supplies had improved, and that they were looking after their many sores and wounds as best they could with whatever rudimentary medicine they could get their hands on. He wasn't telling them to change the position of a particular foxhole out of pure military bloody-mindedness but because, he explained to them, the position he was suggesting would marginally increase their safety and strengthen their defence. They could see the bloke knew what he was talking about and took their cues accordingly.

Meanwhile, Honner had plenty of other things to worry about. Chief among them was preventing the Japanese from finding out just how poorly manned and equipped they were to defend Isurava. He felt certain that if the Japanese knew there were fewer than four hundred Australians to defend the whole plateau, they would either simply come in with all guns blazing, or even more devastatingly, just go around the 39th to cut off their supply lines, and choke them lifeless in nothing flat.

To prevent that, it was necessary to keep the Japanese at as great a distance as possible for as long as possible, and maintain a forward patrol positioned forty-five minutes march along the track. The patrol's job was to provide ample warning of any major Japanese move against the forward position, and also to ensure that the brutes couldn't easily move any of their scouts forward to observe just what kind of a skeletal skeleton crew was actually defending the position at Isurava. With that in mind, Captain Bidstrup's D Company ambush that had been so effective a week before in nailing the Japanese, was now replaced with a constant changing of the guard to ensure maximum alertness.[158] Each platoon manned the position for twenty-four hours before being replaced by a fresh platoon in the first hour of dawn. The relieved platoon then fell back two hundred yards until just before noon, when they were free to head back to Isurava. The next platoon, meanwhile, was on standby to reinforce the duty platoon at a moment's notice, should they come under attack, and so on.

While Honner was delighted with the way this seemed to be working, he was worried about the defensive and offensive capacities of the 53rd Battalion, which had moved up from Moresby and which, at that point, was situated at Alola, the next village down the track towards Moresby and who were protecting the 39th's rear. Since their arrival in New Guinea, the men of the 53rd Battalion had never really seemed much chop, and had in fact spent most of their time in the simple hard labour of unloading ships. One of the main reasons was that at their core they still had around a hundred men who felt, with some justifiable rage in the circumstances, that they had been shanghaied to this God-forsaken land in the first place, and still wanted no bloody part of it. They were intent on doing as little as possible until they could get home again. Such an approach made for very ordinary soldiers, and though there were a few who were exceptions, many of them were very ordinary indeed.

Still another reason for Honner's concern, though, was that the 53rd lacked the experienced leadership of the 39th. Whereas the latter had eagerly absorbed all the veteran AIF officers that they could when the officers had become available earlier in the campaign, the 53rd had continued for the most part with their own militia officers. However well intentioned, these officers had no experience in leading soldiers under fire, and Honner continued to worry about just how well they would hold up when it came to battle. On his own trip north to Isurava he had passed many of the troops of the 53rd Battalion and been appalled at their clear lack of fighting capacity, plus their general lassitude and obviously low morale.

Now though, the problem was that as well as manning the 39th's fall-back position at Alola, it was also the 53rd's job to patrol and defend a tributary track which ran parallel to the Kokoda Track along the other side of the Eora Creek Valley. It was a route that bypassed Isurava entirely before rejoining the main track, and Honner had real worries that the Japanese would get smart and push along this track against the weaker 53rd, all the way to Alola. If that happened, the 39th would be cut off from their supply line and the route by which their wounded were to be evacuated. Simply put, they would be finished as a fighting force.

Meanwhile, the men of the 39th continued to dig in and get ready. On rare occasions when they could get a break, some of the more optimistic soldiers would take time out to write letters home on the back of dog-biscuit packets. Others would sacrifice the paper from cherished letters they had received from home as cigarette paper—the best was airmail letters—to wrap the dried tea leaves they used as tobacco. Certainly, the taste of such 'cigarettes' was deadly, but it did take their minds off what lay ahead, which they all knew was going to be a whole lot deadlier. And sometimes, too, they would do it all, reading and writing their letters, sucking on a cigarette and thinking about what they were fighting for in the first place. They were fighting for home; fighting to stop the Japs getting any closer; fighting to keep their loved ones safe. Someone had to do it, and it was *them*. There was nothing else they could do but get on with it.

The continuing paucity of 'bullets and tucker' as the men constantly referred to the terrible twin, was an ongoing problem. Supplies were so low that the men were severely rationed in what they could eat and when, perchance, a tin of pears, for example, might be scrounged from somewhere, it was often the platoon leader who would dole it out spoonful by spoonful to his section as they lined up. Something as seemingly inconsequential as a small pouch of sugar that had been salvaged from a burst bit of biscuit bombing was guarded like the crown jewels. Craving sweetness, some of the men had tried sucking on bits from the small sugar-cane plants that the village had in their market garden, but all that did was make you thirsty.

At least there was a precious bit of good news that helped to lighten the mood. Just four days after Honner had taken full command, a wonderful message came down the line. The 2/14th Battalion—all Victorians who'd served in the Middle East—had landed in Port Moresby, and were already coming up the track. The

2/16th were just a day behind them. With them would come a whole slew of the hoped-for supplies, and that was just about the finest news of all.

There had also been some indication that the Japs were doing it equally tough. On both sides of the battle it was standard procedure to search the body of every killed enemy soldier to strip them of ammunition and supplies as well as gather information, and time and again the Australians had been amazed to find that the sum total of supplies carried by these blokes for a *whole day's* fighting were the few concentrated vitamin tablets which they always had, and a small, grisly ball of rice wrapped in some kind of seaweed. It was extraordinary how little these blokes could live on. As hungry as the Australian soldiers were, they could barely bear to eat it, but they made themselves anyway. Ditto the vitamin tablets. If those little pills kept the Japs going, then they had to offer *something* in the way of nutrition. When the Japanese found dead Australian soldiers, on the other hand, the principal thing they went after were the sturdy Australian boots, much better than their own canvas and rubber sandshoes which never came to grips with the slippery track— seemingly the single failure in Japanese equipment.[159]

Disaster. Complete disaster. On the night of 18 August 1942, no fewer than three thousand crack Japanese soldiers of the 28th Infantry Regiment, under the leadership of Colonel Kiyono Ichiki, landed at Taivu Point just to the east of the Guadalcanal airbase and carefully moved forward under the cover of darkness. Regarded as Japan's most elite unit, their commitment to their task was total. Each soldier now stealthily moving forward in the darkness had a document stating firmly that if they did not take Guadalcanal they would not be returning to Japan alive. At least this particular mission shouldn't be too hard. Colonel Ichiki had personally told his men that 'Americans are soft—Americans will not fight—Americans believe that nights are for dancing', and in any case his Intelligence had told him that there were only going to be two thousand of the Americans defending the position.

Alas, alas, for the Japanese, well over fifteen thousand American Marines, forewarned of the landing, were waiting for them and all but wiped the invaders out. Most of the Japanese survivors fled into the jungle. Colonel Ichiki didn't. In the tradition of the samurai who had failed at his task, he first burnt his regiment's colours and then committed harakiri. There was no other recourse.

At last, they were getting close and were within just one day's march of Myola. Thank God. After five days footslogging along the Kokoda Track, the men of the 2/14th knew that their destination and the battle true was just up ahead. Which was good. After so many weeks and then months of waiting since returning from the Middle East, and then travelling, and then footslogging, and then more footslogging still, and all the bloody stuffing around, they were ready for the real battle to begin. Even for those who had seen action in such distant climes as Syria, Australia had never seemed further away.

And so, too, relief for the reinforcements from the 144th Regiment, who had left Rabaul by ship on 16 August, and who were getting close, within a day's march of the enemy Australians. It had been a long haul from the landing, making their way through the steaming humidity and overwhelming heat, across raging rivers, up mountains, along muddy tracks, all in an environment never imagined before, but they were getting there. If there was a worry, it was the news filtering back from the front that the Australians were providing more resistance than they had been thought capable of.

As Second Lieutenant Noda Hidetaka noted in his diary on Saturday 22 August, while situated at a point very near Kokoda: 'I hear that the enemy are young, vigorous and brave. Against this enemy we have this terrain also. It will be necessary for us to put forth our utmost endeavour and uphold the prestige of our Imperial Army.'[160] Lieutenant Hidetaka still wasn't feeling as ruthless as he would have liked, but just maybe he was getting there. He was trying, anyway.

•

At last, their papers had come through. The only proper place for a war correspondent of any description was the front and, after a week of waiting Osmar White, Damien Parer and Chester Wilmot now had official permission to trek to the battlefront at Isurava. The three formed a fairly natural trio as each was the leader in his field, and they were good friends besides. The only real condition laid down upon them was that they were not allowed to take native porters, as those crucial members of the war effort were in such short supply that not a single one could be spared for something so inconsequential as journalists. Apart from that, though, so long as they hauled their own supplies they were free to set off immediately up the track. There proved to be just one problem . . .

Just when they were readying to depart, Damien Parer received a cable from the Department of Information, advising him that instead of making this trek to a genuine battlefront, he was required to return to Townsville immediately to make a stunt film for American consumption. Distraught, Damien did the only thing he could think of. He drove out to New Guinea Force HQ to see General Rowell and ask his advice.

It was a wise move. Rowell realised that the best way for both the Australian people and the likes of Blamey and MacArthur to understand what conditions were really like at the battlefront was to have film-makers of the calibre of Parer up there. In his view, such a venture was a more valuable contribution to the war effort than making stunt films for Americans.[161] In a snap decision, he immediately told Damien Parer not to give it another thought. He would cable Australia that unfortunately the film-maker had already left for the battlefront and he was not going to recall him.

It was jolly decent of Rowell to take such action on his behalf and with this blessed reprieve, Damien raced away to tell Ossie and Chester that he could accompany them after all. Only shortly afterwards they were on their way, after hitching a lift to Ower's Corner, and setting off up the track.

•

Up in the village of Efogi, Stan Bisset was just starting to think about turning in for the night, when word was passed to him that his brother Butch was wondering if he'd like to come down to the southwestern corner of the bivouac section and have a singalong with the fellas of his Platoon Company 10. That'd be Butch all right . . . Of course he'd come, Stan assured the private who'd brought the message. Tell Butch he'd be there in fifteen minutes.

It didn't take long to find Butch's platoon, even in the darkness. As always when looking for his brother, Stan followed the sound of the laughter and sure enough, by the glow of the campfire, he found Butch finishing off just one more of his rib-tickling stories as the others of the platoon fell about laughing, marvelling that one man could know so many amazing yarns and keep telling them without repeating himself. They'd all been together nigh on two years now, and Butch still somehow managed to keep it up. On seeing Stan arrive, Butch leapt to his feet, gave his brother a strong handshake, and prevailed upon him to sing some of their favourites, while they all sang along.

And so they did. In the black New Guinea night, the soaring voices of the Australian platoon were soon joined by the voices of others who gravitated there from their own campfires. This close to the front, fires were not allowed unless there was a thick mist, but on this night the fog had rolled in a treat.

Perhaps the high point was when Stan sang the one which had always been Butch's favourite, the Irish ballad, the 'Mountains of Mourne'. In his beautiful, resonant baritone, Stan sang it as never before.

Oh, Mary, this London's a wonderful sight,
With people here working by day and by night,
They don't sow potatoes, nor barley nor wheat,
But there's gangs of them digging for gold in the streets,
At least when I asked them that's what I was told,
So I just took a hand at this diggin' for gold,

But for all that I found there I might as well be,
Where the Mountains of Mourne sweep down to the sea.

As Stan kept singing, Butch kept beaming at him, prevailing upon him to sing just one more song, even though it was now getting quite late. Stan of course obliged and, as his singing of course evoked memories of other times, he beamed back at his brother as they recalled singing around Uncle Abe's old piano on Sunday afternoon after the roast.

Despite the happiness of the moment, oddly enough, Stan felt something like a shadow fall across him whenever he looked at Butch, roaring the songs out by the firelight. It was the shadow of premonition that something terrible was going to happen to his brother, that he was going to . . . well, that he was going to die. Stan shook it off as they kept singing and would give the chorus even more gusto as if to expel that thought forever, but then, he would look at Butch and the thought would come again. Anyway, time to turn in. The fog had suddenly made things very cold.

And the Japanese soldiers sang too, around their own campfires, one of their favourite songs, '*Nankai Dayori*', which, translated as 'Tidings from the South Seas'.

Sekido toppa sakigake wa
Shikoku kenji no waga shitai.
Toku hanarete, nankai no.
New Britain wa Rabaul ni.
Hinnomaru san ni hirugaeru.

First to cross the Equator,
Our unit of vigorous youth from Shikoku.
Far from home, in the South Seas,
The Rising Sun flag fluttering brightly,
Over Rabaul, New Britain.
Like a maiden's breast,

Rising kindly over the gulf,
The fiery volcano beckons.
The pure hearts of young brave men
Think of the smoke of their homeland.
Just below the Equator
We are under the Southern Cross.
The warrior's blood runs hot
As the Rising Sun flag advances.
Ahead the enemy pleads for his life under a white flag.
A brisk divine breeze blowing
Towards Australia at the limit of the south.
The ultimate place to reach.
The dawn of a new world,
Not quickly but faintly.[162]

The wetness was the worry. Apart from the rain and the sweat from physical exertion, Damien Parer also had the remains of a malarial fever, meaning he was completely drenched all of the time. On its own that would have still been manageable, but as always Damien's great fear was that the film in his pack would suffer. First, last, and always, that film had to be protected because if it was ruined, he was wasting his time. In an effort to give the film some protection, Damien took off his hat and got Ossie to put it between his shirt and his backpack, as a rough kind of buffer. Maybe it would help a little.

Despite such measures, both Chester Wilmot and Ossie White insisted on taking turns to help carry Damien's gear, including his heavy tripod, despite his vehement protestations. Not that the thickset Chester Wilmot was himself travelling much better. Way back in Melbourne University days, he had been athletic enough to be the 120-Yard High Hurdles champion, but those days were long gone.[163] Now, taking in huge draughts of air with nearly every stride, Chester was like a Puffing Billy, perpetually straining up the steep inclines which always, almost, very nearly, defeated him, before he would ... finally ... *finally* ... gain a summit and then charge down the other side. Then the whole thing would be repeated again. What he most resented was that every step down would inevitably soon have to be paid for with another wretched step *up*, and in his mind he was just like the Sisyphus of ancient Greek mythology, who was condemned to perpetually push a rock to a hilltop, only to see it roll back at once to the bottom. If there was one small consolation in Chester's suffering, it was that he would hopefully lose some of the spare tyres around his middle which his beloved pregnant wife, Edith, was always gently badgering him to lose. Somehow though, he doubted they would go. Even in the siege of Tobruk, when he had been perpetually hungry for months, he had only lost one notch on his belt, and there was no sign that things were going to be better this time. With Ossie and Damien, he pressed on, with only Ossie—who had long engaged in rock climbing as a hobby—managing the slopes with anything approaching equanimity.

Finally, after a long and arduous journey, and now half a day ahead of the first of his troops, Brigadier Arnold Potts—together with an advance party that now included the Intelligence Officer of the 2/14th, Stan Bisset, whom he had picked up on the way through—hauled himself over the lip of the last hill protecting the vision of Myola below. He stood, then paused. For while there was Myola sure enough, where were the huge mounds of supplies that should have been visible from this distance? If two planeloads a day had indeed been flown in for the last week, where was the evidence of it? He scanned, and scanned again, but all he could see was the precious flat ground of Myola as promised—with the thickly wooded valley walls rising sharply on both sides—and a few Australian Army personnel mooching around, but nothing, *nothing* in the way of a depot bursting at the seams and getting ready to be unloaded to the hungry army that was just around the corner. Hoping against hope, Potts descended to the flats below, praying he was the one making a mistake, only to be told the terrible news.

Despite the promises of Morris, the supplies hadn't been delivered. The transport planes had been bombed at Seven Mile Airfield on

17 August, and alternative arrangements had not yet been made. There had not been a single can of bully beef dropped since the successful Japanese bombing. Things were so disorganised that the ordnance officers at Myola had not even been informed that a thousand men were soon to descend upon them. In the whole place there was only enough food to keep the 2/14th and 2/16th going for five days, not the twenty-five days that Potts had requested and that Morris had promised.

To hasten fresh supplies being flown in, Potts sent messages back to Port Moresby, with a tone of demand just as strong as the stiffness of military language would allow when expressing a grievance to superior officers. There were not sufficient supplies here. They needed them urgently, Suh!

Given the situation, the only way they could manage in the short term would be to hold the 2/16th a little further down the track at the village of Efogi, while bringing the 2/14th on to Myola, and keeping them there until enough supplies arrived—for it would be nothing less than suicide to send a large number of men without sufficient food or ammunition into the teeth of the enemy.

Honner would just have to hold the Japanese a little longer, though Potts himself decided to push on, with Stan Bisset beside him, through the brutal section to Templeton's Crossing and onwards again to Alola the following day. Not being of the MacArthur school of military leadership, Potts intended to go to the frontline of Isurava himself to confer with Honner.

In the meantime, the first of the men of the 2/14th had staggered into the Myola supply depot. After having the weight of their world on their shoulders for the last five days, the majority of them simply dropped their rucksacks as soon as they arrived, and dropped beside them a moment afterwards.

If, a week earlier, Ralph Honner had been staggered by the weak physical condition of the men of the 39th, then so too was Brigadier Arnold Potts when he got through to Isurava on 23 August, though perhaps more so. What most impressed Potts, though, was the 39th's extraordinarily high level of morale and courage under the circumstances, and he was, as author Raymond Paull described it, 'heartened afresh by the spectacle of hollow cheeks and thin lips drawn back in a cheerful grin of appreciation for what "the bloody Nips will cop now!"'[164]

Satisfied that Honner had the situation at Isurava under control in the short term, Potts fell back to the village of Alola, a couple of hours south, where his Brigade Headquarters had been set up by Stan Bisset—who had also set up a bivouac area for the 2/14th just forward of Alola, ready for when they arrived. (Finding a suitable bivouac area was not as easy as it sounded, as along the track it was always difficult to locate a substantially flat place large enough to accommodate several companies of soldiers. Most of the land was on either too steep an incline, or too thickly covered in vegetation. Usually the only solution was to find a spot near a summit, where the track occasionally eased into something roughly approaching flatness.)

That night Potts and Bisset discussed at length the logistics of launching their major offensive against the Japs, as they had been ordered to do. It had become apparent that it was not feasible to follow these orders until all their troops were in place and their supply situation had stabilised, but both still felt confident that they would be ready for serious action from the first days of September. One of the many tasks Potts set Bisset was to use his knowledge of the local topography and skills in intelligence to continue the construction of a 'mud model' of the surrounding ranges and rivers. The map had already been started by the recently relieved commander of the 39th, Major Cameron, who had now been installed in Potts's Brigade Headquarters as a liaison officer. Potts was keen that it be finished so that as many of the shortly arriving troops as possible would not be fighting blind, but would have some idea of the lie of the land, and how best their overall objectives could be achieved.

Here, Stan Bisset was in his element, and with the aid of a lantern he had a look at how the model looked at this point. Already you could see the rough contours of the land as Cameron had set it out.

The Yodda Valley, with the Kokoda airfield squarely in the middle of it, ran from north to south. Eora Creek, which began up around Myola and gathered strength as it flowed down into the valley, ran just to the east of that airfield. On the western ridge of the valley stood Isurava, while on the other ridge perched the town of Abuari. The men of the 39th were assigned to defend Isurava, while the 53rd—still grumbling!—had taken over Abuari. While it seemed that the Japanese were concentrating most of their forces on the main track, which went through Isurava, there remained a great danger that they would push through Abuari and all the way to Alola, in which case the 39th would have its supply line cut and be isolated. As a precaution against the Japanese trying a circling movement to cut them off and isolate them on a tributary track, the 2/16th battalion, when it arrived, would be sent down the western side of the valley to bolster the 53rd. The job of the 2/14th would be to act in relief of the 39th at Isurava and, if all went well, it could stick to the plan of launching an all-out attack on the Japanese on 1 September, and begin to push them back to the sea.

Meanwhile, in his own Brigade Headquarters some three miles to the north, the Commanding Officer of the South Seas Detachment, General Tomitaro Horii, was making his own plans—and he wasn't waiting till September to attack the Australians. Horii was a military officer who liked to remain near the frontline, where he could react quickly to the changing situation, and he was a distinctive figure to his frontline men because of it, not least because he was always recognisable riding his white horse. Many of his men had marvelled at how Horii had managed to get his horse up some parts of the track, which were practically vertical, but they marvelled more at having such a distinctive leader. Streaks of individualism and personal flair were not only not encouraged in the Japanese Army, they were practically non-existent, and yet somehow this squat little man with his trademark owl spectacles and grey hair had managed to get away with it.

For all his natural vitality, however, Horii was already exhausted. Over the previous fortnight he had been massing his troops—no fewer than five battalions, totalling six thousand frontline warriors, together with specialist units of engineers and mountain artillery on the approaches to Isurava—conscious that this was a crucial battle where the result of the whole campaign might well be told. There can be little doubt that had Horii known at that time that the only force stopping his men at Isurava was just four hundred weakened and exhausted Australians—with the main force still a long way back—he would have made his attack immediately; but so strong had been the resistance put up by the 39th so far, he, in fact, thought there were at least five times that number dug in.

Clearly he was going to need more men to force the passage through to Port Moresby. The Australians to this point had been providing far more resistance than he had ever expected, the more so because from the bodies of the dead Australian soldiers it was apparent that they were only *boys*. How was it that they were doing so much damage? There was nothing for it but to push on, harder than before, and with so much overwhelming force that the Australians would simply have to crack. Grim-faced, Horii continued his preparations for the assault he had planned, but was heartened by the information he had just received from Tokyo that the Australians would soon find themselves obliged to defend Port Moresby from *another* front in New Guinea, with any luck distracting their focus from stopping him and his men.

It remained the waiting that was the most wearing. Around the entrenched positions of the Australian soldiers at Isurava, the rainforest brooded, malevolent in its silence. Now experienced in the ways of the Japanese, the men of the 39th were aware that every dark recess could hide soldiers even then moving to slit their throats, every tree was a possible platform for a sniper, every bush possibly a carefully camouflaged killer about to take them down. It was the way of this campaign. Not being able to see the Japs anywhere meant that you inevitably saw them *everywhere*. So the Australians waited, silent as the grave, as hidden as moss on lichen. No easy targets, these blokes. If the Japs wanted to know their exact positions, it was *they* who would have to expose themselves by firing first, and thus they who would cop the first well-aimed shots.

The rain kept on through all of the afternoons and early evenings, drenching men to the core and setting them up for the bitter chill of the night to do its work.

'Only the morning brought a gleam of comfort,' Honner later wrote of it. 'A turn at sleeping and forgetting; a chance perhaps to lie and dry in the warmth of the glowing day. But little light filtered through the leaf-roofed murk where Merritt's men guarded the front creek cliff, pale ghosts crouching in the dank-dripping half-dark, hidden from the healing of the searching sun . . . '[165]

So, too, at home it remained the waiting that was the most wearing. Back in Melbourne, Elaine Colbran just couldn't stop thinking about Joe Dawson, up there somewhere in New Guinea with the 39th Battalion. She missed him so much, and life just wasn't the same without him around, taking her to dances, for a coffee when she finished work, or a simple walk in the park, holding hands. Plenty of her friends in similar situations had consoled themselves by stepping out with one of the many Americans who were now abounding all over Melbourne—blokes who just bowled right up to you and introduced themselves, without being introduced first! But she had never felt remotely tempted. She just wanted to wait for Joe.

And she wasn't the only one who was feeling down, not by a long shot. A general pall had fallen across Australia with the absence of so many loved ones, mixed with the regular blows of terrible news about those killed in action, of battles lost and the Japanese getting closer. All of this news against a backdrop of strict wartime rationing, with even such essentials as soap, sugar and flour sometimes hard to come by. Not to mention, for the men, horse racing, alcohol and gambling were severely restricted, and the skies seemed greyer than ever.

•

Finally, finally, there was a chance for redemption. After well over six months of working as a 'comfort woman' in Rabaul, servicing the sexual needs of roughly 2500 Japanese soldiers, Okryon Park had been put on a ship going back to Korea. In all the viciousness of her experience in Rabaul, there had been one or two men who had been kind to her, including one who had pressed money upon her, to perhaps start her in a new life at home. And now—after she and many of the comfort women who had originally come with her to Rabaul had at last been replaced by a younger, fresher bunch— she was heading home with fifty others.

Okryon just about couldn't believe it. With the crush of Japanese soldiers arriving in Rabaul in the past few weeks, every day had been like Sunday for herself and the other comfort women, as the queue of men was neverending. But now it seemed her agony was at an end and she would soon be with her son again. Okryon was just washing some dishes in the ship's galley when suddenly there was a loud explosion and her whole world was overturned again as water started rushing in. A bomb or a torpedo from an American plane had hit them amidships, and within seconds Okryon was in the water, sinking, drowning, struggling, grabbing on to a piece of driftwood and staying afloat. For nine hours she and just fourteen others drifted around until another Japanese ship picked them up . . . and took them back to Rabaul. There was only one place to stay, back in the comfort station to serve the soldiers again. Not even the fact that she had suffered a bad injury on her forehead in the course of her ship sinking saved her . . .

It had been a long journey but, following in the muddy footsteps of the 2/14th, Osmar White, Damien Parer and Chester Wilmot were now getting close to one of their main destinations, the flats of Myola. It was here, they had already been informed, that the 2/14th were holed up waiting for their supplies to get through from Moresby. The reporters, too, were finding the endless rain to be a total drain on their spirit.

'It is difficult to describe the abysmal depression that had me in its grip,' White later wrote of his feelings as they drew closer to Myola. 'The rain did not vary in intensity for as much as a minute—an endless, drumming, chilling deluge. It roared and rustled and sighed on the broad leaves of the jungletop. It soaked through the green pandanus thatches of shelters and spilled clammy cascades upon the bowed backs of exhausted men. It swamped cooking fires. Creeks ran in every hollow. One's very bones seemed softened by the wetness.'[166]

The following day the reporters had arrived at Myola and, after resting up and lazing like lizards in a rare burst of sunshine, White and Wilmot were right there with their notebooks, and Damien Parer with his cameras, when the transports from Moresby at last began to arrive. Only superhuman efforts in Townsville, Brisbane and Moresby over the previous three days had got them loaded and off the ground. As a matter of fact, Osmar was close enough to the action to be nearly killed by a case of tinned beef, but survived to see from a worm's-eye view for the first time, just how this biscuit bombing was done. The key seemed to be to get the plane to as low an altitude as possible—to maximise the chances of the booty surviving—while still retaining the capacity to pull out of the dive into the saucer and rise above the distant treetops. The planes lined up thus, and roared in, one by one, just a few hundred feet from the ground, with their side door open. At the instant before the drop, the pilot would tilt the plane to make the job of the unloaders easier. Inside, men who were tied to a rope would give the cargo a heave or a kick and it would tumble below. The only things that came down by the very rare parachutes which were available were the mortar bombs, machine-gun ammunition and fuses. Everything else hit the ground at a furious pace and then began to bounce . . . bounce . . . and keep bouncing.

Hence the worst job of all in the whole process. Right next to the designated dropping area was the marker. This unfortunate's job was to stand like a statue and, with the aid of a compass, mark precisely where the bundles came to rest in the jungle, giving compass coordinates and approximate distances from where he stood. Then, when the planes had gone, it would be for the rest of the battalion and the native porters to seek out the booty. It was far from a perfect method, and as much as twenty-five per cent of the supplies were lost forever. But it still served to bring in about fifty tons over the next two days as the sky continued to rain food, bullets, blankets, sweaters, shirts, shorts, cigarettes, grenades and, most impressively of all, five three-inch mortars with three hundred bombs to ram down the Japs' pants. (Now on site, Potts had entirely countermanded General Morris's previous instruction that mortars were of no use on the track, and they had been close to the top of his priority list in his requests back to Moresby.)

By the evening of 24 August, Potts was at last satisfied that they had enough supplies to take the Japs on. Bert Kienzle and his nine hundred odd hardy porters were in full swing, taking the new supplies forward, while in response to Potts's previous urgent requests to Rowell and Allen, another three hundred fully-laden porters were also well on their way towards Myola with yet more supplies.

Potts gave the orders for the first of the 2/14th companies to prepare to move out to support the 39th. Now, if all went well, on 1 September the Australians would begin a full-blown attack on the Japanese positions, and start to fulfil their orders to push them back to the sea. This would be accomplished by the 2/14th Battalion pushing down the western side of the valley through Isurava and Deniki to Kokoda, while the 2/16th would push through on the eastern side along the Abuari–Misima ridge. And so, at dawn on the morning of 25 August, the forward elements of the 2/14th Battalion moved out, towards Isurava, towards their own date with destiny . . .

CHAPTER TWELVE

THE BATTLE OF ISURAVA

*In Ralph Honner's epic view of life and war, Isurava was not merely
a battle on the Kokoda Trail, but Australia's Agincourt . . .*
Peter Brune, We Band of Brothers[167]

*We few, we happy few, we band of brothers,
For he that sheds his blood with me today will be my brother*
Shakespeare, Henry V Part II: Henry V

*In the testing crucible of conflict . . . they were transformed by some
strong catalyst of the spirit into a devoted band wherein every man's
failing strength was fortified and magnified by a burning resolve
to stick by his mates.*
Lieutenant Colonel Ralph Honner[168]

The morning of 26 August 1942 dawned on the village of Isurava
as ever, a bright ball of heat searing down on the slight break in
the intense green jungle. (It was, for the record, the very date that

back in June Major General Basil Morris had asked Bert Kienzle to have the road from Moresby to Kokoda finished, but with one thing and another . . . that hadn't quite happened.)

The first warning to Ralph Honner that the Japanese were on the move came when he heard the sound of booming gunfire rolling along the ridgetop where he had placed the forward patrol to give the defenders at Isurava fair warning of Japanese approach . . . and this was clearly it. When the gunfire continued and intensified it was clear that the battle was underway.

Among the 430 men of the 39th Battalion perched on the Isurava plateau, the effect was immediate. Individually there was a sudden surge of adrenalin, a stiffening of the sinews, a tightening of the stomach, a sudden itch on the trigger fingers, as they checked their ammunition belts and gripped their guns more tightly. It was *on*. The Japanese were coming and they would very shortly be in a fight for their lives. The enormous screeching flocks of parrots suddenly flying overhead—disturbed by either the guns or approaching enemy companies—added to the malice of the moment, as if the bats of hell had just been released.

Yet there was no panic. The 39th's preparations over the preceding ten days had been thorough and, as much as they could be, the men felt substantially ready for whatever the Japs could throw at them. In some ways they took their cue from Ralph Honner, who was now striding around purposefully, talking to the men, giving orders, ensuring that everything that could be done was being done as the gunfire seemed to move marginally closer. One of the first orders that Honner gave was for elements of D Company, under the command of one of his best men, Lieutenant Bob Sword, to march out to reinforce elements of Lieutenant Don Simonson's E Company in their now precarious position in the forward post as Japanese fire rained upon them.

It was as well, because the brave Simonson and his men were now engaged in heavy action, taking fire from the Japanese troops who had suddenly appeared. They were also aware that, at a point about five hundred yards from their current position, a mountain gun had started firing, with the missiles whistling over their heads and heading towards Isurava, where the first indication that the heavy Japanese mountain gun was operational was the sudden sound of incoming . . .

Shells. The Japanese mountain gun—dismantled back at Rabaul, then hauled up in separate bits and reassembled—was now sending round after round down upon those who were blocking their way on the path to Moresby and victory. One happy circumstance for the Japanese artillery unit operating the mountain gun was what an easy target Isurava was; it was the one speck in the whole vista that wasn't green. When the shelling began, Ralph Honner was standing in the middle of the plateau with Lieutenant Keith Lovett and two other officers. As the first shot landed, the officers looked to Honner to see how he would react. Would he be one of those officers who insisted on strutting around in full view of enemy guns, thus making other officers who insisted on ducking for cover look guilty of cowardice . . . or would he be sensible?

Another *whump* in the distance meant that they had five seconds before it landed at some point on the target, of which they were the bullseye.

'Look, there's no point in us just standing around here when a bombardment's going on. We're only going to get ourselves hurt here. What I'm going to do when we hear the preliminary shot fired, I'm going to ground, and I think you'll serve me well if you go to ground with me . . .'[169]

Yes, Sir! They all laughed and, at the next whump in the distance, hurled themselves to the ground like Australian fielders in an Ashes test trying to stop an English drive for four runs. But this was no joke and within two minutes two great mates, Corporal Joe Reilly and Lance Corporal Jim O'Donnell, had been killed by a direct hit on the foxhole they were sharing, their broken bodies hurled ten yards away. With bullets whistling past him, Father Nobby Earl shortly afterwards conducted a simple burial service and buried them both, in adjacent graves, a short distance away.

Against this kind of heavy weaponry, the best the Australians could offer was one all but obsolete Lewis heavy machine gun, which had first seen action on the Western Front of France during the Great War, some twenty-five years earlier. The new supplies at Myola had not yet got through, and the 39th simply had no long-range artillery to get at the Japanese. They would have to wait till they got to closer quarters before trying to inflict damage . . .

Up at the forward patrol post, Lieutenant Don Simonson and his men were trying to do exactly that. Having successfully beaten off the main Japanese thrust through their post, the combined men from E and D Companies now counterattacked and went forward in an effort to silence the mountain gun. This proved fruitless as the Japanese were well dug in beside the track on the approaches to the gun, so for the moment Simonson and his men fell back to their previous position.

Typical of the Japanese tactics, however, was that although they had been stopped on the main track, it did not mean that they had *stopped*. By the middle of the afternoon, other Japanese forces had skirted Simonson and were now attacking the Isurava perimeter from the high ground to the immediate northwest, as the mountain gun continued to rain missiles upon the defenders.

The first of the Japanese soldiers to get within cooee of the lines at Isurava were met by a lone Australian soldier placed a hundred yards forward. He held his fire in a hidden position until they were right upon him, and then squeezed the contents of an entire Tommy-gun magazine into a satisfactorily tightly bunched group of them at a range of just three yards. With a now empty gun, he looked up to see what seemed like a whole *battalion* of Japanese swarming out of the rainforest at him, prompting him to take a running jump—with bullets whistling all around—into the forest and down a ravine to relative safety. It would take him all night to make his way back to his own lines . . . [170]

Meantime, about three hundred miles roughly to the east of Isurava, at Milne Bay, on the eastern tip of New Guinea, fierce fighting was also underway. The strategic significance of Milne Bay—its promising areas of flat ground and geographic proximity to the Coral Sea made it ideal for the establishment of airbases—had not been lost on either side in this war. In late June, General MacArthur himself had ordered the construction of an airfield at a spot known as Gili Gili at the western end of the bay, and a brigade of the Australian Army was placed there to defend it. Throughout August that brigade had been reinforced with soldiers from other Australian units and had enjoyed some of the most inhospitable country in the world, where the air was always filled with one of two things: teeming rain or swarms of malarial mosquitoes. In appalling conditions, the Australian soldiers, with the help and guidance of American engineers, had set about building two more airfields and roads between them.

But on the previous night, at the same time that General Horii was moving his own troops forward to get in position for the attack on Isurava, a convoy of Japanese transports, minesweepers and destroyers had entered the bay. They unloaded two thousand crack soldiers just six miles from Gili Gili where the Australians were dug in under the command of General Cyril Clowes.

The Japanese soldiers had therefore already completed the first half of their orders for this operation, which were clear and to the point: 'At the dead of night, quickly complete the landing in the enemy area, and strike the white soldiers without remorse.'[171]

On that same afternoon of 26 August, at Isurava the Australians were also providing unexpectedly strong resistance to the Japanese attacks. But still Brigadier Potts, at Alola—where he had now taken formal command of Maroubra Force from Honner—signalled Port Moresby that they would likely be needing some help. Advising the Moresby command that they were under attack, he added: 'Condition of 39th Battalion men weak due continuous work lack warm clothing blankets shelters curtailed rations and wet every night.' Later in the day, with a view to who was guarding the 39th's rear and eastern flanks, Potts added: '53rd Battalion training and discipline below standard required for action. For these reasons consider it imperative 2/27th move to Myola as my only fighting reserve.'[172]

As the Japanese attacks continued on the Isurava perimeter that afternoon, Ralph Honner looked at the situation with growing dismay. Ammunition was getting low, the men were totally exhausted and the Japanese kept pressing, pressing, pressing forward, while simultaneously launching endless foraging flanking movements. By Honner's estimation, his men could only survive the Japanese onslaught for a few hours more, and maybe—just maybe—to the following morning. However courageous his men, he had little doubt that if the 2/14th didn't get to them very soon, they would be gone.

For their part, all the men of the 39th knew was that they were in a fight to the finish and, until such times as they were relieved, they had to keep going until either they or their attackers were dead.

There is a noble, if bloody, tradition of such an approach in the Australian Army. Back in World War I, for example, an Australian lieutenant by the name of F. P. Bethune, a clergyman at home, found himself in charge of twenty Australian soldiers in a brutal battle on the Western Front, near the tiny French town of Villers-Bretonneux. In March 1918 it fell to Bethune's platoon to hold the line against the marauding Germans. The Australians were clearly outnumbered and outgunned, and nearby British forces considered their position suicidal. But it was crucial to the rest of the Allies that they hold the line, and the only way to succeed was total resolve. If one man wavered, they were lost. Lieutenant Bethune gathered his men and gave them written orders. 'This position will be held, and the section will remain here until relieved. The enemy cannot be allowed to interfere with the program. If the section cannot remain here alive, it will remain here dead, but in any case it will remain here.

'Should any man through shell-shock or other cause attempt to surrender, he will remain here dead. Should all guns be blown out, the section will use Mills grenades and other novelties. Finally, the position, as stated, will be held.'[173]

In that case, as in so many others, the position was held, and so it was too with the men of the 39th and their commander. Knowing that the 2/14th were on their way, there could be no possibility of withdrawing the men to a safer position. They had to stay, and that was that.

As the light began to fade on this 26th day of August, though, the situation was beyond grim. Moving around the perimeter, Honner became aware that his previous view that they might be able to hold for a few more hours might have been optimistic. If the Japanese broke through just one of his sections then it would be all over. His reserve force was now committed, as was his mobile unit and, like cats on a curtain, the 39th were just managing to hang on with final reserves of strength they hadn't even known they possessed.

Where, oh where, were the men of the 2/14th?

There!

Climbing up the track to meet them in double-quick time came C Company of the 2/14th Battalion, under the command of Captain Gerry Dickenson. Having left Myola at dawn the day before, they were the advance guard of the whole battalion. Soon they took their places beside the men of the 39th, taking over bit by bit the position that had been held by the 39th's C Company on the right forward flank, which included Isurava village.

Both groups of Australian fighting men looked at the other with wonder. The newly arrived saw raggedy scarecrows of men, eyes sunken into their skulls, bodies racked by dysentery and fatigue, many recently wounded, and all of them smelling like latrines in the sun—which was not surprising as most of them had not washed for over forty days. All up, it was a wonder some of them still had the strength to hold up a rifle, let alone fire it, but fire it they did and never let up.

As to the men of the 39th, they looked upon the 2/14th, as one soldier later famously put it, as 'Gods'. At least in comparison to themselves, the newcomers looked fit, strong, tanned, well-fed, and turned out in clothes that were not in shreds. Most of all, the newcomers exuded confidence. Just moments after Dickenson's men had taken up their positions, a furious volley of mortar fire fell nearby and the AIF blokes all started cheering, calling out to each other 'You beaut!' and the like. As later described by Raymond Paull, 'it combined familiarity, a spirited acceptance of an accustomed situation, and confidence in handling it.'[174] All up, it was a moment that would ever after be burned in the memories of the members of the 39th.

That night of 26 August the Japanese unleashed more attacks—one skirmish seeing eight Japanese soldiers killed for no Australian losses. The invaders also made a full-blown attack on Honner's forward patrol, now composed from men of the companies of both Lieutenant Simonson and Lieutenant Sword. The first the Australian soldiers at the forward post had known of it, bullets had suddenly started flying all around them, grenades had exploded in their midst, and from out of the jungle screaming Japanese soldiers had burst, firing as they came. Two of them actually made it all the way to the entrenched Australian position, and for a brief moment had lashed out with bayonets before the attack was beaten off. Lieutenant Don Simonson and three other soldiers were injured in the melee, with one Jap killed and many wounded, which was just as good.

For both sides of the campaign, causing a serious wound in an enemy soldier was almost more effective than a clean kill because every wound was a long-term drain on resources. To care for a wounded soldier on the frontline was debilitating, and to carry a badly wounded soldier out took at least four men many days on a stretcher, not to mention all the subsequent medical care and fuss and bother. If an Australian soldier was killed, though, it only took another one or two fellows perhaps half an hour to bury him and they would be free to fight again. As to the Japanese, their own dead were usually cremated, requiring more effort, but the principle stood.

All up, it was an appalling equation, but real nevertheless, and it was understood by the Diggers themselves. It was for this reason during the Kokoda campaign that time and again, badly wounded Diggers would crawl off quietly to die in the undergrowth rather than draw attention to themselves by screaming for help and so weakening the overall war effort.

On this occasion, though, as soon as contact was made with the 39th Battalion Headquarters and the message passed that four soldiers had been wounded, the instruction came back to bring them in immediately, even though it was still in the middle of the night. Easier said than done. There are few things in this world so pitch black as the middle of a New Guinea jungle in the middle of the night and, while the use of torches would of course help, they also acted as beacons for every enemy gun within miles. The fact was that at this point neither the forward men nor anyone at Battalion HQ had any idea just where the Japanese were, and whether the track between the post and Isurava was clear or not.[175] The severe groans of the wounded soldiers told them there was nothing for it but to give it a try, and Lieutenant Simonson gave the order to move out. Carefully. With their torches shrouded as much as possible from distant eyes, and emitting just enough of a dim glow on the track, they slowly moved forward . . .

As they moved out, Lieutenant Bob Sword watched them go with some trepidation. Not just for them, heading off into a darkness crawling with murderous enemies, but for those left behind, who were now manning the forward post with four fewer of their good men.

As dawn broke on the morning of 27 August, it was soon clear that the solo Japanese mountain gun of the previous day was simply the bass drum of a whole percussion set that now included mortars, as the defenders of Isurava came under sustained bombardment. Out on the southern edge of the perimeter with the rest of D Company, Smoky Howson could hear the individual explosions of the mortars being fired, and then would count to ten. The reckoning of the Diggers was that if you got to ten you *definitely* knew you were still alive, but it was nerve-racking all right, as the mortar bombs continued to explode all around their positions.[176]

And what's that? In the undergrowth about twenty yards in front of them, Smoky and his fellow Diggers could hear a furious crashing as something tore through it.

'Cover me, mate, here the bastards come!' Smoky yelled to the bloke next to him. But then—the sheer relief of it!—out of the thick undergrowth charged a wild pig. Smoky shot him anyway for the valuable meal he would provide for dinner that night, and the soldiers were still whooping over their mistake when the awful truth hit them. What had driven the wild pig at them was something much more dangerous—Japs. Seemingly *hundreds* of them on the charge and just another fifty yards or so behind the pig. A battle royal soon ensued, and not just at Smoky Howson's section.

From all sides of the perimeter, the Japanese forces now attacked, pouring out of the jungle and charging all of the Australian positions, most particularly the ones held by E and B Companies, on the northern and western sections. The most sustained attack came on B Company, dug in at the most crucial position. Wondrously, though, it was clear from the first that Ralph Honner's decision to show faith in B Company was being fully vindicated, as under Lieutenant French's command the men were holding, and giving at least as good as they got. But it was going to be a close-run thing . . .

Based at B Company Headquarters, dug in just back from the frontline behind a large log, Joe Dawson was flat out, first distributing the ammunition, and then going from platoon to platoon to ensure that there was as much order as possible in the chaos of battle.

He was just coming back from one such head-down-and-run-for-it sortie when a runner from one of the platoons caught up with him to say that a couple of Japs had just got through and were loose in his sector. In such a situation of extreme urgency, Joe had no choice but to take immediate action himself and, after picking up his gun, he grabbed another bloke and together they ran full pelt after the platoon runner back to his position to try and stem the flow. They were so hot on the runners' heels that when a shot was suddenly fired from somewhere at close quarters and the runner went down, Joe fell on top of him. It seemed likely the runner had just slipped on the muddy track, but by the gasping, rasping sounds the bloke was now making, it was apparent he had been shot. Joe was about to tend to him when he saw a movement in a bush to his left and fired off two immediate shots, before dragging the runner back to a small depression in the landscape where they could at least get some shelter.

From there he hurled two more grenades into the area of the bush. The runner, it was now clear, was dead, with a bullet to the head. Joe felt bad for him, but that feeling was outweighed by the far more urgent feeling that he needed to complete what he had come here to do. If there were Japs who had broken through and were now inside the perimeter, then they had to be dealt with right now; but circling around to approach the bush from another direction with his gun at the ready he discovered two dead Japanese soldiers, torn apart by one of his grenades. That problem had been solved for the moment.

It momentarily seemed strange that here he was, Joe Dawson of Footscray, having just ended the life of two blokes from Japan— they were *dead* because of him—but that was just the way it was. There and then there was little time to reflect and he had to hare back to B Company Headquarters, where he was certain to be urgently needed. No sooner had he got there than a runner arrived from Colonel Honner at Battalion Headquarters with a message that each company had to hold its position whatever the cost—that if just *one* fell back all would be lost. Now exhausted, the runner who'd brought the message fell to one knee as mortar bombs landed all round and said something Joe would never forget: 'Jeez, they're rockin' in, ain't they!'

They were at that, though it seemed a strange thing to say at the time—as strange as a bloke without a leg being carried past on a stretcher. A mortar or grenade had landed near his feet, blowing one of those feet clear away and leaving the bloody stump. Joe couldn't help but think that it really looked rather like a big red flower had suddenly sprouted from his right leg, just below his calf. Joe thought that maybe he was shell-shocked or having battle trauma or something, but that is what it fair dinkum looked like . . . and he never forgot it.

There were many moments on that morning when other parts of the perimeter were threatened. To stem the fury, Colonel Honner called not only every able-bodied man to duty, but pretty much the disabled as well—in fact, anyone on site who could hold a rifle and fire at the throng was required to do so. Colonel Honner also issued an order for Lieutenant Sword's two platoons from the forward post to hot-foot it back to the plateau and take up positions. The time for keeping the Japs at arm's length was gone and, if it was going to be hand-to-hand, the colonel wanted as many Australian hands as possible on deck.

'There is a problem, Sir,' one of his signallers rushed up.

'Yes, Sergeant?'

'The line to Lieutenant Sword is dead. The Japs must have cut the cables overnight . . . '[177]

At the other end of the severed cable, Lieutenant Sword had just come to the same conclusion. Having heard the heavy firing coming from Isurava, he had attempted to contact Battalion HQ for instruction, with no result. And just as there are few things so black as the black of the New Guinea jungle in the night, there are surely few things so silent as a cut signal cable back to base at a time when the Japanese are swarming and you and your men are suddenly totally cut off and on your own.

What to do then? As a preliminary measure, and as a way of seeing which way the land lay, Lieutenant Sword gave the order for his men to move to their fall-back position some two hundred yards down the track towards Isurava. Bayonets fixed, eyes peeled, they moved out. Carefully. The one thing that gave them some confidence was that the previous night, when Lieutenant Simonson had headed back with the wounded, they had been relieved to hear no shots fired, hopefully indicating that the track was free. Another attempt to contact Battalion HQ from the holding position failed, and so

Lieutenant Sword gave orders for Private Albert Grace to act as a runner and try to make contact.

Shortly after Albie left, Private Jimmy Woods—who had been burning up with fever for the past twenty-four hours—was also given permission to head back to the camp to get some medical attention. No sooner had he rounded the corner though than a massive spate of gunfire broke out.

Hoping against hope, Sword's men were at least relieved to see Jimmy tearing back around the same corner, eyes rolling and tongue spitting with fury: 'The bastards are just down the track and had a go at me.' It wasn't that he was scared, he was *offended* by their pure bastardry. On his back, his rucksack had been shot all to pieces, perhaps saving his life. As to Albie Grace, he was, alas, never seen again, at least not by Australian eyes.

Signals cut. Japs in control of the track. There was only one thing for Sword's men to do, and they all knew it. They would have to head out cross-country, up above the track into thick and densely wooded jungle, to try to cut their way through in a circuitous fashion back to camp. It was a last resort to beat all last resorts, as trying to push through the jungle without a track was pure murder, but on the grounds that it was probably less murderous than staying where they were and starving, or heading straight into massed Japanese guns around the corner, Lieutenant Sword gave the order.

Unbeknown to Sword's men, another patrol, under the command of Lieutenant Bill Pentland—which had gone out to try and stop the Japanese outflanking Isurava by going along another track to its west—was also cut off. These two patrols, separately, now started thrashing their way through the jungle. Given that Isurava was all but surrounded, both groups set off towards Alola. They had little to no food, but more water than they thought they could bear as it continued to tumble from the heavens. They each pressed on through the day and into the night, as to their east the battle rolled on, with Colonel Honner now deprived of some of his fittest men.

•

And that, in General Rowell's view, was a typical bit of bullshit from General MacArthur. On the morning of 27 August, Lieutenant General Rowell the Commanding Officer of all Australian forces in New Guinea, received a direct order from MacArthur, the Supreme Commander of the Southwest Pacific Area: 'The landing force [at Milne Bay] must be attacked with the greatest vigour and destroyed as soon as possible.' (Oh, really? As opposed, perhaps, to simply hauling up the white flag and throwing down their weapons? Or maybe even catching a flight to Australia when things got really grim, as some had so recently done up in the Philippines?) Rowell decided to turn the order into more acceptable Australianese before passing it down the line to his friend Clowes (for whom in a cricket game played by the 1st XI of Duntroon Royal Military College in 1914, they had once combined to make *b. Clowes c. Rowell* that institution's most famous hat-trick): 'Confident you have situation well in hand and will administer stern punishment.'

For all that, Rowell's close colleague, General Tubby Allen, the Commanding Officer of the 7th Division, sent a message quite different in tone to Brigadier Arnold Potts in Alola. In response to Brigadier Potts's request the previous day that the 2/27th Battalion be dispatched forthwith to Myola to act as his reserve as the fighting intensified at Isurava, General Allen's cable advised: 'Enemy force landed at Milne Bay, 26th. Inadvisable send 2/27th Battalion until situation clarifies.' With the Japanese landing at Milne Bay, it meant that Port Moresby had an invasion force coming at it from two directions and would have to protect itself first. The upshot was that the men on site at Isurava, and those racing to get to them, were on their own.

Half a league, half a league, half a league onwards . . . Their's not to reason why, their's but to do and die. Into the valley of Death, rode the six hundred . . .

Many times, as the brave Japanese soldiers launched their full-frontal attacks on the Australian positions, they would shout '*Banzai*!'

and as a matter of principle they usually seemed to make an infernal racket when they were about to make a big front-on charge.

And the Australians? On one notable occasion the many cries of '*Banzai*!' were met with an Australian soldier doing a very impressive Tarzan impersonation à la the Hollywood actor Johnny Weissmuller, but generally their own war cries were a little more prosaic and regional in nature, most particularly given that the men of both the 39th and 2/14th were drawn from Australia's southeastern state.

Sometimes, in the heat of battle, when Australian soldiers burst from their trenches to go at the Japanese with their bayonets, in the midst of the chattering machine guns, the grenades, the screams and imprecations, you could hear it yelled, right in the middle of the battle thunder: 'Up there, Cazaly!'

You knew then that the Victorians were on the job. It was not a password, not a battle cry per se. Rather, it was an intuitively understood shout from one Aussie Rules steeped Aussie to another, which not only had echoes of home and what they were fighting for in the first place, but also served as an inspiration perhaps that this was a time to give it your all, to not hold back, to empty yourself of all you had in the quest for victory. The way the great Roy Cazaly, a VFL footballer from Melbourne in the 1920s had . . . The Victorians, a tribe all their own within the Australian mosaic, were just like that.

'*Banzai*!' was not the only thing the Japanese called out, however. The Japanese practice that the Australians had first noticed at Oivi when they called out to Corporal White was now even more common. For some reason, the Emperor's men at both Milne Bay and on the Kokoda Track now delighted in calling out things in English to their enemies. Some of it was a kind of half-baked attempt to demand surrender, as in: 'Australia man you go, Japan man he come. Withdraw Aussie withdraw. Japan man here. Drop arms surrender . . . ' or 'Don't fire. Troops coming in', and 'We are the Japanese. Order the whole army to stop firing.'

Some of it was amusing, as in when they called out 'Good morning, Aussie,' even though it was the middle of the night, and

'Japanese soldier, he come. Australian soldier, he run like hell.'[178] And some of it was downright bizarre, as in when they had been known to call out: 'Is that you, Mum?'—perhaps one of the few sentences from rudimentary English lessons from many years before that had stuck. With a chortle, some of the men told the story of how at Kokoda a couple of weeks back a stunningly accented Japanese voice had called in the dusk: 'Are you there, Larry Downes?'

'My oath, I am,' Larry had replied, before sending several magazines worth of Tommy-gun lead right in the voice's direction. Larry was there, and on the job.

Of a more serious nature was when Japanese soldiers used stolen uniforms from dead Australian soldiers to get close to the Australian lines. Equally alarming was when in the middle of the night the dim silhouette of a figure moved towards you on the frontline and you had a split second to choose between firing at the figure or—risking your own life—waiting a moment to be absolutely sure whether it was enemy or friend. The Australians soon got around that.

'Woolloomooloo!' one of the platoons shouted as their own password, citing the place whence the *Aquitania* had set off to bring them to New Guinea. If the figure called back 'Woolloomooloo!' it was fine. But anything that sounded like 'Woorroomooroo', or more likely no response at all, risked being met with a hail of lead. Other platoons favoured 'Elizabeth!', the reckoning being that the Japanese tongue had even more trouble with the 'z' and 'th' sound than it did with 'l's. Yet another password was 'Mad dogs and Englishmen!'.

Throughout 27 August the battle continued at Isurava, flaring into full-blooded attacks, fading momentarily as each side regrouped and recovered their dead, and then flaring again. Sometimes, though, as the Diggers learned, the Japs weren't dead at all. There would be one charge seemingly beaten off—with many dead bodies lying prone before your guns—and then when the next charge came in, a lot of the bodies would miraculously rise and charge forward again. They had been simply 'lying doggo', to use the Diggers' term, until the right moment came.[179] The Japs would also send out what the Diggers called 'crawlers', soldiers slithering forward on their bellies, undetected, to a position close enough to the Australians where—when the next wave of their comrades ran forward—they would suddenly jump up and throw grenades at the Australians' entrenched positions. Happily, while an Australian soldier could generally throw grenades about fifty yards, the Japanese were flat out throwing theirs twenty-five yards, limiting the effectiveness of the tactic. Partly, this was because the Japanese grenades were heavier and harder to throw, and partly because the poor bastards had never had a chance to play cricket and didn't know what it was to grow up hurling balls in from the outfield.

Amid the screaming, explosions of grenades and chattering of machine guns there was never a bird to be seen, but curiously the bountiful butterflies seemed entirely unaffected. It was not uncommon for soldiers on both sides to be fixing bayonets to fight for their very lives when, at the moment of highest tension, enormous butterflies of the most extraordinary colours and contours alighted on the helmets of those about to charge. God's own insects wafted away, of course, at the first serious movement forward, but to the soldiers who saw them at such moments, the butterflies always seemed to project a sense that, whatever the hostilities of the moment between man, *they* represented timeless nature, had been there long before man entered their domain, and would be there long after he was beneath the sod.

Though there were moments of great desperation, happily for Colonel Honner, platoon after platoon of the 2/14th Battalion kept arriving throughout the day, taking over from the battered platoons of the 39th, who were then able to fall back, rest, and fill the position of Battalion Reserve, grouping near the centre of the Isurava village. Each newly arrived god of the 2/14th lifted morale even further. In one splendid moment, Honner looked across to see something that he would remember for the rest of his life. It was Captain Claude Nye's 2/14th B Company marching into Isurava to relieve the 39th's valiant B Company, which had taken a terrible mauling over the previous two days, but was *just* holding on.

'I do not remember anything more heartening,' Honner would later write, 'than the sight of their confident deployment. Their splendid physique and bearing, and their cool, automatic efficiency— even the assembly line touch as two platoon mortar-men stepped one on either side of the track to pluck bombs from the haversacks of the riflemen filing past them without checking their pace—made a lasting impression on me.'[180]

It was a veritable ballistic ballet, which could only have been achieved by a team trained to operate like a well-oiled machine, and Honner wondered if the Japanese could possibly have such fine soldiers.

Honner's mood was so improved that only a short time later, Joe Dawson, on a brief errand to Battalion Headquarters, was amazed to see Colonel Honner holding a strange leaf in his hand and explaining its botanical significance to a slightly bemused lieutenant. It was an odd episode, but Joe took heart from it. If the colonel could find time to be talking about leaves, maybe things weren't so grim after all.

Of the newly arrived troops, one was Stan Bisset, and he immediately set to work collating information, moving around the perimeters counting heads and the estimated dead—both Australians and Japanese—and putting it all together so that Battalion Headquarters would always have up-to-date information of the situation. It was because of his grasp of the situation and knowledge of intended orders that Stan realised that his brother Butch's 10 Platoon of B Company—already proven as one of the battalion's finest—was soon going to be put in the toughest position of all, relieving 39th's B Company 11 Platoon on the highest ground of the western side of the perimeter.

Something was wrong. The Australians had not yet crumpled, and the reports coming back to General Horii were full of phrases such as 'unexpected resistance' and 'suffered many casualties'. How could this be? How could such a flimsy force of Australians be holding up his finest troops? Yes, they had provided unexpectedly strong resistance back at Kokoda, but that had surely been an aberration, one of those things that happens in war when through any number of factors a nominally inferior force that is well dug in can hold up a superior one. He most certainly had not counted on that level of resistance continuing at Isurava, and he was worried.

By the late afternoon of 27 August, all of 2/14th Battalion—bar A Company and Headquarters Company—were in place at Isurava. Their confidence remained high. One private from the 39th, Jack Boland, would later recount a significant episode to a fellow 39th soldier and subsequent author, Victor Austin.

'I was in a reserve position when the 2/14th troops arrived that afternoon, and as they were moving past I heard one of them say, "Where are these Japs? We'll have them back in Tokyo by the weekend." A while after that the fighting became hotter and the wounded started coming back. Towards dusk a couple of the 2/14th walking wounded came back through our position and I heard them asking each other how they had "copped it". The gist of the conversation was:

'First 2/14th Digger: "How did you get yours?"

'Second 2/14th Digger: "I don't know. I didn't see any Japs but I got bayoneted. Who said these bastards couldn't fight?"

'First 2/14th Digger: "Who do you mean? The Japs or the Chocos?"

'Second 2/14th Digger: "Both!"'[181]

The newcomers had spent just a small amount of time fighting side by side with the 39th, and their estimation of their abilities had changed indeed. Far from being soldiers who would melt when the heat was on, they had already proved themselves to be 'ragged bloody heroes' to use the tag that the AIF bestowed upon the 39th.[182]

Though the situation remained desperate, it was still considered stable enough that the wounded men of the 39th capable of walking could be evacuated back to Alola, with instructions to make their way to Moresby from there. No fewer than twenty-eight of them were put in the care of Lieutenant Johnston, and limped or staggered southwards to safety. They had done more than their bit, and would be marked for life by the sacrifice they had made. It was now for others to take over.

Shortly after the wounded had left, there was a brief lull in the fighting. It wasn't that the sound of shots had faded completely, so much as it had fallen away from the searing staccato of the morning and early afternoon. Ralph Honner took the opportunity to lead some of his senior officers down to 'rear creek' to shave themselves and have a quick wash. Apart from the virtues of personal hygiene, it was deeply ingrained in the culture of Australian military officers that they had to present themselves well to their men, and that a clean, clear face upped the likelihood that clean, clear thinking was going on just behind it.

Still, the men had only been down at the creek for a short time when a wild-eyed runner arrived in a gallop to inform Colonel Honner that the front being manned by E Company had just been penetrated by the enemy. As Honner would later describe it, 'I looked over at the unsuspecting Merritt. It seemed a pity to disturb him. "Captain Merritt," I said. "When you've finished your shave will you go to your company? The Japs have broken through your perimeter." Merritt didn't appreciate the Drake touch. An astonished look hung for an instant on his half-shaved face; then it lifted like a starter's barrier and he was off like a racehorse.'[183]

Happily, the Japanese penetration into the Australian lines proved to be short-lived as both the 'counter-penetration and mobile units' swung into action, but it had been close.

Back at Alola on this afternoon, Brigadier Potts was greatly worried, for he, too, was receiving reports that wave after wave of Japanese soldiers kept crashing upon the shores of Isurava. He knew that it could only be a matter of time before the Australians would be swamped. And he also felt a growing anxiety about what was happening on the parallel ridge, where the only defence against a developing Japanese thrust was the 53rd Battalion. There remained a dire risk that if the Japs pushed through all the way to Alola, the men at Isurava would be cut off from their supply line and then that would be it for the whole campaign. The only alternative for the Australians would be to melt into the jungle in an effort to save themselves.

Lieutenant Sakamoto was in command of the large body of Japanese men of the 144th Regiment who were making this thrust that Potts most feared, and he had to this point been amazed at the ease with which his men had been able to fulfil General Horii's orders: 'Advance along the eastern side of the valley, deploy to the south of Isurava, cut off the Australians' withdrawal, and annihilate them . . . '[184]

They had first come into contact with Australian soldiers from the 53rd Battalion on 25 August and had completely routed them, forcing them to flee back through the jungle. When another 53rd patrol came looking for them on the following day, they too were sent scurrying by Lieutenant Sakamoto's men.

Now, on 27 August, Brigadier Potts, knowing that the danger to the men at Isurava had never been more acute—and that the whole campaign hung in the balance—sent out two more companies of the all but completely demoralised 53rd to block the Japanese advance. If this failed, the only hope was that the men of the 2/16th could get to Alola in time to thwart the next attack . . .

Up at Isurava, most of the detail of this was blessedly unknown to Ralph Honner, and he was able to give his full concentration to the task at hand. As near as he could reckon, his men were killing the Japanese at a rough ratio of ten to one, by simple dint of the fact that they were dug into well-entrenched positions, and the invaders were not. It was with grim satisfaction that he noted that his men were now, to use his phrase, 'surrounded by a scattered rampart of the enemy dead . . . '[185]

But, not daunted, the Japanese used the same tactics that had worked well for them in the past. Blocked in one area, they probed in another. Now that Merritt's E Company had successfully withstood their attacks, the Japanese turned again to B Company on the high western flank who would now bear the brunt of their full-on assaults.

The tactics of the Japanese were as ruthless as they were costly in casualties. The command continued to send wave after wave of attackers onto the positions of the men of B Company as a clear method of determining the exact location of the Australian guns. Once the Australians fired heavily on the marauding Japanese foot-soldiers, cutting them to pieces, the Japanese mortar-men and mountain gun platoons would zero in and start firing. With every bullet and every mortar fired from both sides, and every artillery shot from the Japanese, the foliage of the jungle progressively thinned as leaves were blown away, small trees fell and the killing fields of fire became ever more clear.

By now the Australians were gaining some familiarity with the ways of the Japanese attacks. From out of the jungle at a distance of what sounded like 150 yards or so, they would hear a guttural shouted order. Closer then would come the gibberish repeated once or twice as the order went down the chain of command and then, as Ralph Honner would write of it, the whole palaver was 'succeeded by a wave of noisy chattering right along the front, almost as if the men in the leading sections were assuring each other that they were all starting out together to do or die. And as the chatter ceased they would crash from their concealment, leaping to the attack in a co-ordinated line.

'In larger scale attacks, by two or more companies, a system of chanting the orders forward from the rear was used, apparently with the same idea of securing a simultaneous assault by all the storming sections emerging from the forest in which they could hear but could not see each other. Away in the distance a powerful voice would chant an order of half a dozen to a dozen words. Somewhat nearer, three or four voices would be loudly lifted together in similar half-sung phrases; and on a closer, wider line a dozen junior commanders would take up the refrain in unison. Then, right along the front, the final, urgent order would rise from half a hundred throats, to be followed by the impressive sight of the serried ranks of Nippon rushing to their doom.

'As they were mown down, and it became apparent that to fight on would result only in heavier losses, the news somehow filtered back into the forest. From its dark recesses, a clear bugle call would ring out, and the attackers would turn and vanish into their jungle fastness as swiftly as they had come.'[186]

And so it continued, with the only advantage for the Australian defenders that at least with all the shouting and carry-on, they were given as much as five minutes warning that an attack would soon be on the way in, and they could set themselves accordingly. The Japanese bodies began to pile up, but so too did the casualties and deaths among the valiant men of B Company. Up at the highest point of this perimeter, Butch Bisset's 10 Platoon came under withering fire, but held their positions, exacting a terrible toll on the unfortunate Japanese soldiers sent to attack them.

Right in the middle of a furious fire-fight, Father Nobby Earl suddenly appeared, walking with a shovel over his shoulder towards an Australian soldier who had just been shot, and clearly killed, in no-man's land between the two forces. War or no war, bullets flying or no bullets flying—but by God it was the former—Nobby was going to give the fallen soldier an immediate Christian burial. As soon as he moved in front of the Australian soldiers they of course immediately stopped firing, and then the most extraordinary thing happened . . .

The Japanese also stopped firing. Yes, Father Nobby was clearly distinguishable as a man of God, with his priestly 'dog-collar' plainly visible; but it was by no means certain that all of the Japanese soldiers would recognise that, and just one easy shot from one of them would have brought him down. But nary a shot. Maybe it was his simple courage that stopped them; perhaps no man wanted to bring down one who was clearly unarmed, taking no defensive or cowering action; or maybe the simple humanity of his action awakened an equal humanity on those all around—whatever the case, not one shot was fired.

The two forces waited in the simmering jungle as Father Nobby dug a shallow grave, manhandled the soldier into it, covered it again and said his prayers. Then, equally purposefully, he put the shovel once again over his shoulder and walked back towards the Australian perimeter. At the very instant he was safely out of harm's way, the Japanese unleashed a fusillade to wake the newly dead. It was back on, and it went through the night . . .

A small parenthesis here. There were other surprising bursts of humanity from the Japanese enemy, even amid all the carnage. One that had come to Osmar White's attention, which had occurred early in the campaign, was when a Digger with a broken ankle was being carried on a stretcher through a large patch of kunai grass at the bottom of a gorge, and a Japanese plane had suddenly appeared from nowhere. The two natives, fearing the murderous machine-gun fire that was surely to come, fled for their lives, leaving the Digger powerless to do anything but lie on the stretcher looking straight up at the man who was about to kill him.

'But,' as White would write, 'the Jap . . . merely leaned out of his seat, waved and left.'[187]

Close parenthesis.

The sickly sweet smell of human flesh burning is unmistakable. This far into the Kokoda campaign the Australian soldiers knew that the smell came from the Japanese practice of burning their dead so that the ashes could be transported home. The difference on this afternoon was that the Australians had three-inch mortars that had been brought forward by the 2/14th. Up on the perimeter held by B Company, the men could clearly see smoke rising further up the hill, and the smell of the human flesh told them it was a funeral pyre. It was too good an opportunity to miss. This was no time to respect the Japanese dead, this was time to add to their number.[188]

B Company commander, Lieutenant French, had much experience with mortars and he knew exactly what he was doing as he gave the men operating them precise ranges and angles. And . . . FIRE! Screams coming from the direction of the smoke told them they had been precisely on target, so they quickly lobbed three more mortars at exactly the same range, just for good measure. Now build a *bigger* fire, you bastards.

Alas, at much the same time, on the opposite ridge, it was the Australians of the 53rd Battalion who were being killed by the rampant Japanese. Those killed included the 53rd's Commanding Officer, Lieutenant Colonel K. H. Ward. Now leaderless, and with neither morale nor even the bare basics of esprit de corps, much of the 53rd did not resist for long when the Japanese launched their main thrust along the parallel ridge line to Isurava. First one man shot through like a Bondi tram and then a couple of others quickly followed suit, running from their dangerous possies down to the comparative safety below the ridge, and it didn't take long before they were joined by a lot more.

The situation was now critical, as the Japanese pushed to within two miles of Alola, and then mysteriously stopped. Although Alola was practically defenceless, as the 2/16th had not yet arrived, the Japanese—not knowing this—dug in at Abuari, and only then began sending out patrols to reconnoitre the country ahead. Complete disaster for the Australians had been narrowly averted by this failure of Japanese strategy.

In all the world, there was surely no stiffness like it. It was the stiffness of one who had gone to sleep wet in a foxhole, partially submerged in mud and filth and water, and then at dawn begun to move his limbs for the first time in many hours. And while breakfast was only sometimes an option, the least the defenders of Isurava could do was ensure that they weren't personally providing breakfast for the many leeches that had settled on them overnight. A key part of the first minutes of the early morning was to put a lit cigarette onto the leeches until they dropped off. Such was life in the trenches.

And such was death . . .

At the first rays of the sun on 28 August, every Japanese mountain gun, every mortar and every heavy machine gun began to again pour withering fire upon the valiant defenders of Isurava, achieving several direct hits. One second a man was a living, breathing Digger— a body who Australia '*bore, shaped, made aware. Gave, once, her flowers to love, her ways to roam*'—and the next, after the whistle of the approaching missile achieved a crescendo never heard before . . . the man was blown apart. The survivors kept firing, perhaps glancing at the torn remains of the body of their mate just three yards away, but firing as if their own life depended on it, because it *did*. There was rarely time for grief, or even shock—that would come later. It was not that another's life was cheap, it was that your own life was precious, and all realised instinctively that in the thick of battle feelings of grief and shock were luxuries you just couldn't afford if you were to survive.

Never in the battle of Isurava so far had the firing on the Australians been so intense as on this morning, as Horii went all out for the knockout blow. And never, once the firing ceased, were the waves of Japanese soldiers coming at them so thickly bunched and committed. A seeming unending tide of them emerged from the jungle . . .

From Divisional HQ in Port Moresby, General Tubby Allen sent a message to Brigadier Potts in the middle of that morning of 28 August, even as carnage and catastrophe were being just kept at bay around the entire perimeter of Isurava: '28 Aug, Allen to Potts. Reports indicate that your patrols are static. Would not fluid fighting patrols with an ambush as a rallying point be better and could not small fighting patrols lure enemy into such ambush?[189]

Now why didn't they think of that!

With respect to Tubby, it seemed extraordinary to Potts that Divisional HQ could be so presumptuous as to think that, from a distance so far away, they could *still* have a better strategic understanding of what was required than the leadership on the spot.

For the defenders of Isurava, however, all such wrangling between their senior officers was neither here nor there as they continued to keep up a steady stream of fire to beat the beggars back. In the Australian trenches, it was simply load and re-fire, load and re-fire, load and re-fire, as the Bren and Tommy guns kept chattering. The key was to ensure that while one gun was in the reloading process, the other guns around it would cover for it and that no matter what, *no matter what*, the oncoming Japanese soldiers would be met by an unending storm of bullets.

The imperative was for the man alongside to grab the gun from a dead man's hands, pick it up and fire it himself. Any Japanese soldier that made it through to the Australian lines was dealt with by bayonet, rifle-butt or whatever came to hand, even if it was only your fists themselves.

With any less ferocity, the Australians would have been overrun in minutes and, as the morning of the 28th whistled on, the piles of Japanese soldiers became progressively thicker on the jungle perimeter. Was there no end to them? How long could the Japs keep this up?

The answer: a long time. In this full cry of battle, the Japanese were in a kind of frenzy unknown to their western counterparts. This was what years of training, of praying, of being inculcated with the belief that their highest calling was to die in the service of the Emperor had prepared them for.

One of the soldiers there at Isurava, Toshiya Akizawa, later told Australian film-maker Patrick Lindsay:

'You need a special kind of courage. When you draw your sword and point it forward like that, this is a display of your own courage as well as a signal to the men. It doesn't just mean right we are going to attack now. In a sense it is a signal but also is deeply linked to your personality and courage. It is like in music when the conductor raises the baton to the orchestra. Instead of raising the baton though, you draw your sword and say "Charge!". You give the order. Obviously you are not trying to cut the opponent. It is in order to get everybody out and into the attack.

'I remember that all my junior officers, my NCOs and most of my men lost their lives. All we could do was leave the place we were in and attack up the hill. And we were being told from behind. Attack! Attack! So there was no courage. Just without thinking, we attacked and attacked and attacked . . . '[190]

CHAPTER THIRTEEN

GUMPTION, GUTS AND GLORY

I remember that an Australian soldier, wearing just a pair of shorts and stripped to the waist, came around and towards us, throwing hand grenades at us. And I remember thinking at the time that this was something that would have been very hard for a Japanese soldier to do . . . I suppose the Australians had a different motivation for fighting but this soldier, this warrior, was far braver than any in Japan I think and when I think about it now it still affects me . . .

Private Shigenori Doi, 144th Regiment[191]

Much was lacking in New Guinea, but the greatest shortage of all was information about the enemy . . . General Headquarters believed we were up against a handful of Japanese . . . In reality we faced a well-trained force of greatly superior strength; yet as late as 7 September MacArthur was insisting to the Prime Minister [Curtin] that we were stronger than the enemy . . .

General Sir Sydney F. Rowell[192]

Finally, Damien Parer, Chester Wilmot and Osmar White hauled themselves to the top of a particularly brutal hill overlooking the Eora Creek encampment, just ten miles from Isurava, and saw a scene that would never leave them. There below, on a small plateau about fifty yards wide by a hundred yards long, was a large dam of mud, on which floated six haphazard huts, all of which looked like they might sink beneath the muck at any moment. Around the huts were hundreds of mud-men emerging from the shins up: Australian soldiers covered from head to toe in the slush that they had been living, sleeping and, in many cases, dying in, in this God-forsaken settlement. On the edge of the settlement were hundreds of panting porters, lying like exhausted and beaten greyhounds after a long race, who with their last ounces of energy were picking at little balls of muddy rice that they were holding in equally muddy banana leaves.

Despite the obvious fatigue of the soldiers, as White soon discovered, there was frenetic activity going on inside the huts, where army surgeons and medical orderlies were working in atrocious conditions trying to save lives that were hanging by a thread.

Their operating tables were stretchers. Their instruments were being sterilised in a biscuit tin suspended by a piece of wire above a small fire.[193] In all, it provided exactly the kind of graphic war footage that Parer sought most and he decided to stay at Eora for the moment, slow down the shutter speed to compensate for the dim light, and capture it all while he could. After a brief rest, Wilmot and White moved forward towards Isurava, which they were told was the frontline.

In the principal Japanese field hospital back at Kokoda, which held many of the wounded and seriously sick Japanese soldiers from the actions at Oivi, Wairopi, Gorari, Kokoda and Isurava, things were even more grim. Takida Kenji, a Japanese officer, who saw it, later described it in this manner:

'On the other side [of the river], a one-metre high wooden sign read in black ink, "Field Hospital Entrance". Lined up on the nearby embankment were countless white sapling grave markers. I passed through and discovered a field hospital in the midst of the jungle. Inside, numerous small wards were lined up like pig-sties. Each was constructed from thick poles with low ceilings. The blackened rotten banana leaves that formed the roof were constantly dripping. The injured and sick were packed in like sardines.

'On the floor were spread green leaves or thin saplings. There were no blankets. The patients lay strewn in their blood-stained, blackened uniforms. Large drops of water fell on their pale faces from the leaves of the surrounding trees. However, they didn't even have the energy to avoid them. They were also tormented from the pain of their injuries, or distressed by high fever. Were they praying for life? Or just waiting for death? Some several hundred of these inmates were probably embraced by unbearable torment. The hospital, where not a word was uttered, had sunk to the pit of a deathly silence.'[194]

At high noon on 28 August, the last of the 2/14th Battalion—A Company and Headquarters Company—arrived at Isurava, and with them came Lieutenant Colonel Arthur Key, their commanding officer. Now that the 2/14th was fully in place, they had planned to withdraw the entire 39th Battalion to safety, but Colonel Honner demurred to Key.

Honner pointed out how precarious the situation was; how there was no sign of Japanese withdrawal, and insisted that the 39th not leave Isurava, but instead stand and fight with their brothers of the AIF. It was a time when everyone who could still wield a gun would be needed to stem the attack of the large force of Japanese.[195] Lieutenant Colonel Key gratefully accepted and together they persuaded Potts back at Alola that this was the only wise decision possible.

It was surely not too difficult a conclusion to come to. For though in one sense the battle was now evenly poised, with the undefeated troops of General Tomitaro Horii's South Seas Force going up against the equally undefeated 2/14th, that did not tell the whole story. Despite the arrival of the 2/14th, the Australians were still vastly outnumbered. In their own battalion they had some 546 active soldiers capable of wielding a weapon, while against them were no fewer than six Japanese regiments, each boasting some eight hundred highly trained soldiers. Potts, Honner and Key were not aware that there were six regiments against them, but they did know that there were so many soldiers that the Japanese could send waves of a hundred men at a time seemingly without fear of running out of men.

It was for this reason that Honner's offer to keep the 39th at Isurava was so highly appreciated. On such an occasion, Potts could not help but look at the reality of the situation he had inherited and try to make it fit with the orders he had been given. Two weeks prior to this the Western Australian officer had attended a meeting with Major General Morris back in Moresby where he had been given orders to check the Japanese advance, turn them around and then retake Kokoda. As it was, in the grimness of the situation, Potts was all too aware that they would be flat out holding the Japanese up for long, let alone routing them and turning their tails for home. For now, there was nothing for it but to make the most of what they had . . .

The sound of gunfire rolling dirty through the jungle from the direction of Isurava told them that there was unlikely to be any let up on this day and, as it turned out, the decision of the 39th to stay and fight with their AIF brothers proved crucial. For in the middle of the afternoon, right on the edge of the sector defended by the 2/14th's mighty B Company, the sheer weight of the Japanese numbers and the ferocity of their constant attacks saw them push their way through the perimeter and—worst of all possible things— fire on the two vulnerable flanks of Australians that had been opened up to them.

In the barest nick of time, with the 39th covering their previous positions, it was Lieutenant Colonel Arthur Key himself with soldiers from A Company and his own Headquarters Company who arrived and, after a bout of furious fighting, were able to push the Japs back beyond the original perimeter. But it was close.

•

For every ounce of Key's elation at stemming the breach, General Horii, sitting on his white horse and watching the whole thing with his binoculars from a high point just under a mile away to the north, felt sheer desperation. Put together with all the reports he had received from his field commanders, Horii had come to a very troubling conclusion. Australia's 39th Battalion which had been opposing his men for some weeks—who had seemed so exhausted and starving they were 'eating stones', to use the Japanese expression—had clearly been reinforced with fresh troops. There was no way the extraordinary number of casualties the 144th Regiment had taken on the previous day could have come from the 39th alone; no way that they could have thrown back his best soldiers once they had breached the perimeter.

What to do? It was out of the question to retreat, and General Horii was becoming ever more aware that time was of the essence. Every day in the jungle weakened them—in these first three days of the battle of Isurava alone, they had lost 350 soldiers and suffered another one thousand wounded. Each passing day strained their supply lines, blunted their thrust and made clear victory less likely. They had to break through, and quickly.

That evening as the fighting lulled, Second Lieutenant Noda wrote in his diary: 'The Australians are gradually being outflanked, but their resistance is very strong and our casualties are great. The outcome of the battle is very difficult to foresee . . . '[196]

Lieutenant Colonel Key and his Intelligence Officer Stan Bisset felt much the same way. That night they had a long meeting in Key's hut where, by the light of the lantern, they tried to collate the many reports that had come in of estimated Japanese strengths on the various sectors, and the number of casualties both sides had taken, to try to work out how best to situate their own forces on the morrow. There was no doubt the Australians had performed well, but the unknown factor was just what resources the Japanese still had to throw into the battle.

When the meeting was over at about eight o'clock on the evening of 28 August, the two decided to personally reconnoitre the frontlines, to see that all was in order. With that in mind they headed off to make contact with the forward platoon on the northern perimeter, where the track led to Deniki. They had gone no more than a hundred yards however, when an Australian voice whispered to them, 'We're the forward troops, Sir.'

At that very instant, both Key and Bisset saw some scurrying figures in the darkness ahead, briefly flitting across the track, and realised they were Japanese. Sweet Jesus, they really were that close.

Assured that all the defensive positions were well manned and all was relatively stable for the moment, both men returned to Battalion Headquarters, such as it was.

It was that very stability that General Horii could bear no more. For it was around this time, completely frustrated by the Australian resistance, that the Japanese general decided to throw his two fresh reserve battalions into the fray. If that didn't shift the Australians, then nothing could. It was time for total assault . . .

29 August 1942. Different day. Same plan of attack. The Australians had missiles and mortars rained upon them, even as heavy fire came at them from out of the jungle. Then there was a sudden pause before the wild Japanese charges began.

It was a measure of the renewed Japanese ferocity, and their sheer weight of numbers due to the two fresh battalions, that by late morning many of them were actually getting through to the perimeter and fierce bayonet battles between Australians and Japanese broke out. It was fast and furious, and very, very bloody.

Early on that afternoon of the 29th, the Japanese very nearly broke through on the right forward sector of the perimeter held by C Company facing Deniki, where the attrition rate among the defenders had been so severe that the level of resistance was thinner. The gunfire and grenades between the two sides had been so unrelenting that most of the lighter vegetation separating them had been all but wiped out, meaning there were fewer and fewer places to hide. Colonel Key sent in a platoon from A Company to bolster the defence, but as the afternoon wore on, they too were in trouble as *still* the Japanese kept coming. Again, the Isurava defenders were only just managing to hold on.

The high ground above the village, now being held by Butch Bisset's 10 Platoon, was taking perhaps the most heat of all, and the number of their dead and wounded had been high as the Japanese continued to thrust for this crucial terrain. Butch's men were a frenzy of activity, covering each other as they kept up their rate of fire and tossing a few grenades Tojo's way for good measure. One thing was certain: this was as unlike their experience in Syria as it was possible to get. In the Middle East it had been all open country with both sides able to get a look at each other and make rapid, sweeping flanking movements. Here . . . well, here you were lucky if you could see the bastards before they were right at your throat.

One way or another, though, this looked like it was going to be a donnybrook to beat them all . . .

Down at Brigade Headquarters at Alola, Brigadier Potts was monitoring the situation as closely as possible, and still endeavouring to convince Moresby of the need for reinforcements, when there was a commotion outside. He emerged from his tent to see what seemed to be a group of walking scarecrows staggering towards them out of the jungle. It was Lieutenant Bob Sword with his two platoons of men who, cut off by the Japanese advance, had been forcing their way through the jungle for three days and nights, avoiding the Japanese positions and endeavouring to reach relative safety . . . and now they had. Along the way they had been joined by another lost platoon from their battalion, and now the whole lot of them were staggering into the compound. Some of the men were barely able to stand as they had hardly eaten in their time in the jungle; all of them had their uniforms torn to shreds and their bloodied feet emerging from boots that were only just hanging together. Clearly they were all in need of medical attention on a dozen different fronts, but . . .

But it was a measure of the commitment that the Australian soldiers on the Kokoda Track had to each other, that once told of how grim the situation was at Isurava, Sword and his men *insisted* on leaving for the frontlines at Isurava again. After Nobby Earl and one of the doctors had done what they could for them, and the men of the 2/16th had given them whatever cigarettes they could spare, together with a cup of tea and some food, they were off, limping gamely up the hill towards Isurava. Brigadier Potts watched them go, his chest swelling with pride. Maybe they were outnumbered. Maybe they were outgunned. But with men like these, with *guts* like the Australians were displaying, they were, by God, still in the fight to give the Japanese something to think about.

Not that there weren't some exceptions. Very early one morning Tom Grahamslaw—who had been attached to Potts's Brigade Headquarters—was on his own and walking fast along the track to Alola when he came across a strange sight. As he would later recount it: 'I saw two soldiers alongside the track. One of them had had it with the war and had prevailed upon his mate to put a bullet through his boot, the idea being to graze the top portion of his big toe at the same time. Unfortunately, his mate's hand must have trembled, because the shot removed most of the toe. Then followed some choice language from the stricken one. No doubt I should have charged the men with having committed a serious offence. However, I couldn't help reflecting that the wounded man would have a torrid time on the long walk back over the Owen Stanleys . . .'

All of the wounded men on the track winding back were indeed having a torrid time of it. But now some of them were needed again. The thirty walking wounded of the 39th who'd been sent back to safety by Colonel Honner a couple of days before, under the command of Lieutenant Johnston, now heard of their comrades' plight. Of the thirty men, twenty-seven immediately turned around and headed back to Isurava. Of the three who didn't, one had lost a foot, one a forearm, while the other had taken a bullet in the throat.

It was not so simple a thing as courage . . .

It was not so simple a thing as discipline which can be hammered into men by a drill sergeant. It was not the result of careful planning, for there could have been little. It was the common man of the free countries rising in all his glory from mill, office, mine, factory and shop and applying to war, the lessons learned when he went down the mine to release trapped comrades; when he hurled the lifeboat through the surf; when he endured hard work and poverty for his children's sake . . .

This is the great tradition of democracy. This is the future. This is victory.

Despite Chester Wilmot's exhaustion, as he walked on with Ossie White his anger continued to grow. As an experienced war correspondent, it was absolutely clear to him that these brave men had been let down by their high command. How could the likes of Blamey have sent up against hardened Japanese veterans these *kids* of the 39th, however valiant they proved to be? How could they be so underequipped? How was it that the 53rd had been sent forward with only a single week's training, after spending all the rest of their time unloading ships? What was the story with the 2/14th and 2/16th heading to the front without their supplies being absolutely assured? And how was it that the *whole lot of them* had been sent into the New Guinea jungle without proper camouflage? How hard could it have been to work out that khaki uniforms in the green New Guinea jungle were going to be an invitation to kill an Australian?

It all fitted in with the overall picture of General Blamey's incompetence that Chester had been building up for some time. It was well known that Blamey was a womaniser and a sot, and not for nothing did the troops sometimes refer to him as 'Brothel Blamey'. Chester's friend and fellow war correspondent and poet, Kenneth Slessor, had even once witnessed the Australian military leader drunkenly carrying on in a sleazy bar in Cairo with an Egyptian woman of low moral fibre, in full view of his senior staff officers.

And while covering the war in Palestine, Chester himself had come across a story that continued to work on him, even though he had never been able to nail it down hard enough to broadcast it and put it in the public domain. The story was that Blamey had done a deal with the provider of films for the Australian troops in the Middle East, a Mr Shafto, whereby Blamey received kickbacks and Shafto was able to provide inferior quality films with no problem from high command.[197] All of that was bad enough, but now, when before Chester's eyes it was clear that Australian soldiers were dying because Blamey wasn't up to the job, Wilmot's anger knew no bounds.

Back at Eora Creek busily filming, Damien Parer was appalled by the continuing stream of wounded men coming their way, but it was at least obvious that he would not be facing the same problem here as he did in the Middle East. In Syria, he found the enemy had often given up before he had a chance to get his cameras into place, thus denying him the opportunity to get the serious action footage he desired. Here, apparently, there was no such risk and it seemed more likely, from what he could gather from the wounded men and officers, that the action of the Japanese would soon be coming towards him.

In a further attempt to reinforce the precarious position at Isurava, Potts ordered C Company—one of the remaining companies of the 53rd Battalion that was still functioning—to leave their position defending the now relatively quiet section of the parallel track down from Alola and move up to Isurava.

And it was at Isurava, at around two o'clock on the afternoon of 29 August, that the Japanese again broke through the perimeter and whole new waves of enemy soldiers suddenly appeared.

About three hundred yards up the hill from where the breach occurred, Colonel Key's Battalion Headquarters was quickly made aware of the urgency of the situation and it was Colonel Key himself who ordered the counterattack. One who quickly volunteered was Private Bruce Kingsbury, a quietly spoken, gentle kind of bloke from Malvern in Melbourne, and as the Japanese soldiers began to surge, he broke into a jog-trot down the hill.

'Where are you going, Bruce?' Key's Second-in-Command, Captain Phil Rhoden, asked him as he passed.

'Just down the track, Skip,' Kingsbury replied, even as he picked up speed, with his best mate Alan Avery right with him all the way, just as he always was.

When Kingsbury got there the situation was a lot worse than he imagined. As he looked further down the hill, he was appalled to see the many clumps of Japanese now beginning to break through, and he also saw that one of his friends, the always courageous Corporal Lindsay 'Teddy' Bear, had been badly hit. Teddy had blood all over his face and front—courtesy of a piece of shrapnel that had gone up his nose—and had then been shot in his left hand. *Still* not beaten, Teddy had whacked the injured hand in his shirt and kept firing with his right until shot twice in his legs he could barely move. He had also been firing the Bren gun so much that it was too hot to hold and he had been obliged to grip it by the tripod, even as he kept one finger on the trigger to keep it firing.

Much of this Kingsbury soaked up in bare seconds as he now sprinted towards Teddy Bear and grabbed the Bren gun from him.

There would afterwards be much debate as to precisely what occurred in Bruce Kingsbury's mind at that moment—whether he was operating within the realms of conscious thought, or simply acting out of staggering, instinctive courage. What he did though became seared deep into the memory of every Australian soldier within cooee who saw it, and they were many.

Firing from the hip, Kingsbury kept charging down the hill, firing at the exhausted Japanese soldiers coming up the hill and scattering them as he went. Whenever a gun was raised against him, he somehow seemed to be able to get off accurate shots before the Japs could do him any damage.

To the observers, it almost seemed as if the bullets must be bouncing off him, so suicidal did his action seem, and yet he was still going! Stunned at what they were seeing, and inspired by it, many of the Australian soldiers charged after him and added their own withering fire to Bruce's. Within perhaps forty-five seconds, it was all but over. Some thirty Japanese had been taken out of commission, and the potential hole in the Australian lines had been blocked. There was little Japanese resistance left on that part of the hillside, and many of the soldiers had turned tail and run back into the jungle in the face of this madman.

The other Australian soldiers were just catching up with Kingsbury—now momentarily stopped before a large rock as he changed magazines—when a Japanese sniper suddenly appeared at the top of the rock and fired off a single shot. Bruce clutched at his chest and went down, with just the slightest groan.

Alan Avery, after unleashing a fusillade of bullets which may or may not have taken out the Japanese sniper, cradled Bruce in his arms. Now that the Japanese had retreated and this part of the battlefront was in brief hiatus, the silence roared all around.

There is a limpness in the dead that is unmistakable and irrefutable, and it was obvious to all the gathered soldiers that Bruce was gone as his head lolled back and his arms flopped loosely while Alan continued to hold him in a kind of rocking motion, whispering, 'No, God, no, please *no* . . . '

Alan didn't want to believe it, *couldn't* believe that he now held in his arms his best friend from childhood onward, who was now, unmistakably, dead. Refusing to accept it, Avery picked Bruce up, put him in a fireman's carry across his shoulders and trudged back for medical help while the other soldiers remained to consolidate the position that Kingsbury had won at such cost.

At the Regimental Aid Post, Dr Don Duffy did not take long in his diagnosis. One look at the red hole where the bullet entered above Bruce's heart told him the truth. If he was alive the wound would be gushing blood, but of that there was no sign. To confirm it, he pulled back Bruce's eyelids and . . . alas. The eyes were the window of the soul, and there was never the slightest doubt when the soul had departed, as was clearly the case now with Bruce.

'I'm sorry Alan,' the doctor said softly, 'he's gone.'

Alan Avery wept, wept as he had never wept before. For his valour and extraordinary courage under fire, Kingsbury would be posthumously awarded a Victoria Cross medal, the highest Commonwealth military award for bravery.

Though Bruce Kingsbury's sacrifice had retrieved the situation that afternoon, the predicament of the surviving defenders was grimly obvious. Despite the heroic nature of the Australians' battle to date, still the Japanese mortars and charges were taking their toll, still there was no sign of the Japanese running out of soldiers to charge at them. Three times B Company had given ground on the high side of the perimeter and three times had taken it back, but they had now lost so many men that it would soon be beyond them to retrieve the situation one more time.

One bright spot at least was when Lieutenant Sword and his men arrived, just before sunset. Honner later recorded his feelings.

'I was surprised to see a grimy, bearded figure leading in a tattered line at twilight. I did not recognise him until he saluted and announced: "Sword, Sir, reporting in from patrol." There was more than mere formality in my answering salute.'[198]

Happily, Lieutenant Johnston's walking wounded from the 39th were only minutes behind them, and the men of the 2/14th were staggered and heartened all at once to see that the same scarecrows they'd seen off two days ago were now, voluntarily, back with them and bearing arms. They looked at these ragged bloody heroes, with their swollen feet, tottering countenance, open wounds and determined expressions with awe. Once again, many of the men of the AIF regretted every barbed joke they might have made at these blokes' expense. Chocolate soldiers, indeed!

Despite their collective bravery, however, there was only one sane move possible and Lieutenant Colonel Key, commanding the 2/14th, requested Brigadier Potts's approval to authorise it. That was to pull back from their present position to a mile down the track to the Isurava Rest House—a small collection of huts to accommodate any travelling missionaries, magistrates and officers, or the like. They would be unlikely to hold their present position for another day, and by carefully withdrawing they would give themselves the advantage of fresh defensive positions that the Japanese would again have to pay heavily in blood to take.

To stay would be to risk annihilation, and that would have accomplished precisely nothing. Potts, though reluctant, deferred to his man on site. He knew that Key would never make such a request unless the position really was untenable, so he sent back the signal that Key could proceed to withdraw that night. Recognising that the front would now be moving towards them, Potts took the precaution of immediately sending back the very worst of the seriously wounded from Alola. All the rest would be needed to hold a gun and stiffen the defence for what was coming.

In the meantime, now that authorisation had been given, Colonel Key requested that Stan Bisset reconnoitre the Isurava Rest House, and determine strategic positions for each company.

Even as Stan was being given his orders out on the western sector of the battlefield, his brother Butch and 10 Platoon continued in a ferocious fire-fight with an onslaught of Japanese. As Butch and his men were the ones occupying the high ground, they were always the ones who were going to be getting the most heat from the Japanese as they tried to outflank the Australians—and so it proved. Over the previous twelve hours, the Japanese had launched no fewer than eleven company attacks on them, with each company comprising around a hundred men. How many of the beggars *were* there? The 10 Platoon didn't budge. A strong, disciplined unit, there was no question of the men retreating, and all knew that this was *it*: do or die.

Butch kept talking to the men, moving among them distributing ammunition and grenades, keeping as low to the ground as he could. He was just handing out the third lot of grenades, though, when in the fast fading light a Japanese soldier of the 144th Regiment spied what he was sure was movement at the exact spot where all the fire from the Australians had been coming, and squeezed off one quick burst of machine-gun fire in hope. He was rewarded with the unmistakable groan of a man who had just been hit, and then what was almost certainly the thud of a body. Well, maybe not a thud. At that distance, and with that level of noise, there was no way you could hear something so relatively placid as a groan or slumping body, but somehow you could *feel* it when you had a hit. He hoped so, anyway.

The strangest thing about being shot is the lack of immediate pain— at least searing, agonising pain. Rather, for Butch Bisset it felt like a very hard punch in the stomach that knocked him off his feet and took the wind right out of him. Then came, *oh mother*, the moment when he put his hand to his stomach and it came away, *oh mother,* wet. That he was hit he knew only too well. That it was bad was apparent from the moment he held his hand up in the wan light to see it completely covered in his own blood. Somewhere within him as many as six bullets were lodged, each one having severed blood vessels which now continued to pump more blood into the menacing twilight with every beat of his heart. Oh *mother*. The disbelief. The shock. Was this a dream? Had it really happened? Was there no way out? Was this *it?* Oh mother. He felt faint, as he sat there, trying to collect himself, trying to hold his intestines in with one hand, while he set up his rifle with the other . . . eager to take out any Jap that came his way. Oh mother.

Around and about Butch at that time, both with his own platoon and other nearby platoons, a furious rearguard action was soon underway to abandon the position while safely retrieving as many soldiers as possible—wounded or otherwise. In all the maelstrom, one man stood stronger and more courageous than the rest.

Corporal Charlie McCallum was the best axeman in Gippsland, his mighty arms capable of chopping through two solid feet of log in just over ninety seconds. It was he who volunteered to be reverse point man—in effect the rearguard for the rearguard—the first man the Japanese would encounter in their pursuit. No matter that he already bore three wounds, to his arm, his leg and his groin. She'll be right. Leave me with enough guns and plenty of ammo and I'll get the job done.

So it proved. The power of his arms was such that he was capable of firing a Bren gun from his right hip even as he hoisted a Tommy gun to his left shoulder and did the same, and that is exactly what the first Japanese soldier was hit by when he came into range. The two soldiers immediately behind him were equally cut down.

When his Bren ran out of ammunition, Charlie kept firing with the Tommy while changing the magazine on the Bren, but even then it was a close run thing. One of the charging Japanese soldiers got to within a yard of him before the axeman cut him down. In a momentary lull while the Japanese regrouped to decide how to take this madman down, the corporal received the signal that the main body of troops was now clear and he could withdraw himself, back past the point where the rest of the rearguard had set up the next ambush point. For his bravery in the face of such massive opposition Corporal McCallum was later awarded the Distinguished Conduct Medal.

At the moment that Butch had been shot, Stan had been just fifty yards away, trying to check that everything was all right with 10 Platoon. Before he could get to Butch, though, and amid terrible fire, he met one of Butch's men, Tom Wilson, who'd had his hand blown off. As Stan led him to the Regimental Aid Post to get medical attention, it was Tom who told him.

'Butch has been hit pretty bad. The boys are trying to bring him in.'

Stan felt like a giant hand had just grabbed his heart and squeezed hard, nearly choking the life out of him.

In a daze, Stan organised the corps medical officer and his close friend, Captain Dr Don Duffy, to be ready for Butch when he arrived, before following his original orders to assess the new fall-back position in the area of the Isurava Rest House.

When he worked out the most defensible position—about three hundred yards back from the Rest House on the Alola side—he found it to be filled with the soldiers from the 53rd Battalion's C Company that Potts had called for the previous afternoon. They had moved only a little way up the track before stopping to have a bit of a rest.

'I am sorry, fellows, but you will have to move from here,' Stan told them. 'These positions will shortly be needed by the 2/14th and the 39th when we fall back here.'

'We're not moving anywhere,' one of the privates replied belligerently, his words backed by the fact that neither he nor his comrades showed the slightest inclination to accede to Stan's request.

'Where are your officers?' Stan responded sharply, amazed at such insubordination to a superior officer.

'Gone . . . dunno . . . gone,' the soldier replied, still entirely uninterested.

'I am *ordering* you to move,' Stan said with some feeling.

'We're *not* moving,' the soldier replied with equal force, while still somehow communicating his complete indifference to what this AIF officer felt about it. They were many, he was one.

Well, if it was like that, there was only way these blokes would understand. Stan drew his gun, cocked it, and pointed it at this recalcitrant soldier who was clearly their spokesman. 'Move.'

They moved.

Nearing 10 p.m., finally, Stan met the stretcher party about a hundred yards and two hours from where and when he had first heard the news about Butch. They had managed to get Butch into a small clearing about fifteen yards off the track where Don could have some space and peace to do what he could.

When they shone the torch on Butch, though, Stan immediately knew it was every bit as bad as he had feared: close to hopeless. The burst of machine-gun fire had sprayed Butch right across his belly, and through the globs of blood Stan could see his brother's intestines. Just the fact that they had got him back down that murderous slope from where he had been hit was extraordinary enough, and in fact 10 platoon had lost one more man killed and one wounded in the process, but it was a measure of how much

Butch was loved by his men that they would take such risks to get him out.

Don did his best, but it was little enough. Though he dressed Butch's wounds, and gave him morphine to ease the pain, the look he gave Stan confirmed the obvious—it wouldn't be long.

They talked of the days on the farm. That time with Uncle Abe. Of Mum and Dad. Their sister and two other brothers. Sang songs of their childhood. At that moment, they knew, Mum would be just likely turning in after making Dad a cup of tea. What about the time during the floods when they were on their raft and Stan had nearly drowned, only to be saved by Butch getting to him in the nick of time? They talked of rugby, of days with the Powerhouse Club, of things that happened in the Middle East.

As Stan and Butch quietly talked, most of the men of the 2/14th and 39th Battalions were quietly filing past on the track, just fifteen yards away, taking up their new defensive positions in the darkness.

Among them was Joe Dawson, with his best mates, Ray Phillips and Wally Gratz. Joe was carrying his own rifle, as well as Ray's highly prized new Bren gun, while Ray and Wally came behind with a heavy ammunition box suspended from a sapling. It was a black hell on earth trying to manoeuvre in the darkness on such a track, tentatively putting one foot forward after another to see if you could put it down on something solid, and at one notably narrow spot Joe stepped off the track for a bit of a breather and to let other blokes pass, while he let Ray and Wally catch up. No sooner had he taken a step back though than . . . *there was nothing there* . . . and he was suddenly falling. Fortunately, a small ledge several yards down the cliff-face stopped him and with great difficulty, and Ray and Wally's help, he was able get back up on the track.

Once he was back, top-side, Ray wasted no time making sure that no real damage had been done.

'How's me bloody *Bren*?' Ray said to Joe, clearly appalled.

'Stuff your bloody Bren, I have hurt myself!' Joe roared back. In fact though, he felt little real pain at all, despite having taken a lot of skin off both knees. In that kind of environment, just finding yourself still alive was usually more than enough to act as a painkiller. The three Digger mates struggled on down the track.

By two o'clock in the morning it was done. Under the very noses of the Japanese, all of the Australians had successfully slipped away and were now dug into their new positions just below the line of the Isurava Rest House.

Back in the tiny clearing, though, it was apparent to Stan Bisset that the life was ebbing out of his brother's eyes. Just when it seemed he was gone though, a sudden spark of something would return, and Stan would sing to him some more. In one brief hopeful moment Butch was even lucid enough to congratulate Stan on his thirtieth birthday, which had occurred just two days earlier. Stan thanked him for the thought and then held Butch's hand all the tighter as a sudden shudder of agony—like something was breaking deep inside the older brother—swept over him. Don Duffy visited periodically and kept the morphine up to Butch, but really there was little to do but talk spasmodically, sing a little, and wait. Sometimes, Stan thought of his mum and dad, back in Victoria, and wondered how they would take the news. It would likely be the near death of his mother especially.

Finally though, at 4.00 a.m., while Stan was holding Butch's hand, there was a sudden slight shudder and then he went limp. Stan squeezed Butch's hand, hoping for some return pressure, a spark of life left, but there was nothing, stone-cold nothing. His brother's hand was already cold and clammy.

Butch was gone. Stan wept.

At dawn, almost on the spot where he died, they buried him. Stan said a prayer over his grave, where he had also lashed together a couple of small stripped saplings into the form of a cross. And then he was back into it . . .

It was later recorded in the official *History of the Second Fourteenth Battalion* by author W. B. Russell: 'Perhaps no other single death could have more deeply shocked the Battalion. "Butch" was one of the most strongly individual men in the Unit, and every man's friend. He had all the manly virtues together with a rollicking sense of humour. Above all, he loved his men unto death and they returned his devotion.'

Sadly, Butch was just one of many who had been either killed or wounded during this terrible period of the battle, among both the Australians and the Japanese. The campaign was so bloody at this point that the natives of Isurava—who had abandoned the village weeks before when the battle had descended upon them and were now gathered at what they thought was a safe point about a mile downstream of the creek on the northern side of the village— were horrified to see that the water now ran red. They refused to drink from it, a sanction that would last for generations.

Osmar White and Chester Wilmot continued to make their way forward. It was hard, grim work to be heading *towards* the cannon's roar and constant *dub-dub-dub* of the heavy Japanese Juki machine guns—the Diggers had nicknamed them 'woodpeckers' for good reason—but if there was action about it was their job to be there and they pressed on. Sure, correspondents were meant to be unarmed and it totally contravened the dictates of the Geneva Convention that they had a few hand grenades with them and a rifle, but it still made them feel a little better that they possessed something with which to defend themselves should it come to it.

What highlighted the seriousness of the Australian situation, however, was the thickening traffic of sick and wounded Australian soldiers coming the other way. To see many of these Diggers it was a wonder that they could still stand, let alone stagger along. For, truth be told, a lot of them were mere skeletons with the skin still attached and still mighty hearts that continued to beat despite everything. More often than not suffering from fever, entirely emaciated, these figures could only proceed a few tottering steps at a time, before gasping for air—'The loose skin on the sides of their necks palpitating like a lizard's throat,' as White described it— resting and then going again.[199] Still, though, there was remaining spirit in them, with each man that was still capable grinning at the oncomers and saying an all but unvaried greeting as the journalists stopped and leaned away each time to try to give the wounded right of way on the too narrow track: 'Good day, Dig. Pretty tough, eh?'

It certainly was that. After salutations and whatever cigarettes and encouragement they could spare, the two non-combatants moved forward. What simply staggered both of them was the stoicism of the wounded, their lack of complaint and their total commitment to sticking together to see each other through.

'Here's a steep pinch and a wounded Digger's trying to climb it,' Chester Wilmot described it for the Australian Broadcasting Commission. 'You need both hands and both feet, but he's been hit in the arm and thigh. Two of his cobbers are helping him along. One goes ahead, hauling himself up by root and branch. The wounded Digger clings to the belt of the man in front with his sound hand, while his other cobber gets underneath and pushes him up. I say to this fellow he ought to be a stretcher case, but he replies . . . "I can get along. There's blokes here lots worse than me and if we don't walk they'll never get out . . . "'[200]

And sure enough there *were* plenty of blokes in a lot worse condition, many of them being carried out on stretchers made from a couple of saplings with a blanket strung between them, bound by lawyer vine—with the worst of them lying in a rough pool of their own blood formed at the bottom of the stretcher and sometimes dripping through. Mostly these stretchers were being borne by teams of eight porters, working as two teams of four to bring their precious cargos back. Though the terminology originally used by the Diggers to describe an assembly of porters was a 'boong line', these natives had now been effectively re-christened as 'Fuzzy Wuzzy Angels', for the dedication to their task was extraordinary. Many of the porters had been working as beasts of burden beneath unimaginably heavy loads since 7 July, when the 39th's B Company had started moving out over the Owen Stanley Range.

The two war chroniclers regarded the capacity of the Fuzzy Wuzzy Angels with amazement and great admiration. Neither was surprised when on one occasion two or three of them were chatting in their own native language when one native suddenly broke into the one English phrase he had heard constantly over the last few days, from just about every digger his stretcher group had passed: 'Bloody awful job that . . .'[201]

It was that, but somehow they managed it. While the correspondents had been on their own long trek forward it was all they could do to keep their feet, and yet the porters—with four times the load—never slipped, their toes seeming to grip the soil and roots like enormous claws, seeking out every nook and cranny to gain purchase. Certainly it was taking them all day to move just one digger back four miles or so, but clearly the efforts of the Diggers' comrades on the frontline was providing the precious time needed to do just that.[202]

And for the record, the New Guinea porters were also doing much the same for the Japanese on the other side of the battlefront. A Japanese soldier, Yoshihara, would later write that the Papua New Guineans, 'Helped by offering food and carrying wounded, and there were countless thousands of Japanese troops who owed their lives to the Papua New Guineans . . .'[203] The Japanese soldiers were usually evacuated from the battle site by what were called Casualty Clearing Units, platoons of fifty to sixty Korean or Formosan conscripts who had been brought to New Guinea for this specific purpose. They would get them back to relative safety where they could be handed to the porters.[204]

The further the duo moved up the track, the thicker the stretcher traffic became, and the more chaotic a process it was for the two opposing streams to pass each other on the exceedingly narrow passage. The reporters' rate of progress was cut down to half a mile an hour in the worst spots. This chaotic nature of men passing each other was in strange contrast to the way the jungle's natural life had organised itself. Right beside the track was the signal wire strung from tree to tree. Going uphill, an endless procession of ants was making its way forward on the topside of the wire, while on the bottomside was an equally thick stream of ants going downhill.[205]

Presently, up ahead, they came across porters who had for a minute gently placed one of the stretchers on a rare piece of flat ground to give both themselves and the wounded Digger a break. This Digger had a bedraggled 'rollie' cigarette dangling from the corner of his mouth and, spying their approach, asked if one of them had a light.

Ossie White, always the best organised, had some waxed matches secreted in an oiled silk tobacco pouch, and gave him one, and rolled another cigarette for later.

'Thanks, mate,' the Digger said with some feeling, as he struck the match on a tin helmet, 'a smoke helps a lot . . . I'll be okay now.' The porters gently lifted him, and he was borne off in one direction while they continued in the other.

Not long afterwards, Chester Wilmot spied a familiar figure limping towards them, a bloke by the name of Bill who he used to go to school with. Back then Bill was a very useful left-arm bowler, though it was clear by what remained of his left arm that those days were now gone forever.

After a warm hail-fellow-well-met, Bill recounted what had happened. His platoon had been defending a patch of ground up at Isurava when three of their blokes were wounded and then another of their blokes by the name of Butch was killed. It had been hell there for a while, and nearly all of them had been wounded in one way or another, but the main thing is that they had got all the wounded safely back. It was an absolute bastard about Butch, though. Now Bill, too, had to press on, with a week's walk still between him and a hospital.

A little further again Chester and Ossie caught up to some men labouring their way towards the front, laden down with mortar ammunition. Just as they passed, a wounded Digger coming the other way said: 'Get those up quick, sport . . . They were lobbin' four inch mortars on us this morning from that ridge on the right . . . They couldn't shift us but we'd like to give them something back . . . '

Through such encounters and the little chats along the way the two were able to glean some idea of what was happening ahead of them, at least as good an idea as many of the wounded soldiers who had naught but their own shocking experience and that of their immediate mates to go on.

By putting it all together, Osmar White was able to report to his readers at the *Sun Pictorial*: 'Gradually the picture of what is happening sorts itself out. All through these hills are two weaving crescents of men seeking out another to kill—blind, trying to achieve invisibility, silence of movement. Sometimes forces come on one another and open fire at ten or twenty yard range or travel parallel below a knife-edge on either side of it, tossing grenades at one another. Uncanny.'[206]

The reporters moved on and soon came upon the man they recognised from their time back at Moresby as Major Cameron, the officer who had been responsible for sending the three companies out to retake Kokoda, and who had now been sent to the rear by Potts to set up a possible next position for Brigade Headquarters.

Wilmot later described Cameron in this moment as, 'Calm, pale with exhaustion, with a bright aware look in his eyes. Up the hillside is a long procession of carriers and stretchers. The machine guns are still going, you can see the tree-tops flutter. The major asks where we're going. We tell him.

'"Well you can't go. The Japs have just done it up. They're coming round behind our fellows, swarms of them. There's no good you can do. You'll only be in the way."

'The private puts it even better: "Better scram. Little shits are all over the place, they love mist and rain."'[207]

A little more uncertainly now, the two journalists *still* kept moving forward.

At Brigade Headquarters at Alola, Honner and Potts looked closely at the situation. Though they had done well to this point to hold off the Japanese on the western ridge at Isurava, and now at the Isurava Rest House—where the Australian forces were once again being pressed on all sides—it was clear that they would be unlikely to hold out for too much longer. The greatest hammering was falling on, who else, but the 39th's B Company which was now down to just thirteen men still standing. Joe Dawson, Wally Gratz, Ray Phillips and their mates had been saved by the blokes from A Company and some more from the 2/14th, but it was obvious that if they stayed too much longer they risked destruction.

Not only that, but it was now increasingly apparent that the Japanese would not be bottled for long on the eastern ridge either, where the remnants of the 53rd, and now the 2/16th were posted. The great danger on this flank was that if the Japs pushed on and regained the track at Alola, then the 39th and 2/14th would be cut off from their supply lines and further reinforcements, and be totally isolated.

The only sane thing to do then, much as it went against the grain, was to withdraw themselves further back from Alola, to a yet to be determined point where they could make a fresh stand. At three o'clock on the afternoon of 30 August, then, the order was given to pull out. Potts sent Honner immediately back to help scout out the best holding positions.

It was in the middle of all this, that Chester Wilmot and Osmar White finally arrived to within just a few minutes of their destination, Potts's Brigade HQ. All was movement and madness. Hurry and hassle. Men moving out. Others wandering around vaguely with vacant eyes, until others gathered them in and sent them in the rough direction of southwards to safety. Follow your nose, Digger, and do your best. The sound of gunfire rolled over them, like unending bursts of dirty thunder. Stretcher case after stretcher case of groaning and bloody men were just starting out on their agonising journey.

'My belly felt like lead,' White later wrote of his emotions as he looked around him. 'I had passed being afraid that a bullet would come out of the leaves and account for me; but I was deadly weary and discouraged—appalled by the sense of being a partisan spectator to a disaster. Also, I felt lonely. Everyone else had a job to do with his hands and his fortitude—except me. My only job was to watch, and nobody cared the price of a matchbox in hell whether I watched or not.'[208]

After having come all this way, both journalists were keen to make contact with Brigadier Potts and get his appraisal of the situation, but under the circumstances it was out of the question. Potts was too busy to deal with the press, and it was another senior officer who *ordered* them to turn around and get out. With the sound of the guns moving closer even in the short time they had been there, they did not have to be told twice.

Up at the battlefront at the Isurava Rest House, the situation was grim and getting grimmer by the minute as the Japanese now pressed on all sides.

When, like Butch Bisset, another young bloke had taken a burst of machine-gun fire in the guts it had fallen to Lieutenant Gough Garland and Private Merv Brown to look after him. One look at him and they knew he wouldn't have long, even though he was still conscious and slowly reaching for something. What was it? It was a letter that had clearly found its way to the young bloke just before the fighting had started, and which he had not yet had a chance to open. Merv opened it for him now and began to read it to him out loud. It was from the young bloke's mother, with news of home.

For the rest of his life Merv would wonder whether the young bloke was conscious enough to hear his words of home, or if he was already too far gone. Probably the latter, he feared, but always hoped the former. In any case, the tragic thing was that they had to leave him as they were about to be totally overrun and it was obvious the lad wasn't going to last long. They took his dog tags, a ring from his finger to return to his family, and moved back . . .

At 5.00 p.m., with his rearguard in place, Colonel Key had the staff of his Battalion HQ, including Stan Bisset, assembled on the track and were mercifully ready to follow Potts's orders to pull back when, suddenly out of nowhere, they came under a withering crossfire. The Japanese were firing at them from two directions, while on the other side, some Australian soldiers in the thick forest who weren't aware precisely where Key's men were situated, were firing back at the Japs. They were stuck in the middle and it was sheer *murder*.

As men all around screamed and fell to the ground, there was only one way out. That was to dive off the track on the low side and tumble down the steep incline into the thick foliage below. Still the bullets whipped around them as they went. At the bottom they gathered themselves and moved quickly through the foliage to get away. Inevitably all the groups became separated from each other. Stan Bisset found himself with Sergeant Bill Lynn, Warrant Officer Les Tipton and ten other men, of whom three were wounded. As the senior officer, Stan took charge, organising for the able-bodied men to go in shifts helping the injured, while he forged ahead with the swinging bayonet on the end of his rifle enabling them to force a slow passage.

On that same afternoon, the men of the 39th, who had been among the last to safely leave the Rest House position, moved back down the track and joined the throng 'withdrawing' from Alola—almost as a point of honour, the word 'retreat' was never used in the Australian Army. Of the 464 who had gathered at Deniki just under a month before, there were now only 150 left, the rest dead, missing, wounded or evacuated sick. As the men clambered up the opposite hill they naturally enough all looked back to see what was happening behind. There, just before dusk, they saw that not only had the forward party of the Japanese taken possession of Alola, but they had already hauled a Japanese flag up from the tallest house off the main square.

It was a bitter, bitter withdrawal, perhaps most of all for the surviving men of the 2/14th. In just four days action at Isurava they had lost more men—forty-eight killed and 150 wounded, with another forty-four cut off and somewhere in the jungle—than in their entire time in the Middle East. Tragically, Colonel Key was among those who would never regain the battalion lines. In the quiet view of the 39th, many of the 2/14th were simply too courageous for their own good, as they were always wanting to stand and fight, whereas from their own experience the men knew that in this kind of environment, striking from the shadows was everything.

Despite the heavy price in blood he had extracted from the newcomers, General Horii was far from rejoicing, for his own price was heavier still. In the course of the previous five days of action at Isurava he had lost at least two thousand frontline troops to death or injury. Having previously planned on a mere ten-day march to Port Moresby, the combination of these severe casualties and the lost time was devastating. The Japanese supplies of ammunition were running low and, even more crucially, their food was running out. *How* had the Australians done this to them? His intelligence maintained that the white devils were outnumbered by at least six to one, they were completely outgunned, with no heavy artillery, and they had at their core completely exhausted men who had been in action for some weeks. Yet somehow they had refused to give in . . .

Out in the jungle, pushing through what the natives called the 'BIKNAIT', the 'big night' of the wee hours, even though his men begged him to slow down, bloody Bisset wouldn't. As he explained to them, in one of the two five-minute rest periods he allowed, it was a matter of urgency that they got out of this jungle as quickly as possible, both because the longer they were in there the more they would be debilitated by hunger, dysentery, malaria and all the rest, and because he was keenly aware that their firepower would be urgently needed by the rest as the Japanese kept pushing hard upon them . . .

All up, Stan knew their best chance was to get ahead of the Japs in their advance along on the track and come out somewhere behind the Australian lines. There was still a rough chance that Alola was in Australian hands, and it was most urgent they get to it as soon as possible before that situation changed.

Stan missed Butch. But he kept going, steering by the sight of the mighty Southern Cross, and constantly consulting his memory of the mud-map he had previously constructed, comparing it to the terrain he was covering. Nearing dawn, Stan figured he was close to Alola and so, leaving the men behind to rest, he and Les Tipton very carefully started to climb up towards the track to see if the Australians or—as he suspected—the Japanese were in control.

The thin whisper of voices carried to them through the thin jungle air. Australian or Japanese? They crept closer, and then closer still. Bugger it. Bloody Japs. Still they crept forward, until they could see about sixty of the brutes lolling around the ammunition dump.

Stan had a very tough decision. They had four grenades between them, and if they lobbed them among the Japs they would be guaranteed to take out as many as ten at once, as well as perhaps wounding the same number. If they got lucky and the grenades set off some or all of the ammo, then it would be Christmas Day and cracker night all in one.

But, disappointing as it was, after reflecting on it for all of five minutes as they lay there, Stan was in no doubt what the correct decision was. His duty lay in successfully guiding the dozen men in his group, including the three wounded, back to Australian lines. If they threw the grenades it would be tantamount to signing the death warrant of the wounded Australians as they just wouldn't be able to get away from the patrols the Japanese would be sure to send out after them.

'No,' he said slowly and reluctantly to Les. 'We can't do it. Let's get back to the men.'

CHAPTER FOURTEEN
FALLING BACK

If you can force your heart and nerve and sinew,
To serve your turn, long after you are gone,
And so hold on when there is nothing in you,
Except the will which says to them, hold on . . .

Rudyard Kipling, 'If'

When some individuals laid down their lives on the Kokoda Trail,
therefore, they did not have the fame of 'Isurava', or 'Brigade Hill'
or 'Imita Ridge' to add immediate substance to their action but, in
all this, they may have died in a most furious fight at an isolated
place that has no real name.

Peter Brune, *A Bastard of a Place* [209]

Back on the track, the bloody track, the survivors of the 2/14th, 2/16th and 39th, and to a far lesser extent the 53rd, were in the process of staging a series of rearguard actions, essentially leapfrogging each other in reverse. Each battalion would move back, dig into a defensive position and allow the other battalions to move safely through them to dig into their own positions a little further back again. And then they would do it again. In this manner all forward elements of the pursuing Japanese were met by Australian soldiers in entrenched positions, further slowing their thrust and, most crucially, allowing the many Australian wounded some time to move back without falling into the Japanese clutches.

And of those wounded there were regrettably many. They were walking, crawling and being carried towards the nearest medical facility at Eora Creek, ten miles back from Alola over treacherous, rugged country. From Eora, the only way back was the way they had come in, back along the track all the way to Ower's Corner.

The Fuzzy Wuzzy Angels continued to do wonderful work in saving the Diggers as they hauled them back towards safety. Many, true, had broken down under the strain, despite the tender ministrations of Doc Vernon who had himself been working on them day and night. And some had indeed deserted, sick of the neverending work and keen to get back to their villages to see their own families and protect them in this 'TIME NOGUT', 'time of turmoil'.

But the solicitude with which the porters who remained treated the wounded would forever remain imprinted on the memories of those they saved. At night, when it was time to rest, the porters would take great care to ensure that the Digger was on level ground with a fire nearby to keep warm, and at least one of them would sit through the night to make sure that the wounded Australian soldier would not want for water, or food, or simple company in his oft-tormented and delirious stages. Gently, oh so gently, for the severely wounded who could not eat, a thin paste of milk powder and water would be fed to them, spoonful by spoonful. Never, no matter how hopeless a Digger's medical condition might have been, was one of them abandoned. Never.

On a single day in the withdrawal from Isurava, Bert Kienzle had forty-two Diggers on stretchers moving back under the steam of 336 porters, who were already exhausted from having carried so much ammunition and supplies towards the frontline.

Of the correspondents, it was never put better than by Chester Wilmot, when he later reported to his listeners: 'When this war is over we should raise a memorial in every Australian capital to the New Guinea natives so that we may never forget how much of the white man's burden was carried by the natives in this roadless jungle warfare . . . so that we may remember how many Australians owe their lives to the natives who bore the wounded in their stretchers across the tortuous trail to safety . . . '210

Right among the wounded and stragglers who did not have the luxury of someone to carry them though, Osmar White made his way back from the frontlines, feeling completely wretched. Chester Wilmot had decided to wait on the track until Brigadier Potts came through, so he could interview him, meaning that Ossie was now on his own and suffering with every step. It wasn't merely his physical exhaustion, nor even the tingling he sometimes felt on his body when he wondered what it would feel like to be taken by a Japanese bullet; for both exhaustion and fear he had more or less learnt to live with. What he had not really got used to was his ongoing feeling of uselessness and fraud when he was among fighting men, when he had not fought himself, and was entirely powerless to affect the course of events.

He trudged on. What made it even worse, somehow, was that he remained able-bodied and uninjured while all around him were men who had taken bullets and had earned their right to withdraw. Like, for example, the bloke up ahead who had lost his leg, but was still propelling himself forward. A mortar bomb had sliced the leg off below the knee, and dropped it like a lump of meat off a butcher's bench, but it hadn't stopped this bloke. Under his own steam he had tied up the end of the stump to stop the blood flow, put a couple of dressings right on the end, and then wrapped the whole thing in the end of an old copra sack. And now he was variously hopping and crawling his way back. Of course Osmar had offered his help, but was waved away. How could a bloke not feel a fraud when face to face with such courage?

Sure Osmar had chosen this course and was confident that his reports from frontline positions made a contribution to the war effort in their own way, but in this specific time and place . . . it was hard to accept that.[211] Time and again his mind turned back to a conversation he'd had with the proprietor of his newspaper, Sir Keith Murdoch, shortly after the war had broken out and Osmar had tried to join the AIF. Sir Keith had blocked it, using the manpower regulations which ensured that essential services were maintained.

'We don't want you rushing around with a pack on your back,' he firmly told Osmar. 'You'll fight the war with your pen.'[212]

You'll fight the war with your pen . . .

You'll fight the war with your pen . . .

And now here he was . . .

Even as daylight turned to darkness there was nothing for it but to keep pushing on in the company of many other groups of straggling men whom he kept passing. Certainly the odd little bundles by the track showed that some soldiers were taking a kip for the night, but the majority had kept going with the view that with the Japs pressing close behind, with no shelter or medical help whatsoever bar the village of Eora which lay up ahead, it was better to stumble and stagger south through the darkness. For the most part White kept himself to himself, nodding to the wretched men he passed— many of them holding blindly on to the belt of the man in front, who was doing the same to the man in front of him, and so on— but not really wanting to talk.

Every now and then the last and weakest man in these catastrophic conga lines would sink to his knees and fall face flat down on to the track, until the leader of the next group would either encourage him to join his own line, or at least move him off the track.

Never, ever, had Ossie felt so alone, so weak. He had only two choices. He could fall to the track himself, or he could keep moving. He kept moving. And sometimes it was surreal. At one point, in the wee hours, he was moving through a notably dark part of the jungle, which had a great deal of a kind of phosphorescent fungus growing all around, meaning that the track showed up as a kind of black highway through the dull luminescence. And here and there, equally all blackness in the glow, was the shape of a man, a fallen Digger who could go no further and had sunk to the side of the track. Some of them were already dead, and indeed, maybe this was what it was like to pass from life into death, all along the blackness and into the netherworld . . .

And then, frequently, one of the black ghosts would speak, in a low, ethereal, appropriately deathly hush, begging to be released from the darkness.

'Dig, I say, Dig . . . are you going to Eora? Then tell them to send a light down the track will you? Tell them to send a light, Digger. Tell them to send a light!'

Men were sinking, and dying, for want of a light in the darkness. Osmar had one, stored against the moment of a life-threatening emergency, and now he could stand it no longer. He took it out. Turned it on. There was a stirring behind him. From the darkness, from places unseen, the mumbling gathered. A light. A light. There was a light in the darkness. First a man who had been shot twice in the chest came up and put his arm on Ossie's shoulder. Behind him a man who had taken a grenade and was now carrying shrapnel in his forearm and thigh. And they kept coming, the black figures rising towards the glowing, and others moving to him from the shadows as they kept on down the track.

In no time at all no fewer than a hundred Diggers had formed up in a line behind him and they were now all gingerly picking their way forward . . . a hundred sons of Australia, a hundred fathers, husbands, brothers and friends, a hundred souls in search of home.

Now and again, Osmar would turn the light back on the men, by way of encouragement—picking out the dull, hollow, half-dead faces as he did so—but mostly he used it for what was absolutely necessary to pick out creek crossings and difficult sections of terrain.

But then the light died. In the blackest hour of the darkest night, it just faded away like a heart that no longer beat and it was impossible to continue on as anything other than a totally blind man feeling his way forward. It really couldn't be done, and Osmar stopped, bringing to a halt all who were with him.

The man who had been shot in the chest, immediately behind said: 'I'm pretty tired. I think I'll wait till daylight.' Osmar gave him a nip from his brandy flask just before he sank to the arsenic weed he had chosen for his bed.

'He was asleep, before I had straightened up from bending over him,' White later wrote. 'I started to cry. The tears rolled down my face, burning. Now there was no light. The line fell away, disintegrated. I was alone.'[213]

And now it was the 39th's turn to dig in and defend, as the 2/14th and 2/16th fought their own rearguard actions against the pressing Japanese ahead and prepared to fall back through. They set up their guns and one working mortar just ahead of Eora Creek, surrounded by the mountains. Exhausted, ravaged by sickness, starvation and, in many cases, wounded as well, they were still a proud fighting force, 150 strong and fully intent on doing their part. It was most particularly a pleasure to help the men of the AIF just as they had been helped at Isurava.

It wasn't easy though. One whose concentration kept wavering, try as he might to bring it to heel and make it stay on the one straight line, was Smoky Howson, manning a Bren gun beside a deep hole on a cleared ridge above the village. Time and again he would peer ahead over the sights of his Bren for any sign of movement, time and again his sight would waver back to the deep pit beside him. Was he looking, right then and there, into his own grave, the place he would rest for all eternity? There was no doubt that if he was hit by a Jap bullet that was where he would land, and equally no doubt that if he were dead that was where his mates would bury him. The bottom of that grave looked so bloody *black*, it was unnerving. There had been times, admittedly, in this campaign, when things were so grim—when he had been so wet, sorry, starving and scared—that Smoky had thought a bullet might be the easy way out, but this was not one of them. He bloody well wanted to *live*. He pulled his eyes back one more time to the sights of the Bren gun, looking for movement. He knew the Japs were coming for them, he just didn't know when.

Just behind him at Eora at this time, and through the long night, the army surgeons were performing major and minor medical miracles in the most atrocious conditions. Life and death operations were being conducted with a lantern for light, mud for a floor, and prayers for hope. A classic form of triage was underway whereby incoming wounded were sorted into essentially three groups: those who could be saved with instant medical help; those who could still likely survive and keep moving south without it; and those who would likely die anyway, whatever treatment they received. It was a distinction designed to ensure that the limited medical resources were not wasted. The upshot was that while some soldiers seeking treatment were just as quickly ushered out again, and others were put in the queue for surgery—often by torchlight—others were taken to the far side of the medical hut, behind a rough curtain, and simply made as comfortable as possible until such time as the last spark of their being had gone. Their lives had begun in a hospital in Victoria, with joy and good cheer all around—'*a son, we have a son!*'—and ended here, in the mud, with a bullet in the guts, despair all around, and their light slowly fading

The combination of extreme conditions and extreme injuries inevitably gave rise to attempts at extreme remedies. Of these, perhaps the most bizarre was to sometimes leave maggots on badly infected wounds, on the grounds that as the maggots were eating rotted flesh they actually gave the soldiers a better chance of not succumbing to gangrene in the time it would take to get back to a genuine hospital in Moresby. The other notable method was entirely up the other end of the spectrum of medical logic. That was to encase all serious wounds in plaster of Paris as a way of keeping all the mud, slush and infection away from them. It was a very messy procedure to put P.O.P., as it was known, on a gaping shoulder wound—and positively wretched for the unfortunate person, hopefully back in Moresby, who would take it off again in perhaps ten days time—but it was a treatment that had apparently worked well in the Spanish Civil War and it was the most prevalent method used now.[214]

This method even applied to head wounds, with doctors applying plaster of Paris skull caps to men who had taken bullets to the head, though usually only if the patient was still conscious. For the firm rule applied, as subsequently stated: 'A patient completely unconscious from a penetrating head wound is not worth operating on if other casualties are waiting. No patient with a penetrating head wound who was deeply unconscious on arrival at the main dressing station lived long enough to be evacuated.'[215]

One thing that often staggered the doctors and medical orderlies was how little the men complained. Despite the most grievous injuries, most of the troops seemed to feel that complaining was beside the point—and that point was either to get well enough to return to the frontline, or to get the hell out as quickly as possible.

Among the men, 'a homer' became the vernacular for a wound that was bad enough to have them sent home, and while it was true that in the course of the campaign some of the men coveted such a wound so badly that they inflicted their own injuries, for the vast majority the aim was *not* to get home, but back to the frontline. The most likely homer was a bad wound in the legs which prevented mobility, for it was truly extraordinary how men with the most terrible injuries in the upper body were able to keep going, so long as their legs were strong enough to get them there.

For most who could not walk properly, or were too weak to do so, the only way out remained to be stretchered by the Fuzzy Wuzzy Angels, but some refused on the grounds that this would unnecessarily strain resources.

One such was Corporal John A. Metson from Sale in Victoria, who was shot in the ankle at the battle of Isurava. Though offered a stretcher, Corporal Metson said 'be buggered', maintaining that he could still crawl, and that was exactly what he was going to do. Wrapping torn blankets around both his hands and his knees, he

set off for Port Moresby, some eighty miles away, across some of
the most inhospitable country on the planet.[216]

When at last Osmar White arrived at Eora the morning after the
worst night of his life, his attention was attracted by one of the
injured soldiers, lying wanly on a stretcher with a bad wound to
his stomach, still waiting to be seen in the tent. He was a young
redhead, probably about twenty years old, and he was seriously
pissed off, muttering that he'd been fighting for weeks and still
hadn't even seen a fucking Jap, let alone been able to fire his gun
at them. Aware now that White was watching him, the redhead
beckoned him over.

'Hey, Dig,' he addressed him, 'bend down a minute. Listen . . .
I think us blokes are going to be left when they pull out. Will you
do us a favour? Scrounge us a Tommy gun from somewhere, will
you?'[217]

White was staggered at the youth's unbelievable courage. This
was not bar-room bravado. This was all too real. One look in this
kid's eyes and you could see it all: he knew he was going to die and
just wanted to do his bit before he went. And his bit was to first
see a Jap and then take him out. That was all. Under any other
circumstance the whole thing might have been appalling, the tragedy
of the whole damn thing, this kid's life ebbing away and all he could
think of was killing another bloke. But this was not appalling. This
was a jungle war without mercy and this is what it was like. There
was a greatness to the kid's approach that took the breath away.

Osmar White wrote this all down later and, after describing the
scene, also invoked his emotions on the spot.

'I was convinced for all time of the dignity and nobility of
common men. I was convinced for all time that common men have
a pure and shining courage when they fight for what they believe
to be a just cause. That which was fine in these men outweighed
and made trivial all that was horrible in their plight. I cannot explain
it except to say that they were at all times cheerful and helped one
another. They never gave up the fight. They never admitted defeat.

They never asked for help. I felt proud to be one of their race and cause, bitterly ashamed to be so nagged by the trivial ills of my own flesh. I wondered if all men, when they had endured so much that exhausted nerves would no longer give response, were creatures of the spirit, eternal and indestructible as stars.'

In a nearby hut at that moment, Brigadier Potts and Colonel Honner were, in their own way, fuming. Back at GHQ in Brisbane, Thomas Blamey and General MacArthur had been apprised of the Australian withdrawal from Isurava and weren't happy about it. Not by a long shot. They were so unhappy, Blamey had personally sent a message to his commanders on site urging them to take the fight to the Japanese, take the offensive, and push right back at them.

'Tired Australians fight best,' he added by way of encouragement, from the comfort of his headquarters in Queensland, with his personal valet always on call.

It was the sort of message that both Honner and Potts did well to keep tight to themselves for fear of the reaction it might produce if it got out. Tired Australians fight best, do they? How about Australians missing arms and legs who had gone without sleep and food for five days straight against an enemy who outnumbered them five to one? How did *they* go?

Ultimately the choice of how to respond to the order rested with the senior man, Potts, and he made the only sane choice possible. To follow the Blamey order was tantamount to murdering his own men in the service of ignorance; to ignore it, and continue a fighting withdrawal, was to preserve as many lives as possible and still weaken the Japanese. Both Potts and Honner were fully aware by this time that every day they delayed the Japanese on their thrust to Moresby was a victory in itself; that the further the Japs moved from their own base the more their supply lines were stretched thin and their meagre resources further strained, while the reverse was true for the Australians. Under these conditions the jungle was at least as great a killer of the Japanese as the Australians, and simply keeping the Japanese stranded in it for as long as possible was a sound strategic move, while equally doing everything they could to preserve the health of their own troops.

Certainly there would come a point where they would make a final stand, but the logical place for that stand was a spot where they could be most easily reinforced, while the Japanese would be as far from their own support as possible.

'We will continue to pull back anyway,' Potts told Honner, perhaps aware that he was likely signing off on his own army career by doing so, but he would be at least able to sleep soundly ever after for making the right decision.

Good God Almighty he hated this job. It had seemed okay at the start of the war, sort of cushy and safe, riding all over Melbourne delivering telegrams to people, meaning he was often the messenger bringing glad tidings of babies born, engagements announced and *'I'll be home soon!'* Now, though, it always seemed to be the same thing. Time and again he would have to bear telegrams from the government. He would knock on people's doors and at the very instant they opened it and saw him in his Telegraph Office uniform, they would start to shake and shudder and often cry, as with trembling hand they opened his proffered telegram, hoping against hope that it wouldn't say what they most feared it would. But when it was from the government, it nearly always did.

Like now. He had knocked on the door of Mr and Mrs G. S. Bisset at their house in Surry Hills, and it had been opened by the kindly looking Mrs Bisset. At the first proper sight of him, though, her hand had flown to her mouth as she had tried to stifle a sob. And then, eventually she had read the government's officious words:

URGENT 212 CARRINGTON 4.30 PM URGENT

MR & MRS G.S. BISSET

IT IS WITH DEEP REGRET THAT I HAVE TO INFORM YOU THAT VVX14631 LIEUTENANT THOMAS HAROLD BISSET DIED ON THIRTIETH AUGUST 1942 AND DESIRE TO CONVEY TO YOU THE PROFOUND SYMPATHY OF THE MINISTER FOR THE ARMY . . .

IT IS WITH FURTHER REGRET THAT WE MUST ADVISE THAT VVX2119
LIEUTENANT STANLEY YOUNG BISSET IS MISSING IN ACTION ...

This lady hadn't fainted on the spot as some of them did, but she had rocked back on her feet and with a strangled cry called for her husband. Enough. He couldn't stand it. Tipping his cap one more time, and mumbling his own regret, he had backed away, only breathing again when the door had closed behind him, muffling too little the enormous cry of anguish that now flowed from behind it. Good God Almighty, he hated this job.

Pulling out of Eora for the push south, Osmar White could barely believe it; for there, up ahead on the slope, was the same amputee he had seen just south of Isurava two days ago, still with his copra sack on his bloody stump, still variously hopping and crawling his way forward. After the barest amount of medical treatment at Eora he had decided to keep going. Again, Osmar White offered his help, this time to see if the bloke would like him to try to round up some stretcher bearers for him, but again the bloke would have none of it.

'If you can get bearers,' he just about snarled, 'then get them for some other poor bastard! There are plenty worse off than me.'

The sad thing is, the bloke was right. The very fact that he was alive and strong enough to snarl so bore testimony that there really were a lot who were worse off.

In fact, by this time there was actually no one still on the track who could be properly defined as 'able-bodied' or 'fit for action'. For even those who had been spared a bullet or shrapnel to this point were starving and almost certainly suffering from dysentery. The latter condition continued to ravage the troops, so much so that it was a common sight for the soldiers heading back down the track to have cast all modesty aside and simply cut the back out of their trousers. Bacillary dysentery was the worst of it, with the men passing a combination of blood and mucus ...

•

The sheer *frustration* of it. After hacking like mad things through the jungle for three days and three nights, Stan and his men came out on a high ridge where a break in the jungle afforded a superb view of the Eora Creek village. They arrived there just in time to see the Japs attack the Australian rearguard. Even at a distance of over a mile, and maybe as much as a mile and a half, they could hear the tiny pops of gunfire, the cushioned WHUMP of the grenades, and the odd scream. Hopefully it was the Japs who were screaming, but either way there was nothing Stan and his men could do. The whole thing was so far away they all looked like ants. At least they knew what the situation was and that the bulk of the Australian forces couldn't be too far ahead. They just had to keep going and try to catch up to them.

By this time several of Stan's men were doing it very tough indeed, but there was no choice. Move out. Move on . . .

Right in the middle of those 'ants' none other than Stan's old mate from the *Aquitania* and the Middle East, Alan Haddy, was in the thick of the action, holding the line against the Japs—and giving the wounded Australians behind them as much time as possible to get out. It was the late afternoon of Friday 1 September and Haddy, typically, was the one the men looked to, even as the battle continued into the night. Through the machine-gun fire and the constant explosions of grenades, it was his voice that could be heard, guiding with calm: 'Hold your fire until they come right up, then give them curry.'[218]

The men did exactly that. Every group of attackers that got within cooee was greeted with a brace of grenades, and it was from the glare of those grenades that the Australians were able to get a bead on the Japanese soldiers coming behind. By the time the Australians had pulled out at dawn the next morning, as the weight of Japanese numbers meant that they were simply unstoppable, there were no fewer than 170 dead Japanese soldiers lying before the position the 2/16th had defended.

In response, General Horii could barely stand it. Every time it seemed like he had the Australians cornered with no chance of salvation, they found a way to get out, to escape, to live to fight another day. Just when he reached for their throat to administer the death grip, somehow, *somehow* they slipped away, and remained between his forces and Port Moresby.

There was a *very* hard choice that had to be made. In his own return from Eora Creek, Damien Parer was struggling. Now severely weakened by ten days of malaria, dysentery and insufficient food and sleep, there was no way he could continue to carry all his film and equipment back. In desperation sheer, going up a particularly brutal hill, he asked Smoky Howson if he would mind carrying some of his valuable stuff.

Smoky, never a man to beat around the bush, gave it to him straight: 'You can go and get fucked,' he said, 'I have enough of my own to carry.' And fair enough too. Damien regretted asking even before he had heard the response, and begrudged Smoky nothing. Still, without help, some things would simply have to be dumped, and it certainly wasn't going to be his precious film.[219] Did he need socks? No. Tripod? He could do without. Ditto a few personal effects, his Graflex still camera, accessories for his Newman camera and leather case, and some rolls of film which he had not yet exposed. At one point Captain Max Bidstrup saw him throwing the film into Eora Creek and offered to carry it for him. No, Damien replied, it was all right.

In the general scheme of things—as highlighted by Smoky Howson's pointed observations—Damien felt rather like Osmar White, that his concerns were as nothing to those of the real fighting men. What he had considered important equipment was essential only to him. And even when he did accept a small amount of help from a nice kind of bloke he met by the name of Tom Grahamslaw, he insisted on parting with a precious bag of dried apricots from his kitbag in return, as something of equal value to the favour done.

Still, when he caught up briefly with Ossie and Chester at Templeton's Crossing, he found that some more film had been dropped for him and he just couldn't help himself. He decided to take more film of the withdrawal, and bade them only leave him some quinine and a change of shirt.

As described by Parer's biographer, Neil McDonald, 'The last the two reporters saw of Parer, he was standing in the rain, clutching his Newman in one hand and his tins of exposed film in the other.'[220]

As to White and Wilmot, the nature of their own journalistic calling was that they needed to get to Moresby at all speed to get their stories out before events overtook them.

Not long after they left Eora Creek, however, they came across a terrible tragedy. Captain 'Tubby' Jacob—the only officer Smoky Howson really liked—had taken over command of C Company after Captain Dean had met his end. As they fell back from Eora Creek, Captain Jacob had seen a soldier ahead of him stumbling blindly through pure exhaustion. In an effort to help the soldier, the captain had taken the soldier's rifle onto his free shoulder, not knowing that the safety catch was off.

A couple of hours later, the now equally exhausted Captain Jacob had slipped while traversing a maze of tree roots and the rifle had discharged, sending a bullet first into his groin and then up through his abdomen. His men had done for him what they could, which was very little, but from the first they knew it was a job for Nobby. Father Earl was shortly on the scene, just in time to administer to the 22-year-old his last rites.

Around and about this tragic scene, the native porters hovered, distressed. Now that the 'WAITMAN SOLDIA EM E DI PINIS', 'the white soldier was die finished', *dead*, they knew that his spirit had just been released. 'SPIRIT BILONG EM I NUW STUP LONG DISPELA PLUS'. His spirit would likely stop for a long time in this place. At least so long as his spirit was properly respected from the beginning. Had Captain Jacob been one of their own, this respect would have manifested itself in quite elaborate rituals to ensure that it not turn into a 'MASALAI', 'evil spirit', but as it was, they let Father Earl do his own ritual in the white man way. For themselves, they simply kept very still, very quiet, only making a slight kind of whistling, whispering sound, as a way of showing their own quiet respect.

Finally, after five days of pushing through the jungle, Stan and his men made it out on to the track. There was only one question to be answered. Were they ahead of or behind the Japanese? Carefully, oh so carefully, they pushed south, looking for signs in the mud. The Japanese bootprint, they had learnt over previous weeks, had two distinct indentations rather like that of a giant stork, and they were searching for it. The problem was that the rain was so strong that no print lasted long and . . .

And it is strange how many emotions can be packed into a single second. In all of one instant, Stan Bisset—in the lead—had turned a corner and become instantly alert at the sight of a man ahead. Then came alarm, that it might be a Japanese soldier; then relief that it was a white man in tattered khaki; then pure joy that it was a man he recognised—his great friend, Alan Haddy from the 2/16th.

Haddy had gone through a similar wave of emotions to realise that there was someone close behind, only to realise that it was his old mate, Stan, and he immediately broke into an enormous grin, and lowered his rifle which had instinctively swung up.

'*Jesus*, Stan! I bloody near shot your head off! Where on earth have you blokes come from? We're the last ones to break contact with the Japs and they can't be too far behind us . . .'

Apprised of the situation, the big Western Australian quickly got his men to share some of their remaining tins of bully beef and biscuits with Stan's blokes, and they set off again, arriving at Templeton's Crossing just as night fell. It was here that Stan was able to meet up with the bulk of the 2/14th and learn, with great sadness, that Colonel Key and some of his senior officers were still missing and presumed dead. Command of the 2/14th had been taken over by Stan's great friend, Captain Phil Rhoden. There was precious little time for any real catching up, though, for within half an hour

of their arrival, the Japs were on the attack. So weakened were
most of Stan's men that they were immediately evacuated to Moresby,
but Stan himself assured Phil Rhoden he was strong enough to
resume his duties. He stayed with the 2/14th then as they carefully
withdrew, leapfrogging ambushes all the way, and being leapfrogged
in turn, back towards Myola.

After arriving in dribs and drabs, by the morning of 4 September
nearly all of the 2/14th had arrived back at Myola and set up some
preliminary defences, as they looked at the possibility of making a
stand there.

The idea of General MacArthur—as communicated in his usual
imperious orders—was that, with a massive supply dump at their
backs, the Australians would for the first time in the whole battle
not have to worry about having enough ammunition or food or
medical supplies to hold on. It was here this American supreme
commander, some 1250 miles from the front, and with no
understanding of the position, insisted the Australians should make
their stand. And, after all, if they lost Myola, the already acute
pressure to keep up supplies to the frontline troops in the New
Guinea highlands would become unbearable as air supply would
be cut off. Myola *had* to be held.

It was fine in theory, but difficult in practice. There were two
problems. One was that the Myola dump was essentially at the
bottom of a topographical saucer, with all approaches around it on
higher ground. A soldier of MacArthur's ilk might have put his
defensive barricades at the bottom of the hill, but most competent
commanders would not contemplate it.

And the second problem was that, if they wanted to, the Japanese
could simply use the old track and bypass Myola altogether, coming
out at Efogi and totally isolating all of the Australian forces so
carefully dug in around their supply dump. This went directly
counter to the brigadier's primary instinct, which was to always
keep his forces between the Japs and Moresby.

After examining it from every angle, Potts ruled it out as absurd. As to the option of placing the forces on the high ground above Myola, that too was looked at but rejected on the simple grounds that the jungle in that area was thinner and it would be completely impossible to put a block wide enough that any competent attacking force could not simply go round. Potts looked at his options and decided there was only one that had any merit. Whatever they might think of it back in Moresby and Brisbane, the fact was that the same thing that had made Myola perfect for biscuit bombing, also made it near impossible to defend, least of all with the mere four hundred men he had at his disposal. (Yes, Potts had been informed that Brigadier Ken Eather's 25th Brigade of the 7th Division was now on its way and would be arriving in Moresby shortly to be able to reinforce them, but they were still too far away to have any bearing on this situation.)

So it was that at 6.00 p.m. on 4 September, Brigadier Potts signalled General Tubby Allen in Moresby: 'Strong enemy attack driven 2/16th Battalion, one and a half hours Myola. Am supporting defence with 2/14th Battalion, but country entirely unsuitable for defended localities. Regret necessity abandon Myola . . . Men full of fight but utterly weary. Plan withdrawal Efogi—take position high ground south of village . . . '[221]

Of course it went against the grain to abandon such a plentiful supply dump to head off once again into the wilderness—rather like leaving an oasis of water to head back into the desert wastelands—but it had to be done. The first instinct of Potts and his senior officers was to blow up all food that they could not carry so as to deny it to the Japanese; but then they had a better idea, an idea which showed that it is not only in the realms of the arts and sciences that genius strikes. It had been noticed during previous weeks that the men who suffered the worst dysentery had often eaten food that had gone off, so . . .

So, after the troops had filled their own packs with everything they could carry, and their stomachs with all the food they could possibly cram in, why not put small punctures in the bottom of all the cans, so as to hasten their ruination? The hope was that the Japanese would be so hungry and desperate that they would eat it anyway and then suffer the dreadful consequences. And so it was done. By the time the last of the troops pulled out on the afternoon of 5 September, all of the cans left behind had been punctured and left in the sun, the rice scattered and pissed on, while everything else had indeed been blown up. *That* would give the hungry Japs something to munch on, all right . . .

The only way he could keep going was to jam a tube into his anus. This, he connected to a small container in his sock, to collect his own waste. It might be all right for other guys to just take the seat out of their trousers and let the shit run down their leg, but it wasn't good enough for Damien Parer. Somehow or other he knew his mother wouldn't want him to do that, however grim the situation got. It wasn't just the mess that was the bother though, it was the agony. Now he knew why the Diggers said that having dysentery was like 'shitting axes'. It really felt like that, like it was tearing your insides apart as it went through.

The main thing though was that, despite everything, Parer was continuing to make his way back along the track, and carrying just enough film and cameras to continue shooting footage. Sometimes he thought he was going to go over in a dead faint; somehow he kept slowly moving back, *willing* himself on each occasion to make the next staging post . . .

Further down the track towards Moresby, Osmar White and Chester Wilmot were at last nearing the southern edge of the jungle that pushed to the low foothills leading down to Moresby. Though they, too, were exhausted beyond all redemption, they were soon presented with evidence that their fatigue was as nothing compared to what others were feeling. For just near Uberi—and right after passing the first troops of the 2/27th Battalion who had at last been thrown into the fray—he saw them. At least a hundred Australian soldiers, with the help of many hundreds of native labourers, were straining on ropes slung around strong trees to bring some 25-pounder guns into position. Slithering, sliding and straining on the ropes with every ounce of their being, they winched the guns into position up the slopes. It was another classic Sisyphean task, where the load was clearly getting heavier the closer they got to the top, but no one doubted that it was necessary. With every successive group of soldiers coming down the track giving ever more depressing reports as to how far south the Japs had moved, these guns were to be the key to the last line of defence. If the Japs got as far south as Ioribaiwa Ridge, these guns—if they could get them into place in time—would be waiting for them. And then we would see how *they* liked being outgunned in the mountains. So heave-ho me hearties, and let's haul.

The correspondents left them to it, now more eager than ever to get back to Moresby and file their reports on the many things they had seen in this extraordinary month.

Different day. Same problem. As ever, Brigadier Potts was looking for a place to make a stand that would give the Australians a fair chance of damaging the Japanese, without the certainty of trapping his own men where they could be massacred. And yet, while the village of Efogi itself was not readily defensible, just over the stream there was a steep hill covered with thick woods, kunai grass and jungle which was much more promising. At the bottom of the hill stood an old and abandoned Seventh Day Adventist Mission hut, thus giving the terrain the name by which the troops would subsequently refer to it: 'Mission Ridge'. (And, in reality, the derelict Mission somehow seemed to fit perfectly with the whole God-forsaken feel of the place. Maybe one time God had done his best in these parts, but had clearly given it up and *gorn*.)

Just behind Mission Ridge, towering over it, was an even more enormous hill. The most important thing from the point of view of Potts was that the western approaches to these convulsions of Mother Earth were viciously steep, giving them a great natural defence à la Isurava, while on the eastern approaches the jungle was extremely dense, which was also similar to Isurava. This meant that for the Japanese to properly advance they would be obliged to take the track, and their usual flanking movements would prove difficult, though of course not impossible. With the Japs, as they had learnt, it never was.

It was Ralph Honner who initially reconnoitred the positions, and had his worthy 39th survivors dig in as the fall-back position for the 2/14th and 2/16th who had yet to arrive. But their blessed relief came from entirely the opposite direction when, at around two o'clock on the afternoon of 5 September, the bulk of the long-hoped-for 2/27th Battalion—some six hundred strong—arrived at Mission Ridge after a brutal four-day march from Moresby.

The new men, too, were goggle-eyed at the vision of the sorry scarecrows whose places they now took over; but the main thing was that, after some six weeks of continuous action, the 39th could now pull back from the frontline of the action.

Scarcely believing it possible, that same afternoon—after leaving behind everything that could be of use to their replacements, including food, ammunition, guns, grenades and blankets—they marched out in the direction of Menari, the next village along the track.

On the following morning, the weary survivors of the 2/14th and 2/16th—some four hundred men—straggled in. For the first time in the whole campaign Potts had all of the survivors of the 21st Brigade in the one place at the one time and was now able to give his orders with his usual decisiveness.

Potts positioned the fresh troops of the 2/27th on Mission Ridge to bear the brunt of the likely Japanese thrust. Further back, as Mission Ridge gradually scaled the ground to the enormous hill behind, he placed the 2/14th and then the 2/16th to back them up.

Potts put his own Brigade Headquarters still higher above Mission Ridge—on a spot which became known as Brigade Hill—in a native hut where he was best placed to survey and direct the battlefield proceedings. Together with Captain Brett 'Lefty' Langridge's D Company, it would be the job of his own staff to guard the whole brigade's rear and ensure that the track to Menari remained clear, come what may.

One who was not happy with the whole set-up was Tom Grahamslaw, and he was the sort of fellow—quietly outspoken, in an odd sort of way—who didn't mind saying so. He told both Potts and his senior officers that their position was way too exposed and that it could too easily be infiltrated. Potts replied that if young Grahamslaw could show him a more suitable place to shelter he would move, otherwise he would remain where he was.

A man of action, in no time at all Grahamslaw and his young police boys began to construct a lean-to in a position nearby, which was marginally less exposed to enemy attack, and Potts and his senior staff moved into it—leaving the hut to some of the more senior officers of the Brigade Headquarters Company, who referred to themselves as the 'Old and the Bold'.

Some good news came through late in the afternoon when the word was sent back to Brigade Headquarters that the 2/16th had discovered another track in the jungle, leading back to Menari by an alternative rough route. If the worst came to the absolute worst, and the Japs did cut off the main route falling back to Menari, then this rough parallel alternative would provide another means of escape.

Ah, the sheer luxury of it. The luxury, for the 39th Battalion, after seven straight weeks of bloody battles and endless trekking, to have been withdrawn from the frontline, to be able to stagger back down the track *away* from the sound of oncoming Japanese guns. It was, of course, a luxury mixed with an enormous sense of sadness; for they were heading south minus 125 of the number who had originally trekked forward all those weeks ago.

(Could it really be *weeks*? The weird thing about this war, many reflected, was that time warped. Sometimes ten seconds could pass like a tortuous ten minutes, as in when you knew a mortar that maybe had your name on it was whistling down towards your vicinity. And yet when an entire day was filled with repelling neverending Japanese attacks, the whole thing passed in a blur that felt like it lasted . . . ten minutes! Under those circumstances, the concept of weeks was a calendar term only, with little meaning for them.)

Nevertheless, in that short amount of time, just under a quarter of the 39th's battalion strength was lost. Now, the 39th regrouped the best they could in the tiny village of Menari, perched on the southern slopes of the Owen Stanley Range.

It was there that Ralph Honner received a message from Brigadier Potts, with his warmest congratulations on their performance, and the request that the message be passed on to the battalion. Colonel Honner went one better. Instead of merely passing the message to his adjutants to tell the men, he decided to call a full parade.

So they formed, a mob of ragged bloody heroes with tattered clothes, odd boots, hollow eyes, crutches, leaning on each other to remain standing, and instead of rifles—which they'd passed on to the 2/27th—holding the sticks they'd used to support their trek back.

But when Colonel Honner came before them they stood to attention like the guards at Buckingham Palace, stock-still and proud, as he saluted them with great feeling. Honner would later record of his feelings at this proud, poignant moment: 'As I glanced along the lines of pallid and emaciated men with sunken eyes and shrunken frames that testified to the hardships they had long endured, I saw no hangdog look—only the proud bearing of tired veterans who had looked death and disaster in the face and had not failed.'[222]

For now, though, Honner simply communicated to them his heartfelt message, and Joe Dawson, standing up near the front with his mates Ray and Wally, listened carefully. Not Joe, Ray, nor Wally, not even Ralph Honner, or practically any of them, noticed the scarecrow figure just twenty yards away who had set up his camera and was now filming, laying down the scene for posterity. Damien Parer had arrived in Menari just a short time before, with the exquisite timing of the born chronicler-for-the-ages he was, and had summoned the last of his strength to stealthily capture these precious moments.

'Men,' Colonel Honner said, standing with the odd combination of perfect military bearing and a warm smile on his face, 'the first

AWM 025597

Major General Basil Morris, General Officer Commanding New Guinea Force.

AWM 139812

'Australia looks to America': General Douglas MacArthur, Supreme Commander Allied Forces Southwest Pacific Area, with John Curtin, Prime Minister of Australia.

AWM 013425

(*Left to right*) Frank Forde, Australian Minister for the Army, General Douglas MacArthur, General Thomas Blamey and General Kenny, during a visit to New Guinea in 1942.

AWM 013009

Native porters provided the Australian troops with invaluable support, carrying supplies up the track and over temporary bridges like this one in New Guinea or by slowly stretchering wounded Australians back down the track, despite the steep slopes and mountain streams *(below)*.
(Top photograph by Damien Parer.)

AWM 013262

AWM 014028

Although not taken on the Kokoda Track, George Silk's enduring image
captures the spirit of the Fuzzy Wuzzy Angels.

AWM 027052

Fresh Australian troops—the 16th Brigade—arrive and make their way up the track (note the customary walking sticks).

AWM 026854

Australian soldiers push a 25-pounder gun up the track.

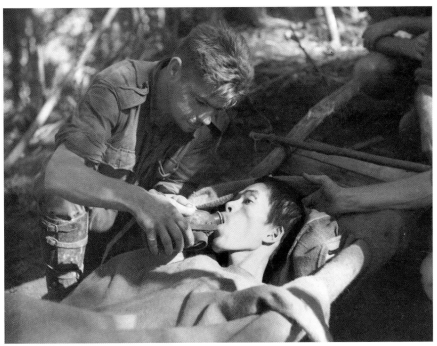

AWM 026824

An exhausted, starving Japanese prisoner captured near Nauro.

AWM 013703

Dead Japanese horses at Wairopi.

AWM 013620

The battle rages on: Australian troops keep moving along the track near Oivi, heading for Buna.

AWM 014082

An Australian soldier carefully clears a Japanese bunker near the beachheads. Australian soldiers were frequently ambushed by Japanese in these bunkers and suffered heavy losses.

AWM 014037

Taken during the actual fighting, Australian machine-gunners and soldiers launched an all-out assault during the final battle at Buna.

AWM 013879

Dejected, wounded and starving, Japanese soldiers are captured during the final assault on the beachheads.

AWM 013731/06

Two Australian soldiers near the end of the war in New Guinea emerge from the jungle covered in mud, just yards from nearby Japanese positions.

thing I want to say to you is "congratulations". Over the last two months you have performed magnificently under very difficult circumstances and have every right to be very proud of what you have achieved. You have done Australia proud, and you have done yourselves proud. Brigadier Potts has specifically asked me to commend you on your performance, and to tell you that news of your magnificent deeds has travelled far. *All of the Australian Army is proud of you.*'

At these last words, there was something of a stirring among the men of the 39th. For so long maligned as 'Chocos' and sometimes 'rainbows'—because they were said to always come out after the storm had passed—to have affirmation that the AIF was proud of them, and claiming them as their brothers in arms, was grand news indeed.

Colonel Honner continued: 'For the rest of your days you will be able to recall these days with the warmth of knowledge that when the heat was on you did not buckle, did not take a backward step. None of us will forget our fallen comrades, but your own efforts have ensured that they will not have died in vain . . . '

At this, a dark shadow of melancholy passed across the 39th, while Parer continued to film, as each soldier remembered individual comrades and the circumstances of their deaths. Honner continued, now a little more forcefully.

'Some things though it may be better to forget. I have heard some talk among you that some of you might feel that you might have been let down by other battalions and companies. While I understand that kind of talk under these difficult circumstances, I ask that you let it go. I remind you that those men are no better or worse than you, but that their circumstances were different. Had they been side by side with you they might have performed magnificently. Had you been side by side with them you might have performed less well. I repeat: the fact that their leaders may have failed them, and yours didn't, doesn't mean they were any better or worse than you are . . . [223]

'The principal thing though is that *you* have done very, very well indeed.'

In the history of the 39th it was a shining moment of redemption that would stay marked in their memories forever more. And Damien Parer captured it all.

By this time at Milne Bay, it was clear that the Japanese thrust had been blunted and turned. For the previous ten days, the dug-in Diggers of the 18th Brigade—handsomely supported by Kittyhawks flown by the pilots of 75 and 76 Squadrons RAAF and a small force of American Ack-Ack gunners—had first stopped the invaders and then pushed them back close to where they had landed, inflicting heavy casualties on the way. Intelligence reports had it that Japanese ships pushing into Milne Bay were not bringing in fresh reinforcements, but were *evacuating* the ones they had.

Still, though, the Japanese had some sting left in them. For the night after Ralph Honner had delivered his jungle oration to the 39th Battalion, a powerful Japanese armada entered Milne Bay and began shelling Australian positions, doing a great deal of damage. One Japanese warship had powerful searchlights and, scanning the newly constructed docks, picked up the vision splendid of the SS *Anshun*, a 4000 ton Australian supply ship, in the process of unloading its stores and munitions. Though the gunners of the Australian ship did what they could, and fired furiously back at the Japanese warship with its vastly superior firepower, in twenty minutes it was all over, with the *Anshun* on its side and half-submerged.

Next the Japanese warship turned its attention to an even easier prize, the HMAHS *Manunda*, a fully lit hospital ship caring for the wounded and dying Australian soldiers. Now the Japanese searchlights swivelled upon the ship for even better illumination, showing up its distinctive green and white hull. The only defence the *Manunda* possessed was a large red cross on its funnel, indicating its status as a non-combatant medical facility. Like a massive lion nosing up to a gazelle paralysed with fear, the Japanese warship hove to, about a thousand yards to the starboard side of the Australian vessel, which was now an easy target for a torpedo or sustained artillery fire.

On the *Manunda*, the entire crew, daring not to breathe, looked straight into the valley of the shadow of death as they stared at the hulking silhouette of the massive Japanese destroyer across the all too narrow patch of water that separated them. Below deck, many critically injured Australian soldiers knew something was up, but they did not know what. On the bridge, Captain James Garden was in full command, but knew that any attempt at flight was pointless. They just had to sit there, and wait.

Hail Mary, Mother of God.

And then the Japanese ship moved off into the darkness, growling softly, until it disappeared out of Milne Bay and all was silent once more.[224]

The invasion of Milne Bay proved to be a complete rout for the Japanese. Of the 2800 soldiers landed, only 1318 were evacuated, while at least 750 were killed during the battle, with most of the remaining enemy troops killed by Australian patrols as they tried to make their way overland to the Japanese base at Buna. On the Australian side of 9000 defenders, the losses were a quarter of that, with 161 killed and 212 wounded.

All up, whatever the casualty count, the fact that the Japanese had pulled out made Milne Bay nothing less than a great victory, which would be hailed as such by many of the Allies around the world. In Burma, the great British leader Sir William Slim would later note that at Milne Bay, 'the Australian troops had inflicted on the Japanese their first undoubted defeat on land. If the Australians, in conditions very like ours had done it, so could we. Some of us may forget that of all the Allies it was the Australian soldiers who first broke the spell of the invincibility of the Japanese Army. Those of us who were in Burma have cause to remember.'

An exception to this prevailing mood of 'all hail the Australian soldiers', however, was to be found back at General Headquarters in Brisbane. There, Douglas MacArthur—impatient for the Australians to deal with the Japanese so they could move on to retaking Rabaul and then on to the main game of returning to the Philippines—had continued to be dismayed to see the markers of the Australian position move back down the track. What was *wrong* with these Australian soldiers?

As soon as the news came through that a resounding victory had been achieved at Milne Bay, MacArthur cabled General George C. Marshall, the US Army Chief of Staff in Washington. 'The Australians have proven themselves unable to match the enemy in jungle fighting. Aggressive leadership is lacking. The enemy's defeat at Milne Bay must not be accepted as a measure of relative fighting capacity of the troops involved. The decisive factor was the complete surprise obtained over him by our preliminary concentration of superior forces.'[225]

Read: the credit was MacArthur's. Just wait till he could throw the American troops, now nearly ready, into action.

For public consumption, MacArthur's communiqué on the subject set the tone, in distinctly unmilitary language: 'The move was anticipated and prepared for with great care . . . The enemy fell into the trap . . . '[226]

Read: the credit was MacArthur's.

One who most definitely did not believe that the highest military leadership was deserving of much credit at all was Chester Wilmot. Now back in the correspondents' hut on the outskirts of Moresby, he was busily turning all his copious eyewitness notes on the campaign into reports for both the ABC Radio network and an ABC feature magazine. As well, he had accepted a highly unusual request from General Sydney Rowell—with whom he got on well and admired—to use his skills as a trained and impartial observer to write a report on the jungle campaign as he had witnessed it. In this task, Chester had not missed his mark and wrote strongly of 'the disorganisation of supply'; the troops abysmal 'lack of camouflage'; and the fact that it seemed that no one at headquarters had any understanding of just what conditions were like up there.[227]

A similar theme showed up in his reports for the ABC, in one of which he got right to the nub. It was difficult to write, but it was heartfelt and he knew it needed to be said:

We must feel proud of the men who fought so gallantly to halt the Japanese in the Owen Stanley Range, but the fight was costly . . .

The main reason for this was a comparatively small one. But campaigns are often lost by little things. Our troops in the mountains were vitally dependent on air supplies. Ten days before the Japanese made their attack, they raided Port Moresby. They found an aerodrome packed with transports and bombers lined up wing-tip to wing-tip on the runway . . . a perfect concentrated target. They didn't miss. On the road to the front our reinforcements were held up four days waiting for supplies to come through. In those four days the Japanese gained the initiative and launched their attack. But for that raid . . . but for our failure to disperse our aircraft on the ground, our troops would have been at the front in time. They would have been in position to stop the Japanese, they might even have been able to seize the initiative from them. In Greece and in Malaya we lost more planes on the ground than we did in the air, because of inadequate dispersion. But we still had to have the bitter lesson of Moresby, before we took real steps to see that it didn't happen again. But by this time the damage had been done . . . a chance had been lost . . . And because of this I felt bitter as I stood on the spur of the Owen Stanley Range looking down on the treetops in the valley that leads to Kokoda . . . I was bitter for I knew that somewhere under those treetops there were unnecessary Australian graves.

Chester Wilmot
War Correspondent
HQ New Guinea Force.
7.9.42.[228]

CHAPTER FIFTEEN

THE BATTLE OF BRIGADE HILL

Strafing and bombing by enemy aircraft became fierce around this time, and resulted in heavy casualties for [us] Japanese. In addition, malaria and diarrhoea plagued us, and many men fell ill. However, it was instructed that those who were required to be hospitalized should be sent forward . . . and should be hospitalized at the field hospital that was scheduled to be built shortly in Port Moresby . . . the physical strength of the soldiers was exhausted day by day due to the food saving requirements. Nevertheless, their morale was still excellent, and they were anxious to capture Port Moresby as soon as possible in order to receive dinner at the enemy's expense . . .

Kengora Tanaka[229]

Look there!

On the night of 6 September, the Australian troops dug in on Mission Ridge, gazing across to the opposite side of the valley, could see what at first glance looked like a long line of glow-worms in perfect formation . . . but then they realised.

It wasn't fireflies, it was some two thousand Japanese soldiers, with burning bits of the insulated signal wire which they had cut up for illumination, massing by night for an attack that would surely not be long in coming. It was absurd that something so dangerous should look so beautiful, but there it was. It was enough to make each of the Australians think of Christmas, but then again Christmas had never seemed further away.

Given the absence of even one gun with the capacity to send lead to the far side of the valley, there was nothing for it but to dig in and prepare for the attack. Once more unto the breach, dear friends, once more . . .

Still, as they watched, mesmerised, in the highlands of New Guinea, it seemed like all the fireflies had gathered into one enormous mass and were now shining as bright as the full moon in the middle of the distant hill. Were the Australians dreaming? No, they were not. What they witnessed was the Japanese forming up an enormous funeral pyre and burning their dead. Such was the way of life, and death, in those mountains so far from home for both sides.

It was something, anyway. At 8.00 a.m. the following day, after Potts's urgent messages to Port Moresby had for once been acted upon, the Australian forces on Mission Ridge had the great pleasure of hearing the roar of eight Boston bombers and four Kittyhawks overhead and then seeing them diving upon the Japanese positions at Efogi, strafing and bombing. They could see the Bostons release their bombs, then lurch suddenly upwards with a change in engine pitch as the planes were released of their burden.

The result of the bombs was even better. With each plume of dust and smoke across the valley, another cheer went up from the Australians. While it helped morale, in the end, though, it changed little.

Proof that the Japanese had been neither destroyed, nor dissuaded from their task came in the late afternoon when the Australians first heard the boom of a Japanese mountain gun from across the valley, and then missiles began to lob among them, almost immediately killing two men from A Company and wounding five others. Clearly, it was *they* who were now being softened up for the attack that would surely come on the morrow, if not before.

Just before sunset, at a pause in the artillery fire, there was a mail call, and the men eagerly scrambled for news from home by the very last rays of light. (Jenny had her first teeth. Jimmy had learnt to ride his bike. Mum was feeling poorly, but had picked up after receiving your last letter, even though she still can't understand why whole paragraphs had been cut out by the censor's scissors! We are all missing you, darling. Auntie Deb sends her love and Uncle Ronnie his best regards. He says to say he's sure you're doing Australia proud and that if your dad was alive he would have been telling everyone you were a chip off the old block, and that he reckons you are too. Please keep your head down and come home safe to us. All my love . . .)

All her love . . .

Beneath a tree on a rare break, the new Commanding Officer of the 2/14th Battalion, Captain Phil Rhoden, read again and again the cable which had just arrived from his girlfriend back in Melbourne, Pat Hamilton. Though for some reason it had arrived in an envelope on which some official or other in Moresby had marked 'Not Urgent', it was the three simple words on the telegram that Phil thrilled to . . . 'Yes I will,' she had cabled in response to his request for her hand in marriage.[230] That wharfie back at the docks in Townsville who he'd been worrying about all this time—the one he'd given the letter to, just before going up the gangplank—had clearly done the right thing.

At first light on 8 September, the Japanese launched a simultaneous, concerted attack on the Australians' positions atop Mission Ridge and Brigade Hill behind. After the bitter battle at Isurava and then Alola, the Japanese General Horii had advanced his tactical approach to fighting such jungle battles and wanted to take out both the forward defensive and rear fall-back positions at the same time. Despite the terrible attrition rate the Japanese had suffered thus far, the attacking force still outnumbered the defenders by more than six to one, so it was always going to be tough for the Australians to withstand the onslaught. But no one had expected it to be this tough.

Within three hours of the first shots being fired at the 2/27th Battalion in the forward positions, the Japanese—in yet one more demonstration of their extraordinary ability to move through jungle previously thought impenetrable—had successfully launched flanking movements which cut the track between the frontline positions and Pottsy's Brigade Headquarters in the rear.

This isolated Potts and his men, and cut them off from the bulk of their force, not that it seemed to worry Potts personally. Tom Grahamslaw was staggered at the way Brigadier Potts continued to walk around with his head held high, refusing to duck for cover like all the rest merely because Japanese bullets were whistling all around. It hadn't even fazed him that the native hut he had originally been occupying had been one of the first targets hit by the Japs, killing one of the men inside.

Still, there was no doubt that the brigadier realised the situation *was* desperate, and was working furiously to ensure that his forces provided maximum resistance. An important part of this resistance, he felt, was to see the track behind the main force cleared. It represented both the supply line and key route for the evacuation of the wounded, whose numbers were already mounting, and it was uppermost in all of their thinking that whatever else, *whatever else*, they had to keep themselves on that track between the Japs and Moresby. Which left them with only one possible solution. The Japs entrenched on the track would have to be removed, blasted out of there by Australian soldiers.

When the news came through, Stan Bisset was in an urgent conference with the new Commander of the 2/14th, Phil Rhoden, and the Commander of the 2/16th, Colonel Albert Caro. The message from Brigadier Potts was that the track was cut between them and they must send a force through to clear it from their end, while he would send a force from his. As part of the same message he ordered that if Brigade Headquarters was wiped out and he, Potts, were

killed, then Colonel Caro was to take over and ensure that the men
fell back to Menari using the previously reconnoitred alternate route.

Both Rhoden and Caro moved swiftly. Each rustled up a group
of men from their own battalions to follow orders. Phil Rhoden
selected Captain Claude Nye and his 2/14th B Company to push
back towards Potts and Brigade HQ, to clear the track. Nye was
an experienced operator and—as Stan would think of it ever after—
surely knew that the order was something very close to a death
warrant. But he merely said 'Yes, Sir . . . ' and proceeded to gather
his men to do what had to be done.

From Brigade Headquarters, Potts personally gave the orders to
Captain Breton 'Lefty' Langridge to do the same thing, to take his
own men and push through in the opposite direction. Lefty simply
removed his dog tags and handed them to his closest friend, on
what was clearly the very good chance that he wouldn't make it . . .

The feeling of each captain was tragically prophetic. Of Nye's
group of twenty-five soldiers, no fewer than seventeen, including
Nye himself and the great Charlie McCallum were killed, though
eight did get through. Gone too, were Lefty Langridge and twenty
of his own men.

Just a small way down the hill from this tragic scene, the 2/16th's
Captain 'Blue' Steward, was working furiously with his medical
orderlies to preserve the life in those who retained a heartbeat, but
were on the edge. And here was a soldier he knew a little, a fellow
by the name of Kevin Tonkin who had been a professional golfer
before the war. A piece of shrapnel had slit his throat as surely and
as cruelly as a bayonet wielded by a Jap, and though the fellow
couldn't speak—as his breaths came in and out of the gaping
wound—his *eyes*, well, his eyes said everything. They were saying
to him now with great urgency and desperation, 'Will I live, Doc?'

'Looking as dispassionately as possible at that man's throat,'
Steward later wrote in his memoirs, 'I hoped he couldn't sense the
lump in mine. Emotion clouds calm clinical judgement, but the

hardest thing is to not flinch from the gaze of the man you know is going to die.'[231]

At another point in this same action, a fellow who was with the 2/16th—a married man with children—stood up to make a charge and was immediately shot twice in the chest. As he fell, his last words were 'I don't want to die'.[232]

The death and destruction was not confined to the Australians. Down the hill from this carnage, one platoon of Japanese soldiers had been all but wiped out when they attacked. Corporal Kohkichi Nishimura's platoon had begun the day with forty-two soldiers, but now, shortly after noon—six solid hours of attacking and rebuttal—there were just eight survivors. Realising the likelihood that they would not get to sundown alive, these eight soldiers made each other a solemn promise: whichever of them survived would return after the war was over and retrieve the bones of all of their original platoon who had died, and return those bones to their homeland.[233]

Smoky Howson thought he was going to die. By now—moving back towards Moresby with the 39th—it was almost more than he could do to stay standing, he was so exhausted he could only just manage to put one foot in front of the other. And he was thirsty too, as dry as a dead dingo's donga, as his water had run out and it hadn't rained for *hours*. At least he was a little lighter than before, having left his gun and ammo with the fresh blokes of the 2/27th on Mission Ridge, keeping only his precious grenades with him—otherwise he would have felt naked. He was just coming down one particularly steep stretch when he saw through the fog of his exhaustion a bloody big red flag. The Rising Sun! The bloody Japs were ahead! It was a fine line, the difference between life and death. Tearing a grenade free, he was just about to hoik it at the bastards when he realised . . .[234]

The flag wasn't that of the Japs at all, but that of the Salvation Army blokes, the forward line of God's Army, who had moved up the track on their own mission to provide sustenance and care where they could.

Now Smoky didn't know if he was Protestant, Catholic or Callithumpian, but that wasn't what this was about. After he'd clipped his grenade back into his belt, the smiling Salvo officers gave Smoky and his mates tobacco, hot tea and a bit of cake. And as it turned out, it was the kindness of them giving him cake that put Smoky over the edge. He burst into tears. This had been a long campaign, and he had an awful lot bottled up inside him. Marginally restored, he kept moving back down the track, vowing that for the rest of his life—however long or short that might be—the Salvos would never have a problem getting a quid out of him.

Back at Mission Ridge, the fight went on. Tragically, despite the many deaths of the likes of Nye, Langridge and their men, and despite the fact that the track was temporarily clear of Japanese because of it, the situation was not retrieved. The Japanese were simply attacking in numbers too great to overcome and, as the blessed dusk began to at last fall on 8 September, Potts gave the orders for his own men to fall back to Menari. The forward forces would get out by the recently discovered alternative route to Menari. Even then, it could have been total disaster bar one thing . . .

In any withdrawals, the key was always to leave behind a strong rearguard who could keep up a withering volley of fire against any pursuers and give the main body of their own troops time to get away. This rearguard position was, of course, one of extreme danger, but it was a measure of the enduring esprit de corps of the Australians that on this occasion there was no shortage of volunteers to do the job.

(And the very act of calling for volunteers marked an important philosophical difference between the Australians and their opponents. The mighty Imperial Japanese Army did *not* call for volunteers. It gave *orders*, and those orders were obeyed, no matter what.)

The most important job of this rearguard was to buy time to evacuate the wounded who simply could not be saved if the Japanese were allowed to quickly come along the track unimpeded.

And sometimes it is just like that in war: ordinary men, do extraordinary things. So it was with just six men from the 2/27th's

B Company, commanded by Captain Bert Lee. Almost as a collective version of what Bruce Kingsbury had accomplished a week earlier, they broke from their precious cover and rose as one charging down the hill at the Japanese troops who had been pressing the remnants of the Australians so hard. Firing their Bren guns, throwing grenades, bayonets flashing in the firestorm, the result was that many of the Japanese simply turned and fled, breaking contact. Thanks to this extraordinary action by their comrades, the rest of the 2/27th—carrying their wounded with great difficulty—had the crucial time they needed to withdraw . . .

With this last thrust of the Australians, Corporal Kohkichi Nishimura's platoon was now down to just one—himself. And it was far from a sure thing that he was going to make sundown. Though the magazine of his own gun was now empty, all around him lay his dead comrades with their own guns by their side. He picked up one of the guns and prepared for the next onslaught.

He did not have to wait for long. For just before dark, an Australian soldier who had been creeping up on his position on the far flank, put the barrel of a Bren gun on to his helmet and gently began to squeeze the trigger.[235]

But at the instant that the metal of the gun touched the metal of his helmet, Corporal Nishimura suddenly became aware that something was amiss and jumped up, just a split second before the bullets came tearing out of the barrel. Though the helmet was blown from his head peppered with holes, his cranium was untouched—it was his right shoulder which took two bullets.

It was do or die, and the Japanese soldier and the startled Australian—who had been expecting an easy kill, but was now faced with a fight to the death—soon came to grips. The Japanese corporal was gushing blood from his wounds, but soon had the bayonet free from his belt and stabbed the Australian. Instead of sliding smoothly into his stomach, however, the point of the bayonet stopped only a little way below the surface as it had hit a rib. The Australian groaned, and kicked the smaller man in the stomach.

Sensing that his only chance was to close quickly on the Australian soldier—and so deny him the chance of getting off more shots—Nishimura grabbed the larger man in a massive bear hug. In the groaning, grunting melee that soon developed, the Japanese man managed to get the bayonet of the Australian free with his good left hand and arm, and satisfactorily plunge it several times into his torso.

The Australian, his strange round eyes suddenly getting rounder and bigger, groaned and fell to the ground in the soft twilight, just a few moments before the Japanese man did the same. The rest of the battle had moved well beyond the two now, and they were alone.

They both lay there for some time, each trying to garner the strength to finish the other off. Both had lost a lot of blood, and were losing more. Every so often the Australian soldier would lift his head up to look balefully at his Japanese opponent, before he would then lay it back down, exhausted. The Japanese corporal would do much the same. On several occasions when it looked like the Australian had mustered the strength to rise, the Japanese man also would start to get up . . . but then sink back down in tandem with his enemy. So it went, all night long until, when the sun finally came up, Nishimura looked over to see that the Australian soldier was dead. Corporal Nishimura was alone. Seriously weakened by his fight with the Australian, he used his remaining strength to secrete himself inside a hollow log, in the hope that his own forces would get to him before the Australians did.

(The earlier experience of Jack Manol, a private of the 39th Battalion, had been entirely the reverse. Pushing through the long kunai grass to be found on the northern slopes of the Owen Stanleys, he had suddenly found himself face to face with a Japanese officer. Each was as startled and scared as the other and there was a split second before each reacted by bringing their weapons to bear. The Victorian managed it just an instant quicker, and fired, drilling the Japanese officer neatly through the heart. He fell dead at Jack's feet. Shaking with the emotion of it, the Australian soldier nevertheless did what he had been trained to do, which was to go through the dead man's pockets, looking for anything that might be of value to military intelligence. There was something, a waxen piece of paper which he retrieved from an inside pocket. Jack turned it over. It was a photo of the officer, clearly back at home in Japan, with his lovely wife and three beautiful, smiling, healthy young children. The perfect family snapshot. Jack wept. Yes, it was 'him or me', and the Japanese officer would have done exactly the same to him if he'd had a chance, but it did not make it any easier to bear.)[236]

Chester Wilmot was disgusted. The report he had penned for the ABC on 7 September, had now returned from the chief censor. Everything that lauded the valour of the Australians had survived all right, but the whole section that had criticised the military administration had enormous slashes of big black pencil through it. 'Not to be broadcast.' Apparently the authorities had decided that it was a matter of national importance that their own ineptitude had to remain a secret. Censored. Chester Wilmot was *disgusted*.

On the alternative track to Menari, the 2/14th had come to a halt in the pitch black as it was impossible to continue. There, Captain Phil Rhoden faced his men—just 150 of whom were left of the 550 who had set out less than a month ago—and made the finest speech Stan Bisset had ever heard.

Rhoden, a former school captain of Melbourne Grammar, as well as captain of the football team and the cricket First XI, had always had a facility for inspiring oratory, but on this occasion he outdid himself, trying to point out that, though they had already accomplished great things, it would all count for nothing unless they went on with it. By the light of a small lantern, Captain Rhoden spoke to the grim-faced men huddled close, here in the back of beyond.

'I know it's been hard,' he said, 'almost harder than we can bear. But we must think of what we've achieved, and know that even though we've been heavily outnumbered we've taken down a lot more Japs, a *lot* more, than he has taken of us. I know that we have been devastated by the losses of so many of our close comrades, but I want each and every one of you to think what they would want of us if only they could speak to us from the grave. They would want us to finish the job they died for. They would want us to keep at the Japs, keep ourselves between them and Moresby, to help keep their loved ones and our own back in Australia safe. They would want us to never give up, while there was still breath in us and *keep going . . .*'

At first light on 9 September, the survivors of the 21st Brigade struggled forward, carrying their wounded trying to get back to Menari. There were no native bearers as they were never expected to stay close to the frontline. Was there no end, no relief from the unending bloody track, some chance to get off it, to rest, to recuperate to have some sweet blessed rest and maybe a cup of tea?

Yes, there was!

For just on the outskirts of Menari the following morning, there were the blessed Salvos again—having successfully moved forward from where Smoky had found them—handing out cigarettes, biscuits, chocolate and a 'cuppa tea'. *Real* tea! Real ciggies! Genuine Arnott's Milk Arrowroot biscuits like Mum used to serve! God bless the Salvos . . .

By late morning of 9 September, as the 2/14th and 2/16th began to make their way into Menari, Brigadier Potts intensified the wrestling with his constant dilemma. Stay or withdraw?

Only shortly after the bulk of the men had arrived, the Japanese were mounting an attack with great force and, though the Australian rearguard was doing well, there was no way they could hold for long. The real problem was that—weighed down by their enormous numbers of injured—the 2/27th Battalion was still out there somewhere on the alternative track, struggling forward. Ideally, Potts wanted to hold till they got there to prevent them being cut off, but within an hour or two the situation had moved well beyond urgent.

Whatever the demands of his military superiors far from the front, it was obvious to Potts that Menari was not ultimately defensible. Like Myola it stood at the bottom of a hill, making it an easy target for the attacking force. Not only that, but when the killed, missing, wounded and those looking after them were taken into the equation, Potts now had only three hundred exhausted men to try and hold an impossible position. Time and again he looked to the track where he hoped the 2/27th would emerge, and every time was frustrated to see no sign. Finally, heavily, he decided that he really did have no choice. After sending out a small patrol to try to make contact with the 2/27th and at least keep them informed, from mid-afternoon on 9 September, Potts moved his available forces back, one more time. The 2/27th would simply have to look after themselves, and get back cross-country. While it was undoubtedly the right decision—and the only sane one possible under the circumstances—Potts's superiors, who continued to have zero understanding of what the true situation was, were dismayed.

Back at Ower's Corner, out of the jungle they came, just over 140 strong. The 39th Battalion. Walking. Staggering. Holding each other up. But still with their heads held high. Their clothes were rags, their wounds suppurating, the results of their dysentery all too apparent down the backs of their legs. But they had made it out, and little could dampen their sense of relief and even joy. Not even the fact that the trucks which were meant to have been waiting for them at Ilolo were not there as they had been shanghaied to help with the more urgent matter of bringing fresh troops up from the dock. No matter. After everything they had been through, this was as nothing, and they simply kept going towards the plantation at Koitaki—about five miles from Ower's Corner—where they were due to recover, wash, sleep, eat and receive medical treatment until such times as they could be thrown back into the fray. After marching five miles down the road—a real *road*!—they passed one of the fresh companies of the AIF newly arrived 25th Brigade marching the other way.

The fresh company stopped immediately on catching sight of

the 39th and stared. God help us all. Just what kind of battle were they going into, when the survivors looked like *this*.

The 39th marched on, their trip at least alleviated a little when, a short time afterwards, a bloke on a supply truck grinding up the hill took pity on them and started throwing out fresh loaves of bread at them. The soldiers fell on them like starving vultures on lost baby ducks. In thirty seconds flat, all of the bread—the first most of them had eaten in well over two months—was gone. That night for equally the first time in many, many weeks, the men could sleep through in relative warmth, uninterrupted, without fearing that the creak of every branch was the possible harbinger of their death. And also, for the first time, they now had the luxury of being able to feel and to grieve. For although among the men there was a great sense of relief that they had survived to this point, this was mixed with a heavy consciousness of just how many of their comrades and dear friends they had lost. It was by no means something constantly referred to—for if they talked of the tragic deaths of their friends, they would have talked of nothing else—it was just a look that would come into a bloke's eyes before he suddenly looked away, and you instinctively knew that he was thinking of a bloke, and a bullet, and what had happened. With Wally and Ray beside him, Joe Dawson set to, trying to recover.

Like all of them, almost the worst of it was when he peeled his boots off for the first time in many weeks. Up in the mountains, against the Japs, you simply never took your boots off because you'd be unlikely to get them back on again. It wasn't as if you had a change of socks anyway—although a few blokes, admittedly, had cut off the sleeves of their jumpers to fashion them into makeshift socks—and it was only sensible to sleep with your boots on at night, knowing you might see action at any instant. Not surprisingly, when Joe peeled his boots off, it seemed like nearly half his feet came with them. The only reason there were no blisters was that there was pretty much no skin left to be blistered. Instead, his feet were simply a putrescent mass of white flesh covered in outbursts of outrage that the medical orderlies called 'boils' for want of a better term. One bloke's right foot was so bad he could put his entire index finger in the hole at the top of his foot, right through to his instep.

At least helping Joe recover a little was a parcel from home which got through in the mail, filled with a fruitcake, biscuits, razors, coffee and cigarettes, sent jointly by his mother and his girlfriend, Elaine.

There was, alas, no such fruitcake waiting for Smoky Howson. Only shortly after getting back with the 39th to Koitaki and, in the blessed Mess Hall for lunch, he decided he'd like another piece of cake. The bloke doling the cake out looked at him quizzically and then, with some irritation, said: 'You've *had* a bloody piece haven't you?' Dismissed. If Smoky had a gun he would have shot the bastard in the guts, just to see him squirm, dinkum he would have. '*You've had a bloody piece haven't you?*'[237] After everything he'd been through! Jesus Christ Almighty.

And he *was* hungry, no joke. As soon as the medical orderlies got a good look at him he was admitted straight to hospital, and one of the first things they'd done was to weigh him, so they would know what their starting point for his recovery was. Bloody hell. In his admission papers to the army Smoky had weighed twelve stone seven pounds. Now, after just nine weeks out on the track, he was down to seven stone five pounds, nothing more than skin and bone, and clearly a very big heart.

Being in hospital was good and all, but Smoky couldn't help but constantly think about the Japs, who he was sure must be coming closer all the time . . .

Up in the Owen Stanleys, there were indeed still hundreds of soldiers facing the might of the Japanese guns as they tried to hold them back. Even further away over the ranges, isolated pockets of Australian soldiers who had either been wounded or—like the 2/27th—cut off, were with great difficulty making their way overland.

One small group of these included Corporal J. A. Metson, with the bullet in his ankle, who was *still* crawling his way back. Every morning the married 27-year-old set off even before dawn, a good hour before the main party he was travelling with, and continued until well after they had stopped for the night and he had caught up with them. He refused all offers of help, including those of a few still strong soldiers who offered to piggyback him part of the way. Finally, however, his condition became so weakened, as were several others, that it was decided to leave them in a friendly native village, under the care of a medical orderly who would stay with them.

At dawn, the morning after the decision was taken, those who could go on paraded before those who were to stay, formally presented arms as a show of respect for their courage and self-sacrifice to this point, and headed off into the jungle. Only a few days later, those who were left behind, including the valiant Metson, were killed by a Japanese patrol.

In the mid-afternoon of 10 September, the order came through. Brigadier Potts was to return to Moresby immediately, for 'consultation', with General Rowell and General Allen, with his position in overall command of the Australian forces defending Port Moresby taken by Brigadier Selwyn Porter. Potts's departure was bitterly resented by his senior staff and the soldiers under his command—most of whom understood how well he had led them and that many of them owed their lives to him. Stan Bisset, for one, was appalled at the treatment of Potts. Yes, it was ostensibly for consultation, but to remove a battlefield commander when the battle was still effectively in progress was an obvious humiliation and it was deeply resented.

Another change was that the decimated ranks of the 2/14th and 2/16th were formed into one composite battalion under the command of Lieutenant Colonel Albert Caro, and obliged to struggle on from there, continuing to carefully leapfrog each other back down the track.

•

Immediately after Ralph Honner had returned to Koitaki with the remnants of the 39th, he was called to Port Moresby and told by General Rowell that he had to 'front the bull'. In army terminology this meant he would have to report to his commanding officer, which in this case was General Blamey, who had himself just arrived for his first look at the situation in Moresby. This was not because General Blamey had specifically requested that Honner come to see him, but because Major General Sydney Rowell was sure that General Blamey would want to consult closely with someone like Ralph Honner who had so recently returned from the battle.

Honner spruced himself up as best he could—polished his shoes and tried to put something that looked like a crease in his trousers— and duly reported to Blamey in the New Guinea Force HQ.

'Good morning, Honner,' the General greeted him pleasantly, if a little vacantly, clearly having no idea who Honner was. 'You've just arrived in Moresby from Australia have you?'

'No, Sir,' Honner replied, staggered at the level of his commanding officer's ignorance, 'I have been in Papua now for some time.'[238]

(Could Blamey be serious? How could the general not even know who had been in charge of the 39th Battalion for the last four weeks, fighting on the frontline against the Japanese? How could he not know something as basic as that, and yet still have been sending orders from three thousand miles away about how the Japanese should be routed? It simply beggared belief.)

The conversation proceeded for the next half hour or so, covering a variety of general matters, not one of which included the actual campaign then underway. Here was the highest officer of the Australian Army, on his one visit to New Guinea, in the presence of one of his leading officers in the field, and yet he posed not a single question. To Honner it seemed as if Blamey had no interest in how the Maroubra Force campaign had fared, what ideas Honner might have for improving Australian performance, or even what weaknesses he might have determined in the Japanese fighting approach. Nothing! After a time, Honner left, shaking his head in wonder as soon as it was safe to do so.

Long had he laboured, great was his suffering, but the time of redemption was near. Now back in Sydney, after hitching a ride on a plane out of Moresby, Damien Parer was showing his bosses the film he had salvaged from his trek, and already sketching out a rough script. Damien was a little disappointed with what he had managed to shoot, but this was perhaps only because he knew just how graphic other scenes were. For his bosses, however, the footage was a revelation. They had simply had *no idea* that conditions were so appalling for the soldiers, and immediately they knew they had a very good documentary on their hands. What's more, they knew who they wanted to front it . . . Damien. He had been up there, he had shot the film, he presented well, he was perfect. Damien resisted, protesting that he was the man behind the camera, and that it wasn't right for him to step in front of it. But his bosses insisted and he reluctantly agreed.

Back at the front, by the morning of 12 September the Australian soldiers had withdrawn to the top of Ioribaiwa Ridge, where the plan was to consolidate before throwing the fresh soldiers of the 25th Brigade—who had just arrived under the command of Brigadier Ken Eather—into aggressive flanking manoeuvres against the Japs.

As was ever the way in war, however, it didn't quite work out as planned. Lacking experience in jungle fighting, the fresh troops who moved forward on the left flank simply became lost, while those on the right flank moved smack bang into a concentration of General Horii's few remaining crack troops and were routed. Even worse, the bulk of the exhausted soldiers dug in at the top of the mountain were easy targets for General Horii's mountain guns which had once again come forward.

It was that rarest and most precious of all things in this war—a real press conference where the likes of Thomas Blamey could be made to answer for what Chester Wilmot, for one, saw as the sheer insanity of some of his actions and orders.

Blamey began, being quite upbeat. 'The Japs are already feeling the difficulties of supply,' he said. 'They have a few light mountain guns, but they have no chance of getting heavy supplies along that terrible track with its precipices and jagged ridges and awful river crossings and great stretches of track that are merely moving streams of black mud. Moresby is in no danger, and I think we shall find that the Japs will be beaten by their own advance, with its attendant problems of supply. It will be a Japanese advance to disaster, an Australian retreat to victory.'[239]

All well and good. But after some preliminary questions by other journalists, the fearless Wilmot got right to the point: 'General Blamey, do you think that green uniforms are necessary for our soldiers in the jungles of New Guinea?'

General Blamey, with a clear flash of anger at the near-impertinence of the very question replied: 'Not at all. It is true that those uniforms were designed specifically for the jungles of India, but I have never seen any evidence that the jungle of New Guinea is any different from the jungle of India. I think the uniforms the soldiers are wearing are quite adequate . . . '

Wilmot continued: 'Well, I can provide several thousand witnesses who have actually fought in New Guinea who can provide evidence to the contrary . . . '[240]

If it wasn't quite a declaration of war from one man to another, it was as close to it as a press conference could allow and, from that moment, both Wilmot and Blamey knew that the other was gunning for him with every means available. Wilmot was outraged by what he had seen in New Guinea and held Blamey personally responsible for a lot of it; Blamey was apoplectic at Wilmot's presumption in not only blaming him, but then endeavouring to broadcast it. For the moment, each took the view that the other would keep . . .

•

How long could the Australians stay on the forward slopes of Ioribaiwa, simply being picked off by mountain guns sending whistling shells right among them? It was absurd, most particularly when their own firepower was now just a few hours march to their rear. The obvious thing to do was to withdraw to the far more defensible Imita Ridge—just four hours march north of Ower's Corner—and bring the Japs to within range of the Australian guns, and to make their 'line in the sand' there. That far, and no further.

So it was, that on the morning of 16 September, Brigadier Eather got a message through to Tubby Allen: 'Enemy feeling whole front and flanks. Do not consider can hold him here. Request permission to withdraw to Imita Ridge if necessary.'

Despite Allen's previous admonition that the 25th Brigade had to draw a line in the sand on Ioribaiwa and never fall back from it, he reluctantly agreed to the request—at least noting that it would bring the Australian soldiers that much closer to the supply lines and stretch the Japs that much further. As well, it would give the brutes a little curry with their rice, once they indeed got within range of the Australian guns.

On his return to Australia, after just three days in Moresby and nowhere near the frontline, Blamey publicly expressed the view that the situation in New Guinea was well in hand, and also evinced confidence in the performance of Lieutenant General Rowell, Major General Tubby Allen and their troops. Yes, the Japanese were now uncomfortably close to Moresby, but on the other hand their exhausted troops were at the end of an extremely long supply line, while the Australians were now well provisioned and daily receiving fresh reinforcements. It was likely that the Japanese would get little further.

This was not a view shared by MacArthur, or at the very least it was not one he expressed. For despite the Australian heroism to this point—fighting successfully against extraordinary odds and managing to weaken the Japanese with every day they kept them out there—back in Brisbane all that GHQ focused on was the markers on the map, which showed the invaders getting closer and closer to Port Moresby. This feeling was compounded after one of the key members of MacArthur's clique, General Kenney, had made his own second trip to New Guinea and returned to tell MacArthur that the fall of Moresby was imminent. Though Kenney did not get remotely close to the actual fighting, he was firm in his view, his words echoing what General Sutherland had expressed to him on his first afternoon in Brisbane, that the Australians simply weren't up to it.

'You've got to get some Americans up there,' Kenney now told MacArthur. 'They don't know anything about jungle fighting, but the Australians don't know that, and the Americans don't know it either. So we'll go up there all full of vinegar and the Australians will be afraid that the Americans will take the play away from them. So both will start fighting, and we'll get the damned Japs out of there . . .'

The scheme would have a bonus benefit, he told MacArthur.

'We've got to stop stories that the Yanks are taking it easy in Australia and letting the Aussies do all the fighting.'[241]

What was clear was that while they were waiting to throw the Americans into the fray, something had to be done, that the situation had to be taken in hand by someone who could turn it around. (And perhaps, a cynic might say, be on site with the failed soldiers of his own nation, to take the lion's share of the blame should Moresby fall.) Blamey was at least part of the answer.

With that in mind, MacArthur called the Australian Prime Minister John Curtin, and they had a strained conversation on the evening of 16 September 1942.

'The retrogressive nature of the tactics of the Australian ground forces defending Port Moresby seriously threatens outlying airfields,' MacArthur told Curtin. 'If they can't stop the Japs, the Allies in New Guinea will be forced into such a defensive concentration as would duplicate the conditions of Malaya.'[242]

In sum: the decimation of both Australian interests and Australian soldiers. The only way around it, MacArthur maintained, was to get American troops involved, which he, MacArthur, would take care of; while General Blamey would have to return to New Guinea full time and give his soldiers the ginger they needed to get cracking. It would be for Blamey to 'energise the situation'.

When MacArthur expressed the same view to Blamey, and insisted that he return to New Guinea, the Commander of the Australian Forces showed no enthusiasm whatsoever, still without quite saying 'no'. It was only when John Curtin, at MacArthur's specific behest, *insisted* that Blamey return that he agreed he would.

(In all of these discussions, the possibility that the military *leadership* wasn't up to it—as shown by putting inadequate and ill-supplied forces up against an enemy overwhelming in its numbers and firepower—was never broached. As the markers on MacArthur's map retreated, there were only two possibilities: that the Australian soldiers were lacking; or the leadership which had put them there in insufficient numbers with inadequate firepower was lacking, and MacArthur was all in favour of the former view.)

So persuasive had MacArthur been with Curtin, that when the Australian Prime Minister heard a few days after their initial conversation that his commanding general was *still* in Australia, he called him and said with uncharacteristic venom: 'General Blamey, I thought that you had gone to New Guinea. If you value your position you will not remain in Brisbane another day!'[243]

The news of Blamey's imminent return to Moresby, essentially to take command so soon after he had returned from an inspection tour, received a mixed reaction. Many of Blamey's detractors all but openly celebrated, in the manner of the Minister of Supply and Development, Jack Beasley, who reportedly exclaimed: 'Moresby is going to fall. Send Blamey up there and let him fall with it!'[244]

On the other side was the likes of General Sydney Rowell whose role as the commanding officer of all forces in New Guinea was clearly being usurped—however much Blamey might have tried to dress it up otherwise when he did in fact arrive. Though they had worked closely together since the war started, Rowell had never liked Blamey, regarding him as a womaniser, a drunk and worse, and in fact was still appalled by Blamey's actions in the fall of Greece where, à la MacArthur, he had taken a plane to safety leaving his troops behind to the mercy of the enemy. And *this* was the man who was now going to take operational command from him, to prove that he was, after all, a great battlefield commander? Rowell could barely stand it . . .

Beware the false dawn. The light of the late wee hours was notorious for tricking those who gazed upon it into thinking that dawn was close, and the men from the Land of the Rising Sun were as susceptible to the phenomenon as any. Dawn meant light, meant warmth, meant the lessening of the evil pressing darkness, meant sure confirmation that they had lived to fight another day, and each sunrise was a tiny triumph. And each time the dawn proved to be false was equally just that little bit crushing.

Bit by bit, though, through the middle of September, the advancing soldiers of General Horii became aware that the faintest of all faint lights to their immediate south was not false at all but was something close to their own version of the Promised Land—Port Moresby. After long weeks, stretching into months of fighting, of disease, of death, of disaster, of dysentery and all the rest, the desired destination of the whole campaign was now so close that as the Japanese dug into the just-abandoned ridgeline of Ioribaiwa, they could even *see* the city and then, wonder of all wonders, the shimmering ocean beyond it in the daytime. They had made it through . . .

The Japanese war correspondent, Seizo Okada—working for the great Tokyo newspaper *Asahi Shimbun*—was in fact among the soldiers when they gained the top of the ridgeline of Ioribaiwa. He reported: 'The sea! It's the sea of Port Moresby! Wild with joy, the soldiers who were stained all over with mud and blood, threw themselves into each others arms and wept.'

The Japanese soldiers were now ninety per cent of the way towards their goal, but had lost fifty per cent of their number through the attrition of battles, jungle, malaria and scrub typhus.

So, too, there were many who had died in the manner of Bruce Kingsbury from a simple excess of courage.

Despite having been pushed to their limits of exhaustion, still the news galvanised the Japanese soldiers as nothing else could. It was possible, just possible, that from here they could see the end of their long campaign and be the authors of as hard fought a military victory as any Japanese troops had ever achieved. A week earlier General Horii had given the order that the wounded were not to be evacuated to the Buna beachhead, and instead were to be kept just back from the frontline in the expectation that they would soon be in real hospitals in the New Guinea capital—and now this decision looked to be a wise one.

Steady though. If the Japanese had learnt one lesson over previous months it was that all advances had to be consolidated, and with their remaining strength the soldiers began to dig in, carving out trenches from the thick soil, branching into weapon pits, together with a massive 'fence' of felled trees placed side by side to give even more cover against the Australians.

Even while this defensive preparation was underway, though, the plan was formulated to attack. Yet so exhausted were the surviving Japanese soldiers who had made it this far—and so starved, as their rations were now only a few stray grains of rice north of zero—that it was all they could do in the first days after arriving at Ioribaiwa to send out a few patrols to test the strength of the Australian defences on Imita Ridge.

The grim pinched faces of the survivors of those patrols told the story: the Australian defences were now, suddenly, very strong. Horii considered his position. So near, and yet still so far.

Where were the supplies that might have made his soldiers a still effective fighting force? His men were now so far from Buna that it had been virtually impossible to carry food and ammunition so far, as every porter would have to have eaten most of the weight he was carrying; and the plan to live off captured Australian supplies simply hadn't worked. The Australians had either destroyed them, or doctored them as they had at Myola, causing an outbreak of the most debilitating dysentery among hundreds of the men. The only thing they had been able to salvage from Myola had been three hundred blankets, which had eased the crippling cold somewhat for a few companies.[245] But that was pretty much it.

The bottom line was that there simply were no supplies, and nor were there any on their way down the track. The situation was grim and getting grimmer, however intoxicating the lights of Moresby might be.

The lack of serious Japanese thrust in this period did not go unnoticed by the Australians. In the previous days the rearguard of the Australians had noted that amid all the mortar fire and the rest, huge boulders, which came crashing and tumbling down the slope through the jungle in their direction had been added to the mix. They were frightening and damaging all at once, sure . . . But *boulders*? In the whole campaign to that point, and despite the fact that the Australians had been fighting up and down mountains, the Japanese had never used this tactic against them. Admittedly it was a good one—one boulder could create havoc and injury among succeeding layers of troops—but the question had to be asked. Were they reduced to using rocks because their own supplies of ammunition were running low?

It was part of a pattern that Stan Bisset for one had noticed. Whereas only a few weeks before every Japanese attack had been full-on and ferocious, now there was something more careful about them—either careful, or more exhausted. Plus, every Japanese corpse the Australians came across was always emaciated and, more often than not, diseased in some fashion. That things were grim for the Japanese, there was no doubt.

It was not long before, in pure desperation, General Horii gave orders that no bullet was to be fired from this point on unless an Australian soldier was actually in your sights . . .

Now ranged against the Japanese, the Australians were well dug into the top of Imita Ridge, with all of the officers well aware of General Sydney Rowell's orders: 'Any further withdrawal is out of the question and Eather must fight it out at all costs.' That much, in fact, was already fairly obvious to all the Australians, given that Moresby lay only a short way behind them, past Ower's Corner, and down the Laloki Road through the rubber plantations to the outskirts of the town itself.

At the same time, now that they were so much closer to Moresby, the Australian forces boasted greater numbers—with four fresh battalions bringing the total defenders to 2500 men—and had more firepower than ever before. Not just bullets either. Now, the Australians had heavy artillery shells. After an enormous and sustained effort, the big guns had been dragged into place onto the high ground between Uberi and Ilolo and on the morning of 21 September—ah, the pure relief of it!—began to do their work. It was the first time in the entire campaign that the Japanese faced artillery attack, and the survivors of the 2/14th and 2/16th could barely contain themselves. Take *that*, Tojo, and now here comes some more. At the time, men cheered as Alan Haddy yelled: 'Mix that with yer bloody rice yer little yellow bastards!'[246]

When Australian patrols carefully moved out from Imita at this time, feeling cautiously for the Japanese front, the word came back fairly quickly: there didn't appear to be any Japs pushing forward from Ioribaiwa. It looked like they were dug in there.

On the night of 22 September—the eve of General Blamey's return to Moresby—Damien Parer's documentary *Kokoda Front Line* opened in Sydney at the State Newsreel Theatrette, on Market Street. The effect was immediate, once the word got out. Queues formed around the block. The public was agog at the conditions in which the Australian men were fighting, and were filled with deep respect— effectively for the first time—for what the Australian militia had proved themselves capable of. 'Chocolate soldiers', indeed!

Damien was able to use the attention that the film attracted to warm to his theme. Just two days after the film opened, he was quoted by his friend and fellow war correspondent Reg Glennie in *The Age*: 'I hear a lot of grumbling here about shortages of this and that. Men are complaining that they can't get enough cigarettes or tobacco. Women are upset because they can't buy silk stockings.

'Up near Efogi in the Owen Stanley Range, a fortnight ago, I saw men smoking dried tea leaves and rushing like madmen to pick up rations that were dropped down to them from our planes. But they weren't complaining. People here have little to complain about. They should make the sacrifices demanded of them gladly. Their men are fighting in appalling conditions. Not so far away, either. Only about 300 miles off the Australian coast . . .'[247]

In the film itself, Damien had been able to slip in support for General Rowell, whom he greatly admired as a military commander. As the narrator of the documentary, Damien looked straight down the barrel of the camera and stated: 'When I returned to Moresby I was full of beans. It was the spirit of the troops and the knowledge that General Rowell was on the job and now we had a really fine command.'

All up, the film made an enormous impression, and it wasn't merely on the public at large. When American troops, at last, were making ready to leave for New Guinea, they contacted General Blamey's Land Forces HQ to determine whether or not green camouflage uniforms were necessary. Despite everything, the firm answer came back: 'No'. And then General Eichelberger and his staff went to see *Kokoda Front Line* and had their eyes opened, as the khaki uniforms of the Australians so clearly stood out. The Americans were concerned and contacted both Damien Parer and Ossie White to get their view, and an even firmer response came back: 'You are mad if you don't'. The Americans subsequently ignored the Blamey view and had their uniforms dyed mottled green.

Blamey himself, meanwhile, sent the following coded cable to MacArthur on the evening of 23 September: 'Assumed command as from 1800 hours today, September 23rd. Consider inadvisable any publicity, may induce enemy to strengthen forces.'[248] As it happened, the likelihood that MacArthur would allow Blamey's presence in Moresby any publicity at all—unless things started to go very badly indeed—was always minimal.

The arrival of Blamey in Port Moresby on a semi-permanent basis proved to be every bit as bad as Major General Sydney Rowell had feared. Blamey arrived with little more than a couple of senior staff, meaning he would have to use Rowell's staff to operate, effectively neutering the previous head of the New Guinea Force. It seemed likely to be untenable, but for the moment Rowell decided to grit his teeth, gird his loins and put up with it.

In the correspondents' hut on this same night—and aware of what Blamey's arrival would likely mean for Rowell—Chester Wilmot did what he could. Banging away on his trusty old typewriter he finished his report for *ABC Weekly* thus:

> *In New Guinea today the lessons of this campaign have been rapidly appreciated, and under General Rowell's direction most of the mistakes, which were the result of previous unsuitable training, have been remedied. Some can only be remedied by training, which takes time, but the most prompt and far-reaching steps have been taken by him to see that our troops can meet the enemy on even terms.*
> *Chester Wilmot*
> *War Correspondent,*
> *HQ New Guinea Force.*
> *23.9.42*[249]

Cooler now . . . Always the blessed darkness brought some relief from the crushing heat beating down on the forward forces of the Imperial Japanese Army at Ioribaiwa as they looked to Moresby on the horizon of their dreams. On this evening, the Japanese war correspondent Seizo Okada decided to visit Major General Horii in his tent. A longtime correspondent, Okada had felt in his bones that something was happening, and naturally gravitated to the highest authority on site. With his friend Sato by his side, they looked into the tent. There was the Major General, looking suddenly very old and extremely emaciated by the light of a single candle, sitting on his heels on a straw mat, facing one of his key officers, Lieutenant Colonel Tanaka, who seemed to be avoiding his gaze. The mood was tense, grim, desperate. The Major General nevertheless courteously bade the correspondents to enter with a wave of his hand, and—after bowing in deference and deep respect—they had just taken their seats on the guest mats, when there was a rustling outside.[250]

In came the always self-important officer in charge of the Signal Corps, carrying a message, which he handed to Major General Horii. It was an order. From Rabaul. They were to abandon their positions, and—because there is no Japanese word for 'retreat'—*advance to the rear*. As quickly as possible, they were to get back to Buna, where they were to consolidate their position. Almost immediately this order was followed by another, which came from no less than Imperial Headquarters in Tokyo, confirming the previous one. The Emperor himself had commanded that they must turn back.

Horii absorbed it all, without displaying great emotion, as was his way, whatever he might have been feeling inside. And in fact, though it was not known to his troops, Horii had received word three weeks earlier from Imperial Headquarters, that he was *not* to attempt to take Port Moresby until such time as the situation was clearer and there was the possibility of getting reinforcements and bulk supplies to him. Instead, his instructions were to find a suitable defensive position and hold the line there. Horii had selected the ridge of Ioribaiwa, and it was for this reason that he had instructed the men—while not telling them the reason—to construct a kind of log palisade at the top of the hill, across the track, behind which defensive trenches were dug in the rich black soil.

Now, though, the order to pull back from even that position was a moment of sanity from a Japanese military leadership which in recent times had seemed more and more suicidal. The Battle of the Coral Sea had meant that the Japanese had lost control of the sea, and their failed action at Milne Bay had lost them all chance of air superiority. Both factors increased the likelihood that the Allies would mount an attack on the Buna beachhead and it was time to strengthen the defences there and abandon the assault on Moresby, which in any case was being slowly strangled by the impossibility of supplying the forward troops. Compounding it all was that the Japanese already were engaged in a deadly war of attrition at Guadalcanal, and therefore simply did not have the spare soldiers to reinforce Horii, even if they had wanted to. So there really was no choice.

Nevertheless, not all of Horii's men viewed it that way when the Japanese commander gave the orders to prepare for withdrawal, leaving behind only a rearguard. Having come so far, many of the surviving soldiers and officers wanted to finish the job and achieve the goal of Moresby. Their proposal was to thrust forward now with total commitment, and see if they could not see their mission through, *regardless* of what the orders said. It was a measure of the extremity of the situation that they could even *think* of counter-manding the orders of their commanding officer.

One of the Japanese officers also present at the time, Captain Nakahashi, later gave this account. 'The order came like a bolt from the blue, causing feelings of anger, sorrow and frustration which could not be suppressed. The dreams of the officers and men of the South Seas Force vanished in an instant. Due to problems of transport and the situation at Guadalcanal, the main body of the Force had to withdraw at once. Accompanied by our prayers, our mountain battery fired several rounds at maximum range in the direction of Port Moresby, thereby somewhat uplifting our downcast spirits and those of our dead comrades. In the evening of the 26th September, our withdrawal began.'[251]

CHAPTER SIXTEEN

THE TIDE TURNS

Shindoi na!

A Japanese expression that translates to 'I'm exhausted'

The Jap is a fanatic with subnormal, animal cunning, but our [infantry man] has been more than a match for him. The Digger asks no beg-pardons. He has adapted himself from the heavy-equipment desert war with the Germans to this individual war in the jungle and he has had to learn the hard and bloody way. He has outfought the Jap with the same spirit as he held the Hun at Tobruk, and smashed him at Alamein. The Jap can commit his hari-kiri for the Emperor and the Imperial Nipponese Empire, but the Digger has fought, and always will fight for his cobbers: for Bluey and Snowy, for Lofty and Stumpy.

Damien Parer, 'A Cameraman looks at a Digger'[252]

With the bitter decision taken, the Japanese return to their Gona–Sanananda–Buna beachhead and possible safety was frenetic. While the decision to retreat was almost unthinkable, the hardest of all things for their men was to abandon the seriously ill and injured to their fate. To this point General Horii had kept the injured just behind the advancing frontline with the intent that they would receive hospital care as soon as his troops captured Port Moresby. But now that the troops were heading back to the beachhead, the wounded would be a terrible hindrance to their journey back over the mountains.

So, just before the still healthy troops pulled out, many of the sick and dying were given two grenades each, with a clear instruction: the first of these grenades is to be thrown at the enemy when they are so close that you can't miss. The second is for you, to ensure that you are not taken prisoner. The groaning men understood. This was the way it was, and it was as good a way as any to go out, with one last chance to serve the Emperor. Their healthier comrades left them, many weeping at the bitterness of what they had to do. (Although this was a slightly better fate than some of the wounded had received, with Diggers maintaining that sometimes at night they could hear the moaning of wounded men behind enemy lines just a hundred yards away, which ended when single shots rang out. Presumably, the Japanese killed their own because there simply weren't the resources to look after or evacuate them in the mayhem of the battle.[253])

The Japanese soldiers were bewildered. Where had this all gone so wrong? How had they, the all-conquering members of the 144th Regiment, got themselves into this position? Had they not fought well and bravely? Yes, they had. Had their tactics and strategies not been effective in shifting the dug-in Australians? Absolutely. Had they not outnumbered the Australians in just about every engagement? Yes, indeed. Somehow, though, it really had all gone wrong and there was nothing to do but try to get back to the relative safety of the beachhead and hope that a victory at Guadalcanal would yet see them reinforced and capture Port Moresby.

Sydney Rowell didn't see this one coming. On the morning of 28 September, just five days after General Blamey had arrived in Port

Moresby, the grim, determined look on the military leader's face was explained shortly after they began their regular morning meeting.

With little ceremony General Blamey told Rowell that he was relieving him of his command, with the firm promise that both John Curtin and General MacArthur would be informed of his inadequacies. Blamey stated that while their current arrangement could have worked if different people had been involved, it simply couldn't work with an officer of Rowell's temperament.

It was to be the beginning of a long and brutal stoush between the two and, furious, Rowell boarded a plane for Australia that very night. Rowell retained a good deal of support within the Australian Government, particularly from those who also deplored General Blamey, and he was far from finished. Despite this widespread support, Rowell did not content himself with leaving the denigration of Blamey to others. He was determined to be an active participant, heading off to see MacArthur in Brisbane as soon as the following day to tear Blamey down, and then to Canberra a few days after that to make the same pitch to Prime Minister John Curtin. Though with both gentlemen Rowell had to use a little diplomatic circumspection, in private communications there was no such need and in a letter to another officer shortly after his effective dismissal Rowell wrote, 'The fight is by no means over and perhaps I can do something to help cut out an evil cancer in the body of the public.'[254]

In the short term, Blamey's presence and total command of the situation in New Guinea had one crucial benefit—for the first time supplies were suddenly plentiful. It had been one thing for Rowell to plead with Land Force Headquarters for more supplies, and quite another when Blamey wanted the same. For the most senior Australian military figure of the day did not plead, he merely ordered, and it came. Ammunition, food, fresh uniforms and boots were suddenly available as never before, at least within the environs of Moresby.

The other apparent benefit was that, in these last days of September 1942, with the Japanese advance stalled at Ioribaiwa, MacArthur decided it was time to throw some Americans into the fray. The oldest battle tactic in American history was to 'cut 'em off at the pass' and that was precisely what MacArthur intended to do on this occasion with the men of the 126th US Infantry Regiment. From the information available on his map, it all looked pretty simple.

The plan was that while the Australians pursued the Japanese back down the main Kokoda Track whence they came, the Americans—starting from the village of Kapa Kapa, forty miles east of Port Moresby—would push north across the Owen Stanleys by a shorter route. This would bring them out at Wairopi, with luck in front of the retreating Japanese and, *bingo*, the Japs would indeed be cut off at the pass. With the Australian soldiers pushing from behind, the crack American troops could block the Japanese retreat and annihilate them. It should be a fairly clean operation.

There were high hopes among the American military leadership for their troops as they set off. On a trip to Australia at this time, a member of the US Joint Chiefs of Staff, Lieutenant General Hap Arnold, privately expressed the view that 'the Massachusetts soldier knew more about the New Guinea jungle in two days than the Australians in two years.'[255]

Fix bayonets. Check grenades. The moment came. As one, the fresh AIF troops of Brigadier Ken Eather's 25th Brigade who had arrived from Australia only a few days before, charged up the Ioribaiwa ridge—if hauling forty pounds of rifle and ammunition straight up a muddy mountain could be so described. The main thing was that even as the Australians ran they kept firing furious fusillades of bullets up at the Japanese defenders, conscious that the more they threw the less dangerous the defenders would be.

Curiously, and for nigh on the first time in the whole campaign, the Japanese defence was scattered at best. Instead of the withering return fire the Australians had been expecting, there was naught but sporadic pot shots, and nothing like the murderous mowing down they had been told to expect.

In fact, by the time the first of the Australian troops breached the perimeters, most of the Japanese defenders had taken off to previously prepared fall-back positions further down the track, leaving behind only a very small rearguard, while the rest were their dead, dying and wounded.

It was only after the Australians had poured past these initial defences that they realised just how desperate the Japanese situation had been. When the Australians had abandoned Myola, they had destroyed or spoiled the bulk of their food dumps before leaving to prevent the enemy from using it. Here, they looked for signs of such destroyed food, yet there were none, quite probably on the grounds that there *was* none.

And there were plenty more indications to come. As the Australians tentatively took hold of Ioribaiwa Ridge—always conscious of the possibility of a Japanese counterattack or ambush or trick, and scarcely believing that all was as it appeared—they became conscious of an all-too familiar stench, but a stronger version than they had ever encountered before. Death. Dead Japanese soldiers were lying all over the ground, some of them dead for many days, and nearly all of them with the pinched and twisted look of the half-starved.

As Australian war correspondent George H. Johnston took notes, one of the army doctors carried out makeshift autopsies on some of the corpses, and reported to the battalion command that many of them had died 'because hunger had forced them to eat the poisonous fruits and roots of the jungle.'[256]

There would be yet more grisly finds to come. As the Australians pushed back down the track they came across their fallen comrades from several weeks before, and some of their corpses appeared to have had flesh hacked away from their thighs and calves. The dreadful suspicion that the Japanese soldiers had been so starving for nutrition that they had eaten their enemies was compounded when the Regimental Medical Officer of the 2/25th Battalion was given a parcel of 'meat' which he examined, before filing a report: 'I have examined two portions of flesh recovered by one of our patrols. One was the muscle tissue with a large piece of skin and underlying tissues attached. I consider the last as human.'[257]

•

As macabre as this apparent cannibalism was, it was one particular Australian death with absolutely nothing to do with Japanese savagery that attracted their attention. Just a little way forward from Menari—where some 'biscuit bombing' had been done to keep the forward troops supplied—there was a fresh grave. It was that of a provost sergeant who had survived bullets, grenades, mortars and malaria, only to be struck dead by a large tin of biscuits. Stone, motherless, *dead*. To this point there had been a lot of near misses, but this was proof positive that it fair dinkum was worthwhile standing well back from any dropping zone when the fly-boys were doing their stuff.[258]

This far into the campaign, however, death did not have the same effect on the soldiers that it once had. At a later point down the track, the men even openly mocked it. At the top of one ridge, from a shallow Japanese grave emerged a skeletal arm and hand at an angle of forty-five degrees to the ground. Each Digger shook that hand as he passed, saying things the like of 'G'day, Dig, how ya goin'?'

Now that the tide of the Japanese advance had been turned, the temptation was for the Australians to turn into a flood of fire rushing after them, but the lessons of the campaign had been learnt. At this point, consolidation was every bit as valuable as helter-skelter harrying, and the Australian soldiers proceeded carefully, aware of the mortal damage a well-executed ambush could wreak upon an advancing force.

In these early stages of the 'advance to the rear', the Japanese soldiers had no such fear of an ambush in front of them, and were constrained only by their own exhaustion and weakness, a result of two solid months of an under-resourced and bitter campaign. At least at their backs they had the 15th Independent Engineer Regiment blowing up the same bridges they'd so recently built, to slow the Australian advance.

The Japanese war correspondent Seizo Okada noted, 'none of them had ever thought that a Japanese soldier would turn his back on the enemy . . .'[259] and the mood of the exhausted Japanese troops was beyond demoralised. Their mission had been to take Port Moresby and they had *failed* in their duty to do so. Under such circumstances, death seemed not an inappropriate end for them, but though some indeed took that option, most who had made it this far were united by a common instinct for survival.

Each tried to find strength in his own way. Some wanted to return to Japan intact to fight again for the greater glory of the Emperor; some so that the 144th would remain an effective fighting force and their battalion colours would once again know glory. One though—Sergeant Yuki Shimada of the 144th Regiment—struggling in the ragged end of the retreat, had a far more universal motivation. With every tortuous step he was reminded of a conversation he had had with his mother just before he left home for the war. 'You *mustn't* die,' she told him, as she held him close. 'You *musn't* die. You must come home. You *must* come home.'[260] Yuki faithfully promised his mother that he would, and somehow that promise and the memory of his mother's words gave him strength.

One by one, the villages of Nauro, Menari and Efogi, slowly, slowly came and went as the Japanese made their long trek back to the beachhead, harassed all the way by the American planes that had now arrived in New Guinea in force and that were constantly, furiously, patrolling, looking for retreating Japs to bomb and strafe.

As they staggered through each village the first port of call for the retreating Japanese soldiers was the vegetable gardens, but this far into the campaign there was simply nothing left. For the previous two months soldiers had been going back and forth and raiding, and now there simply was no more food left. Even when they sent out patrols to fields they knew to be seven miles away, they found them to be picked clean, with nothing to show for their exhausted effort.

Fortunately, ahead of them at Gona, fresh Japanese troops were marching out to meet them, providing a strong rearguard for them, bringing food, and also furiously working on finishing the defensive positions that had been under construction over previous months.

Feeling wretched, Father James Benson was in fear of his life, as he had been for months. Since having been taken prisoner by the Japanese, mostly he had feared that they would kill him, though on this occasion he thought it more likely that one of the Allied planes that were pounding Japanese positions around Buna and Gona would do for him. But, as ever, somehow the danger passed and, extraordinarily, he was still here, still alive. Right now though, there was some kind of commotion outside. There was a new prisoner being brought into their makeshift prison, situated just inland from the coast. An Australian, a lieutenant colonel, as evidenced by the shoulder tabs on his filthy uniform. He was as emaciated as a half-dead dingo, with the haunted look of one who had been through more horrors than he could quite comprehend. He was also nursing a very bad wound on his leg.

Father Benson lifted a careful hand of greeting and softly said: 'Benson, missionary . . . '

Was the figure about to say in reply, 'Lieutenant Colonel Arthur Key, of the 2/14th Battalion . . . '?

Father Benson would never know, as the missionary was suddenly belted in the head by the wretched guard, Fujoka, who roared at him 'Benson! Speak no!', before leading the gaunt officer away again.[261]

For all that, some time *would* be spent at a later point trying to determine if it had been Lieutenant Colonel Key. It just about had to be him, as there was no other Australian lieutenant colonel known to have been captured since Key and several others had disappeared after the attack on the Isurava Rest House at the end of August.

The following day Father Benson received word via an interpreter that the officer was wondering if he could borrow any English books the missionary might have. The missionary sent him every book he had, and also gleaned the information that the officer was so sick he could only take liquids from a tin. Father Benson would never see the figure again and shortly afterwards heard that he had been taken to Rabaul. Soon thereafter Father Benson received another visitor who he really could talk to. It was a journalist, a war correspondent from Japan's foremost newspaper, *Asahi Shimbun*, and in excellent English he said his name was Seizo Okada. They talked for several hours, and did the same over the next few days.

Father Benson found Okada to be an extraordinary fellow, especially for the attitude he expressed about Japan's militaristic culture.

'I feel it is impossible for Japan to win the war,' he told the missionary frankly, 'and what a horrible prospect it would be for the world if she did!'

Uncertain of how far the journalist could be trusted, Father Benson said something noncommital, and the war correspondent followed up.

'Please believe that what I say is genuine. I am no secret police spy. I am an honest man, a writer, who hates all that militarism stands for. Militarism must go.'

When Father Benson carefully put the view that militarism simply went with the territory of Japanese Shintoism and Emperor worship, the journalist was passionate.

'All that must go, too! We of the intelligentsia will stand for it no longer.'

In essence, Seizo Okada made the Christian missionary understand that even in the middle of this war—with planes overhead and men toting guns all around, while other Japanese soldiers worked heavily building fortifications against the coming Allied attacks—there was a new Japan trying to emerge and it couldn't happen soon enough.

'The day of freedom will come,' he said firmly, 'and what a day! I shall be able to speak and write what I feel in my heart.'[262]

The day came. The great American leader, General Douglas MacArthur, the Supreme Commander of the whole Southwest Pacific Area, arrived in New Guinea to inspect the terrain over which he had gained such intimate knowledge—from Brisbane. Well, it wasn't quite the highlands where all the action had taken place, but it was as close as he could comfortably get.

On 3 October, Generals MacArthur, Blamey, Herring and Kenney, accompanied by the Australian Minister for the Army, F. M. Forde (who absurdly was dressed in a pith helmet, and carried a side-arm) visited Ower's Corner. They were there to watch the departure of the 16th Brigade, under the command of Brigadier J. E. Lloyd, as they went up the track to support the 25th Brigade which was right on the tail of the now-retreating Japanese. It was MacArthur who was the focus though. The Australian troops got a look at this legendary military figure for the first time, as the cameras all around snapped and rolled, and the journalists took note. MacArthur always provided terrific copy with dramatic comments.

Drawing himself up into the classic military straight-back posture, the American general told Brigadier J. E. Lloyd: 'Lloyd, by some act of God, your brigade has been chosen for this job. The eyes of the Western world are upon you. I have every confidence in you and your men, good luck, don't stop.'[263] With which, the great man got back in his jeep, saluted and was driven off. General MacArthur proceeded in a southerly direction towards Moresby, where he spent a comfortable night in Government House, before returning to Brisbane. With his men, Brigadier Lloyd headed north, north to the Japanese beachhead and . . . they knew not what.

Over the next weeks the Australian soldiers in the 25th and 16th brigades continued to push the Japanese back along the track, although not without difficulty. Just as they had done to the Japs— setting up ambushes at killing grounds of their own choosing—so too were they now forced to tread warily as it was done to them in return. Sometimes there would be almost no resistance, and then suddenly the Japanese would make a stand, requiring the Australians to blast their way through.

The two critical battles of Japanese resistance came in the familiar territory of Templeton's Crossing and Eora Creek, where the Japanese took shelter in the weapon pits that had been dug by the Australians only a month before.

Flags were important in the Japanese military culture. In the early part of the New Guinea campaign, if a Japanese soldier was wounded severely enough to return to the beachhead, all members of his platoon would sign a Japanese flag for him, as a memento of the time they had spent together. For all the reverence they held for the Japanese flag, however, it was the regimental flag that they regarded as practically holy.

During the retreat, when the Australians made a massive charge on an entrenched Japanese position, one soldier, Yutaka Yanagiba, found himself the sole defender of the regimental flag as the Australians came within just a few steps of it. He knew his duty, which was confirmed by a direct order from his immediate superior officer. The ancient tradition was that when the regimental flag was threatened in that manner, the flag had to be burnt, and the flag bearer with it.

Operating more from atavistic instinct than conscious thought, Yutaka wrapped the flag around himself, threw gasoline all over his helmet and body, and charged into one of the primitive huts in the village where they had been staying, a hut that was now on fire. There was a split second calm as the fumes met the flames and then, with a massive *whoomp*, both the Japanese soldier and the flag were on fire.[264] He writhed in agony on the floor, waiting for the blackness of death to engulf him and end the pain, and send him wondrously to join the spirits of his ancestors. But the meeting was deferred as the Japanese soldier inadvertently fell into a hole in the floor extinguishing the flames. All was suddenly dark and quiet. In agony, he nevertheless remained still, the more so because he now heard the unmistakable gibberish of Australian voices, saying things unknown but seemingly very excited at the success of their attack.

Presently, the voices faded as it became dark outside and the Australians continued their pursuit of his retreating comrades, and Yutaka decided to risk coming out . . . to find that he wasn't alone after all. A Japanese officer had also just emerged from his own hiding place, and upon seeing him asked the obvious: 'What happened to the flag?'

Private Yanagiba apologised profusely, saying he had intended to self-immolate with the flag, but had fallen into a hole, meaning that both he and the flag had survived.

'Well, bring it with you now,' the officer said.

And Yutaka would have, but as he could neither walk nor see, given the severe burns to over fifty per cent of his body, he gave the flag to the officer and told him he would have to advance to the rear with it himself.

As to the badly burnt soldier, he did the only thing he could do: stagger forward, vainly hoping to reach Japanese lines and be evacuated out. (Amazingly, he eventually was.)

The Australians continued to push forward, never knowing at what point the Japanese might have set up an ambush for them. As it always was in battle, the difference between life and death was a hair's breadth. At one point the lieutenant of a company of advancing troops was just making his way down the track, with his men close in behind, when he tripped on a root. At the very instant that he tripped and fell forward, a Japanese machine-gunner opened up, and killed the two men who had been standing right behind him.

The soldiers behind those cut down immediately went to ground as the Japanese machine-gunner sprayed bullets in their direction. One combatant, Sergeant F. B. Burley, later recounted for the magazine of the 2/2nd Battalion, that: 'I spent an eternity of some seconds behind what I considered the smallest tree in all New Guinea. The fire was from a well-known woodpecker, and by the amount of timber gradually being cleared in my vicinity I considered the name woodpecker most apt.'[265]

Now more experienced in the ways of jungle warfare, the Australians knew enough to start moving towards the flanks, and it wasn't long before they were able to shut the woodpecker down, but as always it had come at too great a cost. On this track, advances always came at the cost of blood.

Another common problem was snipers up trees, but the Australians soon learnt that one way of helping to increase their security was simply to spray with machine-gun fire any tree *likely* to hold snipers, and take it from there. If they were lucky, a Japanese soldier would fall from the branches.

Chester Wilmot could bear it no more. Infuriated at the way Blamey had organised the New Guinea campaign from the outset, and appalled at the resulting waste of Australian lives, he had been further outraged at Blamey's treatment of both Brigadier Potts and General Rowell. Wilmot further felt stifled. Not only had the censors kept the truth of what happened in Kokoda from getting out, but Blamey had ensured that the report Wilmot had written for Rowell about what had ailed the campaign was destroyed. (Although, as it turned out later, one copy had survived.)

In this report, Wilmot said that he believed Blamey had lost the confidence of the Australian troops. Specifically on the subject of the New Guinea campaign, Wilmot was blunt. 'It may be argued that the AIF were not trained because their role had been the defence of Brisbane and for this they had been trained. But what of the troops in Moresby? Why were they not trained? It may partly be the fault of the local commander, but it must be remembered that New Guinea Force was directly under the command of Land Forces Headquarters . . .' Step forward, General Blamey.

Wilmot's final line summed up the thrust of his report: 'If the troops sent to the Owen Stanley Range in August had been properly trained, acclimatised and equipped, and if they had had adequate air support, the withdrawal and the consequent considerable losses of valuable personnel need never have taken place.'

Wilmot simply felt that the truth about Blamey *had* to come out one way or another, and that it was up to him to make it happen. And there was, after all, a notable precedent for a journalist taking action. In the Great War, one of the foremost Australian war correspondents and the founder of the Murdoch dynasty, Keith

Murdoch, had decided to ignore the censors entirely to ensure that the truth of the situation in Gallipoli was published.

In this new circumstance, however, there was no way that Wilmot's employer, the ABC, could go against the censorship laws promulgated by the government of the day. So, on a quick trip back to Australia, Chester decided to go directly to the head of that government, John Curtin, and convince him personally that General Blamey was an incompetent commander who had no business filling the Australian Army's highest post. To get to the prime minister, he decided to seek the good offices of the most famous correspondent of the Great War, Charles Bean, who was a good friend. One letter from Bean to the prime minister, and it was done. On a day in mid-October Prime Minister Curtin received Chester Wilmot in his office in Parliament House in Canberra.

Speaking to the prime minister in urgent though still deeply respectful tones, Wilmot, who had never served in the army, listed what he thought were the most flagrant shortcomings of the army's most distinguished and senior officer—an officer whose own military pedigree boasted the white sands of the Gallipoli shore. But let the devil take the hindmost and stand in the queue, Wilmot didn't hold back. With the quiet forensic focus of the superb journalist he was, the ABC man detailed Blamey's most insane decisions, from the saga of the green uniforms to the inadequacies of supply; from the decision to sack Rowell to the insanity of removing Potts, both of whom were among the few good things that the Australian soldiers in New Guinea had going for them.

The prime minister heard Chester out—as was ever his way, throughout his entire political career—and then made a grave, regretful reply. Though John Curtin didn't 'pull rank' and say what he could have—that it was entirely improper and presumptuous for a journalist to speak about the nation's foremost military commander in this fashion—he did make it clear that he effectively had no choice but to side with Blamey in the matter. He told the aggrieved journalist that nothing he had heard here was anything new, and that he was quite aware that Chester had long been a fierce critic of General Blamey.

Nevertheless, it had been Curtin's experience as prime minister that in just about every instance General Blamey had effectively been able to predict what the Japanese were going to do before they did it, and that it was obvious to him that Blamey must have a first-class military mind to be able to do this. That mistakes had been made, he did not doubt. That it could have been done better was of course clear with the benefit of hindsight. But Blamey resided at the head of a massive military organisation of 250 000 men, making decisions on the run for many different theatres of war, and Curtin wasn't going to sack him because Chester Wilmot wasn't happy with the colour of the troops' uniforms. Curtin equally knew that it would be bad for both public morale and the morale of the military men if the prime minister stepped in and sacked the most powerful military figure in the country. What kind of message would that send about how the war was faring?

Case dismissed, and with this the 'power struggle' between Wilmot and Blamey was at least officially over. What remained to be seen was the fallout.

Yet, while the power of radio broadcaster Chester Wilmot in this instance proved to be limited in its capacity to change the course of events, the same could not be said of other radio broadcasters in New Guinea, even though they used different methods and had an entirely different target audience.

Back in June 1942, the Far Eastern Liaison Office, known as FELO, had been set up by the Australian authorities with the specific purpose of winning the hearts and minds of the New Guinea native population, while also lowering the morale of the Japanese soldier through strategies such as leaflet drops. Throughout the following October, as the Australians continued to push the Japanese back along the track, there was a strong effort by FELO to use the power of radio—and many wireless sets were by now dotted around the villages under the auspices of ANGAU and FELO and others—to ensure that the natives remained loyal to the Allies and worked against the Japanese on all fronts.

It was a plan that entirely changed the natives' views of radio, who to this point, believed that the radio was 'SAMTING BILONG MASTA', 'something belonging to the boss man'. Now, on appointed days at specified times, the agents of FELO would gather the natives around the village sets and the program would begin with some favourite SING-SING music. Then to the point . . . As the natives stared with wonder at the amazing box making the wonderful music, an authoritative voice would ring out with a specific instruction for a man named 'Anis', a common native name. To wit:

'MI IGUT TOKTOK LONG ANIS,' 'I have a message for Anis'. 'ANIS YU HARIM MI?' 'Anis, can you hear me?'

Then there would be a long pause, giving every Anis listening across the country the chance to rise up and cry: 'KIAP, MI ANIS! ME HARIM YU!' '*I'm* Anis, and I'm listening to you!'

Now that the box with the magical powers was satisfied that it indeed had the attention of Anis, it would reel off instructions. First and foremost, as Anis was especially selected from the whole village, he must be responsible for telling everyone in that village that the Australian and American soldiers were coming and that they were GUTPELAS, 'good fellows', who were coming to help and the villagers must do everything in turn to help them—get them food, water, shelter and whatever they asked for. But Anis was also charged with bearing the bad news that if the Japanese came they were BADPELAS, they were there to hurt everyone, to take the natives' land and rape the women. Everything must be done to deny them, to damage them, to make them go away—*Everything*, Anis.

'ANIS YU SARWEY WUNEM MI TOKTOK?' 'Anis, are you listening?'

'MI HARIM YU!' 'I can hear you!'

More SING-SING music and then goodbye, until the same time next week . . .

It was a popular program at all levels.[266]

MacArthur was furious. Yes, the markers on his office map showing 'Allied' positions—read Australian—were now moving forward along the track and it was clear that the Japanese were in full retreat. But one thing he would not abide was any pause in this retreat. For the life of him he could not understand how the Australians were being held up at Eora Creek. (The Australians on site had no trouble understanding. The Japanese were now closer to their own supply lines and were being reinforced by fresh troops; all up they had gathered the necessary wherewithal to mount something of a rearguard action.) But MacArthur wouldn't hear any of it. He had a very strong opinion about what was *really* going wrong with the leadership of Tubby Allen, and he passed it on via General Blamey in Moresby.

On 8 October General Blamey issued the following missive to Allen: 'General MacArthur considers quote extremely light casualties indicate no serious effort to displace enemy unquote. You will attack enemy with energy and all possible speed at each point of resistance. Essential that Kokoda airfield be taken at earliest. Apparent enemy gaining time by delaying you with inferior strength.'[267] Again, it was extraordinary the kind of vision MacArthur had some three thousand miles away, but Allen now took the view that if his men weren't dying in sufficient numbers to gain the respect of the American general, then that was just too damn bad.

Allen's return message noted that the attacks made by the Australians had been very energetic indeed, and 'I respectfully submit that success in this campaign cannot be judged by casualties alone.' This was at least a lot more politic than a message he formed up a short time later, when the missives from MacArthur and Blamey kept coming: 'If you think you can do any bloody better come up here and bloody try.'[268]

And fair enough too. Of all the men on the planet at the time, there were few with as much experience in commanding men—all the way from platoon level to battalion to a division—as Tubby Allen. He had fought with great distinction in World War I, was now deeply involved in another world war, and his battlefield experience was several times the combined total of MacArthur and Blamey. As a matter of fact, Allen had more or less already shown his feelings to MacArthur back when the American general had visited Ower's Corner in early October, and Allen had been there. On that occasion MacArthur had made some grandiose comment about the need for Allen to push through hard, and the Australian had simply been unable to contain himself, informing the American that when *American* troops started to do a bit of pushing through themselves, they would earn his respect, but not before.

On this occasion, though, Tubby Allen was dissuaded from sending the 'come up here and bloody try'—message by his chief of staff. Yet tragically, when it came to casualties one would have thought there were soon enough to satisfy even MacArthur, as in devastatingly bitter fighting, Brigadier Lloyd's 16th Brigade lost a total of three hundred killed and wounded, over ten days fighting at Eora Creek.[269]

Nevertheless, it was now clear that Allen remained right on the edge of being dismissed, as certified by Blamey when he told one member of the press: 'If it wasn't for the fact that it takes six days to send in a relief I'd sack the old bastard.'[270]

As it turned out, Blamey was in the mood for doing quite a bit of sacking at this time, and not just Tubby Allen. For now Pottsy was in his sights. And if it wasn't Blamey's last bit of bastardry, it was among the most hurtful. After calling him back to Moresby for consultations, and briefly returning him to command 21st Brigade, on 22 October Blamey relieved Brigadier Potts of his command, just as he had Rowell, though in Potts's case he was sent to Darwin.

Before leaving, Potts penned a letter to his men.

Special Message to Officers, NCOs and men,

HQ 21st Aust. Inf. Bde,
23 October 42.

On relinquishing my command of the 21st Brigade, it is impossible to express my feelings adequately to all its members.

Though in command of you for only six months, my association has been for the full period of service of the Brigade. It has so grown to be part of my life, that even when not facing you or speaking directly to you, the task of saying goodbye is the hardest job in my life and one I flunk badly.

This much I can say—that I regard this Brigade as the best fighting formation in the AIF and second to none in this war or the last. Your new cmd. will be proud of it. Its discipline and tone is obviously high and that is not meant as praise—it is as it should be.

Be loyal to all the ideals we have built up around this Brigade of three hard-hitting, hard-marching and hard-living Battalions, and nothing in your lives will ever give you half so much pleasure as belonging to it or so much pain as leaving it.

Thanking you for your loyalty and cooperation; you are a great team and I'm proud that I was one of you. Thanking you and goodbye.

A. W. Potts. Brig.[271]

Still not done, on 27 October, Blamey wired to his commanding officer in the field, General Tubby Allen: 'Consider that you have had sufficiently prolonged tour of duty in forward area. General Vasey will arrive Myola by air morning 28 October for tour of duty in this area. Will arrange air transport from Myola forenoon 29 October if this convenient to you . . .'[272] It was a bitter blow to Allen, but as a soldier to his core he followed orders and thus ceded his command.

In Blamey's view, General George Vasey had more of the right stuff for this kind of operation, as witnessed by one of Vasey's first commands to his most senior officers when he arrived in New Guinea. 'The Japanese . . . are vermin and like vermin they must be destroyed . . . we must not expect the Japanese to surrender. He does not. He must be killed whether it is shooting, bayoneting him, throttling, knocking out his brains with a tin hat or by any means our ingenuity can devise.'[273] And that was General 'Bloody' George Vasey all over, so-called because it was his favourite, if not only, adjective. One way or another, he would find a way to get the job done.[274]

Have you heard? Women are arriving! *White* women! *Real* sheilas! Seventy Australian Army nurses have just docked on the hospital ship *Manunda*. They reckon they're going to be staying for a while.

From everywhere, all over Moresby, the word spread, on this 28th day of October 1942. Sick men, injured men, crippled men, healthy men, strong men, men who were so fit and strong they were dangerous . . . all found sudden reason to head down towards the harbour, and maybe mosey along towards the *Manunda* to see what they could see. It had been a long, long time since they had been so blessed, that's for sure. Nurse, I have a sudden stabbing pain in my chest . . . I think you're breaking my heart.[275]

It was 1 November 1942, and in the war correspondents' compound at Port Moresby, the chap from the *Daily Mirror*, Geoffrey Reading, was chatting to his friend Chester Wilmot, who had just returned from Australia after his failed attempt to get rid of General Blamey. By Reading's later account, it was then that George Fenton, the officer commanding the war correspondents, came up to them.

'Chester,' Fenton said, 'Blamey would like to see you. You can take my jeep.'

'Righto,' the ABC man replied, and took his leave of Reading.

Half an hour later he was back, looking a little vague and shell-shocked.

'Well, Chester, what happened?' Reading asked pleasantly.

'I've just been disaccredited . . . ' Wilmot replied, still trying to grasp the implication of what had just happened to him.

'Why, what did he say?'

'He said: "Mr Wilmot, when you were on furlough in Melbourne did you or did you not say [to friends while in Melbourne recently] that I had been involved in rackets in the Middle East?"'

'What did you say?'

'I said "I can't remember, Sir".'

'What did he say?'

'He said: "Well, Mr Wilmot, you are hereby disaccredited".'[276]

And that was it! After all Chester's struggle, all his dedicated reporting, all his high-minded ideas about bringing the *real* story to the Australian public, a single stroke of the pen from Blamey could end it all and shut him down! It was hard for such as Wilmot—raised with an acute sense of justice and an inclination to right wrongs—to think straight, when in his view he was now *himself* the victim of extreme injustice but was powerless to do anything. By the following day Chester had gone the way of Rowell and Potts before him, flying back to Australia simply because he had fallen foul of Blamey. Given that Chester now no longer had accreditation, which had formally provided him with access to the Australian Army and the right to ask questions, there was no point in remaining in New Guinea.

As if to make it more bitter, this was the same day that after a long and bitter campaign against the retreating Japanese, the most forward of the Australian troops spied Kokoda ahead in the near distance.

The impending arrival of those advancing Australian soldiers precipitated terrible scenes in the Japanese field hospital at Kokoda, as later described by one Japanese soldier, Takida Kenji: 'When the order to retreat was received, the seriously ill patients had to get up and walk. They all rose using walking sticks. However, many were too weak to support themselves and toppled over. The immobilised and seriously ill officers and troops took their lives one by one under the roar of enemy air attacks. The forest around the field hospital became a forest of grim death.'[277]

Despite such misery among the Japanese, the forward Australian troops into Kokoda were met by many smiling natives—some of whom had previously worked for the Australians as porters—bearing flowers and fruit, and clearly delighted at their return. The Australians embraced them in turn, most particularly the former porters who had saved so many Australian lives. Stories of their maltreatment at the hands of the Japanese came to Australian ears and there would clearly be no struggle for the hearts and minds of the populace in these parts, as there had been in other parts of New Guinea.

But there was no time to tarry. A message was quickly sent from General Vasey to Eather and Lloyd: 'Occupation of Kokoda is expected by our troops 2 November. Congratulations to you and the fine troops under your command for their rapid advance, you have made under shocking conditions which include hunger. The enemy is beaten. Give him no rest and we will annihilate him. It is only a matter of a day or two. Tighten your belts and push on.'[278]

The key importance in regaining Kokoda was as before: the airfield. Within a day, enormous DC3 aircraft were taking off and landing, bringing forward in twenty minutes supplies that had been taking eight days by land.

At this point, the Allies believed the final capture of the remnants of the Japanese forces would be a cake walk. Intelligence estimated the enemy at about 1500 debilitated and sick soldiers across the whole Gona–Sanananda–Buna beachhead.

They were in for the shock of their lives. There were nine thousand. The battle for the beaches was to be a bloodbath.

Personally, MacArthur was so confident that victory would soon be at hand that, arriving in New Guinea on 6 November 1942, he moved his whole headquarters north, to Government House in Port Moresby, nominally so he could be close enough to lead more effectively, but perhaps so that he could be on site when the Japanese raised their flag of surrender.

CHAPTER SEVENTEEN

TO THE BITTER END

The Jap is being more stubborn and tiresome than I thought and I fear the war of attrition is taking place on this front. The Jap won't go till he is killed and in the process he is inflicting many casualties on us. I am beginning to wonder who will reach zero first.

General George 'Bloody' Vasey to Ned Herring, 23 November 1942

There is no doubt in my mind, that the Gona campaign was the worst and most horrific battle the 39th Battalion fought.

Joe Dawson, 39th Battalion veteran

It was 9 November 1942, and it was time for another parade. This one was up at the Koitaki sports field, just a few miles from Ower's Corner and the start of the track. On this day General Blamey had travelled up there to talk to the men of the 21st Brigade—the 2/14th, 2/16th and 2/27th battalions. Having substantially recovered from their previous gruelling experience on the track, they were now thought to be ready to go again, despite the dreadful losses the battalions had already suffered.

In the 2/14th, for example, only 73 men remained of the 550 brave souls who set off up the track just under three months before. The rest were known to be either lying beneath the sod of the New Guinea jungle, or injured and recovering in a New Guinea hospital or now at home, or still missing in action, meaning that they were more than likely dead.

Though all three of the battalions were of course devastated by their dreadful losses, they were also justifiably proud of what they had achieved, and if they had bothered to think about it at all, they were of the opinion that Blamey had probably gathered them together to tell them so in person. They formed up before him then, at ease, with straight backs and clear eyes to await his words. Certainly, the bloke was less than popular for many reasons—not least because he was known as the one who had sacked both Rowell and their beloved Pottsy—but he remained their commanding officer and it was instilled in them to listen carefully to what he had to say.

Australia's highest ranking military officer was set up on a wooden platform and began to speak in that notably imperious manner which had never sat well with Australian soldiers. Perhaps it was because of the time he had spent with the British, or because he had just risen so damn high, but in their view Blamey never seemed to display any empathy for their lot, any warmth, any remnant of the knockabout manner that Australian men admired in each other, whatever position they held. Rather, he had a lecturing tone which grated.

There would be no further retreats, he intoned imperiously, no fall-backs. They would do as they had been ordered and *attack*. They were to advance at all costs. They really were going to push the Japs all the way back to the sea this time, and there could be no excuses, for the campaign to date against the Japanese had been nothing short of appalling.

A shocked atmosphere suddenly descended on the troops as they realised they were being *criticised*.

Blamey went on . . . 'You have been defeated, I have been defeated, Australia has been defeated,' he said.

There was a stirring among the soldiers, a murmur of mutiny, of *outrage* . . .

Then they heard the words that would never be forgotten, and Stan Bisset—as adjutant to his battalion, and therefore standing at the front of the men of the 2/14th—was well placed to hear Blamey's next words clearly.

'Always remember, it is the rabbit who runs who gets shot . . . '[279]

At these words, there was a real *rumble* in the ranks, a gasp of disbelief that Blamey had really said what he did. But the fact that they had all heard it confirmed it, and the disbelief soon gave way to barely contained white fury at his colossal presumption in saying such a thing to them. *They* who had fought so valiantly against a force that had outnumbered them by at least six to one. *They*, who had marched forward with impossible loads on their backs in good faith, only to find themselves totally outnumbered, outgunned, overwhelmed and undersupplied, as missiles and grenades were lobbed on them through the blizzard of bullets that was their most constant accompaniment. *They* who lost one by one and then two by two, and then *platoon* after *platoon* of their own beloved brothers-in-arms?

Just who the hell did Blamey think he *was*? He was a bloke who to this point—holed up in his luxurious digs in Brisbane—hadn't demonstrated that he could lead a bunch of blowflies to a cow pat, and he was criticising *them* for the effort *they* had put in!

As the mutinous rumble continued, progressively more audible, like a volcano that was about to erupt, Blamey was incredulous. He could not believe that such ill discipline could go unchecked, but then perhaps he realised that he really had gone too far for he suddenly cut the speech short and left the podium. Shortly afterwards, he at least composed himself well enough to call a group of senior officers to a meeting to discuss the forthcoming campaign.

But Stan Bisset, for one, was so molten with rage that—together with other officers who felt the same—he simply refused to go. This refusal was partly in protest, and partly because Stan just did not trust himself to control his rising and violent rage towards the general. It was much better that he put a mile between himself and Blamey for the remainder of his time in New Guinea.

Word of Blamey's disgraceful speech soon spread well beyond those who had heard it. A while later, when Blamey visited a Port Moresby hospital to visit wounded Diggers, he was amazed to see each one sullenly staring back at him, refusing to talk, and each munching a lettuce leaf . . .

Rabbits were they? Fucking rabbits that had got shot because they were running away, while the clever foxes like Blamey were safely sheltered thousands of miles away? Well cop *this*, mate![280]

Some time later when Blamey and an entourage of his senior officers visited an open-air theatre packed with five thousand Australian soldiers, first one man, then another, then ten more, then seemingly the whole lot of them started booing and whistling in a derisory manner. Once it began there was no stopping it, as their collective rage burst forth in a cathartic release at the brute who caused it. Fearing that it would get completely out of hand, the organisers quickly rolled the movie, whereupon the whistling and cat-calling died down relatively quickly. Hating Blamey was one thing, but getting to watch Betty Grable in *Song of the Islands* quite another.

Back in Sydney, a good while later, Chester Wilmot was not at all surprised to hear of Blamey's words—he had always detected precisely that aloof yet ignorant attitude in Australia's most senior military commander. It was one of the many reasons he detested Blamey. Despite Chester's extreme antipathy, however, after much soul-searching and tossing and turning through the night, Chester had decided to lower himself enough to write a letter of apology to Blamey. He wrote that he was terribly sorry for any misunderstanding there might have been; that he fully accepted that the general had never engaged in any improper activities, and humbly asked that he be reinstated with his accreditation.

It didn't work. And nor did all the ABC's representations to Blamey to get him to reverse his decision. In fact, Blamey's own antipathy remained so strong towards the ABC journalist that before he was done he would try to use the power accorded to him by the Manpower Act not only to get Chester into the army, but also to put him on latrine duty with his own Land Forces HQ, wheresoever they were at any given time.

Despite Blamey's now well-publicised views of their shortcomings, on 11 November 1942, the Australian forces in the lead on the track finally overwhelmed the Japanese soldiers defending Oivi and moved closer to the Wairopi Bridge over the flooding Kumusi River. Here, though, they started to come up against fresh Japanese reinforcements who had landed and were now stiffening the resistance considerably.

And what of the crack American troops of the 126th Regiment whom MacArthur had unleashed from Kapa Kapa to cut the Japanese off at the pass and block the Japanese retreat at that point? They had done it tough. After forty-two days of stumbling through the jungle where they had seen precisely *no* Japanese soldiers, and fired not a single shot in anger, they indeed made it through. If not to Wairopi as originally intended, they had managed to get to the other side of the Owen Stanleys. Most of them, anyway. Several had died en route from the privations of the jungle—beset by the all too common maladies of malaria, malnutrition and dysentery—while most of the rest had to receive urgent medical attention. As described by the Australian author Jack Gallaway, they became known as the 'Ghost Battalion',[281] and were unable to resume any effective action for months after returning.

Not that any of this showed up in MacArthur's controlled press. Back in Sydney on 9 November 1942, beneath a headline of 'Enemy Almost Out of Papua: Americans Near Buna', the *Sydney Morning Herald* reported, 'American forces have penetrated central and northern Papua to a point near Buna and the Japanese troops

defending the strip of land from the Owen Stanley Range to Buna
are menaced on several sides . . . '282

Frankly, the Australians who really were there on the ground would
have loved to see them. The bottom line was that there were actually
no Americans fighting alongside the Australian troops as they forced
their way to the Kumusi River against a fanatically ferocious Japanese
defence. But fight across it the Australians did, and a particularly
odd sight greeted them as they did so. There, on the right bank,
was the flyblown carcass of a white horse.

In an attempt to ford the flooded river during the retreat after
Allied bombing had once again taken out the bridge, General Horii
and his steed had been put on rafts that had been hastily constructed
by lashing fallen logs together. The horse had fallen from the raft
and drowned immediately, while Horii's fate was still in the balance.
After his raft had got caught in a large tree, he and some of his
senior officers had transferred to a canoe. In his haste to get back
to the main beachhead, Horii decided he would stay with the canoe
right down to the mouth of the Kumusi River and then paddle up
the coast from there to save time. Though the Japanese general
made it to the mouth of the river, once he was in the open sea an
enormous storm suddenly hit and neither he nor the senior officers
with him were ever seen again. It was the afternoon of 19 November
1942.[283]

And finally, it had come to this. The Japanese had now returned
to their beachhead at Gona–Sanananda–Buna and were dug in.
Really dug in. For months the Japanese soldiers who had remained
at the beachhead had been preparing these defences, based on crawl
trenches joining up carefully constructed coconut log bunkers with
thickly made roofs that were placed in mutually supporting positions.
For added protection the bunkers had, just within their walls, many
44-gallon drums filled with sand, making them all but impregnable
fortresses against mortars and small-arms bullets alike. In some of
the most strategic positions, the bunkers had been made out of

concrete and steel and all had been built long enough before that the jungle had grown back over them, making them all but impossible to see until you were right upon them. The area so fiercely defended by the Japanese formed a rough triangle, with the Solomon Sea as the long base, the coastal village of Gona at one end and Buna, some twelve miles to the east, at the other end.

It was going to be a brutal task to get the Japanese out, but America's 128th Regiment and 32nd Division were assigned the primary task of cleaning them out at Buna, and it was for the Australians—led by what was left of Brigadier Ken Eather's 25th Brigade—to blast them out of Gona.

Beyond the bunkers, trenches and so forth, Gona's natural defences against an attack were so formidable that a Japanese general would have been proud to call them his own work. A very narrow beach of only ten yards depth gave way to thick groves of coconuts, among which were dotted many banyan trees. This made for a very thick canopy that detonated most of the explode-on-impact shells sent by the Allies way too high to do any damage to anyone sheltered below. On the western edge of the Japanese hold-out, a deep, wide creek also made any attack from that direction out of the question. And on its eastern edge another creek made an attack difficult. On the southern approaches, fetid swamps would effectively catch any attacking force in treacle, preventing them from moving quickly or with stealth. Where there wasn't swamp, there was either open killing fields of burnt kunai grass, which the Japanese concentrated so much of their firepower on, or thick scrub.

All up it meant that unless the Allies were lucky enough to make a direct hit by a bomb or an artillery shell that penetrated the canopy, the only way to take out the Japs was to find some way through the massacre-maze and sneak close enough to get a well-aimed grenade through the wide slots the Japanese troops used to poke out their heavy and light machine guns—a hairy task. Populating the bunkers alongside the bitterly battle-hardened veterans of the 41st and 144th Regiments were fresh Japanese soldiers brought in from Rabaul.

They were just over a thousand in total, superbly commanded by Lieutenant Colonel Yoshinobu Tomita, who had done for his men much what Ralph Honner had done for the 39th at Isurava. He had organised them so that their arcs of fire supported each other, their ability to move between defensive positions was maximised and every yard of ground gained by the Australians would have to be paid for in blood. Even if any of the Australian soldiers *could* get close to the zig-zagging line of bunkers, Tomita had dozens of snipers up in the thick coconut trees just waiting to pick off Bren gunners and officers in equal measure.

At the Buna end of the battlefront, the Japanese were equally well dug in; not that that fazed the likes of MacArthur. His command of 20 November, ordering the beachhead bastions stormed, was a classic of the genre: 'All columns will be driven through regardless of losses'. A simple or unthought-through decision by MacArthur, safe in Port Moresby, and dozens of soldiers died in a flash, hurling themselves too hastily at defences that had not been properly reconnoitred. No matter. MacArthur's orders the next day were more of the same. Directed at his own General Harding, he commanded: 'Take Buna today at all costs. MacArthur'.[284]

Despite MacArthur's expectation that once the mighty US Army was involved the Japanese would not be able to hold out for long, it was not to be . . . After the initial carnage, it barely seemed to matter *what* commands MacArthur made, his men weren't inclined to advance to their almost certain deaths. Untested in battle, many of these farm boys from Iowa and Idaho had been thrown into one of the toughest theatres of the war and, not surprisingly, were proving to be incapable of effective action.

True, at their end, the Australians had not been making huge advances against the Japanese dug in at Gona—and Brigadier Ken Eather's 25th Brigade, which had the first crack at them had in fact taken horrendous casualties of 17 officers and 187 soldiers killed—but they were having a go, which was more than could be said for their American counterparts. They, as defined by George 'Bloody' Vasey in a letter to Blamey, had 'maintained a masterly inactivity'.[285]

The situation became so bad that in the final week of November, Blamey felt that he simply had to go to Government House to discuss it with MacArthur and his senior staff. The relationship between the Australian general and the Americans by this time had become so strained that the Bataan Gang apparently sometimes privately referred to him as 'Boozey Blamey',[286] and it was an antipathy that Blamey himself could not possibly have been unaware of.

This time, though, it was very much Blamey who had the upper hand.

'It is a very sorry story,' Blamey told the American general, perhaps with some secret satisfaction at the American's discomfort. 'It has revealed the fact that the American troops cannot be classified as attack troops. They are definitely not equal to the Australian militia and from the moment they met opposition they sat down and have hardly gone forward a yard.'[287]

When at one point Blamey reported on the appalling casualties that the Australian troops had taken, MacArthur offered the 41st American Division as reinforcements. Blamey pointedly declined, saying he would prefer to get the Australians of the 21st Brigade— now under the command of Brigadier Ivan Dougherty, who had replaced Potts—because, 'I know they'll fight'.[288]

Just how MacArthur reacted to these words is not recorded, but only shortly after that meeting, the American general summoned one of his most senior commanders in General Robert Eichelberger.

On the broad verandah of Government House, with the vista of Port Moresby harbour spread before them, MacArthur said in a grim voice: 'Bob, I'm putting you in command at Buna. Relieve Harding. I am sending you in, Bob, and I want you to remove all officers who won't fight. Relieve regimental and battalion commanders. If necessary put sergeants in charge of companies—anyone who will fight. Time is of the essence. The Jap may land reinforcements any night . . . I want you to take Buna, or not come back alive.'[289]

•

Plenty of Eichelberger's men didn't. For as Eichelberger indeed whipped his men forward without adequate reconnaissance being carried out, or sufficient artillery support to cover them, the fatality rate was appalling.

As to the 21st Brigade, which was once again thrown into the fray to relieve the 25th Brigade—just as the 25th had effectively relieved them at Ioribaiwa—they too did it tough.

They had flown from Moresby, over those green hills far away, and gazed silently down upon the valleys, ridges and gorges where they had so recently had to fight for their lives. Then just thirty minutes after taking off they'd landed at Popondetta, just a few hours march from Gona, knowing little of what to expect, with the only near-certainty being that there was no way that the coming battle could be any worse than the trials they had known.

But they were wrong.

Still scarified by what Blamey had said at Koitaki, the Australian commanders were determined to show that neither they nor their men were fucking rabbits and, also stung by MacArthur's ongoing orders, they pushed forward too hurriedly. When the likes of Stan Bisset and his comrades of the 2/14th Battalion were just about to come to grips with the Japanese at Gona right before dusk on 28 November, they had neither aerial photographs of the enemy's defences, nor even a rough plan of where their bunkers and machine guns were. Nothing at all.

It was *insanity* to hurl themselves at the well-entrenched Japs but they had been given orders and those orders had to be followed. So in the last gasp of the twilight then, the Australians of the 2/14th pushed forward on a tortuously slow approach, through two hundred yards of waist-deep swamp, to they knew not what . . .

Watching them move forward, a heavy concentration of Japanese soldiers from the 144th Regiment focused intently, picking their targets and scarcely believing that the Australians, whose fighting abilities they had come to respect and even fear in recent months, could present themselves thus. But there they were—proverbial sitting ducks in the swamp. The Japanese held back until the moment was perfect . . .

As the first clump of Australian soldiers approached the shoreline, a single shot rang out from the Japanese commander, followed a split second later by the mass of Japanese guns, coming from seemingly a dozen different directions at once. From their hidden bunkers the fierce defenders simply poured lead into the Australian soldiers, as from the high treetops, Japanese snipers methodically picked off the soldiers who hadn't been cut down in the first fusillade. Within minutes, six Australian officers and forty soldiers were wiped out, and for the most part the survivors didn't even know where to direct their fire back at the brutes.

Stan, in a cold rage at the sheer futility and *needlessness* of what had happened, moved as quickly as he could to organise for the wounded to be picked up, and for the whole lot of them to get out of there. Lieutenant Colonel Challen at this point was nowhere to be seen, and Stan knew it was up to him to take charge. With the help of two other surviving officers, Stan gathered the rump of the 2/14th together and—having located a signal wire in the now all-but-pitch blackness—led them back through the swamp, away from the Japanese guns. They spent the night camped on the track, listening to the Japs' weird, unworldly screaming, occasional shots and, most tragically, the groans and sometime death throes of their own grievously wounded men. In the final count of that terrible day, the 2/14th lost a tenth of their men, and a third of their officers.

Coming at Gona from the western side, the men of the 2/27th fared almost as disastrously. Though the 2/27th at least had air support, there was no communication between the men on the ground and those in the air, and it is debatable if the air support made any difference at all. They had seven officers killed or wounded, fifteen soldiers killed and another thirty-three wounded.

Though the following day the 2/14th had a modicum of success by gaining some bitterly contested ground, the price they had paid in blood was one that could never be redeemed. And while it was one thing to follow orders, it was quite another to be part of a process where women and families in Australia were being deprived of husbands and fathers, without doing something to try to stop the madness.

Feeling a rising anger at the tragedy of it all, Stan decided that he simply had to get through to the highest reaches of their military command and *make* them understand that following their orders was killing the men, and that there was a better way ... It took some time, but using the field telephone at Battalion Headquarters, Stan was at last able to get through to Brigade Headquarters, situated some three miles to the rear, and was able to speak to Brigadier Ivan Dougherty.

'Sir, it is Captain Bisset, Adjutant, 2/14th,' he said in quite strained tones, conscious that if he was not successful in changing the mind of the brigadier then the whole lot of them would likely be massacred. 'Sir, I do hope that you will permit me to speak freely and frankly, because there is something that needs to be said. Sir, simply charging the Japs without adequate care and reconnaissance beforehand is not working. We are being killed and wounded in massive numbers. Sir, I respectfully submit that we need more time before going on with the attacks; we need time to work out precisely where they are before going in with our guns blazing. Otherwise ... ' Stan didn't finish, aware that he had said what needed to be said, but half-expecting that it might be going too far to take it any further. If it at this point the brigadier had blasted that it was a damn impertinence for a lowly captain to presume to tell a brigadier his business, Stan was not sure what he would have done, but as it turned out he didn't have to worry.

The brigadier was cordial in reply and said that he would take Bisset's views into consideration when HQ formed up the battle plan for the morrow. And maybe it really did have an effect; for the following day, the 2/14th was not obliged to make a suicide assault and was able to gain a little more valuable ground, this time losing only three mortally and two injured. It wasn't great, but compared with the carnage and slaughter they had known on previous days it was something. But nothing could change the fatal wound the battalion as a whole had suffered, and Stan knew that with so many men lost they didn't have a lot left in them as a fighting force and might soon be finished. As it turned out, just a short time later, Stan was only a whisker away from being finished himself, when a Japanese bullet creased his right eyebrow and the blood flowed freely. It was really little more than a scratch, but had his head been an inch forward he would have been dead before he hit the ground. On such an inch did the difference of destinies of two brothers rest.

Other battalions found themselves in continued difficulties, none more so than the valiant 2/16th. At one point on 1 December, some of the 2/16th men made an extraordinary charge straight into fierce Japanese fire, with enough surviving to get to grips with some of the Japs for the first time, only to find themselves suddenly under a sustained artillery bombardment from their own guns! Everywhere was disorganisation, destruction, disaster and death. Never in the course of the whole New Guinea campaign would Rowell's previous words to Osmar White—'We need a victory in the Pacific and a lot of poor bastards have got to get killed to provide it'—prove more tragically prophetic.

By 3 December, the 25th Brigade, which had fought across the Kokoda Track against the retreating Japanese, and then been first into the battle for Gona, had lost two hundred men in six days, while the so-called 'rabbits' of the 21st Brigade had lost 340 Australian souls out of a total of 874 soldiers. What to do? How to proceed? Four months before, it had been the men of the 39th Battalion who'd been hanging on like grim death until the men of the 2/14th and 2/16th could relieve them. Now? Now it was time for the 39th to return the force-of-arms favour.

Again, this time several DC3s—also known as 'Biscuit Bombers'—took Honner and his men across the Owen Stanley Range, and again the veterans among them looked out, remembered, and didn't speak. In recent times their numbers had been bolstered by one hundred of the best soldiers from the disbanded 53rd Battalion, as well as three hundred or so fresh troops from Australia, but the wistful air of the men with the thousand-yard stares was all to do with the men who they'd replaced, down there in their graves. And now it was on again.

'*Once more unto the breach dear friends, once more . . .*'

They landed at Popondetta and almost immediately set off in the pouring tropical rain, through ankle-deep mud. As Joe Dawson and his mates Ray Phillips and Wally Gratz trudged—like all the rest with their eyes on the boots of the man in front—they were slightly unnerved by the dozens upon dozens of little wooden crosses made from Kraft Cheese boxes that lined the track, crosses that became more numerous the closer they got to Gona. Many of the crosses had a helmet at their base, and marked on the crossbar was usually the name of a soldier and his army number. Bloody hell, it was a hard thing to walk like that, past the graves of the blokes who had gone before you and fallen down dead. It made a fellow wonder if there was a plot of ground up ahead with his name on it, but this far down this bloody track, there could be no turning back.

At last they came out somewhere near Gona, because the track kind of fizzled into nothing but swamp, and then they were on a clearing right on the beach, bunched up with the 2/14th. And there was a bit of a lark . . .

The exhausted men watched intently as two of their own planes, Beaufighters, went back and forth strafing a half-submerged Jap supply ship just off the coast, finishing it off as it were. Look, maybe it was the equivalent of putting bullets into an already half-dead dingo, but it was something to ward off the tension and some of them even raised half a cheer as bits of the ship started to fall in the sea. But then one of the Beaufighters broke off and started heading their way . . . *right* at them. Jesus Christ, you don't think . . . ? He's not going to . . . ?

He *is*! The stupid bastard must have mistaken them for Japs, because before the men could do anything the plane was swooping just fifty yards above the ground, with its machine guns raising pockmarks of sand in straight lines leading right at . . . *jump for your lives*!

Joe jumped one way, Wally and Ray the other, as everyone in the two battalions did the same. Amazingly no one was killed and, when they'd all picked themselves up, only five soldiers and two native carriers were wounded, none too seriously.

'Typical air force—couldn't hit a barn door!' someone yelled out. Welcome to Gona.

They settled in, a bit back from where the main action was, and awaited orders. Not surprisingly, this wait was something close to hell on earth. It wasn't just the heat, nor the humidity, nor the rain, nor the stench of death somewhere near. It was the fucking flies. Flies like they'd never seen before. Green flies, a bit bigger than a normal housefly, but with a sting on them that could kill a brown dog and stay itchy for *days*. Each sting left a mark on your skin, and it really looked, and felt, as if they had taken a chunk out of your flesh. And what the flies left, the mozzies and ticks were free to have a go at.

The 39th were soon issued with two bottles of liquid each, which the boffins said would help. The bottle the troops called 'Mary' was meant to keep the mozzies off, while the bottle they called 'Betty' was supposed to keep the flies at bay. As bloody *if* . . . What was dropping like flies was not the flies, but the men of the 39th, with everything from dysentery and malaria to the dreaded killer, scrub typhus.

Waiting. Waiting. Waiting. *Sweating.* Waiting for the order to action, Joe, Wally and Ray stuck together, as much as possible, talking. They took their turns at various duties, but really they just wanted to get into it, one way or another.

At the 39th's command, Colonel Ralph Honner did what he had done at Isurava—that is, surveyed the lie of the land minutely to see if it would yield anything to aid their cause. This time, though, his aim was to see how best to attack. What was immediately obvious was that attacking the Gona mission by way of the swamp was close to mass suicide, and so too was heading across the cut kunai grass where his men would be totally exposed to the massed Jap firepower. There seemed to be only one way and, in many ways, it was surprising that it hadn't already been tried.

Just to the east of the track, leading from the south into what had been the Gona compound, a thin finger of jungly scrub reached into the heart of the Japanese defences. It seemed to Honner that the only way to get at the Japanese was to take advantage of the cover offered by the scrub, and the firmer footing it was situated on. Why had this route been overlooked? Quite possibly, Honner thought, because for the previous few days the area had been occupied by an Australian force under the command of Lieutenant Colonel Alan Cameron—the same man he had relieved from commanding the 39th at Isurava—and he had misreported the situation. The way Cameron had reported it to Brigade Headquarters, his men were so close to the enemy that they were having grenade-throwing jousts with them. And yet when Colonel Honner put his own A Company in there to relieve Cameron's group, A Company's Captain Gilmore soon requested permission to move his men to a much more forward position where they could be in basic contact with the enemy. 'Grenade-throwing jousts', indeed![290]

It was one thing to know what was the right thing to do, and quite another to be allowed to do it. Unbelievably, on 6 December, Honner was ordered to send in a dawn attack over the killing field of the sixty yards of cut kunai grass. It was to be supported by a three-inch mortar barrage and a smoke barrage, but it was still against every military instinct the Western Australian possessed. But an order was an order, and it was done.

The assault was led by Captain Max Bidstrup and his D Company and, while the smoke barrage was indeed laid down, the problem was that they couldn't see the Japs, while it was clear that the Japs could see them only too well.[291] The whole thing was a tragic fiasco, and resulted in twelve good men dying and forty-six being wounded for the net gain of nothing but a few dozen yards of kunai grass. The Australians were simply cut to pieces by the totally committed Japanese soldiers, who were fighting for their lives to the point of losing their lives if necessary, so long as they killed more of the enemy.

Still there was to be no respite. For the assembled Australian forces, their one standout fear at this point—amid so many fears—was that the Japanese would get reinforcements to their now besieged men at Gona. One of the obvious ways for them to do that was to land on the coast just to the west of Gona and move these reinforcements to the rear of the Australian forces who were now massing on the western side of Gona Creek. To prevent this, it had been necessary to place a defensive force beyond the western perimeter of the Australian forces which could strike at any such Japanese landing and, in so doing, give warning to the rest of the massed Australians that the Japs were on their way.

For such an important job, there had been none better than Stan's old mate, Alan Haddy of the 2/16th, the big smiling Western Australian who had so distinguished himself in the war to date. Haddy had taken twenty of his best blokes and set up in a small village two miles to the west of Gona that had instantly become known to the troops as 'Haddy's Village'. In truth, Haddy was now only a pale shadow of the man he had been, racked by malaria, lack of food, lack of sleep and sheer exhaustion at having fought so hard for so long, but his mighty spirit remained intact and everyone felt better for the fact that Alan was on the job. They knew if the Japs did land west of Gona, Haddy had 'em covered, and would give 'em hell the way he always had—usually first up with the two-inch mortar that he operated personally, before then using his Bren, then his rifle, then his bayonet, then his fists as they got progressively closer. That was just Haddy.

And sure enough, sure enough . . . The night after the 39th's first disastrous assault on Gona, a storm that would wake the dead had blown up out of the Solomon Sea. Whatever gods New Guinea had were clearly all angry at once as the lightning cracked just a split second before the thunder crashed and the rain lashed down as the wind blew the palm trees almost horizontal to the ground. And in the middle of it all each flash of lightning around Haddy's village suddenly revealed dozens, *hundreds,* of scurrying Japs, all converging on Haddy and his men. Suddenly there is a flash and an explosion and one of Haddy's men is killed outright, while four others are severely wounded, of whom Haddy is one. But it was going to take more than a grenade to take out the likes of him and, though bleeding profusely, Haddy soon organised his men to drop through the floors of the flimsy huts, get into their entrenched positions beneath and return fire, even as he sent one of his men immediately back to warn the troops behind that the Japs had landed and were coming their way.

Propping himself on the edge of his trench, Haddy was soon timing his every shot to the flashes of lightning, which in every split second revealed more and more targets coming for them. In the intensity of the Japanese return fire it was extraordinary that any of the Australians survived. When it was clearly hopeless, and there was just no way to hold back the Jap tide for much longer, Haddy ordered his few able-bodied men to gather the wounded and get back to safety, while he mounted a rearguard. And that was Haddy, too. On the track, in dangerous country, he had always insisted on taking the most dangerous position of forward scout, the one who always copped it first, and now that they were in trouble, he was insisting he'd be the last man out, while they got to safety.[292]

What goes through a man's mind when he does this? What does he think as he sends others to safety, surely knowing that he is signing his own death warrant by doing so? What was Haddy thinking? The soldiers making their retreat to safety didn't know, but they would never forget the vision offered by their last backward glance. There was Alan Haddy, a proud mother's son from Western Australia, now a skull's head by the lightning's glow, loading his Bren, gathering his grenades close and getting ready to take as many of the bastards with him as he could. And then, as they limped away, he was lost to them.

It was a measure of the respect that the Australian troops had for Haddy that as soon as the word got through that he had been left behind and was in trouble, two groups immediately went to the rescue, one of which included the 39th's Lieutenant 'Kanga' Moore and ten of his men from 18 Platoon. Both groups soon encountered swarms of Japanese, and neither was able to get through, but at the very least Haddy's mission was accomplished. No one knew if the Western Australian warrior was alive or dead, but the fact that he and his men had put up such a fight meant that Brigadier Dougherty had time to move more men of the 2/14th west of Gona Creek to prevent the Japanese reinforcements from getting across that creek to relieve the Australian siege.

The following morning, Ralph Honner could barely believe it. He had been ordered to mount *another* attack just like the disastrous one the day before, to send men over the same killing field that was now soaked with the blood of five aborted attacks that had got precisely nowhere. It was almost more than Honner could stand. It was one thing for him to follow orders, but how could he order men to their certain deaths? *Could* he do that?

Salvation came from heaven, or at least the heavens, for this attack was going to be supported by an aerial bombardment. It fell to Joe Dawson and a couple of other soldiers to guide the bombers. Standard practice in such cases was for the troops on the ground to construct a massive white T, with the top of the T pointing to the target site. Strangely, Joe didn't have any starched white sheets on him, but he managed to gather in the towels of all the blokes and quickly construct a 'T'hat-a-way T for the Wirraway bombers, while keeping his head down.

But then came the supposed salvation. Whether they didn't see the T or were just bad shots would never be known, but the bombs when they came simply went everywhere, including *behind* the gathered 39th. No one was hurt, but it gave Honner precisely the excuse he was looking for. He was quickly on the field telephone to Brigadier Dougherty to inform him that he wanted to cancel the attack. When Dougherty agreed, Colonel Honner used the opportunity to *implore* the brigadier to let him put into action the plan he had formulated to get to the Japanese via the finger of jungle leading to their heart. Choosing his words carefully, but acutely conscious that the lives of many men depended on him mounting a convincing argument, Honner respectfully pointed out the folly of heading out once again over terrain that was already soaked with Australian blood when there was a good alternative at hand.

Dougherty, who had fought with Honner in Greece and Crete—and knew him to be absolutely top drawer—listened, and roughly acceded, although without wanting to abandon the attack on the left flank altogether. Perhaps the fact that Honner was free of the Koitaki slur meant that Dougherty was more free to follow Honner's advice and not simply command. Extraordinarily, in all of the Gona campaign to this point, this would be the first time that a commander in the field would be executing a plan entirely of his own creation, instead of following the dictates of someone operating solely from maps and situated well removed from the action.

Honner spent the time before the attack began scanning the ground with his binoculars, making notes and plans, and working out precise tactics for his men. One thing among many that he soon worked out was that if his men could get through, the Japanese defences really would be split for the first time, with the Jap defenders to the west entirely cut off from those on the eastern side.

They found Haddy. Dead, beneath the house, surrounded by a ring of equally dead Japs. If he had to go, that was precisely the way he would have wanted to go, defending his mates and giving the Japs hot curry right to the end.

All was now in place for the 39th's attack on Gona. Colonel Honner's plan was for A Company to lead the attack, followed hard by D Company and then . . . C Company. Ah yes, C Company. Though Brigadier Dougherty had insisted that C Company mount their attack across the kunai killing fields, for the first time in his military career, Ralph Honner disobeyed a direct order. Quietly, he told the C Company commander, Captain Seward, to make a feint only—send in some limited fire, but risk no lives at all—and get ready to back up A Company and D Company in the eastern sector, through the finger of jungle, when the moment came.

And still Honner had yet one more ace to play. His close examination of the Japanese military method had revealed that while the Japs were being bombarded, they didn't bother firing but simply kept their heads down till it passed and then proceeded to let forth their withering fire.

What if his men, then, advanced right to the Japanese throats while the bombardment was on? What if the 39th took the risk of being blown apart by their own bombs, on the reckoning that, however dangerous, it was a whole lot less dangerous than going straight into the teeth of a Jap who was aiming directly at you? The more Honner thought about it, the more he liked the idea. Refining it a little more, he arranged with artillery to fuse their shells so that they would explode a couple of feet into the soft soil. That way if they got into the roof of the bunker they would damage the structure, and if they landed beside they'd still stun the defenders. Either way the Japs would be heavily distracted.[293]

By split-second timing, the 39th would be able to begin its move on the Japs two minutes before the bombardment finished, giving them one minute to get among the bunkers, and one minute to do damage while the bombs were still dropping and all was confused.

It was a plan of extraordinary daring, the more so because there was a very real chance that an enormous bomb would drop right on his own men and take out twenty at once; but the point was that it was so daring that the Japanese surely wouldn't anticipate it.

The key was to get the timing precisely right, and not to tell the men that the barrage would continue for two minutes after they launched their attack. To do so would have troubled them unnecessarily, and simply lifted their anxiety. All they needed to know was that when the time came, they were to attack with everything they had.

There was a rumble in the jungle. Aeroplanes overhead. American aeroplanes. This time they were not dropping death and destruction on the Japanese, but propaganda pamphlets. It was an initiative from Brigadier Dougherty, and the hope was that the pamphlets might weaken their resolve. Each photo showed dozens of Japanese soldiers being guarded by a single Australian soldier holding a rifle, with the subtitle in Japanese characters saying: 'This is to inform the Emperor's soldiers that thousands of their comrades have already laid down their arms, so you too should surrender.'[294] The soldiers of the 39th wistfully watched the pamphlets flutter down, and the worse they had dysentery the more wistful they were. All that paper, *wasted*—though it was a fair bet that all the Japs suffering from dysentery, which was surely most of them, would put the paper to good use.[295]

Not surprisingly for the men of the 39th, the pamphlets did not make the Japanese do what five straight months of starvation, bullets, bombs, death and disease had not been able to accomplish— that is, make them throw down their weapons and come out with their hands up—and the attack by the 39th had to go ahead.

And the time came soon enough. It was 12.42 p.m. on 8 December 1942, and the bombardment just ahead made the ground shake like it had thunder in its belly. At Honner's signal the men of the 39th did what they did best, which was to get to grips with the Japs. And how sweet it was. Four months before, it was the 39th who had dug themselves in, waiting for the Japs. But now, now it was their turn . . .

With the roar of the exploding bombs obviating any need for a cautiously quiet advance, they just up and ran straight at where they knew the Japanese bunkers to be, where Lieutenant Colonel Honner's reconnaissance had told them they would be found. Cannon volleyed and thundered—to the left of them, to the right of them, and cannon right out in front.

    'Forward, the Light Brigade!
    Charge for the guns!' he said:
    Into the valley of Death,
    Rode the six hundred . . .

What ensued was happy carnage. Happier still, not one bomb killed any man of the 39th.

The Japanese had no idea that the Australians were on them, and many died where they sat, their heads between their hands, waiting for the barrage to stop. By the time they knew that the game had changed, an Australian grenade had either hurtled surprisingly through the gun slot of their bunker—*'mail call, special delivery!'*— or the muzzle of an Australian Bren gun was spitting death at each and every one of them. Some Japanese soldiers did manage to rally a little, but they, too, were wiped out in the course of the day and into the night, as the men of the 39th moved ruthlessly from post to post, secure in the knowledge that they now had the yellow bastards isolated from their reinforcements.

Not that the Japs didn't have some fight left in them. In the last post to fall, the gallant Lieutenant Bob Sword—he who had gone so far beyond the call of duty at Isurava, and who Colonel Honner had saluted with such respect—was mortally wounded by what was close to the last shot fired in the clean-out.

All around Gona Mission now on this morning of 9 December, the detritus of a long battle was apparent. Walking around among it all, Joe Dawson came across the bodies of two Australians with their heads within a foot of Japanese pillboxes. Just one more yard and they would have made it, killing the Japs instead of being killed by them. And, obviously, they weren't the only ones. Joe was a bit worried at the time, as he was yet to catch up with Wally and Ray, and had some fear they might have been killed or injured. Never mind, he was sure they would show up soon.

In the meantime, many dead and rotting bodies of the recently killed Japanese soldiers lay nameless in the tropical torpor. In these conditions a dead body could start to be on the nose in a matter of an hour, but that wasn't where most of the unbearable stench was coming from. Nor did it arise from the fact that the Japs in their trenches for days on end had to do their ablutions a step away from where they subsequently died. The real putrescence came from the Japs who had been killed *weeks* before, and who had just been piled up, sometimes almost as part of a barricade, before being blown apart in this new battle. Their remains now lay all over the place. Not for nothing were some of the dead Japs wearing gas masks. It wasn't because they feared a gas attack, it was because they too, couldn't stand the smell.

Shattered palm trees lay every which way. At a Regimental Aid Post a member of the 39th was screaming as they tried to remove a bullet from his stomach. And yet he was one of the lucky ones who had survived. The first duty of the victorious 39th was to bury their own men who hadn't made it—six had been killed in the action— and of these the gallant Lieutenant Sword was among the first to be buried, before the bowed heads, silent prayers and tears of his comrades.

A God-forsaken place it seemed. Just a short distance away, the old Gona Misson house and church were blown to bits, though, oddly enough, the only thing in the whole place that didn't seem to have a mark on it was the one large white cross out the front.[296]

Ralph Honner got a message through to Brigadier Ivan Dougherty, commanding 21st Brigade back in Moresby. It was as simple as it was appropriate: 'Gona's gone'.

Later that morning, Joe was leaning on his backpack trying to get some sleep, and trying not to worry that Wally and Ray still hadn't shown up, when suddenly someone shouted: 'Hey Sarge, there's a couple of wounded Japs over here.' Joe grabbed his Owen Gun, which he'd just recently taken over from one of his wounded comrades, and ran towards the voice.

And sure enough, there they were. It was strange to suddenly come across, face to face, two soldiers he'd likely been fighting against for months and then see them so helpless. But that was the case. One Jap was lying face down, breathing heavily, while the other was sitting crosslegged, using his right hand to hold together what remained of his left bicep, which looked as if it had been torn apart by shrapnel. It must have happened at least a day or two before, because the whole thing was rotten with maggots. Joe put down his pack and pulled out a field dressing, bound up the wound and was just about to turn his attention to the other Jap, when the bloke who had first called out to him asked the question.

'Why don't you just shoot 'em, Sarge?'

The question hung in the air for a moment, before Joe made reply. 'You found them, so I suppose for the same reason you didn't.'

'What do you mean?'

'Probably because you don't want to be like them!'

It was a good thought, but evidence that some didn't mind being 'just like them' was soon upon them. Just when some native porters had the wounded man on a stretcher, an Australian lieutenant came up with a .38 pistol and shot him dead. Just like that. The Japanese soldier was almost certainly going to die anyway, but Joe found it brutal and shocking.

Gona had been a long, brutal and bloody fight, but even then the Australians were far from done. The Japanese remained in possession of Buna. By 18 December, MacArthur got what he deserved, which was the humiliation of asking for help from the Australian Army and senior officers he had criticised, ridiculed and indirectly sacked. For by this time it was clear that the Americans couldn't on their own capture Buna—the Japanese holdout that *they* were supposed to take, the place where they were going to show the Australians how it was done. They retained a masterly inactivity, and at MacArthur's humble request it was the Australian 18th Brigade, the heroes of Milne Bay, who, with the help of the the survivors of the 39th, began to move in on Buna to save the day . . .

Lost. Wandering. Exhausted. Where was he? *Who* was he? Joe. Joe Dawson. Snatches of things came back to him. Two nights before, he'd shown a sore on the inside of his leg to a medical orderly, who had taken his temperature and diagnosed him with scrub typhus—an often fatal infectious disease common in Southeast Asia, transmitted to humans via the bites of mites. Shocked at how hot he was, the bloke had given it to Joe straight: 'If it goes up any more, mate, you're on your way out.' Then Joe had sweated through the night. Then the next day too. He needed Ray or Wally to look after him. But they were gone. Dead. Killed by the Japs at West Gona, near 'Haddy's Village'. At the news of Ray and Wally's death, Joe had wept. Then he'd tried to get to the Regimental Aid Post on his own, but had got lost in the fog of his own sickness. He kept wandering. Was he near Jap positions or his own? Was Christmas yesterday, or next week?

And then someone had grabbed him, one of his own blokes fortunately, and led him to this place and gave him some pills, and put something around his neck to identify him, and then they'd tried to walk him out some more, till he collapsed and the next thing he knew it was later, much later, days later, and he'd been roasting all that time on some hospital bed, and then the fever had started to get even *worse* and he was burning, burning, burning for days and days and days . . . and then it was cooler, a little cooler, and he'd opened his eyes and a nurse was looking down at him, a kind nurse, a very kind nurse, and now she was speaking to him. He had to concentrate because his hearing had never really come back properly since his near bombing on the *Macdhui*. But he could make out her words, all right.

'They brought ten soldiers in with you the day you came in, all with scrub typhus . . . ' she said. 'They're all dead, and everyone thought you were going to die too, but I didn't think so. I thought you were going to live, and I'll tell you why . . . ' And then she smiled, reached under his pillow, brought out his rosary beads, and put them on his chest. He clasped them, and rested his hands on his chest. He wanted to go home. He wanted to be with Elaine.

Finally, on 22 January 1943, it was over. In one of the great feats of arms in Australian history, the Australians had captured the critical ground at Buna, allowing the Americans to come in over the top and take the Buna Government Station—meaning that the last Japanese resistance was now wiped out in the area. Yes, there were many Japanese still on the loose along the beachhead, but they were foodless, and fleeing west in the hope of eventual evacuation. They had to be found and killed or captured—mostly killed. It would take months. But the war was effectively over. In their previous six months' fight to control the track and its approaches, Australia had mortally lost 2165 troops, with another 3533 wounded. The United States, which had only come into action very late in the piece, had 671 troops killed and 2172 wounded. It was the Japanese, operating so far from their homeland, with military officers perhaps less concerned with the sanctity of their soldiers' lives, who suffered most. Some twenty thousand Japanese troops were landed in Papua and New Guinea, of which it is estimated that some thirteen thousand were killed, with nearly *all* the rest wounded or debilitated in some fashion.

On that last day, Ralph Honner led his survivors away from the battlefield. It was a wonder they could stand at all. The bulk of the men had been in battle for most of the previous six months with only short respite. They had been shot at, bombed, wounded, starved, deprived of sleep, frozen and boiled, they had suffered malaria, dysentery, scrub typhus and the constant trauma of seeing their dearest friends killed and blown apart, while always wondering if they were next . . . Yet standing they were. And walking. And *marching*.

'Higher authority refused us vehicles for the less fit,' Honner later explained to his biographer, Peter Brune. '[They ruled] that no one could ride unless he fell out on the march. In the 39th's book, marchers didn't straggle, so we all marched, all the way, to Dobodura—for some a long torture on the verge of unconsciousness.'[297]

It was at this point, coming into Dobodura that an amazed bystander, staggered at the sight of such exhausted, ravaged and debilitated men marching in this fashion, was heard to enquire, 'What mob's this?'

Honner's men didn't flinch, but kept marching with their eyes straight ahead. But Honner's second-in-command, who had heard the remark, couldn't contain himself.

'This is not a mob!' he barked. 'This is the 39th . . .'

EPILOGUE

How do we remember them? . . . They died so young. They missed so much. They gave up so much: their hopes; their dreams; their loved ones. They laid down their lives that their friends might live. Greater love hath no man than this.

Ralph Honner[298]

In Papua New Guinea the war was especially more painful for the Japanese. 'I hate war. Peace is a must.' This was a shout that rang out from the bottom of their heart for the soldiers and sailors who participated in the Papua New Guinea campaign . . .

Kengora Tanaka[299]

Nothing will ever be the same again in Papua. Anyone who toiled over the Owen Stanley Range in wartime knows, it will never be the same silent, sweet-smelling jungle track where man and his indecencies were almost unknown. It is a trail of blood and iron now, and in the memory of this generation will remain so.

Geoffrey Vernon[300]

In July 1943, the word came that the 39th Battalion was to be disbanded, with its survivors broken up and scattered to units of the AIF. For two years they'd withstood everything the Japs and the jungle could throw at them, never buckled and always given more than they got, and now they were wiped out by the stroke of some bureaucrat's pen.

Most of the soldiers, like Smoky Howson, were disgusted. Because that would be about fucking right, wouldn't it?[301] The bloody government didn't want a militia battalion coming home with all those battle honours when most of their AIF units would be coming home with Sweet Fanny Adams. Here they were, they'd fought their bloody *guts* out, shown the AIF they weren't the only ones who could fight, and this was their reward. Broken up. Made to join the AIF. Seriously, *made* to join the AIF. They were told that if they wanted to go home, then they'd have to join up with one of the AIF units that would shortly be posted there, but otherwise they could stay and rot with one of the other militia battalions.

Well, Smoky had to do it, didn't he? He told them they could go and get fucked, he was *not* going to join the AIF. So he ended up staying in New Guinea and rotting, while most of the others went every which way, and eventually home.

It just *gutted* Smoky to split up from his comrades-in-arms, who were now closer to him than brothers. When he'd joined up with this mob, he'd barely had a friend in the world, he'd been so bloody busy working in the market garden, but in this caper you always made friends just a bit faster than you buried them, and you ended up bound tight as a drum to the ones who stayed above the sod, while you'd miss forever the ones who were under it. Yes, they told each other they'd be in touch, that they'd catch up after the war was over—see you in such-and-such pub, and so on and so forth—but no one was fooled that much. It was over. They were scattered and would never be as they were—one unit of men, fighting under one flag. The 39th was finished.

With the men going in different directions, Ralph Honner took over command of the 2/14th Battalion, and was still at their head in October 1943 when, during the 2/14th's campaign in the Markham Valley and Ramu to clear out the last remaining Japanese in New

Guinea, he was caught by enemy machine-gun fire, taking bullets in his hand and thigh. After recuperating for ten months in a hospital back in Australia, he took a senior administrative role with the Directorate of Military Training in Melbourne. For his wartime achievements he was awarded a Distinguished Service Order and a Military Cross.

Another day, another landing, another assault, another chance for Damien Parer to capture graphic images of Allied forces doing the business, fighting on the beaches, fighting on the landing grounds, defending their islands, continuing to turn the tide against the Japanese. But by now, September 1944, Damien was no longer a relatively anonymous newsreel man, but had taken his place among the most acclaimed documentary-makers in the world.

Kokoda Front Line had not only filled theatres around Australia, it had gone on to be joint winner of the Academy Award for best documentary in 1943—the Australian film community's first such recognition. The citation said that Damien Parer's film had won 'for its effectiveness in portraying, simply yet forcefully, the scene of war in New Guinea and for its moving presentation of the bravery and fortitude of our Australian comrades in arms'.[302] Of course it was terrific, but as was his way, Parer continued to pursue his passion without pause. (Or just pause enough to have married Marie just a few months before. Already she was pregnant, and he couldn't have been more thrilled.)

The current action he was filming was with the marines of US Task Force as they protected MacArthur's eastern flank for his grand 'I-shall-return' gesture to the Philippines by invading one of the outlying islands where the Japanese had a base. Just before dawn on 15 September 1944, the battleship on which Damien had journeyed thus far, the USS *Pierce,* along with the many other ships in the battle group, plastered the beaches of Peliliu with heavy fire to knock out whatever coastal defences the Japanese had set up. Typically, Damien was with the first group of marines to storm the beaches and he remained with them, shooting all the while, over the next two days.

On the third morning he went out with them again, but never came back . . . A deeply distraught fellow film-maker, John Brennan, found him that afternoon, dead on the beach, and was able to work out what had happened by talking with the marines who had been with him. The Americans had been pushing across a stretch of relatively open ground and, because they had been under such heavy fire, the only possible way for the grunts to advance had been behind the shelter of lumbering tanks. Damien had always taken the view that to film advancing troops properly you had to be out in front of them, so had been walking backwards behind the lead tank, capturing the advance of the marines when a burst of fire from a hidden pillbox had cut him down. A small mercy was that in all likelihood he was dead before he hit the ground. He was a great Australian, an artist in his craft, and he was gone.

The sequel was beautifully described by Damien Parer's principal biographer, Neil McDonald, in his book *War Cameraman: The Story of Damien Parer*.

'Six days later, Marie's mother and her sister, Doreen, came over to the flat in Wollstonecraft on Sydney's lower north shore. "I've got some bad news," Agnes Cotter said.

'"He's dead isn't he?"

'"Yes."

'Tears started to run down Marie's face. She thought, "I'm crying and my life's over."

'Two hours later [the] telegram was delivered. Marie's father had worked at the cable company so they had known where to contact her parents before sending out the notification. Still the young girl who made the delivery asked first whether Marie had someone with her before handing her the envelope.'[303]

It was an agony that would not pass. Even twenty years later, Marie was quoted in the Sydney *Sun*: 'I would give the whole of my life for another five minutes with Damien . . .'[304] That life was a long one. She lived quietly in suburban Sydney, with the support of her son, the baby she was carrying at the time, Damien Parer Jnr, himself now a film-maker, until she died, in December 2003.

John Curtin continued in office working as hard as ever, but in November 1944 he suffered a heart attack that was serious enough to put him in hospital for two months. Though he was able to return to his duties in January 1945, and was mightily gratified to be in office when Germany unconditionally surrendered on 7 May 1945, Japan was still holding out and Curtin's overall health continued to spiral downwards, as he paid the toll for the crippling workload he had taken on over the years. By early July 1945 he was clearly ailing badly and had been put to bed.

On the night of 4 July, his driver, Ray Tracey, to whom the Australian Prime Minister was very close, went up to Curtin's bedroom in the Lodge to wish him goodnight. Curtin had just enough consciousness left to ask who had won the football. Alas, there had been no football. It was a Wednesday. But Tracey didn't care and told his boss what he wanted to hear.

'Fitzroy won, Sir,' he said, nominating the team that Curtin had followed all his life.

'That's fine,' Curtin had replied. 'A very good team, Fitzroy.'[305]

Just before midnight his wife, Elsie, took a cup of tea into him, and had a cup herself, sitting quietly by his bedside until just before midnight when he said to her: 'Go on, Mrs Curtin. It is best that you go off to bed now.' She got up, gave him his nightly sedative and he said to her, 'I'm ready now.' A final kiss, and she left him. Just before dawn, she was summoned by a nurse to come back to be there with him as he passed away.

From the Philippines, where he had now successfully returned, General Douglas MacArthur issued his last communiqué on the subject of the man who had become his friend.

'Mr Curtin was one of the greatest of wartime statesmen, and the preservation of Australia from invasion was his immemorial monument.' To Elsie Curtin personally, MacArthur sent a telegram stating: 'He was of the great of the earth.'

The prime minister's funeral was held in Canberra with great pomp and ceremony and two of his pallbearers were Artie Fadden and Robert Menzies. Just after they had put the coffin down on the gun carriage Menzies said to Fadden, 'I don't want all this fuss when I go, Artie.'

'Don't worry,' Fadden assured him. 'You won't get it.'[306]

From there, Curtin's casket was slowly taken to Canberra Airport, where an enormous Dakota aircraft awaited, with six Kittyhawks and six Boomerang fighters for escort. The planes took off. The Dakota, on a brief solo excursion, circled Parliament House twice slowly, and then headed west, with the other planes moving into respectful formation behind. John Curtin is buried in Perth's Karrakatta Cemetery.

Did they look up? Unlikely, but had they, some of those few Japanese soldiers from the 144th Regiment who'd managed to get back alive from the Kokoda Track to recuperate at home on the island of Shikoku, might have just been able to spot a few flashes passing high above. For at that moment, at an altitude of some 28 000 feet, three American planes were on their way to complete what would ever after be noted as the most important mission of the war. The lead plane was piloted by one Paul Tibbets—flying his soon-to-be-famous *Enola Gay*, named for the mother who had encouraged him, against the wishes of his father, to pursue a flying career with the American Armed Forces. Yes, his father had wanted him to be a doctor in a hospital and save people's lives, but that was not the way it had turned out . . . not by a long shot.

Only shortly after crossing Shikoku, the planes traversed the Iyo Sea and then, up ahead, at last came into view the city of Hiroshima, gleaming in the morning sun. It was coming time to drop the cargo in *Enola Gay's* bomb-bay, a bomb the likes of which the world had never seen—the culmination of the ultra-secret Manhattan Project. It was an atomic bomb, which they called 'Little Boy', capable of delivering a blast the rough equivalent of 20 000 tons of TNT.

And now the men could see the curious T-shaped bridge which they knew to be the effective cross-hairs of their target in downtown Hiroshima. Tibbets flicked the switch and reminded all of the crew to quickly put on their heavy dark Polaroid goggles to shield their eyes from what was coming. No one could quite believe it, but the scientists had said this thing was going to go off with an intensity the equal of ten suns.

Lining it up, lining it up . . . lining it up and . . . *now*.

The bomb doors opened and Little Boy hurtled down onto the oblivious city below. At the instant of release—suddenly unburdened of 10 000 pounds of weight—*Enola Gay* lurched upwards, and Tibbets quickly put into effect long months of training. In as tight a turn as *Enola* could manage without breaking up, he immediately put as much distance between them and the coming explosion as possible. And sure enough just forty-three seconds from the moment of release, as Tibbets would describe it later, 'I look up there and the whole sky is lit up in the prettiest blues and pinks I've ever seen in my life. It was just great.'[307] The other thing he noticed was the tingling in his teeth, as his fillings interacted with the bomb's radioactive pulses. When the shockwave hit them from the mushroom cloud billowed up behind them to an altitude of 45 000 feet, *Enola Gay* again briefly lurched, but steadied and then continued on its way.

The bomb was only slightly off target. Instead of exploding above the Aioi Bridge as planned, it vaporised the Shima Hospital, some three hundred yards to the southeast. Some 140 000 citizens of Hiroshima were all but instantly killed. One of the few in Japan who was not entirely overwhelmed by the news when it got out, was the recently deposed prime minister, Hideki Tojo. According to his biographer, while all the rest of Tokyo and most of Japan was panicking in the face of the bomb, Tojo calmly said to his wife: 'Our ancestors must have lived in caves at one time. So can we.'[308] If the worst came to the worst and Tokyo itself came under attack, Tojo's simple plan, he said, was to live underground by night, and forage for sweet potatoes by day.

•

And so, it had come to this . . .

In 1853, it had been the great American naval officer, Commodore Matthew Calbraith Perry, who on his flagship USS *Mississippi* had steamed into Tokyo Bay, and become the first to forge a genuine passage through centuries of splendid isolation and open negotiations with Japan for trade. From that point on, Japan had indeed opened itself up to the West, but for the most part it had been on Japan's terms. This however, was very much the reverse.

For this was the ceremony of Japan's surrender, and the same flag that had flown on that day on the USS *Mississippi* was on this morning of 2 September 1945 framed in the boardroom of the mighty warship USS *Missouri*, also moored in Tokyo Bay. There assembled on one side were many Allied commanding officers, including General Sir Thomas Blamey of Australia and Lieutenant General Arthur E. Percival of England, the latter of whom had surrendered Singapore and had now just been released from a Japanese POW camp. On the other side of the room, representing Emperor Hirohito, was Japan's Foreign Minister, while the Chief of Staff of the Army represented Imperial General Headquarters.

Presiding, of course, was General Douglas MacArthur, gazing imperiously as one by one, the representatives of each nation signed the documents that formalised the terms of surrender. After weeks of negotiations, Japan had fully accepted all of the West's conditions, with their sole demand in return being that their Emperor should survive and not be tried as a war criminal. Though there was a strong view among some of the Allied leadership that this condition be refused, and Hirohito tried for war crimes, MacArthur—now installed as commander of the Allied powers occupying Japan—had overruled them. MacArthur allowed Hirohito to remain Emperor, as a symbol of continuity and cohesion for the Japanese people, his only insistence being that the Emperor acknowledge that he was indeed mortal and *not* a divine being. This admission was contained in the surrender documents, and they were now signed. After all the blood, all the tears, all the lives lost and families torn apart, it was over.

•

On the day that Damien Parer was killed, his great friend Chester Wilmot was in France, in the thick of action himself. After losing his accreditation at the hands of Blamey in the spring of 1942, Chester had spent all of 1943 writing a book about the valour of the Australian forces at Tobruk, before the BBC had invited him to join them in early 1944. Even then, General Blamey had tried to block the appointment, sending a cable to the British War Office asserting in the strongest of terms that Wilmot simply was not fit to be a war correspondent *anywhere*.[309] Even the Australian Government initially denied the necessary permission. Eventually though—with the help of political pressure applied by Robert Menzies, whom the well-connected Chester had known since he was a child—Wilmot prevailed and joined the BBC, moving his young family to Britain.

It was to be a very propitious appointment for all concerned. On D-Day, 6 June 1944, Chester was with the Sixth Airborne Division as it landed at Normandy, and remained with the Allies all the way to Berlin over the next twelve months. Right at the death of the Third Reich, Wilmot achieved his greatest scoop. It so happened he was at Field Marshal Montgomery's HQ when the word came through that the Third Reich's General Jodl was ready to sign the surrender terms, so long as it was first approved by Field Marshal Wilhelm Keitel.[310]

When Montgomery organised to send one of his senior officers to see Keitel with these surrender terms, Wilmot talked his way into being allowed to accompany him. They made their way through the mass of armed sentries into Field Marshal Keitel's headquarters, and the highest ranking surviving German officer did indeed sign the terms. On their way out, there was only one sentry still on duty, and he was eating an apple. The world had changed. Wilmot had a scoop to beat all scoops, he thought as he raced away to write it. Unfortunately, the army censor didn't allow a word of it to be published.

•

Father James Benson, who was the sole survivor of the three principals of Gona Mission, finished the war as a Japanese POW, and when Rabaul was liberated, he walked free. He eventually made his way back to the ruins of the Gona Mission and and began to rebuild it. Once it was established again, he handed the running of it to his nephew and concentrated his energies, and considerable artistic talents, painting a mural in the nearby cathedral at Dogura. In 1955, he returned to England and for six months was the presiding priest of St Paul's, Knightsbridge, before dying in September of that year. He was sixty-eight. At his request his ashes were sent back to Gona, and scattered in the rich fields around.

Lieutenant Colonel Arthur Key did not emerge from imprisonment in Rabaul, and it is presumed that he died in Japanese captivity. On the subject of Key, Brigadier Potts wrote to his wife: 'It looks as if Key is gone. Oh hell. And he did such a good job and made his battalion for all times. Makes me want to howl like a kid . . .'[311]

The end of the war found Doc Vernon working in the main native hospital at Port Moresby. He left the army in March 1946, and died of tuberculosis and a stroke just two months later at sixty-five years of age.

General Douglas MacArthur stayed on in Japan for six years, entirely undisputed as the most powerful man in the land. At one point it looked like he might become the most powerful man in the world when he stood for the Republican presidential nomination in 1948, but when that fizzled with a bad showing in the Wisconsin primary, he returned his attention to purely matters military.

Though MacArthur's benevolence had spared the Emperor, the American general showed no leniency at all to longtime Prime Minister Hideki Tojo. When the American forces came to take Tojo into custody, just a little over a week after the surrender documents were signed, the prime minister tried to commit suicide by shooting himself. The Americans, though, would allow him no such easy exit, and considerable resources were put towards ensuring that he survived . . . for the moment.

He was to be the star turn at the forthcoming trials for war crimes, and from that point on Tojo was placed on suicide watch. Only when the United States was ready would he be allowed to die, and that day came just before Christmas 1948.[312]

Of the many charges for which Tojo had been found guilty, the catch-all was that he had promoted a scheme of Japanese conquest that 'contemplated and carried out . . . murdering, maiming and ill-treating prisoners of war and civilian internees . . . forcing them to labour under inhumane conditions . . . plundering public and private property, wantonly destroying cities, towns and villages beyond any justification of military necessity; perpetrating mass murder, rape, pillage, brigandage, torture and other barbaric cruelties upon the helpless civilian population of the over-run countries.'

Tojo was dressed in US Army fatigues with a large capital 'P' for prisoner on his back, when the trapdoor dropped beneath him in Sugamo Prison just after midnight on the rising day of 23 December. As the son of a samurai, who had built his career on espousing the values of the samurai, Tojo met his fate calmly, seemingly fulfilled by dying bravely at the hands of an enemy who had defeated him.

Six decades on from that death, it is his principal biographer, Edwin P. Hoyt, who notes—as an example of how much Japan has changed since that time—that the 'name of Hideki Tojo is anything but a household word. Indeed it is scarcely recognised by three new generations of Japanese.'[313]

In 1951, General Douglas MacArthur while still the Military Governor of Japan, fell out with the man who had replaced Franklin Delano Roosevelt as President of the United States, Harry Truman. The two men had disagreed from the beginning of their professional relationship, which culminated in Truman summarily dismissing MacArthur from his post.

Truman later explained why, precisely, he had taken this extreme action. 'I fired him because he wouldn't respect the authority of the

President. I didn't fire him because he was a dumb son-of-a-bitch, although he was, but that's not against the law for generals. If it was, half to three-quarters of them would be in jail.'

Despite his dismissal, MacArthur remained as a kind of *éminence grise* of the military establishment, though he never again held command. He died at the age of eighty-four on 5 April 1964 in Bethesda, Maryland, and his body now lies in a veritable MacArthur shrine, situated in Virginia.

Chester Wilmot's career continued to prosper after the war, in no small part on the basis of his wide experience in the European theatre of war. His extensive work covering the Nuremberg trials had unearthed a lot of valuable documentation, and in 1952 he would publish a highly acclaimed book about the campaign that confirmed him as one of the most distinguished correspondents of the day.[314] One of his innovative ways of presenting history was to constantly change perspective in his narrative, interweaving what was happening in Germany and Britain at much the same time, to tell the whole of the story and not merely a part. Writing in the London *Daily Telegraph* on 21 January 1952, Malcolm Muggeridge enthused that Wilmot had '[put it all together] so brilliantly, so conscientiously and so imaginatively that the result, published today—*The Struggle for Europe*—becomes at once a classic of contemporary history.'

It was at the height of his career, then, that in December 1953, Chester Wilmot visited Sydney to anchor an around-the-world radio program that preceded the Queen's broadcast on Christmas Day from Auckland. From Sydney, Wilmot introduced speakers from all parts of the British Commonwealth, before heading north, back to his wife and two young daughters at the home the family had settled into in Buckinghamshire.

Just a few days later, a fisherman by the name of Giovanni di Marco was pulling in his nets in the Mediterranean waters just south of the island of Elba when he heard three quick explosions and looked up to see on his far horizon a seeming silver meteorite flashing out of the clouds and heading to the sea, where it disappeared in an enormous spray of water. It proved to be a BOAC Comet jet airliner, which had, for reasons unknown, just twenty minutes after taking off from Rome on its last haul from Sydney to London, exploded in mid-air. By the time the fisherman arrived at the point of impact all was calm, and all he could do was retrieve some of the floating bodies from the water. Chester Wilmot was one of the thirty-five passengers killed. It was the third such accident involving a Comet since they had been introduced into service just two years before.

Of the three journalist friends who had forged their way across the Owen Stanley Range to the front in mid-1942, only Osmar White would live to make old bones. After the New Guinea campaign, White covered the Allied action in the Solomon Islands in 1943, until wounded when he was travelling in a landing craft that was bombed. From there he went to cover the less physically strenuous European campaign, and stayed with General George S. Patton's Third Army as they invaded Germany, liberated concentration camps and stormed first into Berlin. Later he remained close to his great friend Chester Wilmot as they covered the Nuremberg war trials. In his post-war career he continued with journalism initially, but then expanded his interests to books and writing screenplays, including episodes of the television series *Homicide*. In 1957, he was the only Australian journalist to accompany the Australian National Antarctic Research Expedition and his work was so valued that there is an Antarctic island named after him. He died in May 1991, at the age of eighty-eight.

Bert Kienzle, who had done such a sterling job ensuring that the supplies got through—and who was awarded a Member of the British Empire for his trouble—returned to New Guinea's Yodda Valley after the war was over, and started running three thousand cattle on a property just fifteen miles to the west of Kokoda, which he continued until 1980, when he retired and moved to Queensland. Aged eighty-three, he died in January 1988 in Sydney.

There was a postscript to the murders of Sister Mavis and Sister May. On a morning in September 1943, at a time when the village that had betrayed the Sisters was back under Australian control, the ANGAU officer in charge of the district, Tom Grahamslaw, did what he felt had to be done. Accompanied by a large group of native policemen and several other ANGAU officers, he had gathered the villagers of Higaturu, together, so they could witness it. 'It' was the hanging of the seventeen men, including the original traitor, Embogi, who had reported the presence of the Sisters and the other white men to the Japanese. The natives had to be given a strong message that this would not be tolerated by the Australian authorities, and as a large group of village women and men wailed, the job was done. Seventeen traitors were left twisting in the wind. After the war, Tom Grahamslaw moved to the Central Coast in New South Wales, where he took up life as a farmer. He survived until the late 1990s.

A few of the Fuzzy Wuzzy Angels survive. One of them, Ovuru, is now the Headman at Nadi village, at the approximate age of ninety-two. With his son, he was brought to Sydney in 2002 by the Australian actor and film producer Yahoo Serious, himself a devotee of the Kokoda story. Yahoo and his wife, Lulu, took Ovuru to, among other places, the Imax Theatre in Darling Harbour where the older man donned special three-dimensional glasses and watched a film about travelling in space. Ovuru returned to the highlands, thrilled, his proud boast to his villagers and fellow chieftains that he was the first man from their parts to have travelled to the heavens.

Okryon Park, the comfort woman from Rabaul, finally made it home to Korea on New Year's Day of 1944, but not until she had suffered another ill-fated trip, when yet one more ship she was travelling home on was bombed and sunk by Allied planes. When she did make it back, it was to find that her parents were still alive, but her son was back with his father. Her mother prevented her going to her son for fear of what her husband would do to her. She became the mistress of a man who worked for the town office and twice fell pregnant to him, bearing him two healthy babies. This man was under the impression that she had worked as a nurse in Rabaul.

When her parents died and this man fell bankrupt, Okryon became effectively a 'non-person', shunned by what was left of her original family, though still supporting her children. She found some domestic work, and sold vegetables at the markets, but ended up living on welfare. She survived at least into the 1990s, when the issue of 'comfort women' was acknowledged for the first time, and she told her story. 'Our country should never be controlled by anyone in the future . . . ' was one comment she made to the journalists who interviewed her.[315]

And Kohkichi Nishimura, the Japanese soldier who made the pact with his fellow platoon soldiers that whichever of them survived would return to retrieve the remains of the others and bring them back to Japan? For three and a half decades after the war ended, Nishimura worked as a successful businessman, without ever forgetting his promise. Sometimes in the middle of an important business meeting, the memory of that day on Mission Ridge would suddenly come back to him, and he would again remember the vow that they had all taken. He would hear the grenades exploding, see the Australians charging, watch his comrades fall and die and think of them still there, see their faces beneath the sod, lying, waiting for him to return. Waiting. Waiting for him to fulfil his promise. He would have wanted them to do it for him, had he fallen. And he knew they wanted him to do it for them. That he *had* to do it for them. He could bear only so many of such thoughts.

In 1979 Nishimura could bear it no longer. He knew that he must redeem his vow—whatever the cost. Despite the protestations of his wife and child, he sold his land and all his assets and at the age of sixty-eight left his family to return to Papua New Guinea to search for his fallen comrades. Certainly it was a tremendous wrench to do so, but knowing that the task ahead of him would take years—and that he had no choice but to do it—he felt it would be the best thing for his wife and son in the long run.

Basing himself at Popondetta, he became a familiar figure to the natives along the track, who always saw him using a kind of silver stick to probe the ground, looking for bones. And over fifteen long years he found them, too. Most of them, at least. Strangely, four to five decades on, the upper bodies had disappeared and all that remained was the legs, with their boots on, ready to go home with him. He took them, as promised, for a proper Shinto funeral. Home, home to Japan, and most particularly the beautiful city of Kochi, surrounded by its high mountains, on the wondrous island of Shikoku. 'Home is the hunter, home from the hill, and the sailor home from the sea.'

Very shortly after the war ended General Sir Thomas Blamey lost his position as head of the Australian Army and, after a brief reign by General Sturdee, was replaced by . . . Sydney Rowell, who went on to hold the post from 1950 to 1954.

Nevertheless, one day in late 1950, the Heidelberg Repatriation Hospital in Victoria received a very important visitor, no less than the Governor General, Sir William McKell. He was there with a delegation of official guests, including Prime Minister Robert Menzies and the Minister for the Air, the Minister for the Navy and Army, to present Blamey—who had just suffered a stroke, and also had pneumonia—with his field marshal's baton. This was a great honour, largely pushed through by Menzies, but the role was effectively ceremonial only. Rowell now ran the show, and Blamey never recovered his health. He died on 27 May 1951, and was accorded a state funeral. Rowell, as the army's chief of the general staff, had the official role of chief mourner at the funeral, and one can only wonder what went through his mind as Blamey was at last lain to rest . . .[316]

•

Joe Dawson and his beloved Elaine married a few months after his return from Kokoda and are still going strong. Joe is now eighty-two, and in May 2003 he and Elaine celebrated their sixtieth wedding anniversary in the beautiful seaside town of Forster, just north of Newcastle. (It was a far happier day than the one just a few months after their actual wedding, when Joe informed the newly pregnant Elaine that, despite everything, he was going *back* to New Guinea to fight some more. He did so, but mercifully returned safe and sound at war's end.)

Smoky Howson went back to the market gardens before marrying, becoming a builder and raising children, but was always marked by his experience in the war. Haunted by events such as his killing of the Japanese soldier who was staring up at him, he spent a good deal of time over the years in institutions devoted to mental health. Though he had just about never cried during the war, sometimes after it, he just couldn't stop. Many was the night he'd wake in a cold sweat, looking intently into the eyes of the Japanese soldier, who was *still* looking straight back at him, and sometimes he'd wake to the sound of his wife screaming, only to realise that he was choking her. Other times he'd relive his grisliest work of all during the war, sawing the tops off dead blokes' heads, and ripping their chest cavities open with a sharp knife, with the blood and muck getting all over him. This was all so that they could send the brains and hearts of dead soldiers to the University of Melbourne for testing and God knows what. Some damn thing anyway. He hated working in Moresby's military morgue—with all those bloody great big foot-long rats running around everywhere—but that was what they asked him to do after he'd refused to join the AIF, and that's what he did. It was just that it was so damned hard to forget it. The world was back at peace, but he wasn't. He would never be. At least the grog helped, a little . . . Smoky Howson lived until June 2003.

•

After the war, Ralph Honner soon returned to civilian life, and continued what he'd started before the war, which was raising a family of four with his beloved wife Marjorie. A sign of just how long he'd been away, though, came a few days after he got home, when his two small sons reported to the nuns at their school that a strange man had come into the house and was cuddling their mother all the time, even in her bedroom!

Back in the swing of civilian life, Ralph moved to Sydney with his family and became very active in the Liberal Party and the United Nations Association among other things. Professionally, he became the long-time Chairman of the War Pensions Assessment Appeal Tribunal, and also had a stint with the Diplomatic Corps as he became Australia's Ambassador to Ireland from 1968 to 1972, after which he retired.

Ralph Honner died at eighty-nine, on the morning of 14 May 1994, not long after doing what he did every morning—raising the Australian flag on a specially constructed flagpole in his garden. His funeral at St Mary's Catholic Church in Miller Street, North Sydney, was standing room only. And one was there, an old Japanese gentleman, who had, unannounced, arrived the day before from Shikoku. He walked up to the coffin and bowed low and long, before handing a letter to Ralph's sons, noting the enormous respect he and his fellow old Japanese soldiers had for Colonel Ralph Honner, the warrior.

In some ways Alan Avery never recovered from the death of his best friend, Bruce Kingsbury, who had died so valiantly in the defence of Isurava. Every day he thought of Bruce, every day he missed him, every day something felt empty inside. Alcohol helped fill the hollow a little, but never for long enough. After the war he worked in a nursery and married, but the marriage broke up in 1965. The one place he seemed to find calm, oddly enough, was up in the same area of Queensland where the 2/14th had done so much of its preparation before heading off to New Guinea. It was more or less the last place he'd felt pretty good, so maybe it was natural enough. Alas, after a bout of prolonged ill-health, Alan finally gave up on living, and at the age of seventy-seven in May 1995, shot himself dead.

For his courageous efforts at Gona, Stan Bisset was awarded the Military Cross. After the war, he returned to Melbourne to marry, and he and his wife Shirley raised four children, as he worked with great success in the administrative side of a business that built gas and combustion furnaces. In 1970, when his marriage ended, he moved to Gladstone in Queensland, where he met the woman who was to become his second wife, Gloria. He now lives in quiet retirement in Noosa with Gloria, not far from where he and the rest of the 21st Brigade were training in preparation for their embarkation for New Guinea. It is Stan who organises the annual reunion of the 2/14th Battalion, and helps keep everyone in touch.

When I asked him in July 2003 what the greatest satisfaction of his life had been, he said that apart from seeing his children grow, it had been to help ensure that a memorial was built for his fallen comrades and brother up on Mount Ninderry, near Yandina, as well as feeling like he had some part in the wonderful memorial at Isurava being built through his own lobbying.

Speaking of which . . .

The village of Isurava, as it was, is no more. In 1988 the villagers decided to change sites and upped sticks to move about an hour and a half's walk closer to Kokoda, not too far from the place where Colonel Honner had placed his first standing patrol forward of Isurava to give fair warning when the Japanese soldiers were on their way. It was a place that had closer access to water and more flat arable land for their gardens—a place, too, where killing on a massive scale had not taken place.

In 1992, Paul Keating was the first Australian Prime Minister to visit Kokoda itself. On the helicopter ride from Moresby he discussed the significance of the Kokoda campaign with Professor David Horner of the Australian National University, one of the foremost experts in the field. Flying over the track on which so much blood had been spilled, looking down upon the gorges and cruel spurs that his fellow Australians had fought across fifty years before, clearly affected the prime minister. Upon emerging from the helicopter, which landed just near a modest memorial in honour of what the Diggers had accomplished in these parts, he immediately fell to his knees and kissed the ground. It was a symbol of the fact that Australia was finally recognising what had been achieved in this place. Here, Mr Keating said, the Australian soldiers were *not* fighting for Empire, they were fighting 'not in defence of the Old World, but the New World. Their world. They fought for their own values.' Which was in turn why, he explained, 'for Australians, the battles in Papua New Guinea were the most important ever fought.'[317] Amen to that.

And the New Guinea jungle? The butterflies that fluttered around despite the battle—on the reckoning that their own world would soon win, whatever happened here—were right, and the jungle continues to exert its primeval timeless force, returning all that is, to what it once was. The deep weapons pits, once big enough to hold two men with machine guns, are now only shallow depressions on the jungle floor as year by year the ground has crumbled and the thick undergrowth grown back. The rough huts that were built as the staging posts have now rotted and disappeared. The skeletons of Japanese and Australian soldiers have both, for the most part, simply enriched the soil, while old bullets and shell casings continue to corrode into nothingness, their anger entirely spent.

Not so long from now there will be little left physically in the highlands to show that a great battle was once fought there. Spiritually though, the legacy of the 39th Battalion, the 2/14th, the 2/16th, the 2/27th and all the rest, will endure. At the very least, in their native Australia, the understanding of what they achieved, and the sacrifice they made has never been stronger, and it will get stronger still.

There remain, too, a handy group of survivors who treasure the memory of the fallen and will continue to do so to their own dying days. It was well put by one Private Burton, a veteran of the Kokoda campaign from first to last, who wrote in his diary: 'Now on Kokoda Day, when the names are read out of those killed in action, I know them all and still see them as they were. They will never become old or embittered. Just laughing kids forever.'[318]

They shall grow not old, as we that are left grow old. Age shall not weary them, nor the years condemn. At the going down of the sun, and in the morning, we shall remember them.

We shall remember them.

AFTERWORD

It was late on a shining Sunday afternoon in early August, 2009. They were old men, all nudging 90 and beyond, gathered in a circle under the beautiful dome of Melbourne's Shrine of Remembrance. The filtered afternoon light bathed their faces in an ethereal glow as they bowed their heads and the old Lieutenant of 'B' Company, 'Kanga' Moore, uttered those precious, poignant words: 'Age shall not weary them, nor the years condemn. At the going down of the sun, and in the morning, we shall remember them.'

'We shall remember them,' the old men rasped in unison. 'Lest we forget.'

All over Melbourne and in parts north on that same afternoon, nine much younger people were mostly with their families, engaging in last minute preparations, getting ready for a long journey ahead, first by plane and then by foot. The unifying focus of both the old ones and the young ones was, of course, events on the Kokoda Track in 1942. The old men were the surviving veterans of the 39th Battalion who had so courageously fought there in 1942, and formed such bonds that they have regularly seen each other since. The younger people were trekkers, wanting to honour what those older men and their fellow Diggers had accomplished in thwarting the Japanese invasion, by walking the Track . . .

Alas, at 9.56 am on the following Tuesday morning, the twin Otter plane bearing them to Kokoda from Port Moresby crashed into a cliff, just north of the iconic battle site of Isurava, where the 39th Battalion had made their heroic stand against the Japanese in the last days of August, 1942.

In an unfathomable tragedy, all of the trekkers were killed, and for days the news dominated the front pages of the papers and led the news bulletins. So many young Australians losing their lives was always going to produce great national emotion. But this accident, occurring in a place as significant as the Kokoda Track, a place made iconic by Australian soldiers – a fair number of whom were still alive – saw an outpouring of extraordinary national grief, far beyond what might have been expected had the same tragedy occurred in a non-descript jungle in another land.

Certainly, there was some muted questioning of what possessed the trekkers to be there in the first place, what made them go to an inherently dangerous country, to get into a small plane flying over such mercilessly rugged and unforgiving ground, all in the hope of putting themselves through nine days of an agonising walk . . . but most Australians understood.

The trekkers were wanting to pay homage to, if not a new Australian legend, then at least a relatively newly *acknowledged* Australian legend. Twenty years ago, for most Australians younger than sixty, 'Kokoda' was little more than a recognisable name for some battle or other that occurred somewhere up New Guinea way, probably during World War II. But as to detail, as to feeling a great passion for what occurred, the broad mass of the country knew little and cared less. It is only in the last twenty years that the story of 'Kokoda' has resonated with broad swathes of the country.

And yet, how could that be? Gallipoli was legendary almost from the moment news of it got out, and has barely wavered since. So why was Kokoda so different? How could a battle fought in 1942 have been largely ignored for half a century, only to roar back into favour to take its rightful place as pre-eminent in all Australian battles?

For decades, Kokoda was a legend denied. The first denial, of course, came at Koitaki on 9 November 1942 when, instead of lauding the veteran Australian troops of the mighty 21st Brigade for their heroism and stunning achievement in thwarting the Japanese thrust, General Blamey had the hide and the colossal lack of judgement to lecture them on cowardice, and utter those infamous words: 'Always remember that the rabbit that runs is the rabbit that gets shot.'

The troops stared back, stunned, scarcely believing their ears.

'You have been defeated,' he went on, 'I have been defeated, Australia has been defeated.'

This, to the very men who had just handed to the previously all-conquering Japanese army their first defeat!

It was an insult that those troops would never forget. When I raised the subject with the great Stan Bissett some sixty years later, *still* he turned white with rage.

The next denial, effectively, came with the disbandment of the 39th Battalion in July of 1943. By any measure, their achievements over the previous twelve months had been staggering, and under different circumstances they might have had the reasonable expectation of returning to Australia, lauded as heroes forevermore. But that is not the way it turned out.

With the politics of the time, it simply did not suit to have the Australian public realise that in the face of a grave threat, the only troops that the government had to put on the front line in the first instance, were so-called 'chocolate soldiers'. And nor did it fit to have a mere militia outfit perform at least as well as the Australian Imperial Force battalions.

So that was the end of the 39th and any true appreciation of their achievements.

And yet, even those mighty battalions of the AIF who had stormed to the 39th's aid at Isurava and then fought the Japanese all the way back down the Track were not particularly honoured for their achievements either. For one thing, when you had their commander in Thomas Blamey saying they had been 'defeated', it was unlikely the public would easily be able to arrive at a different conclusion on their own. Certainly, the emphasis in everything said from headquarters concentrated on the counter attack. For much of the Australian public at the time, Kokoda was just one more campaign of many, in an obscure part of the world that was immensely difficult for journalists to reach, let alone cover and get their stories out – and there was certainly no official effort to change that.

It simply didn't suit to make much of what they had done, particularly at a time when the most powerful force abroad in the land were American forces, led by one General Douglas MacArthur, who was eager that most of the glory for Allied victories against the Japanese in New Guinea go the Americans generally, and himself specifically.

And even allowing for the famous notion that 'history is written by the victors', the official history was not particularly kind to the Kokoda veterans. There were some especially glaring omissions in its account of the fighting on the Kokoda Track and beyond.

Dudley McCarthy's *South-West Pacific Area First Year: Kokoda to Wau,* was published in 1959, and though it helped to shed some light on what had been achieved, it was nowhere near enough to bring the story of what had happened at Kokoda to wider public attention.

When I asked my historical and intellectual mentor on this book, Neil McDonald, how that could be, he was passionate in his answers. Neil's strong view is that if you were the Official Historian in the 1940s or 50s when the histories were being written you could hardly state that the man who was by then Chief Justice of Victoria, Sir Edmund Herring – formerly General Ned Herring – had needlessly sacrificed his troops in the attacks on Gona, Buna and Sananda by launching ill-considered frontal attacks without adequate reconnaissance and sufficient artillery support, or that the man ultimately responsible for this tactical and strategic idiocy was Australia's first Field Marshall, Sir Thomas Blamey.

Soon Blamey was dead, but men who owed their careers to him were still in positions of power and influence. Neil points out that Dudley McCarthy was himself, by his own admission, a 'Blamey man' whose career had been helped by the late Field Marshall.

McCarthy took the word of other Blamey men at the Koitaki Parade that Sir Thomas was misunderstood and intended no disparagement of the 21st Brigade.

To be fair, *Kokoda to Wau* is still a very good book, and McCarthy did expose Blamey's lies about Rowell's conduct of operations. (He also discovered why Rowell detested Blamey. 'Because he was debauched and I would not join him in his debaucheries,' Rowell told McCarthy.) But still the legend was denied.

Despite those steps forward however, and the fact that McCarthy's understanding of the terrain is on every page, it was never going to be the book that would alert the public at large to what had happened – even if subsequent writers like myself owe it a great debt. Of course there were also several official battalion histories that covered the campaign but, again, they were limited publications that did not enter the mainstream consciousness.

Earlier writers who *did* want to research Kokoda and tell the story were denied access to the official records until the Official Historian completed his volume. And even when Raymond Paull's first popular history of the campaign was released shortly before McCarthy's official history, the title chosen, *Retreat from Kokoda*, could only have been more downbeat had it been called *Defeat at Kokoda*.

Still, in terms of information on the battle, it was big step forward.

Paull had been a junior officer who had served with Potts in Darwin after he had been removed from command of the 21st Brigade. There he had heard Potts' very impressive lectures on Kokoda. Paull, a journalist in civilian life, realised that there was a great book in the Kokoda story. He interviewed Potts at his farm in Konjonup in Western Australia and was given access to Potts' diaries and correspondence. Sydney Rowell and Tubby Allen gave Paull 'their reminiscences and access to personal documents', while Chester Wilmot got his family to unearth the original drafts of his dispatches. Paull also interviewed a number of senior and junior officers as well as soldiers from the key battalions that had been on the track. Included was the first accurate account of Blamey's conduct at Koitaki. And as the foremost of the modern Kokoda authors, Peter Brune, has observed, it was a brave book to have been written just sixteen years after the events it was describing.

When *Retreat from Kokoda* appeared, Osmar White, the one remaining of the three correspondents who had covered the retreat, wrote a ringing endorsement in which he insisted Paull's book told the story as he, Damien Parer and Chester Wilmot would have wanted. But there was a serious backlash. John Hetherington, another former war correspondent – himself the author of a biography published four years earlier, *Blamey* published a review attacking Paull's depiction of Blamey. Then, as Neil McDonald has detailed for me, Sir Edmund Herring organised a letter to the *Age* signed by himself and other Australian luminaries of World War II who had been broadly in the Blamey camp – even if not fighting beside him during the events in question – deploring the way Paull had seen fit 'to assail the honour, capacity and reputation of the late Field Marshall Sir Thomas Blamey in a most bitter and partisan fashion'. The men said they had written the letter, 'so that some measure of justice may be done to the memory and motives of the Field Marshall'.

And yet they advanced no evidence, only the preposterous claim that after Chester Wilmot had been disaccredited Blamey had found him a position with the BBC. (As is a matter of historical record, Blamey had of course done the exact opposite.)

While Paull's book was nevertheless a great step forward in offering due acknowledgement to those who fought there, the fact remained that Hetherington's review and the Herring letter were a strong warning to all who might presume to follow: far more important than elucidating the truth of what happened, was protecting the reputation of some of the leadership involved. This factor even ensured that some modest battalion histories were, effectively, censored. Though it is staggering to contemplate from this point in our history, the truth is that when the authors of the volume on the 2/27 Battalion wanted to include a description of what had happened at Koitaki, they were told by Official Historian

Gavin Long that if they did they would lose their War Memorial grant. (Peter Brune confirms this story in his book, *Those Ragged Bloody Heroes*.)

The decades passed. The defenders of the likes of Blamey and MacArthur fell away, the issues became a whole lot less sensitive to deal with. It was time for a fresh look.

Step forward, Peter Brune. For it was not really until 1991, when he released his classic *Those Ragged Bloody Heroes* – which gave a complete account of Kokoda campaign – that the public at large began to be aware of the stunning details of the campaign.

Following Brune's wonderful book, the true breakthrough, of course, came on Anzac Day 1992, when the Australian public, watching the evening news, was greeted with the exceedingly curious image of our newly installed Prime Minister, Paul Keating, on his knees, kissing the ground at Kokoda and soon after making his famous speech.

As I write, in 2010, in my view that speech neatly encapsulates a poignant truth, widely, if not universally, acknowledged. At the time that Paul Keating said those words, however, they were practically revolutionary. 'For Australians, the battles in Papua New Guinea were the most important ever fought . . .' Hang on, sport, what about Gallipoli, the story all of us were born and raised on?

For that, of course, was the other factor that to this point had acted as a severe brake on the Kokoda campaign by the Australian forces receiving the reverence that was its due. Simply put, the Australian Military Legend Lodge was full, with practically every room filled with Gallipoli battles, Gallipoli soldiers, and even Gallipoli donkeys.

I do not exaggerate.

At the time that Paul Keating kissed the ground of Kokoda, the truth is that if you had assembled all of the nation's knowledge of our military history in one pile, then few could doubt that a full 90 per cent of it would start at dawn of 25 April 1915, and go till dusk of that same day. The story of the Gallipoli landing, with a few honourable mentions for what happened afterwards had so consumed the nation for so many decades – telling the same story, year after year after year, to our children and our children's children, just as we heard it from our parents and our parents' parents – it really did mean that there was little room for the nation to be collectively aware of *anything* much else that happened!

Personally, while I was vaguely interested as a young boy to know that my father had fought at the battle of El Alamein and in battles in New Guinea, and that my mother had served in Bougainville, Lae and Darwin, I was under no illusions. Yes, yes, yes, that was all well and good, but it was hardly Gallipoli.

And yet, after Brune's book, and Prime Minister Keating kissed the ground, things really did start to slowly change. Brune's book was soon followed in 1994 by Neil McDonald's *War Cameraman – The Story of Damien Parer*. This included the first account of the reporting of the Kokoda campaign not just by Parer but his friends and colleagues, Chester Wilmot and Osmar White. A few more Australians began to pay attention, to understand the story, to begin to appreciate what had happened there. Veterans of the Kokoda campaigns who had lived in obscurity for decades, at least insofar as their wartime exploits were concerned, suddenly found their recollections were of a little interest again and they were occasionally sought after to recount them. It was just a small flicker of interest at first, a small candle in a dark valley – 'send a light, Dig, send a light!' – but it really would begin to grow.

In my own review of Peter Brune's second book, *A Bastard of a Place,* in 2004, I particularly praised his line where he noted the arbitrary nature of where history's accolades fall. The man who gave his life in the defence of Kokoda or Gallipoli, for example, is not inherently better or more worthy of our reverence than many a man who lies forgotten in a ditch by some long forgotten battlefield in faraway foreign climes. Against that, there really was something about the Kokoda story that captured the Australian imagination. and the more we found out about it, the more we wanted to know.

Here were ordinary Australian soldiers – very good men, fighting in a very good cause – who, despite being badly outnumbered and poorly equipped, succeeded in defeating a barbaric enemy.

The story offers mateship, sacrifice, a last minute rescue and, after a brilliantly executed fighting withdrawal, final victory. There are extraordinary heroes – men like the commander of the 39th Battalion, Ralph Honner, who takes over when all seems lost at Isurava, who alters the dispositions then proceeds to cut the Japanese attackers to pieces; Staff Sergeant Jim Cowey waiting for his men in the darkness outside the Kokoda plantation and coolly picking off one Japanese gunner after another as they vainly tried to man a machine gun; Brigadier Arnold Potts switching from the offensive to a fighting withdrawal then making the enemy pay in blood for every foot of their advance.

There are many ordinary Australian soldiers, just like Joe Dawson, who were with the action from first to last who, while they may not have returned with a swag of medals, never wavered in their duty from first to last. Personally, while despairing at the death of his brother, I also loved the story of Stan Bisset – among other things, now the nation's oldest living Wallaby – who, after being ambushed, managed to lead his patrol on a five-day trek through the jungle, to get his men safely back to their own lines. I found great inspiration in the story of Corporal Metson who, despite being grievously wounded, refused the offer of a stretcher back to safety, on the grounds that there were other blokes who needed it more than him, and so *crawled* for the next three weeks back down the Kokoda Track.

There is Damien Parer who, wretchedly sick with dysentery, throws away all his equipment except for his bulky Newman Sinclair movie camera, and – no greater love for his craft, hath any many but this – shoved a tube up his anus that drained into a bottle in his sock so he could continue filming the withdrawal, come what may. We have Chester Wilmot who was prepared to risk his career, after first risking his life, to get the truth about the battles to the Australian public and to prevent the Commander-in-Chief from sacking General Rowell just as the tide was beginning to turn

And, of course, no great legend is complete without its villains. In the story of Kokoda they are spectacular. First and foremost there are the Japanese, great soldiers but with an appalling record of atrocity in the field, starting with their atrocious treatment of Australian prisoners on the Burma Railway and spiralling all the way down to hell from there, including the torture and murder of women and children in Papua.

Then there are those who were on our side: Sir Thomas Blamey, blaming everyone but himself for the logistical foul ups of the campaign, prepared to lie, cheat and deride the men who had served so heroically on the front-line so he could pretend to re-energise the situation, all to secure the credit for the Australian successes for himself; or Douglas MacArthur who, after misreading the intelligence telling him the Japanese were heading for Port Moresby, then tried to blame the Australians for his own failures, before trying to manoeuvre things so that both himself and the American troops would get the glory to win the final battles.

None of which is to say that when I was approached to write this book back in 2002, I knew all about it and immediately leaped at the chance. I didn't. I knocked it back on two grounds. Firstly, despite its growing reputation, I personally knew next to nothing about it. Secondly, I didn't think the nation, and most particularly its reading public, cared about it.

It was only chance conversations with Kim Beazley – a heavyweight student of military history and former Minister for Defence – and others that turned me around. I listened, and then began to read. Wonder of wonders, I, too, slowly began to *get it*, began to understand just how great the story was and one more thing besides . . .

That was that as a story from our past, it really did resonate much better with the Australians of the 21st century, than the Gallipoli legend did. With the greatest respect to those who revere the sacrifice of our soldiers in the Great War (as indeed we all should), the more I got into the writing of this book the more I came to passionately believe that Paul Keating was right. At Gallipoli,

Australia was fighting for Great Britain and lost; on the Kokoda Track, the Australian soldiers were fighting for Australia, and won!

If, as is claimed by many historians, Gallipoli was where the nation was actually born – as soldiers from six former colonies were forged by the fierce heat of battle into one coherent whole for the first time – to emerge as the mother country's proud son from the southern seas ready to fight at her command, then Kokoda is the battle where the proud and loyal son had grown up enough, and become independent enough, and even strong enough, to be fighting his own fights in his own interests!

Again, as Paul Keating put it at Kokoda: 'There can be no deeper spiritual basis for the meaning of the Australian nation than the blood that was spilled on this very knoll, this very plateau, in defence of the liberty of Australia. This was the place where I believe the depth and soul of the Australian nation was confirmed. If it was founded in Gallipoli, it was certainly confirmed in the defence of our homeland.'

And they were doubly confirmed by our troops being there in the first place!

After all, had the British Prime Minister Winston Churchill had his way, those troops of the 2/16th Battalion, 2/17th Battalion, 2/27th Battalion *et al* from the AIF, would not have been at Isurava, serving Australia's interests. Rather, they would have been in Burma, trying to block the Japanese thrust towards the jewel in the crown of the British Empire, which was India. In just a little over two years, Australia had gone from Robert Menzies' 'loyal son' notion – Great Britain is at war, and *as a result*, Australia is also at war'– to an entirely new stance. From early 1942 onwards, the new Prime Minister John Curtin took the position that while it was extremely noteworthy that Great Britain wanted Australian troops to defend against Japan's westward thrust towards India, what was far more important was where the *Australian Government* wanted them to go. And that was home, home to Australia, to defend against Japan's downward thrust towards Australia. The Kokoda campaign was of course where those very troops met that downward thrust head on, and so blunted the attack the Japanese were obliged to withdraw.

Clearly, rather than just an extraordinary saga in its own right, when viewed through the prism of modern times there is a special resonance to it. I cite particularly those of us – and I certainly put myself in the heart of the movement – who yearn to see Australia cut its formal ties with Great Britain, to at last become a free-standing republic. It was Paul Keating who formally put Australia on the road to becoming a republic at the very time he kissed the ground at Kokoda, and it's not a large leap to think that he was effectively the first to recognise how powerful a story it was for the new age he wanted Australia to enter into.

For a fierce monarchist of yesteryear, the Gallipoli story was a wonderful example of the strength of the bond between Great Britain and Australia, where Australian blood was spilled in Great Britain's service.

But, as republican, I personally cherish the Kokoda story as the essence of Australia not only forging a path independent of Great Britain, but doing it with staggering courage and with brilliant effect.

Of course, the story itself is strong enough that it may stand alone as deserving of our reverence, regardless of one's politics seventy years later.

But while all of us can take inspiration from different parts of the story, I do think there are some lessons to be learned from it that ought to be universally acknowledged. Kokoda and the battles on the beachhead to capture Gona, Buna and Sanananda, raise important questions about our relationships with our great and powerful friends, the USA and Great Britain.

While having displayed commendable independent mindedness in resisting Churchill's attempt to send our troops to Burma, almost immediately Curtin became subservient to the Americans, in particular General Douglas MacArthur. Yet at that time just about any Australian senior officer had more experience of combat than the American commander! What's more, they had been much more successful. While MacArthur had just lost the Philippines,

Australian troops had been winning battles against the Italians, the French and the Germans – at Tobruk the Australians gave Rommel his first bloody nose in the desert war. They did not deserve to be disparaged by this failed American general when, outnumbered five to one, 21st Brigade were grinding down the Japanese in a superbly executed fighting withdrawal. Indeed, in 1942, the Americans were sorely in need of advice from us – not the other way around. Yet the only Australian general to give MacArthur a much needed dressing down was 'Tubby' Allen.

In fairness, after a second explosion by the peppery Australian, MacArthur became apologetic, an indication of what might have been achieved if Curtin had been prepared to back the judgement of his military advisors. (Blamey did put the boot in later when, on being offered American reinforcements, he told MacArthur, 'I'd rather have Australians, at least I know they'll fight,' but that was kicking a man when he was down.

All of this needs to be part of the Kokoda story along with the battles of the beachhead. This is why this book concludes with Ralph Honner and his 'boys' of the 39th Battalion capturing Gona. Increasingly I have come to believe that we have much to learn from the later battles too, and I am glad Peter Brune and Neil McDonald insisted to me that I had to include them in my book as part of the one campaign. Taken as a whole, they teach us to be more independent in dealing with our allies. If we hadn't been so anxious to prove ourselves to the Americans there would not have been so many unnecessary Australian graves.

Like Gallipoli it is a dark story, but one that remains vitally important. The habits of subservience that cost us so dearly in 1942 remain with us. That kind of dependence was there when we decided to send troops to Iraq on the basis of American and British intelligence reports that the Iraqis had weapons of mass destruction.

The same thinking had previously led to our involvement in Vietnam. To be sure, Australian troops performed admirably. But, in my view at the time, and I think more and more in the long view of history, they should never have been there in the first place. We now know Australia's involvement came about because the government of the day believed it was essential to Australia's security for America to be deeply committed in South-East Asia. Military and strategic folly!

This is why we need to remember the Australian soldiers in Papua 1942. We can take a legitimate pride in their achievements on the Kokoda Track. We should never forget the Australian soldiers inflicted Japan's first land defeat of the Pacific War at Milne Bay. Having wrested the initiative from the Japanese, the Australians annihilated their remaining forces in the bloody battles of the beachhead. Papua New Guinea 1942–43 is also a cautionary tale that should teach us to be wary of our allies and to have confidence in our own judgement.

But in the wider scheme of things were our victories in New Guinea *really* that significant? Did our 'ragged bloody heroes' really save Australia from Japanese invasion? Certainly if you are writing a history of the war in the Pacific the Kokoda/Beachhead battles have to be viewed in a wider perspective that includes the Battle of the Coral Sea, and Guadalcanal. And yes, no one to date has found specific Japanese plans for the invasion of Australia.

For me, this is irrelevant.

In 1942, the soldiers fighting on the Kokoda Track, the government and the commanders, and the Australian public, believed they were preventing an invasion of the mainland. The Japanese had invaded Australian territory and that was it. This is the reality the writer must first imagine then recreate.

To deny this reality is profoundly offensive to the survivors, their families and the descendants of the men who fought and died in New Guinea. I am not suggesting that we should make ourselves comfortable with lies and half truths. But it is absolutely certain the Diggers believed they were fighting to protect Australia.

Was that belief so wrong? The Japanese were undoubtedly heading for Port Moresby. Had they reached their objective they would have launched devastating air raids on northern Australia.

The Japanese tended to only make short term plans, and a victorious commander would have been obliged to exploit such an important victory. This exploitation would at least have included raids on Australian coastal towns. The ragged bloody heroes of Maroubra force made certain that did not happen.

Should Anzac Day therefore become Kokoda Day?

I'm not sure I'd want to go that far, but I would like to see less emphasis on the Gallipoli landing and more on Kokoda and beyond.

This does not imply any disrespect to the memory of the Great War diggers.

It is beyond dispute that the Anzac legend has enriched our culture; it has never detracted from our achievements in nation building or involved the denigration of our allies. The battles at Kokoda and beyond remind us that Australians properly led are capable of winning through against overwhelming odds. They underscore the vital importance of relying on our own judgements and retaining a healthy scepticism about our allies. After New Guinea and Tobruk, Australian soldiers really didn't need to prove themselves to anyone. Moreover, in New Guinea 1942 they fought our enemies on Australian territory for the first time. They demonstrate that while fighting against Australian soldiers is always a formidable proposition, when those soldiers are on Australian territory and believe they are defending Australian soil, they are nothing less than mighty.

BIBLIOGRAPHY

A book of this nature has involved drawing on a wider than usual range of material: published and unpublished, interviews and oral history. I have tended to cite the original edition of books used, and I have relied greatly upon the generosity of many to give me access to much unpublished material. Many have been thanked elsewhere in this book—and my apologies for any I have neglected to name. As mentioned previously, Neil McDonald and the ABC were especially helpful in relation to material relating to Chester Wilmot—and sincere thanks are due to them.

Austin, Victor *To Kokoda and Beyond: The Story of the 39th Battalion, 1941–43*, Melbourne University Press, Melbourne, 1988.

Benson, James *Prisoners Base and Home Again: The Story of a Missionary P.O.W*, Robert Hale, London, 1957.

Bergerud, Eric *Touched with Fire: Land War in the Pacific*, Viking, New York, 1996.

Bertrand, Ina (ed) *Cinema in Australia: A Documentary History*, NSW Press, Kensington, 1989.

Bleakley, Jack *The Eavesdroppers*, AGPS Press, Canberra, 1991.

Brune, Peter *A Bastard of a Place: The Australians in Papua*, Allen and Unwin, Sydney, 2003.

——*Those Ragged Bloody Heroes: From the Kokoda Trail to Gona Beach 1942*. Allen & Unwin, Sydney, First edn 1991, 2nd edn 1992.

——*We Band of Brothers: A Biography of Ralph Honner, Soldier and Statesman*, Allen & Unwin, Sydney, 2000.

Charlton, Peter *The Thirty Niners*, Macmillan, Sydney, 1981.

Chatterton, Percy *Papua: Day That I Have Loved*, Pacific Publications, Sydney, 1974.

Day, David *John Curtin: A Life*. HarperCollins, Sydney, First edn 1999, 2nd edn 2000.

——*The Politics of War*, HarperCollins, Sydney, 2003.

Dornan, Peter *The Silent Men: Syria to Kokoda and on to Gona*, Allen & Unwin, Sydney, 1999.

Edgar, Bill *Warrior of Kokoda: A Biography of Brigadier Arnold Potts*, Allen & Unwin, Sydney, 1999.

Gallaway, Jack *The Odd Couple: Blamey and MacArthur at War*, University of Queensland Press, St Lucia, 2000.

Hall, Tim, *New Guinea 1942-44*, Methuen, Sydney, 1981.

Hetherington, *Blamey: The Biography of Field Marshal Sir Thomas Blamey*, Melbourne, Chesire, 1954.

Horner, David *Blamey: The Commander-in-Chief*, Allen & Unwin, Sydney, 1998.

——*Crisis of Command: Australian Generalship and the Japanese Threat*, Australian War Memorial, Canberra, 1978.

——*General Vasey's War*, Melbourne University Press, Melbourne, 1992.

——*Inside the War Cabinet. Directing Australia's War Effort 1939–45*, Allen & Unwin, Sydney, 1996.

Hoyt, Edwin P. *Warlord: Tojo Against the World,* Cooper Square Press, New York, 2001.

James, Bill *Kokoda 1942: A Trekker's Guide to the Lost Battlefields,* First draft published June 2002.

Johnston, George H. *New Guinea Diary,* Angus and Robertson, Sydney, 1943.

Lindsay, Patrick *The Spirit of Kokoda,* Hardie Grant, Melbourne, 2002.

Manchester, William *American Caesar: Douglas MacArthur 1880–1964,* Dell Publishing, Boston, 1978.

McArthy, Dudley *Australia in the War of 1939–1945: South West Pacific Area First Year, Kokoda to Wau,* Australian War Memorial, Canberra, 1959.

McAulay, Lex *Blood and Iron: The Battle for Kokoda 1942,* Hutchison, Sydney, 2nd edn, 1992.

McDonald, Neil *War Cameraman: The Story of Damien Parer,* Lothian, Melbourne, 1994.

——*Damien Parer's War,* Lothian, Melbourne, revised edition 2004.

McDonald, Robert James *Kokoda Trail: McDonald's Corner,* Self-published, 2003.

McInnes, Dianne, *A Tribute to the Brave: 1941 to 1945, Papua New Guinea.* South Pacific Post, 1992.

Mehan, Russell *An Unrewarded Hero: The Alan Haddy Story,* Self-published 1996.

Milner, Samuel *Victory in Papua: United States Army in World War II, The War in the Pacific,* Center of Military History United States Army, Washington D.C., 1989.

Murphy, John J. *The Book of Pidgin English,* Robert Brown & Associates, 1943.

Nile, Richard & Clerk, Christian *Cultural Atlas of Australia, New Zealand and the South Pacific,* RD Press, 1996.

Paull, Raymond *Retreat From Kokoda: The Australian Campaign in New Guinea 1942,* Mandarin Australia, 1958.

Perrett, Geoffrey *Old Soldiers Never Die,* Random House, Sydney, 1996.

Pollard, Jack *Australian Rugby Union: The Game and the Players,* Angus & Robertson, Sydney, 1984.

Reading, Geoffrey *Papuan Story,* Angus & Robertson, Sydney, 1946.

Rowell, S. F. *Full Circle.* Melbourne University Press, Melbourne, 1974.

Russell, W. B. *2/14th Australian Infantry Battalion,* Angus & Robertson, Sydney, 1948.

Steward, H. D. *Recollections of a Regimental Medical Officer,* Melbourne University Press, Melbourne, 1983.

Stone, Peter *Hostages to Freedom: The Fall of Rabaul, New Guinea 1941–1945,* Oceans Enterprises, 1995, 2000.

Sublet, Frank *Kokoda to the Sea: A History of the 1942 Campaign in Papua,* Slouch Hat Publications, 2000.

Tanaka, Kengora *Operations of the Imperial Japanese Armed Forces in the Papua New Guinea Theatre During World War II,* Japan Papua New Guinea Goodwill Society, 1980.

Vernon, G. H. *1942: A War Diary, The Owen Stanley Campaign, July–November 1942,* 253/5/8 AWM 54.

Watson, Don *Recollections of a Bleeding Heart,* Vintage, Sydney, First edn 2002, edn 2003.

White, Osmar *Green Armour,* Angus & Robertson, Sydney, 1945.

Wilmot, Chester 'Kokoda Road' Disc. No. C.W.311

NOTES

These notes contain sources of information where these are not obvious in the text, together with some information on the research process. Information that has not been referenced either here or in the text has been drawn from the author's interviews and correspondence.

   i Paul Keating quote from 'Diggers Put Australia First' Michael Gordon, *The Sunday Age*, 26 April 1992.

   x Chester Wilmot quote from Kokoda Front, ABC Field Unit, Disc No CW 309 Side A

xxii Osmar White quote from *Green Armour*, Angus & Robertson, Sydney, 1945

IN THE BEGINNING

1 From Albrecht Furst von Urach, *Das Geheimnis Japanischer kraft*, Berlin, Zentralverlag der NSDAP, 1943. *The Secret of Japanese Strength* by Albrecht Furst von Urach. Drawn from www.calvin.edu/academic/cas/gpa/japan.htm.
2 As reported in *The Medical Journal of Australia*, 15 December 1945, p.427.
3 Account of Damien Parer growing up, adapted from the opening pages of Neil McDonald, *War Cameraman: The Story of Damien Parer*, Lothian, 1994.
4 To understand the constitutional structure of Japan, I found http://www.wikipedia.org/wiki/Emperor_Hirohito very useful.
5 Account of Damien Parer's involvement in *Forty Thousand Horsemen* drawn from Neil McDonald, *War Cameraman*, p.22.
6 Hetherington, *Blamey: The Biography of Field Marshal Sir Thomas Blamey*, Melbourne, Chesire, 1954, p. vii. cited by David Horner, *Blamey: The Commander-in-Chief*, Allen & Unwin, 1998, p. 129.

STORM CLOUDS GATHER

7 David Horner, *Crisis of Command: Australian Generalship and the Japanese Threat*, Australian War Memorial, Canberra, 1978, p. 16.
8 Prince Konoye's address was delivered before the 76th session of the Imperial Diet in Tokyo, 21 January 1941.
9 The account of the meeting between Dupain and Parer is from Neil McDonald, *War Cameraman*, p.35.
10 Alan Gill, 'Damien Parer: the unlikely war hero who was true to his faith', *Sydney Morning Herald*, 19 October 1988.
11 Neil McDonald, *War Cameraman*, p. 38.
12 This editorial appeared in the *New York Times* in early June 1940, and was subsequently reprinted in a 9th Division News Sheet in Egypt in 1942, where it was read and memorised by the author's late father, Lieutenant Peter McCloy FitzSimons, who was serving with the 9th Division of the Australian Infantry Forces at the time.

13 Neil McDonald, *War Cameraman*, p. 111.
14 This article was quoted in a seminar paper written by Professor Hank Nelson 'Payback: Australian Compensation to Wartime Papua New Guinea', Australian National University, Canberra, 1999.
15 David Horner, *Blamey*, p. 53.

BATTLE STATIONS

16 Edwin P. Hoyt, *Warlord: Tojo Against The World Book*, Cooper Square Press, New York, 2001, p. 43.
17 David Horner, *Crisis of Command*, p. 17.
18 Edwin P. Hoyt, *Warlord*, p. 79.
19 William Manchester, *American Caesar: Douglas MacArthur 1880-1964*, Dell Company, Boston, 1978, p. 237.
20 Edwin P. Hoyt, *Warlord*, p. 225.
21 This is from 'By Jingo', the music-hall song by G. W. Hunt, which appeared at the time of the Russo–Turkish War (1877–8).
22 Quoted by Kim Beazley in a speech about leadership, October 2003.
23 Told to the author by Neil McDonald in a conversation between him and the former Head of News for the ABC at the time, Frank Dixon.
24 Information about Templeton's background is drawn from Dudley McCarthy, *Australia in the War of 1939–45: South West Pacific Area First Year, Kokoda to Wau*, Canberra, Australian War Memorial, 1959, p. 115.
25 Victor Austin, *To Kokoda and Beyond: The Story of the 39th Battalion. 1941–43*, Melbourne University Press, 1988, p. 11.
26 Information on communiqués drawn from Jack Gallaway, *The Odd Couple: Blamey and MacArthur at War*, University of Queensland Press, St Lucia, 2000, p. 21.
27 David Day, *The Politics of War*, HarperCollins, Sydney, 2003, p. 28.
28 Drawn from the the reminiscences of the 39th's Sergent Kevin Grey on the Patrick Lindsay and George Friend film released in 1992, *The Bloody Track*.

MUD, MOSQUITOES, MALARIA AND MONOTONY

29 Osmar White, *Green Armour*, Angus & Robertson, Sydney, 1945, p. 34.
30 David Horner, *Blamey*, p. 355.
31 John Farquharson, 'Crucial Force in the PNG Campaigns', *The Canberra Times*, 30 August 2003.
32 Dianne McInnes, A Tribute to the Brave: 1941 to 1945, Papua New Guinea, South Pacific Post, 1992, p. 34.
33 Peter Stone, *Hostages to Freedom: The Fall of Rabaul, New Guinea 1941–1945*, Oceans Enterprises, 1995, 2000, p. 44.
34 Quoted in a seminar paper by Hank Nelson 'Payback: Australian Compensation to Wartime Papua New Guinea', Australian National University, Canberra, 1999.
35 George H. Johnston, *New Guinea Diary*, Angus & Robertson, Sydney, 1943. p. 25.
36 Peter Stone, *Hostages to Freedom*, p. 48.
37 David Day, *John Curtin: A life*, HarperCollins, Sydney, First edn 1999, This edition published in 2000, p. 444.
38 Peter Stone, *Hostages to Freedom*, p. 46.
39 Dianne McInnes, *A Tribute to the Brave*, p. 15.

40 Dudley McCarthy, *Australia in the War of 1939–45*, p. 54.
41 Victor Austin, *To Kokoda and Beyond*, p. 34.
42 *The Sydney Morning Herald*, 28 August 1989.
43 George H. Johnston, *New Guinea Diary*, p. 18.
44 ibid, p. 11.
45 David Day, *John Curtin*. p. 448.
46 ibid, p. 440.
47 David Day, *The Politics of War*, p. 21.
48 David Day, *John Curtin*, p. 451.
49 David Day, *The Politics of War*, p. 280.
50 Raymond Paull, *Retreat From Kokoda. The Australian Campaign in New Guinea 1942*, Mandarin Australia, First edn 1958, this edition 1985, p. 3.
51 Peter Charlton, *The Thirty Niners*, Macmillan, Sydney, 1981, p. 218.
52 Neil McDonald, *War Cameraman*, p.468.

SWEATING IT OUT

53 The Australian War Memorial, *Khaki and Green, With the Australian Army at Home and Overseas*, 1943, p.86.
54 David Day, *John Curtin*, p.468.
55 Osmar White, *Green Armour*, p.36.
56 George H. Johnston, *New Guinea Diary*, p. 62.
57 Osmar White, *Green Armour*, p. 43.
58 Quoted in a speech by Kim Beazley about leadership, October 2003.
59 There is a photo of this in Dianne McInnes, *A Tribute to the Brave*, p. 51.
60 This story of comfort women is drawn from *http://www.hk.co.kr/event/jeonshin/w2/e_jsd_3.htm*
61 Jack Gallaway, *The Odd Couple*, p. 27.
62 ibid, p. 28.
63 David Day, *John Curtin*, p. 459.
64 Richard Nile and Christian Clerk, *Cultural Atlas of Australia, New Zealand and the South Pacific*, RD Press, 1996, p. 191.
65 Peter Charlton, *The Thirty Niners*, p. 215.
66 A full account of MacArthur's arrival in Australia can be read in Geoffrey Perrett, *Old Soldiers Never Die*, Random House, Sydney, 1996, p. 282ff.
67 An account of this episode can be found William Manchester, *American Caesar*, p. 310.
68 ibid, p. 312.
69 Geoffrey Perrett, *Old Soldiers Never Die*, p. 283.
70 Victor Austin, *To Kokoda and Beyond*, p. 49.
71 This is material drawn from an extensive interview conducted with Lawrie 'Smoky' Howson, on 5 November 1988, by Harry Martin and Milissa Byrne, for the Australian War Memorial.
72 George H. Johnston, *New Guinea Diary*, p. 59.
73 Victor Austin, *To Kokoda and Beyond*, p. 45.

THE DYNAMIC DUO

74 Hetherington, *Blamey*, p.223.
75 Geoffrey Perrett, *Old Soldiers Never Die*, p. 284.
76 Jack Gallaway, *The Odd Couple*, p. 3.
77 Geoffrey Perrett, *Old Soldiers Never Die*, p. 285.

78 Minutes of Prime Minister's War Conference, Melbourne, 1 June 1942, p.2: JCPML. I read this whole account on the AWM website, which has the copy of a paper presented by Peter Edwards at the 2002 History conference, entitled 'Another Look at Curtin and MacArthur'.
79 Jack Gallaway, *The Odd Couple*, p. 64.
80 William Manchester, *Caesar*, p.332.
81 Victor Austin, *To Kokoda and Beyond*, p. 68.
82 David Day, *John Curtin*, p. 474.
83 Greg Bearup, 'The Country At War: Remembrance Day', *Sydney Morning Herald*, 9 November 2002.
84 Osmar White, *Green Armour*, p. 74.
85 David Horner, *Blamey*, p. 293.
86 ibid, p. 301.
87 ibid, p. 302.
88 Osmar White, *Green Armour*, p. 74.
89 Neil McDonald, *War Cameraman*, p. 121.

UP THE BLOODY TRACK

90 Both soldiers were from the 3rd Battalion of the 14th Australian Infantry Brigade and this is from a report they made after crossing the Kokoda Track in mid-June of 1942. It was quoted in an unpublished paper written by Maclaren Hiari.
91 From a pamphlet issued by the Formosa Jungle Training School in preparation for the departure of the South Sea Forces. Attributed to Masanobu Tsuji (translated by Margaret E. Lake) and cited as an epigraph by Steven Bullard, 'The Japanese Medical System in the Campaigns in Papua (Kokoda and Buna) in 1942 and Early 1943', Paper delivered at the 5th Symposium, The Pacific War in Papua New Guinea, Perceptions and Realities, Australian National University, 7–8 August 2003.
92 Peter Brune, *We Band of Brothers: A Biography of Ralph Honner, Soldier and Statesman*, Allen & Unwin, Sydney, 2000, p. 128.
93 Peter Brune, *Those Ragged Bloody Heroes: From the Kokoda Trail to Gona Beach 1942*, Allen & Unwin, Sydney, First edn 1991, Paperback edition 1992, p. 10.
94 David Horner, *Blamey*, p. 294.
95 Sydney Rowell, *Full Circle*, Melbourne University Press, Melbourne, 1974, p. 110.
96 Victor Austin, *To Kokoda and Beyond*, p. 37.
97 Osmar White, *Green Armour*, p. 174.
98 *The Sydney Morning Herald*, 'The Guide', 17 October 1988.
99 Osmar White, *Green Armour*, p. 174.
100 Neil McDonald, *Damien Parer's War*, Lothian, Melbourne, revised edition 2004, p.181.
101 Dudley McCarthy, *Australia in the War of 1939–45*, p. 114.
102 ibid, p. 115.
103 Hank Nelson, *The Journal of Pacific History*, Volume XXXVIII, 1 June 2003, p. 113.
104 *Jungle Trail. An Official Publication. A Story of the Australian Soldier in New Guinea*, Brochure Number Two, The Australian Army at War, published by the Australian Commonwealth Military Forces, 1943, p. 20. Though this

description was not made for the Kokoda Track itself, the experience of the 39th Battalion walking it, was certainly very similar.

105 David Horner, *Blamey*, p. 315.
106 Chester Wilmot, *Kokoda Road*, Disc No. C.W.311.p. 3 (No date visible.)
107 Peter Stone, *Hostages to Freedom*, p. v.

ATTACK!

108 This comes from Eric Bergerud's definitive account of Allied operations in World War Two's Pacific Theatre in *Touched with Fire: Land War in the Pacific*, Viking, New York, 1996.
109 A full account of this can be seen from p. 118 onwards of Tim Hall's *New Guinea 1942-44*, Methuen, Sydney, 1981. See also, James Benson, *Prisoners Base and Home Again: The Story of a Missionary P.O.W*, Robert Hale, London, 1957.
110 From Albrecht Furst von Urach, *Das Geheimnis Japanischer kraft*, Berlin, Zentralverlag der NSDAP, 1943. *The Secret of Japanese Strength* by Albrecht Furst von Urach. Drawn from www.calvin.edu/academic/cas/gpa/japan.htm.
111 Dudley McCarthy, *Australia in the War of 1939–45*, p. 125.
112 George H. Johnston, *New Guinea Diary*, p. 168.
113 *Lessons Learnt from New Guinea Operations 42–43*. Issued by Imperial General Headquarters, Army Section, 18 November, 43, AWM 55 [5/25], pp. 3 and 9.
114 Victor Austin, *To Kokoda and Beyond*, pp.90-1.
115 This episode was also reported in *the Moresby Army News Sheet*, August 1942, Vol 1, No 28, p. 2.
116 Peter Brune, *Those Ragged Bloody Heroes*, p. 43.
117 An account of this murder can be found in Tim Hall, *New Guinea 1942-44*, and Issue 21 *Wartime*, Official Magazine of the Australian War Memorial.
118 Osmar White, *Green Armour*, p.127

STRIKE-BACK!

119 Opening quote from paper by Steven Bullard, 'The Japanese Medical System in the Campaigns in Papua (Kokoda and Buna) in 1942 and Early 1943', delivered at the 5th Symposium, The Pacific War in Papua New Guinea, Perceptions and Realities, Australian National University, 7–8 August 2003.
120 G. H. Vernon, *A War Diary. The Owen Stanley Campaign, July–November 1942*, 253/5/8, AWM 54.
121 Peter Brune, *Those Ragged Bloody Heroes*, p. 45. (From a interview Peter Brune had with Bidstrup in 1986).
122 ibid, p.54.
123 Australian War Memorial, Allied Translator and Interpreter Section, 12 October 1942, Captured Documents Nos 32–35.
124 Raymond Paull, *Retreat From Kokoda*, p. 65.
125 Lex MacAulay, *Blood and Iron: The Battle For Kokoda 1942*, Hutchinson Australia, Sydney, 1st edn, 1991, 2nd edn 1992, p. 53.
126 Bill Edgar, *Warrior of Kokoda: A Biography of Brigadier Arnold Potts*, Allen & Unwin, Sydney, 1999, p. 127.
127 A full account of this can be found in Peter Brune, *Those Ragged Bloody Heroes*, p. 59.

128 This is material drawn from an extensive interview conducted with Lawrie 'Smoky' Howson, on 5 November 1988, by Harry Martin and Milissa Byrne, for the Australian War Memorial.
129 The best account of this action can be found from p. 74 onwards of Lex MacAulay, *Blood and Iron.*
130 Peter Brune, *Those Ragged Bloody Heroes*, p. 62.
131 An account of this episode can be found in Raymond Paull, *Retreat From Kokoda*, p. 77.
132 This account based on diary entry displayed in Dudley McCarthy, *Australia in the War of 1939–45*, p. 135.
133 Bill Edgar, *Warrior of Kokoda*, p. 130.

HOLDING ON

134 *Jungle Trail. An Official Publication. A Story of the Australian Soldier in New Guinea*, Brochure Number Two, The Australian Army at War, published by the Australian Commonwealth Military Forces, 1943, pp.3-5.
135 Dudley McCarthy, *Australia in the War of 1939–45*, p. 147.
136 An account of this meeting is contained in David Horner, *Blamey*, p. 318.
137 A good account of this retreat is in Raymond Paull, *Retreat From Kokoda*, pp.77–82.
138 Information on Tsukamoto can be found in Dudley McCarthy, *Australia in the War of 1939–45*, p. 144 and Peter Brune, *Those Ragged Bloody Heroes*, pp. 72–73.
139 Australian War Memorial, Allied Translator and Interpreter Section, 12 October 1942, Captured Documents Nos 32–35.
140 Victor Austin, *To Kokoda and Beyond*, p. 77.
141 David Horner, *Blamey*, p. 319.
142 Victor Austin, *To Kokoda and Beyond*, p. 125.
143 This is material drawn from an extensive interview conducted with Lawrie 'Smoky' Howson, on 5 November 1988, by Harry Martin and Milissa Byrne, for the Australian War Memorial.
144 Victor Austin, *To Kokoda and Beyond*, p. 129.
145 William Manchester, *American Caesar*, p. 317.
146 Osmar White, *Green Armour*, p. 152.
147 Neil McDonald, *War Cameraman*, p. 144.
148 This letter published in Bill Edgar, *Warrior of Kokoda*, pp. 166–7.
149 Osmar White, *Green Armour*, p. 154.
150 ibid.
151 Australian War Memorial, Allied Translator and Interpreter Section, 12 October 1942, Captured Documents Nos 32–35.

A WEARY WAY TO GO...

152 Peter Brune, *Those Ragged Bloody Heroes*, p.77.
153 ibid, p. 88.
154 Peter Brune, *We Band of Brothers*, p.134.
155 Drawn from an article written by Ralph Honner, 'This is the 39th', in *The Bulletin*, 3 August 1955.
156 Ralph Honner recalls his feelings on this subject at some length in *The Kokoda Interviews*, a collection of interviews conducted for the Australian Army.

157 Ralph Honner, 'This is the 39th', in *The Bulletin*, 3 August 1955.

158 ibid.

159 Information on Japanese desire for Australian boots drawn from Chester Wilmot report contained on p.3 Disc no. CW 300. Japanese Mastery of Movement. Side B, 6.9.42, from the Australian War Memorial.

160 Australian War Memorial, Allied Translator and Interpreter Section, 12 October 1942, Captured Documents Nos 32–35.

161 This letter written by Sir Sydney F Rowell to Damien Parer's wife, Marie, on 26 April 1964.

162 'Tidings from the South Seas,' Australian War Memorial, Captured Documents Nos 32–35, pp. 15–16.

163 As recorded in the Sydney *Daily Mirror*, 13 April 1952.

164 Paull, *Retreat from Kokoda*, p.109.

165 Ralph Honner, 'This is the 39th', *The Bulletin*, 3 August 1955.

166 Osmar White, *Green Armour*, p. 162.

THE BATTLE OF ISURAVA

167 Peter Brune, *We Band of Brothers*, p.134.

168 Ralph Honner, 'This is the 39th', *The Bulletin*, 3 August 1955.

169 Peter Brune, *We Band of Brothers*, p. 146.

170 Ralph Honner, 'This is the 39th', *The Bulletin*, 3 August 1955.

171 Tony Stephens, 'Held at Bay', *Sydney Morning Herald*, 3 August 2002.

172 Dudley McCarthy, *Australia in the War of 1939–45*, p. 201.

173 A copy of this can be seen on the Australian War Memorial website, AWM exdoc 40.

174 Raymond Paull, *Retreat From Kokoda*, p. 125.

175 Peter Brune, *Those Ragged Bloody Heroes*, pp.98-99.

176 Victor Austin, *To Kokoda and Beyond*, p. 156.

177 A full account of the whole episode with Lieutenant Sword's platoon can be found on p. 148 of Peter Brune, *We Band of Brothers*.

178 Accounts of what the Japanese called out can be found on p.28 of *The Jap was Thrashed: Milne Bay, Owen Stanleys, Buna, Gona and Sananda 1942–43*, The Australian Army at War series, published by The Director General of Public Relations Under the Authority of General Sir Thomas Blamey. Also p. 5 of Chester Wilmot's report 23 September 1942 for *ABC Weekly*, entitled 'Japs are Strange Mixture of Primitive and Modern'.

179 Chester Wilmot, 'Japanese Jungle Tactics', *ABC Weekly*, 17 September 1942.

180 Ralph Honner, 'This is the 39th', *The Bulletin*, 3 August 1955.

181 Victor Austin, *To Kokoda and Beyond*, p. 155.

182 As reported by Raymond Paull, *Retreat From Kokoda*, p. 90. It was subsequently made more famous when Peter Brune used it as the title for his book *Those Ragged Bloody Heroes*.

183 Ralph Honner, 'This is the 39th', *The Bulletin*, 3 August 1955.

184 Victor Austin, *To Kokoda and Beyond*, p. 146.

185 Ralph Honner, 'This is the 39th', *The Bulletin*, 3 August 1955.

186 ibid.

187 Osmar White, *Green Armour*, p.176.

188 Victor Austin, *To Kokoda and Beyond*, p. 156.

189 Bill Edgar, *Warrior of Kokoda*, p. 143.

190 Patrick Lindsay, *The Spirit of Kokoda* Hardie Grant Books, Melbourne, 2002, p. 61.

GUMPTION, GUTS AND GLORY

191 Reminising to Patrick Lindsay for the Patrick Lindsay and George Friend film released in 1992, *The Bloody Track*.
192 Sydney Rowell, *Full Circle*, p. 116.
193 Chester Wilmot, *Kokoda Road*, Disc No. C.W.311.p. 3 (No date visible.)
194 Steven Bullard, 'The Japanese Medical System in the Campaigns in Papua (Kokoda and Buna) in 1942 and Early 1943', Paper delivered at the 5th Symposium, The Pacific War in Papua New Guinea, Perceptions and Realities, Australian National University, 7–8 August 2003, p. 4.
195 Ralph Honner, 'This is the 39th', *The Bulletin*, 3 August 1955.
196 Victor Austin, *To Kokoda and Beyond*, p. 157.
197 An account of the Wilmot allegation about Blamey's cinema contract can be sourced to an article written by Chris Masters, *Sydney Morning Herald*, 14 August 1995.
198 Ralph Honner, 'This is the 39th', *The Bulletin,* 3 August 1955.
199 Osmar White, *Green Armour*, p.164.
200 Neil McDonald, 'Reporting the Papuan Campaign', *Quadrant*, November 2002, Volume XLVI, No. 391, Number 11.
201 Chester Wilmot, *Carrier Line*, Recorded for ABC on 20 October 1942, p. 5.
202 From transcript of Chester Wilmot broadcast, 'And our Troops Were Forced to Withdraw', DISC No. 311 CW Side B, 11 September 1942.
203 Dianne McInnes, *A Tribute to the Brave*, p. 21.
204 This information drawn from Steven Bullard, 'The Japanese Medical System in the Campaigns in Papua (Kokoda and Buna) in 1942 and Early 1943', Paper delivered at the 5th Symposium, The Pacific War in Papua New Guinea, Perceptions and Realities, Australian National University, 7–8 August 2003, p. 4.
205 Chester Wilmot, *Kokoda Road*, Disc No. C.W.311.p. 3 (No date visible.)
206 Neil McDonald, 'Reporting the Papuan Campaign', *Quadrant*, November 2002, Volume XLVI, No. 391, Number 11.
207 ibid.
208 Osmar White, *Green Armour*, p. 168.

FALLING BACK

209 Peter Brune, *A Bastard of a Place*, Allen and Unwin, Sydney, 2003, p.172.
210 Chester Wilmot, *Carrier Line*, Recorded for ABC on 20 October 1942, p. 5.
211 This account of Osmar White's walk towards Eora Creek can be found in *Green Armour*, pp.169ff.
212 Daniel Oakman, *Wartime*, Official Magazine of the Australian War Memorial, No. 23, p. 57.
213 Osmar White, *Green Armour*, p. 170.
214 This method is detailed on p. 156 of an article by Gwynedd Hunter-Payne entitled 'From the Other Side: The Patient Experience of Outpost Medicine In New Guinea During WWII', *'Outpost Medicine' Australasian Studies of the History of Medicine*, Third National Conference of the Australian Society of the History of Medicine, Hobart, February, 1993.
215 *The Medical Journal of Australia*, 14 October 1944, p. 405.

216 Mention of the Metson saga is made in *The Jap was Thrashed: Milne Bay, Owen Stanleys, Buna, Gona and Sananda 1942–43*, The Australian Army at War series, published by The Director General of Public Relations Under the Authority of General Sir Thomas Blamey, p.48.

217 This account drawn from Osmar White, *Green Armour*, p. 173.

218 Russell Mehan, *An Unrewarded Hero: The Alan Haddy Story*, Self-published, 1996, p. 45.

219 Neil McDonald, *War Cameraman*, p. 155.

220 ibid.

221 Bill Edgar, *Warrior of Kokoda*, p. 158.

222 Ralph Honner, 'This is the 39th', *The Bulletin*, 3 August 1955.

223 It was the ABC journalist Chris Masters who in his *Four Corners'* program, 'The Men Who Saved Australia', broadcast on 27 April 1998, first documented the fact that Honner sought to deflect blame from the 53rd Battalion in his address to the troops at Menari.

224 An account of this can be found in *The Jap was Thrashed: Milne Bay, Owen Stanleys, Buna, Gona and Sananda 1942–43*, The Australian Army at War series, published by The Director General of Public Relations Under the Authority of General Sir Thomas Blamey, p. 25.

225 Jack Gallaway, *The Odd Couple*, p. 118.

226 Geoffrey Perrett, *Old Soldiers Never Die*, p. 306.

227 An account of this is contained in an article by Chris Masters, *Sydney Morning Herald*, 14 August 1995.

228 'Kokoda Front', Chester Wilmot, ABC Field Unit, Disc No. CW 309, Side A.

BATTLE OF BRIGADE HILL

229 Kengora Tanaka, *Operations of the Imperial Japanese Armed Forces in Papua New Guinea Theatre During World War II*, Japan Papua New Guinea Goodwill Society, 1980, p. 21.

230 This was drawn from *The Kokoda Interviews*, a collection of interviews conducted for the Australian Army.

231 H. D. Steward, *Recollections of a Regimental Medical Officer*, Melbourne University Press, Melbourne, 1983, p. 127.

232 Peter Brune, *A Bastard of a Place*, p. 206.

233 The story of Corporal Nishimura and his platoon is drawn from Patrick Lindsay and George Friend's film *The Bloody Track*, 1992.

234 This is material drawn from an extensive interview conducted with Lawrie 'Smoky' Howson, on 5 November 1988, by Harry Martin and Milissa Byrne, for the Australian War Memorial.

235 Drawn from Patrick Lindsay and George Friend's film *The Bloody Track*, 1992.

236 The experience of Jack Manol comes from an interview conducted by ABC journalist Chris Masters for the *Four Corners'* program 'The Men Who Saved Australia', 27 April 1998.

237 This is material drawn from an extensive interview conducted with Lawrie 'Smoky' Howson, on 5 November 1988, by Harry Martin and Milissa Byrne, for the Australian War Memorial.

238 As recounted by Ralph Honner in the Patrick Lindsay and George Friend film *The Bloody Track*, 1992.

239 George H. Johnston, *New Guinea Diary*, p. 156.

240 David Horner, *Blamey*, p. 324.

241 Geoffrey Perrett, *Old Soldiers Never Die*, p. 307.

242 ibid, p. 307.

243 David Horner, *Blamey*, p. 328.

244 ibid, p. 327.

245 This information drawn from Steven Bullard, 'The Japanese Medical System in the Campaigns in Papua (Kokoda and Buna) in 1942 and Early 1943', Paper delivered at the 5th Symposium, The Pacific War in Papua New Guinea, Perceptions and Realities, Australian National University, 7–8 August 2003, p. 4.

246 Chris Masters, *Four Corners*, 'The Men Who Saved Australia', 27 April 1998.

247 Reg Glennie, *The Age*, 23 September 1942.

248 David Horner, *Blamey*, p. 329.

249 Chester Wilmot, 'Japs are Strange Mixture of Primitive and Modern', *ABC Weekly*, 23 September 1942, p. 5.

250 This account drawn from the writings of Seizo Okada, the Japanese war correspondent for *Asahi Shimbun*. It was reported in Dudley McCarthy, *Australia in the War of 1939–45*, p. 304.

251 Victor Austin, *To Kokoda and Beyond* p. 180.

THE TIDE TURNS

252 Damien Parer, 'A Cameraman Looks at the Digger' article, Neil McDonald and Peter Brune, 200 Shots: Damien Parer, George Silk and the Australians at War in New Guinea, *Allen & Unwin, Sydney, 1998*.

253 *The Jap was Thrashed: Milne Bay, Owen Stanleys, Buna, Gona and Sananda 1942-43*, The Australian Army at War series, Published by The Director General of Public Relations Under the Authority of General Sir Thomas Blamey, p. 28.

254 David Horner, *Crisis of Command*, p. 184.

255 Jack Gallaway, *The Odd Couple*, p. 126. A full account of this exercise can be found in Samuel Milner, *Victory in Papua: United States Army in World War II, The War in the Pacific*, Center of Military History United States Army, Washington D.C., 1989, pp. 101-124. It is also coverd in Kengoro Tanaka, *Operations of the Imperial Japanese Armed Forces in the Papua New Guinea Theater During World War II,* Japan Papua New Guinea Goodwill Society 1980, pp.30ff.

256 George Johnston, *New Guinea Diary*, p.164.

257 Jack Gallaway, *Odd Couple,* p. 135.

258 As recorded on p. 83 of *Nulli Secundus Log*, the magazine of the 2/2nd Infantry Battalion of the AIF. It has no date upon it, but was most likely published in 1945.

259 Dudley McCarthy . *Australia in the War of 1939-45*, p. 305.

260 As recorded by Tetsura Danjo on the Patrick Lindsay and George Friend film *The Bloody Track*, 1992.

261 A full account of this episode can be found in James Benson, *Prisoners Base and Home Again*, pp.70ff.

262 ibid, p. 71.

263 As recorded on p. 83 of *Nulli Secundus Log*, the magazine of the 2/2nd Infantry Battalion of the AIF. It has no date upon it, but was most likely published in 1945.

264 Drawn from the Patrick Lindsay and George Friend film *The Bloody Track*, 1992.

265 As recorded on p. 85 of *Nulli Secundus Log*, the magazine of the 2/2nd Infantry Battalion of the AIF. It has no date upon it, but was most likely published in 1945.

266 This story is detailed in Dianne McInnes, *A Tribute to the Brave*.

267 Jack Gallaway, *Odd Couple*, p. 136.

268 Peter Brune, *A Bastard of A Place*, p.414.

269 Victor Austin, *To Kokoda and Beyond*, p.185.

270 Peter Brune, *A Bastard of A Place*, p.414.

271 This letter is recorded in Bill Edgar, *Warrior of Kokoda*, p. 199.

272 Dudley McCarthy, *Australia in the War of 1939-45*, p.307

273 Professor David Horner, *General Vasey's War*, Melbourne University Press, Melbourne, 1992, p.196.

274 Raymond Paull, *Retreat From Kokoda*, p. 87.

275 Drawn from Dianne McInnes, *A Tribute to the Brave*, p. 91.

276 The account of this exchange was contained in a Letter to the Editor, written by Geoffrey Reading of Castle Hill—who was a newly arrived war correspondent in Port Moresby at the time—and published in the *Sydney Morning Herald* on 16 August 1995.

277 Originally from p. 209 of Takida Kenji, *Taiyo wa moeru*, [The Pacific is Burning], Tokyo, 1955. From Steven Bullard, 'The Japanese Medical System in the Campaigns in Papua (Kokoda and Buna) in 1942 and Early 1943', paper delivered at the 5th Symposium, The Pacific War in Papua New Guinea, Perceptions and Realities, Australian National University, 7–8 August 2003.

278 Horner, *General Vasey's War*, p.209.

TO THE BITTER END

279 A full account of this episode can be found in Horner, *Blamey*, p. 353.

280 Both this story and the one following were drawn from *The Kokoda Interviews*, a collection of interviews conducted for the Australian Army.

281 Jack Gallaway, *Odd Couple*, p. 134.

282 Horner, *Blamey*, p.352.

283 A full account of General Horii's drowning can be found on p.32 of Kengora Tanaka, *Operations of the Imperial Japanese Armed Forces in the Papua New Guinea Theatre during World War II*, Japan Papua New Guinea Goodwill Society, 1980.

284 Peter Brune, *A Bastard of A Place*, p.435.

285 ibid.

286 David Day, *John Curtin*, p. 477.

287 Jack Gallaway, *Odd Couple*, p. 144. Footnoted to McCarthy, *Australia in the War of 1939–45*, p. 352 and Milner, *Victory in Papua*, p. 138.

288 Horner, *Blamey*, p. 361.

289 ibid, p. 364.

290 Peter Brune, *We Band of Brothers*, p. 195.

291 Dudley McCarthy, *Australia in the War of 1939–45*, p. 437.

292 ibid, p. 439.

293 Peter Brune, *A Bastard of A Place*, p. 476.

294 Victor Austin, *To Kokoda and Beyond*, p. 200.

295 Peter Brune, *We Band of Brothers*, p. 200.

296 Peter Brune, *A Bastard of A Place*, p. 485.

297 Taken from Peter Brune's obituary of Ralph Honner, published in *The Australian* on 24 May 1994.

EPILOGUE

298 Ralph Honner. As quoted by the Hon. Charlie Lynn in *Hansard*, 23 November 1995.

299 Kengora Tanaka, *Operations of the Imperial Japanese Armed Forces in the Papua New Guinea Theatre During World War II*, Japan Papua New Guinea Goodwill Society, 1980, p. 98.

300 G. H. Vernon, *A War Diary. The Owen Stanley Campaign, July–November 1942*, 253/5/8, AWM 54.

301 This is material drawn from an extensive interview conducted with Lawrie 'Smoky' Howson, on 5 November 1988, by Harry Martin and Milissa Byrne, for the Australian War Memorial.

302 Ina Bertrand (ed), *Cinema in Australia: A Documentary History*, University of NSW Press, Kensington, 1989, p. 214.

303 Neil McDonald, *War Cameraman: The Story of Damien Parer*, Lothian, 1994.

304 *The Sun*, 22 April 1963.

305 David Day, *John Curtin*, p. 575.

306 From an article by Tony Stephens, *Sydney Morning Herald*, 13 May 1998, about Geoffrey Serle's book *For Australia and Labor*, John Curtin Prime Ministerial Library, Curtin University of Technology.

307 *The Guardian*, 6 August 2002.

308 Edwin P. Hoyt, *Warlord*, p. 212.

309 This account is taken from a radio documentary made by Phillip Knightly, 'Chester Wilmot: War Correspondent', ABC Parliamentary and News Network, 5 March 1995.

310 This account is drawn from *The Daily Mirror*, 17 January 1954.

311 Bill Edgar, *Warrior of Kokoda*, pp 181–82.

312 An account of Hideki Tojo's death can be found in Edwin P. Hoyt, *Warlord*, pp. 1ff.

313 ibid, p. 224.

314 Chester Wilmot *The Struggle for Europe*, William Collins, London, 1952.

315 This account is drawn from the website: http://www.hk.co.kr/event/jeonshin/w2/e_jsd_3.htm

316 Horner, *Blamey*, pp. 581–82.

317 Michael Gordon, *The Age*, 26 April 1992.

318 Frank Walker, *The Sun-Herald*, 2 July 1995.

INDEX